From Oral to Written

ALSO BY TOMSON HIGHWAY

PLAYS
Dry Lips Oughta Move to Kapuskasing
*Ernestine Shuswap Gets Her Trout**
*The (Post) Mistress**
The Rez Sisters
*Rose**

FICTION
Kiss of the Fur Queen

NON-FICTION
Comparing Mythologies
A Tale of Monstrous Extravagance: Imagining Multilingualism

FOR CHILDREN
Caribou Song
Dragonfly Kites
Fox on the Ice

* Published by Talonbooks

FROM **ORAL** TO **WRITTEN**

A Celebration of Indigenous Literature in Canada
1980–2010

TOMSON **HIGHWAY**

Talonbooks

Talonbooks
278 East First Avenue, Vancouver, British Columbia, Canada V5T 1A6
www.talonbooks.com

First printing: 2017

Typeset in Arno
Printed and bound in Canada on 100% post-consumer recycled paper

Interior and cover design by Typesmith
Cover painting: *The Masterpiece* by Norval Morrisseau. Image courtesy the Coghlan Gallery. © Gabe Vadas and The Estate of Norval Morrisseau

Talonbooks acknowledges the financial support of the Canada Council for the Arts, the Government of Canada through the Canada Book Fund, and the Province of British Columbia through the British Columbia Arts Council and the Book Publishing Tax Credit.

LIBRARY AND ARCHIVES CANADA CATALOGUING IN PUBLICATION

Highway, Tomson, author
    From oral to written : a celebration of Indigenous literature in Canada, 1980–2010 / by Tomson Highway.

Includes bibliographical references.
ISBN 978-1-77201-116-6 (SOFTCOVER)
ISBN 978-1-77201-188-3 (HARDCOVER LIBRARY EDITION)

    1. Canadian literature – Indigenous authors – History and criticism.
2. Indian literature – Canada – History and criticism. I. Title.

PS8089.5.I6H54 2017   C809'.8897071 C2017-900704-1

To all Indigenous writers of this
beautiful country, always my heroes

I am an Indian. I am proud to know who I am and where I originated. I am proud to be a unique creation of the Great Spirit. We are part of Mother Earth ... We have survived, but survival by itself is not enough. A people must also grow and flourish.

—CHIEF JOHN SNOW
  in *These Mountains Are Our Sacred Places* (1977)

CONTENTS

PROLOGUE

How, kaachimoo-staatinaawow (I'll tell you a story). *Kayaas, igoospeek kagee-awaaseewiyaan, ootee waathow keeweet'nook Manitoba kaa-ichigaateek aski, keegaach mawch awinuk maana keen'tayschooloo-oo. N'paapaa, n'maamaa, nimoosoom, noogoom, apoochiga nimis igwa nistees mawachi kaak'seewee-ayawichik, mawch keen'tayschooloo-iwuk. Oosaam waathow keeweet'nook eegee-ayaa-ak, kapee maana eegeep'mooteewee-aak, eemaachiyaak, eewanee-eegiyaak, eepagitawaa-ak. Igwa ithigook waathow saawaanook maana eegaa-ayaag'wow igoospeek ischooliwa. Apoochiga keespin keen'taytheetaag'wow tantay-schooliwichik, mawch tageegaskeetaawuk. Igwaani, mawch awinuk keeschooloo-oo igoospeek, mawch awinuk keegaskeetow taagathaaseemoot. Nigeegeenee-hithiwaanaan maana poogoo, igaachi nigee-oocheepawnee-imoonaan. Maw maa-a nigeegathaaseemoonaan. Anooch maa-a igwa peetoos. Neet'naan ooskip'maat'suk, neet'naan igwa nigeeschooliwinaan athis p'mithaagaana igwa igootee waathow keeweet'nook eesithaag'wow. Athis waathow keeweet'nook eesithaag'wow igwa oo-oo p'mithaagaana, nigaskeetaanaan igwa neet'naan tantayschooliweeyaak. Igoochi anooch kaageesigaak kaagaskeetaa-ak tagathaasi-mooyaak taayameechigiyaak meena. Taamasinaa-igiyaak meena. Igoochi meena igwa mawaachi kaatigaskeetaa-ak taweecheewaa-ag'wow n'tooteeminawuk maawaachi kwayas tagaskeetaachik tapami-isoochik. Igoochi kaamasinaa-igeeyaak. How, n'gagaathaaseemoon igwa...*

Now sign here with an X: _____

Thank you. You've just signed your house away. When can I move in?

You see? It's all in the perspective. It's all in who is telling the story. About whom. And whose language in which that story is being told. Because to us Indigenous peoples, when we first heard English, which in my case was within the past fifty years, it was like Greek to our ears. We understood it about as much as you've understood what you've just read. Or tried to. Because you can't. Understand *or* read it. Just as we couldn't understand *or* read *your* language when all those treaties were being signed, for example. Or what's more, when the Bible was being read to us in archaic English.

In any case, that is what our language, or at least one of them, sounds like – or would look like if it were written down on paper, which, thankfully, it now is with increasing frequency. Which is why this book. Its mission? Record the emergence of a written form of storytelling from the ashes, so to speak, of an oral tradition. And it purports to back this thesis with a generous selection of Indigenous literature written and published, for the most part, in the thirty years between 1980 and 2010. I say "for the most part" because, though there were some twenty books by Indigenous authors published in Canada prior to 1980, including one as early as 1851, they constitute a kind of overture to what I call the first wave. Because that first wave started only with the big explosion that happened in and around the year 1980. This is when Indigenous literature in Canada became a genuine movement, a genuine wave, a genuine phenomenon, though one that wouldn't have happened, it goes without saying, *without* that overture. For thousands of years before that, our stories, just as with our languages, were *not* written down. They were simply passed by word of mouth from one generation to the next and then to the next. And would have been indefinitely if the white man's schooling hadn't come along to suppress, if not try to eradicate, the languages in which these stories were being told. In a sense, that would have amounted to the killing of an entire body of literature, much of it so ancient it can be said to go back to pre-Biblical times. And you'd pretty well have to speak at least one of those languages, with complete fluency, to be able to back up such a claim.

When I was growing up in the paradise I was born to in the province of my youth, some 1,100 kilometres north of Winnipeg, some three hundred kilometres south of the Nunavut border, and about ten kilometres east of Saskatchewan, Cree, my mother tongue, and Dene, the language of the neighbouring "Nation," were the only languages heard and spoken. In fact, that paradise on Earth was so far north that Inuktitut too was heard and spoken. As caribou hunters regularly dogsledding into the far north, some among our people inter-married with the Inuit, which is how the blood of these igloo-dwelling, seal-hunting, High Arctic people found its way into our families. *I* have relatives who are part Inuit. All by way of saying that my homeland was trilingual, just not in French or in English, tongues that are spoken, by the way, in a mere 1/1000th of the country when that country is taken in the context of land mass only. That other 999/1000th, in any case, is where I was born and raised, a part of the country so remote that no one but our people – the Cree, the Dene, and the Inuit – have seen it to this day – northern Manitoba where it meets Saskatchewan, the Northwest Territories, and what, since 1999, has been known as Nunavut ("Our Land" in Inuktitut).

The truth, however, is that, for us, there *were* no borders. For us, there *was* no Manitoba, Saskatchewan, Northwest Territories, or Nunavut. There was just this extraordinary land that stretched from Manitoba's northern extremity clear to the North Pole (or almost), a distance of some 3,400 kilometres, equivalent to that from Vancouver to Toronto. When you consider that Nunavut alone, with its population of some 37,000, is the size of all western Europe, with its population of nearly half a billion – and that's just *one* territory of Canada – you get an idea of the unpeopled vastness of the land that is my trilingual home.

My point here being language. And languages. If linguists tell us that there exist on the planet some 5,500 languages, then Indigenous Canada alone has fifty-two or, at least, up to recently, *had* fifty-two for those that aren't dead already are dying very quickly, thanks, these days, to television. And the Internet. And of those nearly five dozen languages, all spring from eleven linguistic families each as distinct one from the other as Latin is from Slavic, Chinese from Arabic, and the four major members of the eleven linguistic families lie east of the Rocky Mountains. So just as Spanish, Italian, and French (to name but three), are Latin languages, all different but similar, coming as they do from the same linguistic root, then Cree is an Algonquian language, just as are Ojibwa, Mi'kmaq, and Algonquin (to name but three), all different but similar coming as they do from the same linguistic root. (Algon*quin*? A language. Algon*quian*? A linguistic family.) Dene, on the other hand – like Dene Tha (Slavey), Tlicho (Dogrib), and Gwich'in (to name but three) – is an Athapaskan language, in the same sense that Russian, Polish, and Czech (to name but three), are Slavic and not Latin. As for Inuktitut, it is a language *and* a linguistic family all on its own just as are Magyar languages Finnish and Hungarian. So that when one is trilingual in Cree, Dene, and Inuktitut, as was my father – actually, he spoke some self-taught English as well, making him *quadri*-lingual – it is not like one speaks French, Spanish, and Italian or English, German, and Norwegian. It is more like one speaks English, Arabic, and Cantonese or French, Korean, and Zulu, truly a virtuosic feat. Of linguistics. Northern Canada? A maelstrom of languages, an embarrassment of linguistic richness. And therefore of wisdom.

The Indigenous languages of North America, for one thing, are structured in a manner dramatically different from – some would say diametrically opposed to – their European counterparts, major among which difference is the concept of gender. Where European languages divide the universe into genders, where objects and beings are either male, female, or neuter, with the hierarchy of power descending from the first to the second to the third, the Indigenous languages ignore it entirely – there is no "him," there is no "her"; there is just "her/him" (a rough translation but the closest one can get to the idea in English). If gender is defined – the biological difference between men and women, for instance – it is done according to dynamics that would take a book of its own to do justice to its explanation. Suffice it to say for now that, in Indigenous languages, the universe is divided into that which is animate and that which is not. Beings either have a soul or they do not, granting, in this way, equal status to a man, woman, tree, ant, and even rock. There is, most expressly, no hierarchy. Looked at from another angle, in one linguistic superstructure, nature lost its soul when humanity (and language) was evicted from a certain garden and therefore is a foe to be dominated. A female foe? A neuter foe? The answer is moot – *it* is a foe, a victim. In the other linguistic superstructure that has no experience of eviction from a garden – *any* garden – nature is an equal, a friend to be talked to, if not, in fact, a friend to be thanked, to be consulted. One linguistic superstructure thus lives outside the garden – the garden of pleasure, of beauty, of joy, which, in just one sense of many, is the human body – the other *still* lives inside it. Which is why one system negates pleasure – any activity remotely smelling of pleasure is suspect, pleasure is a crime, an obscenity, especially sex – while the other marries it: pleasure is a joy, laughter is gold. Which is how we arrive at this stunning equation – in one linguistic superstructure, North America is a hell to be hated, to be conquered; in the other, it is a garden to be tilled and cared for.

In another context, one linguistic superstructure is monotheistic in architecture, with one god only, a god that is male; the other is pantheistic, a system where divine energy has not yet left nature, so that nature – trees, grass, air, even one drop of water, even the aforementioned ant – virtually bristles with divine energy. In this latter design, god is biology, womb, female; god is the land. Another way of putting it: structurally, one linguistic notion is phallic – a straight line; the other yonic, womb-like, a circle. So that one system defines existence on planet Earth as a curse from an angry male god – we are here to repent, to suffer; the other a blessing, a gift from a benevolent *female* god: we are here to laugh, we are here to celebrate. Which is why one god laughs and the other doesn't. And which is why Cree, to name but one Indigenous language, has got to be the world's funniest language, English its most serious. I kid you not when I say that the second you utter even one Cree syllable, you start laughing, and laughing from the gut – your entire body jiggles; the second you switch back to English, you stop. As does your body.

This pantheistic design, in any case, is the "map" that has steered our culture over the eons. Just as Christianity has its map, its signposts, its light that guides, then we have ours, the point to remember being that the route the human soul takes across either map is seldom perfect. Virtue exists inside both systems just as evil does; people do get lost. But there is, at least, a map, a grand design.

Most of the writers documented in this book will not, however, remember the paradise from which came their parents, their grandparents, or their great-grandparents. Most live in cities. Most do not know their language. They speak English only. Or French. I was just lucky to be was born where I was born *when* I was born … before the circle was broken. For first had come the land, which the ancestors of these writers had been part of since time immemorial. (As was I when I was born hundreds of kilometres from the nearest urban centre, hundreds of kilometres from the nearest English word.) Caribou, moose, geese, ducks, loons, ptarmigan, trout, pike, pickerel, whitefish and their caviar, eggs from Arctic terns, herbs and wild berries by the kilometre – direct from the bush, direct from the lake; we ate better than at five-star restaurants in Paris; in Paris, you pay three hundred dollars per person, for such meals, for us, they were free – tracts of forest by the tens of kilometres, a million lakes and the rivers and waterfalls that fed them, drinkable water, air so breathable it made lungs gasp, snow so white it made eyes ache, northern lights that stole one's breath, a silence so enormous you heard Earth's heartbeat, the richness and beauty of our extraordinary land is beyond human imagining. Lean years aside, spring-time blackflies aside, illness aside, the usual tawdry human politics aside, there was nonetheless a balance, a partnership between humanity and nature that functioned and functioned well. The only way it can be described in terms that are adequate is to say it in Cree, Dene, or Inuktitut. God as woman? Said in English, it sounds ridiculous, obscene, dangerous. In Europe, in the years leading up to and immediately following Columbus's arrival in the Americas, thousands of women lost their lives for even thinking such a heresy; ultra-efficient, ultra-male organizations such as the Spanish Inquisition ensured that. In Cree, in Subarctic Manitoba in the middle of a lake on a starlit August night, bugless, windless, the lake glass-smooth – or, in winter, the aurora borealis reflected in that now iced-over, snowbound lake, that snow micro-shards of crystal – it makes perfect sense to say "God as Mother."

Depending, however, on which part of the country a people was living, in when they first encountered European thought, European language, some experienced that first contact earlier than others. In eastern Canada, that would have been as early as 1534 when Jacques Cartier came sailing up the St. Lawrence River with his motley, starving, scurvy-ridden crew. In southern Manitoba, that contact would have come some 350 years later, circa 1870 when the province of Manitoba came into being and towns like Winnipeg were first constructed. For me, personally, it would take another hundred years. It would take, in a sense, until 1973 when I was twenty-one, the summer electricity – the telephone, television, the air strip, and English – arrived in earnest in our home base of Brochet (pronounced "Bro-shay") on the Barren Lands First Nation in northern Manitoba, it was too late to "stain" me, too late to "bend" me, making me the last of a breed, the *pre-contact* breed. In a sense. In a sense because, in point of fact, Catholicism had already "touched" me, as had the little bit of time I had spent on the reserve, as had the "white" education I had thus far acquired, including speaking, clumsily, the English and French languages. But if it's true that a human being is made in the first six years of his life – I didn't go to "boarding school" until I was almost seven – then the circle of Cree wisdom had been planted already so deep inside me that it could not be broken. It has been strained, yes, strained to the limit, but broken? No.

Which sets the stage for a look at the two physical realities in which live Canada's Indigenous people today: the north and the south. Southern reserves are hemmed in by cities and have been for three, five, eight generations. Some, in fact, stand right next to them, on the outskirts of major cities – Québec City, Montreal, Kamloops in British Columbia, and Brantford, Thunder Bay, and North Bay in Ontario – just six of many. At least one reserve I know of stands inside an urban centre's city limits – the Squamish Nation in North Vancouver. Eroded by English (or French) over the course of several generations, the original language of these Indigenous communities no longer lives or, at least, no longer thrives, is no longer the *lingua franca*. In contrast, northern reserves are isolated, in some cases so much so that the only way to reach them is by canoe and dogsled – and now, of course, skidoo – modes of transport that can take a traveller weeks to cross any distance. Or by bush plane. In Brochet's case, when I was growing up, the nearest centre of white civilization, so to speak, was Lynn Lake, a mining town seventy-six miles to the south as the crow flies. There being no road, one had to fly there, by bush plane with its pontoons in summer, its skis in winter. To us as children, Lynn Lake with its population of some three thousand white people was the Emerald City: New York or Paris! All by way of saying that Indigenous languages on reserves like Brochet remain intact. To this day, there are people up there – my godmother, aunts, uncles, cousins – who speak no English. My mother didn't speak it. The four eldest of my eleven siblings didn't (and don't) speak it. That's how well Cree – and Dene and Inuktitut – have survived on northern reserves, in northern communities. I myself speak Cree fluently (and Dene with effort). I write my plays, books, and cabarets in Cree – *taapwee, kwayus ooma neetha nineetaani-ithoowaan*. As a northern Indian, that is my privilege.

Reserves, moreover, are not laid out like towns or cities. Whether they are northern or southern, most resemble farming communities with their large tracts of land interspersed by dwellings so that, in this sense, they are not so much urban as rural. What distinguishes northern reserves from their southern counterparts in terms of this rural/urban dichotomy is that southern reserves, because they are hemmed in by cities, have limited access to true rural areas for hunting and fishing, to name but two "traditional" Indigenous activities. With northern reserves, that access is limitless. From Brochet, you can drive your dogsled (a mode of transport still practised by some) 3,400 kilometres in one line direct to the North Pole without laying eyes on another human being.

Which brings us to the question of economy. Traditional Indigenous economy was based on the land. People hunted, fished, and trapped and the land gave abundantly. Our lives – that is, the Highway family's – as Subarctic hunters and fishers between Brochet and the Nunavut border were blessed; we lived in heaven, a hard-working heaven but a heaven nonetheless. Confined to reserves, people lost that livelihood, earlier in the south than in the north. The tax-exempt status that reserves are cursed with – blessed, some would say – only made it worse. Motivation to make things work locally – the water system, street maintenance, house construction, community-controlled education – was neutered. As for economic development, its complete absence proved lethal. Dependence on the government became the new reality; welfare *is* the economy. And there is nothing more soul-destroying than welfare. It kills ambition. It kills dreams. Still, we are here. And life goes on. Many of those who have elected to stay on their reserves are managing to carve out a future for themselves and for their people, at least in the south with their urban centres right there at their doorstep – you can live in Six Nations and work in Toronto, in Peguis and work in Winnipeg, in Cape Croker and work in Owen Sound. Northerners can't do that; a two-way plane ticket from Toronto to the lake two hundred kilometres north of Brochet where I was born would cost you close to four thousand dollars. For that amount of money, you can fly from Toronto to Rio de Janeiro, Brazil, five times easy. So that those of us who come from the north and want to help make life better for our people have had no choice but to leave our communities, and our families, for the south and its cities.

Then there's religion. From the very beginnings of colonial history, the various branches of Christianity have, of course, been engaged in a race for the souls of Indigenous people. In some regions, the Anglicans won. In others, it was the Methodists, in others, the Evangelicals. In northwestern Manitoba – in Brochet, that it to say – it was the Catholics. Fortunately, there were some regions that the missionaries either overlooked or didn't know existed, with the result that the original Indigenous religion – female-based, nature-based, circular in structure – remained untouched. *Or* if it was threatened, went underground – medicine men, medicine women, mid-wives, and such would continue their practice behind closed doors, away from the eye of the watchdog church who, most distressingly, had a way of equating nature worship with devil worship, equating, in effect, nature with hell. Kill the Indigenous idea of divinity in female form and replace that energy with the monotheistic, male, Christian God, is what such work amounted to. And is the cause, at base, of the social ills that are eating away at our communities – if the goddess is sick, then so are her children; it only makes sense.

But then came the era of the residential schools in which sexual abuse at the hands of church personnel came to public light on a scale unprecedented. The breach of trust couldn't have been more spectacular, more definitive, more effective. The fallout? Wholesale rejection of Christianity by an entire generation of Indigenous people out of which rejection has come the move back to the ancient religion – out with the straight line and in with the circle. Out with the phallus and in with the womb. Out with God and in with his Wife.

The watershed year was 1960, the year the Indigenous people of Canada were given the right to vote in their country's federal elections. Where the Indian Act of 1876 had pretty well confined us to those zoo-like compounds they called Indian reserves, the right to vote – that is, the right to decide our own lives, own destinies – also finally made it legal for us to leave the reserve and migrate to cities. This we did for three reasons: employment, education – and alcohol, so we could drink. All of which made the 1960s the era that saw the mass migration of Indigenous people from reserves to cities, from rural to urban reality, a social revolution that was not entirely dissimilar to England's Industrial Revolution where land-based peasants migrated to cities in numbers so unprecedented that the English social structure came near to collapsing. And human misery ballooned to proportions unimagined before then.

Prior to this move, whether Christianized (as most of us were at one point) or unilingual in English (as most of us are), Indigenous people still functioned, at a fundamental level of their inner consciousness, in circles:

the drum, the round dance, the sun dance, the four directions, the four seasons, the tepee, the sweat lodge, the circle of Elders and councillors that governed a village, the "roundness" of Earth as mother goddess, the endless circle of life and death, consensus (as opposed to choice by election) as circle, time as a circle, even the languages – Cree, Blackfoot, Dene – which define life in, and as, a circle. Outwardly, Indigenous people may have "semi-functioned" in those straight lines – marched to the beat of the drummer, so to speak – but, inwardly, they still functioned in curves. Now for the first time, they had to walk through the streets of cities whose blocks were square, whose buildings were square and rectangular. The rows of desks in a classroom, the rows of pews in a church, the vertical straight line of male, female, and neuter as social hierarchy, the straight line of life and death – that is to say, the vertical line from heaven to Earth to hell – the board of directors that governed communities and organizations (which, in itself, is one of those straight lines, that is, the straight line of the electoral system), the straight line of budgets, the straight line of a Western economy, time as a straight line, even the language, French and/or English, as tongues that define life in, and as, straight lines. All these changes were too much for us; connection with the "roundness" of nature was severed; this was our "eviction from the garden." And what little "white" education we had managed to acquire on the reserve armed us poorly. We couldn't get jobs so we went on welfare. And the kiss of death? Alcohol.

Prior to 1960, alcohol had been illegal on reserves. The result? Binge drinking. Binge drinking on a scale unprecedented. People would sneak off the reserve and into the nearest town that had a bar or a liquor store, drink as much, and as quickly, as possible before they got caught, arrested, and thrown in jail, spending, in the process, the little money they had for their children's food and clothing. By the time fetal alcohol syndrome became known as an illness, it was too late. A people whose bloodstream had not known alcohol had just had their circulation electrocuted. The French and the Italians with their endless square kilometres of vineyards may have drunk wine for centuries; drinking it with lunch, dinner, and even breakfast, every day, was as normal as breathing. Alcohol ingestion was bred into the bone, the blood thereof inured to the substance. In Indigenous Canada, it was not.

I *have* to qualify: the northern Manitoba I speak of as paradise is *not* Thompson. It is *not* Lynn Lake. It is *not* The Pas or Churchill. And it is most certainly *not* reserves like Pukatawagan, Shamattawa, or Brochet. It is just unfortunate that you have to go way beyond such hellholes to find it. The remotest sign of urban life, of linear thinking, and the result is disaster. Reserves, in particular, are the places where circular thinking clashes most brutally with linear thinking, though northern frontier towns such as those just named are not much better. Some, in fact, would say they are worse. The flames of violence domestic and otherwise were fanned by frustration, by rage, by family breakdown – with people so poor they eat from garbage dumps, as did the Dene in Churchill in the late 1960s and early 1970s. Those flames were fanned by loss of language, loss of pride, dignity, ambition, and spirit, by third-generation fetal alcohol syndrome that will take six generations to heal, with the result that the current victims are no longer human – come to Lynn Lake, Manitoba, and see for yourselves the walking dead, the classic image of the "drunken Indian," the ultimate victims. The least of the results of this lengthy list is the complete degradation of the languages, Cree in this instance, just as German, I might add, was stripped of its dignity in the 1940s. Even the houses traumatize us, standing cheek by jowl as they do in cities; when you have lived in huge open spaces for generations, the claustrophobia this causes is, in itself, a kind of mental illness. People don't even know how to deal with garbage. In the old way of life, everything was biodegradable; after you'd eaten the fish, you left the bones on the ground, moved on to the next campsite, that fish skeleton melted back into the Earth, one year later you were back at that campsite which had returned to its former pristineness, you ate another fish and left its bones on the ground and moved on and thus the circle completed itself. Plastic shopping bags, glass, tin cans, Styrofoam, disposable diapers, they don't do that; they function – dysfunction? malfunction? – outside that circle.

Before I get accused of trashing my own people, let me qualify again ... Throughout the greater bulk of their history, Europeans were no better off than the Indigenous people just described here. Canadian writer, Heather Robertson, in her 1970 book, *Reservations Are for Indians*, may, after all, have written: "A stone age people who had not yet invented the wheel could not compete with Victorian England or with the sun King of Versailles without running the almost certain risk of extinction." What she neglected to include as part of her thesis is that the Sun King came from a family that was so inbred, whose bloodline was so degenerate, that his father, Louis XIII, had a double row of teeth. What Robertson neglected to include as part of her research is that while 3 percent of France's population lived like the Sun King throughout that era, the other 97 percent ate scraps of rotting meat thrown from its kitchens, *if* they were lucky. What she neglected to include as part of a character assassination so insulting it made one verge on suicide – and, in too many cases, among our youth especially, *did* actually cause it – is that, while 4 percent of the population in Victorian England was busy constructing its megafactories, the other 96 percent ate garbage thrown from its kitchens, just as did the Dene in Churchill in the 1960s. Or while a handful of absentee landowners feasted on roast beef and French wine in an Ireland being ravaged by the potato famine of the mid-nineteenth century, one million Irish starved to death while another million fled for their lives to North America, men ate dogs who themselves had eaten human flesh, there exist eyewitness reports of a woman, driven mad by hunger, eating her child. According to respected Italian writer Carlo Levi in *Christ Stopped at Eboli* (1945), to cite another lustrous example, people in the south of Italy lived in three-storey homes right up to the 1950s. The goats and the pigs lived under the bed; that was the first floor. An eight-member family slept *en masse* on that bed; that was the second floor. And the geese and chickens hung from cages above that bed; that was the third floor. The streets of Paris, today, are littered with the passed-out bodies of filthy, drunken Frenchmen, for God's sake, bodies the rich just step over on their way to the opera. All one has to do is pick up novels by Hugo, Zola, Dickens, and Dostoyevsky to read about the abject misery in which grovelled 95 percent of Europeans from one century to the next. That's why they came here, to our garden: so they could eat. And that's why writers write: to expose such social ills so that politicians, social reformers, educators, and such can cure them. So it was with Dickens, so it was with Hugo, and so it is with Canada's Indigenous writers.

Fortunately, for those Indigenous writers who have not known the paradise I speak of *or* speak their language, there is such a thing as ancestral memory. A case in point: as a playwright, I once worked with an actor who was Cree but spoke English only. At the time, he was in his mid-thirties, too late most would say, for him to begin to learn a second language; one does that as a child, most would say. Still, I had given this actor eight pages of Cree text, most of it in the form of rapid-fire monologue. Not speaking the language, he had no choice but to learn the lines by rote. Hard work for him. Committing to memory syllables that make no sense to one? Try this: *kanagee mootha neetha n'pagit'naawuk n'chawsimisuk taganaw-pimichik meegwaach lapwachin eepagaasimuk keetha maa-a taanspeek iskwiyaaneek kaageepati'naachik kichawsimisuk taganaw-pimiskwow meegwaach lapwachin eepagaasimut?* First memorize it. And then deliver it – adding another seven pages – at lightning speed. *And* know what you're saying. In front of fifteen hundred people every night for ten weeks. Next to impossible, most would say. But he did it, God bless him. By opening night some four weeks later, he was ready. And wonder of wonders, his accent was flawless northeastern Alberta, the land of his birth. *That's* ancestral memory. All by way of saying that, if all these Indigenous writers have been forced by circumstance to write in a language that is not theirs by birthright, then at least they have ancestral memory working for them. If they have been torn from the circle of their birthright, then at least they have ancestral memory working for them. Languages live inside ancestral memory. The paradise that is Canada lives inside ancestral memory. The circle that is North America lives inside ancestral memory.

Then came our second watershed year within living memory. Following fast on the heels of the first, this one was artistic. On September 14, 1962, Ojibwa visual artist Norval Morrisseau mounted his first exhibition of paintings in Toronto. Up to this point, the non-Indigenous world had been under the impression that we were a people without a history, a religion, a philosophy, a mythology, a theology, a soul, a dream, or even a language. We were just blanks waiting to be filled in by European "civilization," fresh in from the potato fields of Ireland, one might add. Now here at this gallery in downtown Toronto, white society was being ushered into the world of magic that is Indigenous mythology, a dream world inhabited by the most extraordinary beings and events. The Trickster (Wesakechak in Cree, Nanabush in Ojibwa, Glooscap in Mi'kmaq, Raven, Coyote, and so on), the Windigo (in Ojibwa, Weetigo in Cree), the Little People (Memekwesiwak in Cree, Memequasit in Ojibwa), the Son of Ayash, the Woman of the Rolling Head, Oh-ma-ma-ma (the Great Mother Goddess) – not the Christian god but his wife – giving birth to the planet and *then* to the Trickster, that cosmic clown, all came tumbling out of the closet one after the other after the other, if not by the hand of Mr. Morrisseau himself then by those of the small army of visual artists who followed in his wake. The Woodland School of Painting, this movement was called. (Mr. Morrisseau's people, by the way, comes from one of those areas of Canada – northwestern Ontario some five hundred kilometres north of Thunder Bay – that the missionaries missed, a loophole through which, one could say, some of that magic, that classified information, managed to leak.) The non-Indigenous world was astonished. Here was a vision that went back centuries, perhaps even to a time before the Bible was written. Here was a narrative tradition that went back to the beginnings of human consciousness not only in North America but on this planet. Here was a storytelling tradition that defined a land whose power was as seminal as the first cell that took root on Earth to spawn, eons later, a land so beautiful it made men weep to see it. This exhibition was the spark. And some two decades later, that spark would jump to another medium – writing.

And the third watershed event within living memory? Then-Prime Minister Pierre Elliot Trudeau's infamous White Paper of 1969. This policy paper which, that year, verged on legislation, proposed the elimination of the reserve system and the wholesale assimilation of Indigenous people into white society. The reaction on the part of Indigenous people was extreme – they did not want it. In fact, the anger was such that, inadvertently or not, it awoke the embers of a voice that had lain dormant for a hundred years with writings by the likes of Ojibwa Methodist Minister George Copway (1851), Louis Riel (1886), and E. Pauline Johnson (1912). Those embers lit up into a spark with a book entitled *The Unjust Society* by a Cree man from northern Alberta named Harold Cardinal. It was published that year: 1969. And it would be another decade of sporadic production on the part of a handful of more Indigenous writers before that spark would burst into full flame.

Still, it is geography that stands as the first reason this spark took so long to make the leap from oral tradition to visual expression to written. For a city kid, the nearest public school is two blocks down the street, the nearest high school five blocks away, the nearest university an hour's bus ride away. To go to these schools, you can walk home for lunch and if you can't, then you can at least go home for dinner *and* for the night. That holds true for 1/1000th of the landmass that is Canada, for that very narrow strip that hugs the U.S. border. The farther north you get from this strip, the greater the distance to the nearest school. For us in the extreme northwest corner of Manitoba just south of Nunavut, the nearest school was seven hundred kilometres away. We had to fly – albeit by bush plane, which was fun – to get there. We had to leave our home, parents, and language seven hundred kilometres behind us just to learn the English words, "See Spot run." When I was a child, finishing grade seven for a kid from Brochet was like getting a degree in rocket science. The cost of bush plane travel aside, the distance alone made it impossible for us to come home even for Christmas. For kids in the High Arctic Northwest Territories, even coming home for the two months of summer was doubtful. So once you left home for school, you were gone for ten months, which was my case. Or for ten years. Some kids would come home from school and not even recognize their parents. Having lost their language, many couldn't even talk to them. All this was too hard on too many of us. So we dropped out, in grade five, seven, nine. No one ever made it to grade twelve. No one ever learned to write, at least not well. Our geography made it impossible.

The second reason was that there was nothing for us to read in the textbooks they gave us at those schools in far *maameek* (south). Even up to grade four, they remained indecipherable – we did not speak the language they were written in so why would we understand them? Why should we care? Even the drawings had no relevance to us. We had never seen a car, a white picket fence, a lawn, a cow, or even a cat. Where were the dogsleds, the tents, the canoes, the great herds of caribou? Where was the Cree *or* the Dene? Instead, here were these white kids, God bless them, with blond hair and blue eyes named David and Ann and their dog, Spot, who lived on a farm somewhere in Kansas with its fields and its cows and its tractors and its white picket fences. By the first year of high school – those few of us who made it that far – we were learning that civilization had arrived in North America in 1492 and that, before that, the continent was empty. There was no one here. We did not exist. All the great adventures, all the great love stories, even the bloodiest of murders, all happened in New York, London, or Paris. Nothing ever happened in Flin Flon or Sudbury. No one in Kispiox, British Columbia, ever ate steak. No one in Saskatoon, Saskatchewan, ever fell in love. No one in Dildo, Newfoundland, much less Brochet, ever had sex.

And if Indigenous people were in those textbooks, we were nothing but bloodthirsty savages who scalped poor innocent – and perfect – white people and then ate them, live. This from John Richardson, author of *Wacousta* (1832) and later *Wau-Nan-Gee* (1852), wherein he writes: "Squatted in a circle, and within a few feet of the wagon in which the tomahawked children lay covered with blood, and fast stiffening in the coldness of death, now sat about twenty Indians, with Pee-to-tum at their head, passing from hand to hand the quivering heart of the slain man, whose eyes, straining, as it were, from their sockets, seemed to watch the horrid repast in which they were indulging, while the blood streamed disgustingly over their chins and lips, and trickled over their persons. So many wolves or tigers could not have torn away more voraciously with their teeth, or smacked their lips with greater delight in the relish of human food, than did these loathsome creatures, who now moistened the nauseous repast from a black bottle of rum ..."

Great for self-image, one that, unfortunately, has touched off suicide among our youth in far too many of our communities. The way we were portrayed, by comparison the impalings, beheadings, quarterings, witch-burnings, and Auschwitzes of Europe were civilized. Somehow scalping one man at a time was an act of savagery, but cooking six million in an oven, including toddlers, live – or lynching "niggers," by the thousand – acts of kindness. Only years later, after sleuth work that rivalled Sherlock's, did we learn that the Pope in 1492 was a Borgia who revelled in the services of eleven mistresses and had six children by five of them, among these offspring one of the greatest murderesses of all time, a woman named Lucrezia. And here we were being taught that God in the person of the Catholic Church had finally arrived in North America. And that his Prince on Earth, this Pope, Alexander VI, had given Christopher Columbus *our* continent as a gift for having discovered it. No one ever told us that, at the same time as this was happening, the Catholic Church was busy ethnic-cleansing Spain of its Jewish population. No one ever told us that, within fifty years of Columbus's arrival in North America, the three Americas had lost ninety million of its Indigenous people to war and disease spread, on purpose, by smallpox blankets. And if Cherokee writer Thomas King writes that this statistic has never been proven, then I submit: all one has to do is look at hard-core data that apply to three representative Indigenous populations, that of Haida Gwaii, Newfoundland, and Argentina. In the first, 90 percent of the population was lost to smallpox within mere months of the year 1862 (read Bill Reid's entry in a coming chapter), in the second and third, the loss was 100 percent. In the latter two territories alone, the program was outright extermination – Indigenous people, including children, were hunted down with high-powered rifles. Like moose. Even I remember stories about the 1920s and 1930s when a third of Brochet was mowed down by tuberculosis, including two of my seven sisters. Now if you average these statistics out and apply the result to all three Americas, then it is almost certain that what is left today is a mere 4 percent of what there once was, which would explain our very low population numbers. Even 10 percent would be a figure to be gawked at, the point here being: the statistics say it.

But no one ever told us that North America harbours a history of germ warfare. There was nothing about it in the books we were taught from. What was pounded into our heads, quite on the other hand, was that historians tell the truth, that they swear to a kind of Hippocratic oath that applies to their discipline. There was something fishy here. We were *not* being told the truth and, deep down inside, we knew it. To set the record straight, just for instance, my father died at age seventy-nine in 1988 as fit as a gymnast and kinder than Jesus; in contrast, bloated to the size of a walrus, Pope Alexander VI first rotted to his death and then burst like a cyst. Historical fact. The question here being: which of these two men was the savage? *We* would be told the truth and, until we were, we would drop out of school and continue wreaking havoc on Canadian society until that society screamed with embarrassment. And drop out we did, in grade nine, ten, eleven. And filled to capacity the jails of our country. Few ever made it to grade twelve, even fewer to university. I was one of them.

When I entered the University of Manitoba in the fall of 1970 – a first for Brochet – there was no such thing as Canadian literature. At least there wasn't in the public mind. If it did exist, few knew about it. Certainly as a body of work, as a national voice, it was unknown. Not like the Americans had with their Melvilles and Faulkners and Hemingways and Dickinsons. Not like the Irish with their Yeatses and Shaws and Joyces and Becketts. And not like the English and the French and the Germans. Margaret Atwood's seminal assessment of Canadian literature as it existed up to that time changed all that. Published in 1972, the book was titled *Survival*, and

I picked it up in third-year university (in 1973) in what was one of the first courses in Canadian literature ever to be offered at a university anywhere on Earth, so far as I know. I was astonished. Here, all of a sudden, were writers such as Susanna Moodie who had written, *in Canada*, as early as the 1850s. Sir Charles G.D. Roberts, E.J. Pratt, Frederick Philip Grove, Sinclair Ross, Gabrielle Roy, Al Purdy, Earl Birney, Sheila Watson, Margaret Laurence, James Reaney, Robertson Davies, the names popped out one after the other, after the other. I was astonished. Here, finally, were stories that took place in Neepawa, Manitoba, on the prairies of Saskatchewan, in London, Ontario, in Montreal. I was walking, one day, on a stretch of road where a Donnelly (from James Reaney's famed Donnelly trilogy of plays) had driven a stagecoach, I saw Margaret Laurence's stone angel at the cemetery in Neepawa, I walked one day on Mordecai Richler's St. Urbain Street in Montreal. And as I studied this material – still struggling with the English language as I was – a voice inside me said: "if they can do it, maybe I can, too, one day, with Brochet, with Reindeer Lake, with the Guy Hill Indian Residential School in The Pas, Manitoba, with Winnipeg." And one of those writers, poet-playwright James Reaney who taught at London's University of Western Ontario to which I had transferred for my fourth year (in 1974), gave me the courage. And the encouragement. So I started writing, secretly, timidly, clumsily, but I started. As had other young Indigenous people in other parts of Canada who, like me, had survived impossible geographies and suicidal self-images.

They started telling their own stories about their own people in their own voice from their own perspective. And suddenly, things were happening in Indigenous communities, including – wonder of wonders – on reserves, in Cree, in Ojibwa, in Inuktitut. Our people were having love affairs *inside* books and on stages. They were walking, they were dancing, they were singing, they were arguing, they were getting drunk, they were fighting, playing hockey, playing bingo, baking pies, they were laughing and crying. And looked at through the warp and weave of languages and linguistic architecture, their ancestral memory went back way beyond the year 1492, to the very dawn of time itself, some might say – for Cree, as it turns out, is older than English, Blackfoot older than French.

If as recently as forty years ago, there was no recognizable body of work by Canadian writers, as recently as *thirty* years ago, there was no

Indigenous literature in this country. There were, perhaps, five or six books that had made a dent on the national consciousness, so few that one can practically count them on the fingers of one hand: *The Unjust Society*, by Harold Cardinal, *Halfbreed* by Maria Campbell, and the poetry of Pauline Johnson and even Louis Riel. And there were a handful of others much less well-known. As recently as thirty years ago, there was no such thing as a professional Indigenous writer in this country, "professional" meaning one who makes a living at a profession, in this case, the profession of writing.

Now, thirty years later, there exists an entire community of Indigenous writers that stretches all the way from Cape Breton Island, Nova Scotia, to Old Crow, Yukon. Professional, semi-professional, it doesn't matter, we are here by the dozen if not by the hundred, writing in English, in French, *and* in Cree, Innu, and other Indigenous languages. Against all odds, this handful of intrepid revolutionaries had learned the English and French languages to the point where they could write their own novels, that most British of narrative forms, their own plays, own books of poetry, own books of non-fiction in the form of biography, autobiography, history, and social and political analysis. The floodgates had opened. The sparks that Riel, Johnson, Cardinal, and Campbell had lit had at last burst into flame. And out of that flame came an entire industry, one that employs small armies of workers in the form of publishers, editors, booksellers, teachers, university professors, social workers, agents ... Out of that flame came this voice that is now heard not only clean across the country but clean around the world.

Still, in all this excitement, one must not forget that the most important element is this: finally, there is something for Indigenous children to read and something to hold the interest of adolescents going to school. If before 1980, we couldn't have cared less about what we were reading, now we couldn't wait to turn that page and see who was doing what to whom, how many times they were doing it, how hard, why, when, where, and what the results were. Finally, Spot was barking in Cree – "*Eemik'simoot* Spot, *'neeeee,' kaa-itweet*." ("Barking, Spot said, "neeeee" ["good grief"]). Finally, his master, David, was talking to trees – "*taansi igwa keetha, mistik*?" ("How are you, you creature of wood?)

If in my part of the world when I was a child, acquiring grade seven was a miracle, to be able to say "I saw you stoling" or "you want some the coffee" an act of magic, that situation has changed dramatically. If thirty years ago, it was rare that Indigenous people finished high school, that situation has changed dramatically. If when I was a teenager it was almost unheard of that an Indigenous person went to university much less finished an undergraduate degree much less a master's, that situation has changed dramatically. When I entered the University of Manitoba in the fall of 1970, there were only fifteen Indigenous students in a student body of some 22,000 white students. And believe me, they were white – all them coloured folks came later, God bless our country's immigration policy. When I transferred to the University of Western Ontario in the fall of 1974, same thing – fifteen Indigenous students in a student body of 22,000. That's a ratio of less than .10 percent. Today, Indigenous students at university are legion. At Brandon University alone, eight hundred of the 3,500 students are Indigenous, a ratio of nearly 25 percent. Lakehead University in Thunder Bay, Laurentian University in Sudbury, Trent University in Peterborough, the University of Manitoba in Winnipeg, they're all there. Indigenous students are getting B.A.s and M.A.s. They are getting Ph.D.s in English literature, Ph.D.s in *Canadian* literature, Ph.D.s in *Indigenous* literature in Canada, Ph.D.s in *northern Manitoban* Indigenous literature in Canada. Thirty years ago, not a single university in Canada had an Indigenous Studies program. Now they all do.

There are, of course, several reasons for this sea change. There are those, Indigenous *and* non-Indigenous, who say that Indigenous literature was born as a reaction to the threat of 1969's White Paper, that this was the final spark that lit the flame in the aftermath of which followed the politicians, social reformers, social workers, and teachers, some Indigenous, many not. Maybe yes, maybe no. Still, I doubt that they could have done what they did without Indigenous writers. Because for the first time in history, those Indigenous students in those universities have a literature that does not portray them as savages, as cannibals, as losers, as drunks, as perpetual victims. They have a literature that gives them four-dimensional characters and not just cardboard cut-outs that spout sounds like, "ugh," "how," and "white man speak with forked tongue."

They have a literature that paints them in colours that are psychologically complex and sophisticated. They have a literature that validates their existence, that gives them dignity, that tells them that they, and their culture, their ideas, their languages, are important if not downright essential

From **Oral** to **Written**

to the long-term survival of the planet. And when they have finished school, they will go back to their communities – as they are doing already – to enrich them, to empower them, to help heal those that are still so in need of healing that, without it, they will die. And they are doing it so that the next generation of Indigenous people will be healthier, stronger, more functional people, a people who will contribute in a manner so significant and so positive to the life of their country that they will help transform it into one that is even better than it already is, a country where their people will not be forgotten, will not be locked up in zoo-like, apartheid-inspiring enclosures, a country that is a true, a visionary leader on the world stage.

"When the white man wins, it's a victory. When the Indians win, it's a massacre." "The only good Indian is a dead Indian." "Indians are a dying race ..." "White Canada is in love with the image of the Indigenous as victim." "'Indian' is a dirty word ..." We've read all the rubrics. We've heard them all. It's in the newspapers every day in some form or other, if between the lines. As Métis writer Olive Patricia Dickason says in *A Concise History of Canada's First Nations* first published in 2006 (and included here): "As recently as 1951, when major changes to the Indian Act of 1876 were undertaken, the old idea that Amerindians were human in form only and could not reason may have gone underground, and perhaps even taken on new forms, but its essence was alive and well." As an Indigenous citizen of this country myself, this information hits me over the head like a sledgehammer day in and day out. And it is particularly infuriating because most of it is simply not true. Contrary to what non-Indigenous writers like *Wau-Nan-Gee*'s John Richardson would have the world believe about us, we do *not* eat human flesh. We never have.

To cite another instance, and this from firsthand experience: regular as clockwork, when someone finds out that I am a successful Indian – waiters, shopgirls, real estate agents, strangers waiting for planes at airports, even Indigenous people themselves – they get upset; there's something wrong there; Indians are supposed to be losers, not winners. When a taxi driver pulls up to my house – which to me is a mansion – in leafy, middle-class, suburban Gatineau, Quebec, from the Ottawa airport after a flight from Rio de Janeiro and I tell him that this "mansion" with its six-foot Steinway concert grand piano (which I play like a dream) is not only *my* house but only one of four, the second one being a luxury cottage in northern Ontario, a third a penthouse in Rome, the fourth an apartment in Rio de Janeiro, Brazil – yes, right there on Copacabana Beach – his eyes bug over. His eyes bug over because he himself, a white man, can barely afford one tiny apartment beside a parking lot in downtown Ottawa. When I bought my first house, in Cabbagetown, arguably Toronto's fourth or fifth most affluent neighbourhood, back in 1991, people – including Indigenous people – were so upset they wanted to kill me. They didn't want me to have that house. Why? Because Indians don't do that kind of thing; they are *not* supposed to be successful. And to imagine that I bought that beautiful house with the proceeds of just one play!

This is a survey of Indigenous literature *published* in Canada in the thirty years between 1980 and 2010 with, as I say, an overture featuring the handful of books that first sparked the embers of a dormant voice. It addresses, first and foremost, the victimhood that the forces of colonization have reduced us to as a people. Then it addresses the rage that rises from that victimhood. Then it addresses the overcoming of that victimhood and that rage. And it touches here and there on the greatest challenge that we have as writers, which is not to be able to write in our own Indigenous languages, which is to have to write in the language of the colonizer, which is to be forced to write in French and in English, two languages that simply cannot capture the insane magic of our mythology, the wild insanity of our Trickster thinking. For the entries in French, I have simply written the chapters in English. And to beef up on their quantity – for there hasn't been, as yet, that much written by Indigenous people in that language – this is where I've included the bulk of the writing "for young people."

In so doing, in any case, this book asks the questions: What happened here? Why that period? Why that voice, that culture, that literature? What previously had quietened that voice? What was it beginning to say, what is its point, its objective? Where is it going? What has it accomplished? Has it made a difference in Canadian society, in Canadian thinking, in the life of Canada? If so, what? In what way, what form? Beyond that, has it made a change to the way the world thinks of itself and of its inhabitants, its land, its environment?

This is our story, our newly minted written tradition, being written, as we speak – in Innu, in Cree, in French, and in English – by a brave, committed, hard-working, and inspired community of exceptional individuals, our current generation of visionaries, our cultural warriors, our writers, our women, our two-spirits … from the Haida of Haida Gwaii (British Columbia's former Queen Charlotte Islands) to the Mi'kmaq of Nova Scotia's Cape Breton Island to the Ojibwa of central Ontario to the Innu of North Shore Quebec to the Loucheux of Old Crow, Yukon to the Mohawks of southern Ontario to the Secwepemc of south interior British Columbia to the Cree of central Saskatchewan to the Inuit of Nunavut to the Métis of Alberta to the Tlicho (Dogrib) of the Northwest Territories and even – surprise, surprise – the Beothuks of Newfoundland … they are the cream of our crop, our most gifted people, our heroes …

POSTSCRIPT

1   This is not an academic book. I am not an academic. I don't use academic language. I am an artist. I use artistic language.
2   Readers are not obliged to read the whole volume. Think of each page as an entry in an encyclopedia. All one has to do is leaf through the table of contents, choose an entry, and ignore all the rest or, rather, save it for another time.
3   Think of each entry as a snapshot. Having seen that snapshot, not only should the reader's curiosity be piqued to the point where he will want to buy the book seen in that snapshot, he will want to read more books written by the same author.
4   Think of this as a sort of *Gilmour's Albums*. In this much-loved show that ran for forty years – from 1957 to 1997 – on CBC Radio, this amiable man named Clyde Gilmour would chat warmly about and then play his favourite records to a devoted audience. Think of this book as *Tomson's Books*, which would be this fascinating collection of writings by Indigenous writers whereby this ridiculous Cree man from northern Manitoba chats warmly about and then "plays" his favourite books to a devoted readership. Look for more than that and you will be disappointed. Think of it as no more than that, however, and, guaranteed, you will enjoy, you will be enriched.

SOURCES CITED IN PROLOGUE

Atwood, Margaret. *Survival: A Thematic Guide to Canadian Literature*. Toronto: Anansi, 1972.

Campbell, Maria. *Halfbreed*. Toronto: McClelland and Stewart, 1973.

Cardinal, Harold. *The Unjust Society: the Tragedy of Canada's Indians*. Edmonton: Hurtig, 1969.

Dickason, Olive Patricia, and Moira Jean Calder. *A Concise History of Canada's First Nations*. Toronto: Oxford University Press, 2006. 226.

King, Thomas. *The Inconvenient Indian: A Curious Account of Native People in North America*. Toronto: Doubleday Canada, 2012. Chapter 7.

Levi, Carlo. *Christ Stopped at Eboli: The Story of a Year*. Translated by Frances Frenaye. New York: Farrar, Straus, 1947. 122.

Parliament of Canada. Department of Indian Affairs and Northern Development. Statement of the Government of Canada on Indian Policy (The White Paper), 1969. 28th Parliament, 1st session, June 25, 1969.

Richardson, Major John. *Wacousta or The Prophesy: A Tale of the Canadas*. 3 vols. London: T. Cadell and Edinburgh: W. Blackwood, 1832.

——. *Wau-Nan-Gee or, The Massacre at Chicago: A Romance of the American Revolution*. New York: H. Long, 1852. Chapter XXII.

Robertson, Heather. *Reservations Are for Indians*. Toronto: James Lewis & Samuel, 1970. 1143.

A NOTE ON CREE AND
OTHER LANGUAGES

Cree is one of the easier languages to pronounce. You simply follow the syllables as you see them. I use Roman orthography for just this purpose – so that Cree and non-Cree speakers alike can read my text. Japanese written in Roman orthography works much the same way. If I, by contrast, were to use Cree syllabics with their geometric cuneiforms or a Japanese writer were to use Kanji script with its complex squiggles, this wouldn't be the case.

In Cree, there are three traits that stand out from the rest. The first is that the soft *g* as in "gene" or "gem" doesn't exist. Only the hard *g* as in "gag" or "giggle" does. In fact, the only time the soft *g* is heard in Cree is if names like "George Bush" or "Gina Lollobrigida" happen to pop up in the conversation. The second is the preponderance of the double consonant. Examples are *"neet'naan"* ("us" or "we"), *"n'gaskeetaan"* ("I can"), or *"pag'waani-gamik"* ("tent"). Then again such words are much easier to get the tongue around than is the French triple vowel as in *"feuille"* ("leaf") or *"accueil"* ("reception"), to cite but one European language. And the third is that the stress generally comes on the second syllable of both two-syllable and multi-syllable words. Examples of the former are *"ooskaat"* ("leg") or *"kapee"* ("always"). Examples of the latter are *"n'chawsimisuk"* ("my children"), *"pag'waa-tee-oon"* ("belt"), and *"waasee-namaa-win"* ("window"). As in most languages, however, there are always the exceptions to the rule. English, in particular, is notorious for this oddity. If anything, so rife with exceptions-to-the-rule is that sterling language that a person encountering it for the first time in his life might as well learn every one of its words by heart. At least, this was my experience.

Last, if you find Cree difficult to read, even in its Roman orthographized incarnation, then I challenge you to read Russian, Arabic, Greek. Or Mandarin.

Other Indigenous languages used in the book descriptions that follow are also set in Roman orthography. To confirm spelling, we have consulted the website of the relevant author or community. Every effort has been made to be as accurate as possible. Apologies in advance for incontrovertible errors. Please contact the publisher if correction is needed.

A glossary is included at the back of the book to explain key terms that repeat throughout the book descriptions.

FICTION

In Search of April Raintree

BEATRICE CULLETON MOSIONIER

Métis from Winnipeg

Published in 1983

April and Cheryl Raintree are Métis sisters who, as children, were given up for adoption into white families. Now young adults living in Winnipeg, their struggle to adjust is made doubly difficult by their heritage. In the relationship between the sisters, we also see the relationship between Indigenous and non-Indigenous people in Canada's west in the 1960s. Neither relationship is easy. Both are marked by a yawning racial divide, one that threatens to capsize the sisters at every turn. And one sister does, in fact, go under while the other just barely makes it through.

At first, the younger sister, Cheryl, is the stronger of the two. Encouraged by kind foster parents to appreciate her heritage, she enters university to study social work. Her intention? To help people like herself find the strength to carve out successful lives in the face of routine racial discrimination. Her failure to achieve this goal stumps her. Her discovery that her father was a drunk – a "gutter creature," she calls such people – and that her mother killed herself, which is how she ended up a foster child, don't help either. These combined experiences are so painful that Cheryl resorts to heavy drinking – and to prostitution to feed her addiction. As to the much fairer April, her foster home experience was, by comparison, traumatic. She was tortured psychologically by a mentally unstable white foster family both for her race as well as for her "half-breed" alcoholic parents. Cheryl survives in later life by passing herself off as white. She avoids, for example, being associated with "Indians" or anyone who looks like one. Unfortunately, this includes her darker younger sister. Still, April succeeds in her posturing insofar as she marries into a bourgeois family. But she, too, meets misfortune. She finds herself completely out of place, her situation exacerbated by having lost touch with Cheryl. The marriage fails and the sisters reunite, but their reunion explodes from tensions that have been accumulating since childhood. Cheryl falls apart first. Her fall from grace is so powerful that she binges herself to an early grave, in effect a suicide. This leaves April to search within herself for her identity and purpose in life. Amid great anguish, she accepts her heritage and works toward the healing not only of herself but also of her people.

Through the circumstances of their birth and their race, these sisters are victims from the word go. Their parents before them were victims too, as more than likely were their grandparents, and so on right up to the clash of Indigenous and non-Indigenous cultures that began when the first white person arrived in that part of the world. Cheryl fails to overcome her traumas. April, in the end, does prevail but only after she makes a life-changing decision. It turns out that, before she died, Cheryl had given birth to a boy, Henry. April decides to adopt him and bring him to a place where pride in his heritage will be central to his life. Thus is victimhood defeated.

Slash

JEANNETTE ARMSTRONG

Syilx (Okanagan) from Penticton, BC

Published in 1985

A young Syilx (Okanagan) man named Thomas Kelasket sets off on a journey from innocence to experience and comes home a changed man. Among his adventures is a violent showdown with drug dealers in a Vancouver dive where he gets "slashed" with a knife. Hence his nickname. At first, he knows little about himself, about his people, about the world. To change this, he crosses the continent, immersing himself in political activism. Seeing the undignified treatment his people have been subjected to, he aims to change that treatment. At the end, he learns about himself in a way he never expected. This is a coming-of-age story set in the mould of a political novel.

The story begins in the early 1960s. That decade's social revolution has just launched so it is a fertile time for Slash to set off on his journey of discovery. He has grown up in a secure, traditional Syilx family at the south end of the Okanagan Valley. When he leaves, he gets involved with Indigenous organizations. Some, like the American Indian Movement (AIM), are radical. Others, like the National Indian Brotherhood, the precursor to today's Assembly of First Nations, are less so. Involving himself in such organizations, he criss-crosses the continent. From Vancouver to Ottawa to Toronto to California to Washington, D.C., and back to Vancouver, he sees it all. Gradually, Slash gains the ability to articulate his own ideas about his people's place and political destiny. Among those he meets along the way is a young Indigenous woman named Maeg with whom he falls in love. But his aim remains focused – topple the tower of oppression erected on Indigenous land by the European system of thought. According to this system, Indigenous people have two choices: assimilate or disappear. Slash tries to find a third option but his efforts are disappointed. The frustration drives him to drink and drugs and to use his maleness to wield power over women. Still, true confidence and self-affirmation arrive only when he acknowledges that there is, in fact, a third option: "the Indian way." Only by functioning on their own terms will Indigenous North Americans survive. That, however, has certain implications, the major one of which is land and access to it – land as the source of balance, security, and wholeness.

Rage against colonial subjugation is evident on virtually every page of this novel. Which, of course, is one way of fighting back, of exposing the spiritual corruption that lies at the root of colonization. Despite all the pain and anguish he goes through, however, in fact, because of it, Slash emerges as a man who sees that his culture has value. It has something of importance to offer the world. It has its place; it is necessary to this very world's survival. The baby born to him and Maeg at the story's end symbolizes hope for the time when that value will be given its due. And rage is laid to rest.

Whispering in Shadows

JEANNETTE ARMSTRONG

Syilx (Okanagan) from Penticton, BC

Published in 2000

Penny Jackson, a Syilx (Okanagan) artist, goes out into the world to address the wrongs that have been done to her people. Not only has their dignity been taken from them, as she sees it, so has the dignity of their land, of their environment. Following a period studying fine arts and political science at university, Penny spends a lifetime engaging in activism. But all this time, she is actually in search of the peace of mind and well-being she felt as a child living with her family in the hills above her beloved Lake Okanagan. In her fifties, she develops cancer and comes home to die.

As an adolescent, Penny takes part in a protest against logging of old-growth forest on Vancouver Island. The spark is lit. From that moment on, she dedicates her life to travelling the world to attend conferences that address the relationship between Indigenous peoples and the Earth. When she sees the destruction that free trade agreements and globalization are wreaking on that relationship, her anger hardens. She is convinced that the world view and cultures of those very Indigenous peoples offer a much wiser way of dealing with the planet's resources. But those world views are not being heard. Her life is devoured by such impassioned activity that she barely has time or energy to raise her three children from a failed marriage. Eventually, the wear and tear get to her and she develops cancer. On one level, she understands that the illness has its roots in the chemicals that have been forced on her diet by these global empires. On another, she understands that it also has its roots in her anger. Her now-grown children in tow, she goes home to heal. Here, it turns out that one sister has maintained a traditional Syilx lifestyle while the other is battling addictions. Penny concludes that if individuals cannot change the world, then showing that world that one cares deeply is a step in the right direction. Political activism is one thing but community, laughter, and love have at least as important a role.

Penny Jackson is angry, so angry that it makes her ill to the point of death. She is angered by seeing her people being devastated by corporate greed. She is angered by seeing her land – and the environment – being destroyed. She is angered that her way of life, and human life itself, is coming to an end at the hands of mechanisms hell-bent on maximizing financial gain from natural resources. Those resources are the lifeblood of a people, she says. Not just Indigenous people, but everyone, so those mechanisms have to be stopped. Still, there is hope. Penny, and by extension the author, sees how, given the chance, Indigenous people can contribute to a system beyond the idea of exploitation, a system where natural life retains the paramount place. Until that happens, one must wait in one's ancestral community quietly practising tradition, thereby blessing the land that gave one birth. In giving her life to the cause, Penny conquers "the monster." And as in all Indigenous cultures, death, by its nature, is celebration, celebration over anger.

Brothers in Arms

JORDAN WHEELER

Cree from Victoria, BC, George Gordon First Nation, SK, and Winnipeg, MB

Published in 1989

This volume collects three short stories about brothers, all of whom are Indigenous. "Hearse in the Snow" describes two brothers transporting their father's body home to his funeral, an odyssey on which they reconnect. "Red Waves" tells of two brothers caught on opposite sides of an Indigenous terrorist case. Revenge for a mother murdered many years ago drives the tension. And "Exposure" address the issue of AIDS in the Indigenous community.

In "Hearse in the Snow," widower Harry Cochrane has just frozen to death on a road on the Berens Landing Reserve. His children, now adults, have to deal with his body. Walt lives on the reserve with his wife and children. Still single, Brenda has moved to nearby Regina. And Billy has long left for Vancouver where he is a successful businessman. From the funeral home in Regina where their father's body has been taken, Walt and Billy have to drive it back to the reserve. En route, a blizzard maroons them in the hearse. Here they confront their relationship with their father and with each other. Like too many such relationships, theirs has been paralyzed by tension if not outright abuse. With their deceased father as their spirit guide, they repair their bond as brothers, a bond that had been broken while in their youth. In "Red Waves," Wayne Weenusk is a journalist who is working on a set of three terrorist cases. The most recent is taking place at the department store in his adopted city of Winnipeg. Unknown to him, his brother, John, is the terrorist group's leader. As in any good spy thriller, the plot grows in complexity until the motive is revealed. Their mother was raped and killed when they were boys. An eyewitness to the crime, John has hidden it from his brother all his life. The racist perpetrator, then an RCMP officer, is now the Minister of Indian and Northern Affairs. He is, moreover, trying to push through a bill that will stop Indigenous people from achieving self-empowerment. When things come to a head, John is about to blow up the Indian and Northern Affairs building with the minister inside and Wayne is brought in to talk him out of it. Their mother's killer before them at gunpoint, John now has his man. Except, it now turns out that the minister is calling the shots for the terrorists. His objective? He hopes that their acts will nullify sympathy for Indigenous people and allow his bill to be passed. In "Exposure," Martin Morris has AIDS and wants to die on his Saskatchewan reserve. The community shuns him. His brother, Kris, flies in from his successful career in Toronto to nurse him to his death. For a straight man to do this in the face of all-out homophobia – from their own community, including their mother – is well-nigh impossible. But Kris does it – his love for his brother is just too strong.

All three pairs of brothers are survivors of dysfunctional relationships. This, however, is not so much because they are Indigenous but because they are human. Love as the final, and only, panacea to surviving abuse is the common theme to these stories.

Moose Meat and Wild Rice

BASIL JOHNSTON

Ojibwa from Chippewas of Nawash First Nation at
Neyaashiinigmiing (Cape Croker) and Toronto, ON

Published in 1978

As the author states in his introduction, these short stories are fiction based on real-life events. The twenty-three stories, which all take place in the mid-twentieth century in Ojibwa Ontario, address many subjects. If there is one central theme that ties them together, however, it is humour. For if Indigenous culture is known for anything, that is it. So deeply embedded in the culture is this humour that each syllable of the language, or languages, is a burst of laughter.

In "Indian Smart: Moose Smart," a group of Ojibwa are crossing a lake in two canoes after a failed hunting expedition. Suddenly, they spy a moose in the distance. As the animal swims across, one member of the group suggests lassoing his antlers thus bringing him to heel. The trick, however, will be to keep the other end of the rope attached to their two watercraft. This they do. Once the moose reaches lands and finds solid footing, the result is predictable – and hysterical. In "The Honey Pot," three Ojibwa decide to get honey from a beehive they've spotted. Lacking the paraphernalia of professional apiarists, they improvise with foul-smelling sacks used normally to hold fish. Their improvised protection gear fails miserably and all three end up in a hospital where they refuse to eat the honey offered with their toast at breakfast. In "What Is Sin?" the residents of a village keep getting stopped by the local missionary from doing something they enjoy. Each time they stage a square dance, the priest appears at the doorstep to send them packing. It turns out that the priest also forbids the eating of meat on Fridays. When he catches a parishioner eating bologna on the day in question, the latter defends himself by arguing that bologna is not actually meat but something resembling it. When the priest orders firewood, the sinner delivers sawdust. His argument? If bologna is meat, then sawdust is wood. Another story: at a time when cars were still a rarity in Indian country, a man mistakes the headlights of a car for a Windigo-like monster, a belief he has been forbidden by the church to subscribe to. One drunken night on his way home, on foot, from the nearby city of Blunder Bay, he batters the vehicle to shreds with a club. The car's owner? The local missionary. And so go these stories.

With names like the Moose Meat Point Reserve (where these characters live), Thick Blanket, Fish-Eggs, Mottled Cloud, and Big Tit, the angle is slapstick if not cartoon (though, of course, all these names are rendered into English from their original Ojibwa). Which is the author's point – reality in Indigenous culture is not what it is in non-Indigenous culture. In one culture, laughter is sin; in the other, it is the heart, the culture's foundation. And that is the message we get here. Kicking sand – wryly – in the face of the colonizer is this writer's approach. Who is the loser here? he asks in so many words. The one whose culture is based on guilt, or the one whose culture is based on laughter?

Stones and Switches

LORNE SIMON

Mi'kmaq from Elsipogtog (Big Cove) First Nation, NB

Published in 1994

A fisherman named Megwadesk Ligasudi struggles to make sense of his identity as a Mi'kmaq living during the depression in Maritime Canada. His confusion arises from the fact that, although he was raised with the traditional stories and customs of his people, he lives in a world that is thoroughly Christianized. One system is based on nature and women, the other on humanity and men, and they leave his soul a battlefield of conflict. Only a crisis that threatens to destroy his personal life shows him the way out. On one level, this novel tells the story of a man at odds with himself. On another level, it is about two systems of thought which, if not reconciled, can destroy entire societies.

In many Indigenous communities, even today, there are people who still practise traditional medicine, that is, engage in shamanistic practices – they deal with the spiritual life of their communities. So it is in Megwadesk's village. His prospective wife, Mimi, for instance, works with the power of stones and crystals. And a village Elder is believed to be a *buowineskw*, a Mi'kmaq term that translates loosely as "dream woman." She is a medicine woman, a shamaness. From the Christian point of view, that makes her a witch. All of this Megwadesk dismisses as so much superstition – until his nets stop catching fish. From this point on, he becomes convinced that they have been cursed by this *buowineskw*. The situation is compounded by the fact that she is the mother of his good friend Skoltch. It turns out that, fearing the old woman, Mimi had refused to teach her the nature of her powers. In tandem with her backstabbing son, the woman retaliates by taking Megwadesk's *deumal* – an object that contains the life force of its owner, in this case his tobacco pipe – and placing a curse upon it. She diverts fish away from his net and into her son's. Another complication is that Mimi is pregnant. For a woman to be pregnant out of wedlock and, what's more, have her offspring-to-be raised in the "old ways" gives her Catholic community two reasons to ostracize her. Fortunately, Megwadesk solves the problem of his threatened livelihood when he finally heeds Mimi's advice and sleeps with a spirit weapon. With this, he cripples the *buowineskw*'s power. The fish come back. His life stabilizes.

Through this maelstrom of spiritual confusion, Megwadesk slowly realizes that, if Mi'kmaq stories and beliefs are mere superstition, then so is all of religion, including Christianity. It would thus also follow that all religions have the capacity to act as signposts, as guides to the living of human lives. Only after understanding this simple equation is he able to heed Mimi's advice and accept the ancient beliefs of his people, thus killing the curse. The author portrays an individual being abused by his community, as well as one spiritual system being abused by another. And if the individual can redeem himself from his abuse, then so can the system that anchors his life. This is a story that pinpoints the abuse that eats at the base of Indigenous communities. Suffice it to say that one book that defines that problem is one step taken in the right direction.

The Lesser Blessed

RICHARD VAN CAMP

Tlicho (Dogrib)* from Fort Smith, NWT

Published in 1996

Larry Sole is growing up in a fictional town called Fort Simmer at the southern extremity of the Northwest Territories. His hormones are boiling, his thoughts confound him, his feelings upset him, and his relationships are plagued by uncertainty. This makes him a typical teenager. What makes him atypical is that his father is dead, his mother is single, and he is an only child in an era when Indigenous families often had a dozen or more children. In his life, rock and roll music is first, sexual awakening second, experimentation with soft drugs third. Fortunately, he is gifted with a sense of humour and a wit that have their roots in his Tlicho (Dogrib) heritage. I say fortunately because, underneath the circus that is his life fester wounds that will take him a lifetime to heal.

It is the 1980s and Larry and his mother have just moved to Fort Simmer from Fort Rae, a town a hundred kilometres northwest of Yellowknife. Widowed, she is studying for a teacher's diploma at a local college while having a fling with a Dene Tha (Slavey) adventurer. Larry is a new student at the local high school. At first, he has no friends, just incipient enemies who become all-out torturers. When Johnny Beck, a young Dene Tha man appears at the school from Hay River, Larry's life changes. Johnny is tough, cool, and good-looking and the girls are impressed. So is Larry whose physical attributes are not what one would call macho. Larry witnesses Johnny giving the school bully, Darcy McMannus, a beating, and Larry is smitten. From that moment on, he and Johnny are blood brothers. Together, they experiment with soft drugs, listen to heavy metal music, and discuss and are affected by Dene Tha and Tlicho creation mythology. They go after girls, though it turns out that Larry and Johnny go after the same girl, the winsome Juliet Hope. That is to say, like most high school students, they have fun. Through it all, however, Larry is haunted by two childhood events. The first is an accident where, sniffing gasoline with six cousins, he accidentally set fire to the liquid and killed all six. His own body was scarred for life. The second is brutal sexual abuse at the hands of his father, now deceased; in recurring dreams, Larry beats him to death with a hammer. The story ends with three threads: Juliet Hope gets pregnant – though not by Larry or Johnny but by Darcy McMannus – and moves to Edmonton. When Johnny's single father finds a job in Yellowknife, he takes his son with him. And Larry buries a ptarmigan in the snow. The bird was killed by someone we never see, an incident that harks back to one of the Tlicho creation myths that Larry and Johnny shared one giddy evening, a story that symbolizes rebirth.

This novel is filled with hijinks and mirth at the same time as it is laced with pain and sadness. The jokes make you laugh even as the blood splashes. The secrets are dark and the sadness unbearable, but what saves the hero from self-destruction is the sense of raucous hilarity inherent in his people's mythology. In that tradition, there is no eviction from a garden; evil and virtue, laughter and tears co-exist in the same space.

---

* Tlicho (Dogrib) is the name of one of the six Dene (pronounced "Day-nay") nations who speak a tongue that comes from what is known as the Athapaskan family of languages. The European equivalent would be the Latin family of languages of which French, Spanish, and Italian or the Slavic family which include, among others, Polish and Russian. Athapaskan land in southern Nunavut and the Northwest Territories also separates that of the Inuit of the High Arctic from that of the Cree to the south. And if any one factor renders this separation distinct and incontestable, it is language. Inuktitut comes from a linguistic family that is every bit as unusual as Hungarian is in Europe, Cree, like Ojibwa, Blackfoot, and others, from the much larger family known as Algonquian. So that, while Tlicho and Dene Tha, like Spanish and Italian, may be similar yet different, neither has a word in common with Cree or Ojibwa which, in their turn, are similar yet different, just like Polish and Russian. These days, of course, there is much mixing and mingling of all the Athapaskan-speaking peoples in such northern hubs as Whitehorse and Yellowknife, *ergo* the Tlicho-Dene Tha relationship described in this novel. Such a friendship would thus be like one between a Spanish and an Italian youth or one between a Pole and a Russian. If all three sets of friends – that is, Tlicho-Dene Tha, Spanish-Italian, and Polish-Russian – were to speak their respective languages to each other, they may be able to get just enough information across to make the effort worthwhile.

From **Oral** to **Written**

Angel Wing Splash Pattern

RICHARD VAN CAMP

Tlicho (Dogrib) from Fort Smith, NWT

Published in 2002

All but one of these eight short stories (with one poem and a myth tacked on) transpire in the Northwest Territories in or close to the territory's capital city of Yellowknife or in Fort Simmer, a fictive take on the author's hometown. The territory is one of the largest, least-populated expanses of land on Earth. Its climate is just as imposing, its winters long with nights that never end and its summers short with days that never end. On that land and in that climate live a people whose lives may be of the twentieth century but who are haunted, still, by Tlicho (Dogrib) mythology, a magic that goes back eons. Caught in a place where these two realities collide, people feel the pressure to the point where explosion is a daily possibility. And in these tales, such events occur with a regularity that makes them almost banal.

In "Mermaids," a young man's gay, elder brother, unable to deal with the AIDS that is killing him, has just shot himself. The deceased's surviving younger brother, Torchy, finds succour for his grief in a story he relates to a young Dene girl he finds abandoned on the streets of Yellowknife. She, too, is in mourning, for a father just lost, and she goads Torchy into telling her why God killed the mermaids. Because they were more beautiful than He, says Torchy. And because his dead brother's love for the mermen was greater than it was for God, God killed his brother – and the girl's father. His rage at his brother's fate, in other words, is epic. In "Let's Beat the Shit out of Herman Rosko!" young men experimenting with sex learn that mints and ice cubes inserted in the mouths (and others parts) of prospective partners can yield great pleasure. "Why Ravens Smile to Little Old Ladies as They Walk By" relates the Tlicho myth of the time the Trickster lost his beak. Tired of his antics, irate hunters tear it from his face and hide it under the skirts of a blind old woman. Whereupon the woman goes into unprecedented paroxysms of pleasure. The cause? When the bird's beak was torn off, the tongue came with it. Another story, "the uranium leaking from port radium and rayrock mines is killing us," draws an apocalyptic picture of a world devoured by radioactivity, a very real possibility in Tlicho country. The metal, mined for years from the shores of Great Bear Lake north of Yellowknife, is blamed for much of the cancer in the local population. "Sky Burial" describes the death of an Elder at a shopping mall in Edmonton. Related from an interior perspective, his spirit flies off, at death, "with an explosion of white feathers. "Snow White Nothing for Miles" tells the story of a secret, and very dangerous, pact between a medicine man and a cop, both Dene.

The co-existence of comedy and tragedy found here is classically Indigenous. Jive talk, psychedelic juxtaposing of images, ancient Dene magic superimposed on pedestrian, modern-day reality, strands of narrative that interweave as in dreams, all of these elements are crucial to the narrative technique. But foremost is the Dene magic, the medicine, for it still exists. So long as the land lives, the author says tacitly, it will never go away. It, biology, *is* that magic, that medicine. With the sheer virtuosity of the manner in which he adapts a foreign language, English, to serve a Tlicho imagination, a Tlicho heart, he soars like hawk above pain and pathos.

Sundogs

LEE MARACLE

Stó:lō from North Vancouver, BC, and Toronto, ON

Published in 1992

A young Indigenous woman named Marianne struggles to prevent her family's implosion from events that mark all families: birth, love, death, marriage, familial strife, domestic violence, getting an education, earning a living. What sets this family's story apart is the background against which it is told. By the end, two events with national impact, both transpiring in the summer of 1990, will have dramatically changed Canada's relationship to its Indigenous population. One is Elijah Harper's symbolic blockage of the Meech Lake Accord. The other is the Mohawk standoff at Oka, Quebec, against the Canadian army over the building of a golf course on their people's burial grounds. From this vortex of emotions, personal and national, Marianne emerges with a newfound consciousness.

At their humble home in east Vancouver, Marianne's mother jousts with her TV set as it spouts reports on events related to her great obsession, cultural genocide. This television and the radio will serve as our main points of contact with the two national debacles. Out of this image emerge the figures of the matriarch's eight children, central among them, Marianne. A sociology student at a local university, she is writing a paper on marriage and divorce. Her younger sister, Rita, meanwhile, gives birth to twins even as Rita herself plots separation from their father. Marianne's own father is absent; her mother is enjoying a relationship with an older man named Johnny. Early one morning, a sister-in-law enters with her children. All three have just been beaten by her husband, Marianne's brother. The dramas amass in fury and complexity. The feeling in the family is that much of this spiritual disorder is due to the "non-person" treatment the government of Canada foists on Indigenous people. Marianne resolves to do her bit to change things – she joins a marathon of Indigenous people who will run an eagle feather from Vancouver to Quebec to demonstrate to Canada their solidarity with the Mohawks at Oka. "Canada has not only erased us as a people" – Elijah Harper's words stick to her – "but it has cut its own people off from learning from us, and Canadians have much to learn from us." That is what Marianne sets out do to on that run – to show Canadians that her people cannot be ignored.

At the end of the novel, Marianne may not have changed the world. Still, she believes, each step taken is one step forward. "Purgatory is where I live," she says to a white cohort early on. "Your ancestors conjured into being its design and location, then consigned all of my ancestors to be its permanent residents." And she says to a sister at the end, "Elijah's small 'no' may have shaken us from a deep sleep, but we still have a distance to travel, not least of which is to alter our perception of ourselves." And that is what the author accomplishes with her book – she has altered our perception of ourselves and altered Canadians' perception of us as losers. Sun dogs are a trick the sun plays on surfaces; at the height of the sun's intensity, objects can appear in double, giving the viewer a depth of vision they would not have had before. On that run across the country, Marianne had such a moment of transcendent clarity: she saw sun dogs – twin suns, twin images of her family and her community.

Ravensong

LEE MARACLE

Stó:lō from North Vancouver, BC, and Toronto, ON

Published in 1993

Stacey's Indigenous community just outside Vancouver is in the middle of a flu epidemic. The only medical assistance available is tightly sequestered in the non-Indigenous town just across the river. As the only Indigenous student attending its high school, Stacey ends up representing her people in their struggles with the racism inherent in that co-existence. This harks back to 1954 when Canada's non-Indigenous community was almost all white, not yet the multicoloured mix it would later become. Above the drama circles Raven, the West Coast trickster. A kind of offstage commentator, if not master of ceremonies, he has the final word.

Using the learning that she is acquiring at the white school, Stacey dreams of opening her own school in her village for two reasons: so that children from her community won't have to leave for residential school, and to shield them from the racism the town's school is rife with. When she has to work with members of her community to deal with the flu epidemic, she becomes painfully aware of the gulf that separates the cultures. Raven's sage advice is that disaster must transpire before people can reconcile. When Stacey is finally able to instill a sense of shame in a white classmate whose father, a doctor, has neglected to treat her people, she sees hope. But tragically, the epidemic shatters her village's family clan structure in a way that leaves its members out in the cold. How are they to deal with life in a modern urban world that has no place for them? For instance, even with the university education she later acquires, Stacey fails to get permission from government authorities to start her school. In the end, we see the life of an Indigenous community in the Vancouver area in the 1950s.

This novel is driven not so much by plot as by theory. Stacey, for example, has to balance her family's traditional values with the radically different values of white society. Aware that both communities have something to offer, she knows that she somehow must combine both sets of values. The Indigenous community could share its strong spiritual relationship with nature, something the white community lacks. The author pulls no punches in criticizing the culture of the colonizer. But in order for the Indigenous community to wake up to those values, it has to be struck by catastrophe. And the non-Indigenous community, for its part, would share its intellectual and technological know-how with the Indigenous community. Old Dominic, the community's philosopher and guardian of traditional law, promulgates this concept. It's too bad, the author suggests, that Canada wasn't ready at that time and place to absorb such wisdom. It is fascinating to see this view not only through the eyes of a teenage girl but also through those of a spirit (the Trickster) who is the underpinning of all Indigenous thinking. The rage against subjugation fuels the principal character's way of doing things. But her victory over it is her awareness that her people's culture, though imperfect, is nonetheless beautiful. And the song that Raven sings more than amply proves it.

Daughters Are Forever

LEE MARACLE

Stó:lō from North Vancouver, BC, and Toronto, ON

Published in 2002

Marilyn is a Salish woman living in Vancouver in the 1990s who finds herself alienated from her culture, her family and, finally, herself. Only by listening to the forces of nature around her, and to the voices of deceased ancestors, does she begin to heal the wounds she has inherited from a fractured childhood and a fractured culture. We see her searching through her past with a fine-tooth comb and, little by little, recovering that culture, her spirit, her life. In the process, she redeems her relationship with the people she most values: her daughters. This novel is about reconciliation with oneself and about the courage and honesty it takes to effect it.

  Marilyn was born into a family torn by alcohol abuse and marital violence. As a toddler, she remembers her mother's bleeding nose, a result of her father's drunken rages. She remembers an elder brother, still a child himself, being hurled against a wall by this same father. She comes close to witnessing her father's violent end – getting hit by a truck while under the influence after yet another fight with his wife, who was likewise drunk that terrible night. As an adult, Marilyn's own life replicates these patterns – marriage to a drunk, marital violence, spousal abandonment, extreme poverty. This results in loss of self-worth, which, in turn, manifests itself in violence against her own children. Later on, after some schooling, she finds employment as a social worker helping single mothers in similar straits though her past still haunts her. She soldiers on against the odds. Marilyn tries to contribute to her people on much more than a personal level, engaging, for example, in the struggles at Mount Currie, Ipperwash, and Oka.* Through her internal monologues, she grapples with the doubts that plague her – her tortured spirit resonates in dialogue with her grandmother, her mother, and her stepfather, all long deceased. Still, even if her ability to love men has been frozen by violence and abandonment and even if, at age forty-five, she is a respected professional in her chosen field, she craves male company. Accordingly, toward the novel's end, she meets a man who thaws her heart. Only in this way can she, once more, feel human emotions. Through it all is woven her relationship with her daughters, now adults, one an actress, one a student. Ultimately, all these pieces gel – the daughters forgive her her abuse and she embraces them to embark on a healthier life.

This author has insisted in interviews that even though she writes in English, she still thinks in her native Salish. The technique she employs in the story, that is, going back and forth from present to past, she has described as coming from the Salish narrative tradition. Still, the feature that is most striking is the manner in which the forces of nature – the four winds, for instance, and even the birds – conspire to guide Marilyn through her darkest periods. Nature is very much a living organism, very much a part of the living fibre that is Indigenous culture. It is not a foe, as it tends to be in much of non-Indigenous literature, but a friend, an ally. And hanging on to this intrinsic belief is what delivers Marilyn from feeling like a loser and enables her to celebrate her dignity.

---

* Mount Currie, Ipperwash, and Oka are three instances (of many) in which Indigenous communities were forced to make a stand against, respectively, logging companies, the Canadian army, and developers on the question of land rights. In all three cases – the first in British Columbia, the second in Ontario, the third in Quebec – these powers attempted to use force to take Indigenous land away from its owners, in order, in the first case to clearcut, in the second case to build an army base, and in the third case to build a golf course. In all three cases, Indigenous people took a stand that became a national, and even international, *cause célèbre*, a scandal.

Honour the Sun

RUBY SLIPPERJACK

Ojibwa from Whitewater Lake First Nation and Thunder Bay, ON

Published in 1987

This novel explores community and family life in an Anishnabe* village in remote northwestern Ontario. Each chapter is an entry in a girl's diary. It begins in the summer of 1962, when the girl is ten, and ends in the summer of 1968, when she is sixteen. In the process, we see an Ojibwa girl growing from the innocence of childhood to the challenges of adolescence and, once her older siblings have left home, the responsibility of taking a leading role in the welfare of her family. And we see the inner workings of an Ojibwa family and community in that time and place.

In the diary, Owl describes relationships within her family, seasonal activities, and the joys and frustrations of any ten-year-old girl. The first part of the book is a celebration of her childhood. Reflecting the innate sense of humour that lives in the structure of Indigenous languages, laughter abounds. The campfire smoke and the forests of spruce and pine are redolent. The sun glinting off the lake in the dying light of a northern Ontario summer is described so richly that we see it. Fishing for one's supper or blueberry-gathering expeditions explode into larks filled with pranks. Nighttime falls with the hush of child whispers and giggles and mother cooing age-old Ojibwa myths until Owl and her bedmates have slid into dreamland. In the waking world, Owl's mother deals with her five children and her two foster children in a manner that meets mistakes and misdeeds with humour, not anger. It is only later that an undercurrent of pain, discomfort, and even violence becomes apparent, not so much in Owl as in the lives of ancillary characters. For instance, she is hesitant about involving herself with boys because of the violence she sees in certain marriages. The cause is usually alcohol; even her mother hasn't escaped its curse, at least for certain periods. Her mother's slide into negligence forces Owl to mature before her time – she starts looking with closer attention at her family's situation. How can she save it? One thing that is certain, however, is that, through thick and thin, she is loved. This – and a land that is beautiful beyond compare – is what gives her the power to survive.

Suffering at the hands of the colonizer is not this writer's focus. Indeed, the few non-Indigenous people who appear are depicted simply as people; they have their faults and their virtues, just as do the Indigenous. Rather, maintaining a balance in life as in love is what moves the author to write such paeans to her culture. What she is saying, if tacitly, is that our future as a people lies somewhere between taking the best of the new while keeping the best of the old. As Indigenous people, we cannot live without the latter, at the same time as which we cannot live in a modern world without the former. In other words, it is a high-wire act we are engaged in. At story's end, Owl finds it within herself to pay heed to her mother's long-standing counsel: to honour the sun for its gift to our lives. Our spirituality, our land, our culture that's what will save us, for good, from our status as the colonized.

---

* The term "Anishnabe" means "people" or "humans" in Ojibwa. Or Chippewa, as the southern, State-side extension of the nation is called. If the latter two appellations were hoisted upon them by the colonizer at one point in their history, then the first is one they have always given themselves. Anishnabe and Ojibwa are thus terms that are interchangeable in Canada in the same way that Anishnabe and Chippewa are in the United States.

From **Oral** to **Written**

Silent Words

RUBY SLIPPERJACK

Ojibwa from Whitewater Lake First Nation, and Thunder Bay, ON

Published in 1992

Fleeing a violent father, an Ojibwa boy named Danny Lynx seeks refuge in his absent mother's home community some distance away. Failing to locate her, he finds that refuge in the community. People come together to care for him, including to shield him from his father, a man they know. After much inner turmoil punctuated by interludes of beauty, Danny makes peace with him. Years later, as an adult, it is Danny's turn to care for his father.

The novel begins in Nakina, a small Ojibwa community in northwestern Ontario some three hundred kilometres northeast of Thunder Bay. Eleven-year-old Danny is unhappy living with his father and his father's girlfriend because they treat him abusively. So he runs away. He walks down the railway to his mother's community where he is certain she will care for him in a way his father never did. Instead of finding her, however, he finds people who pitch in to offer him shelter, food, and guidance. Danny, meanwhile, is determined never to see his father again. Through this story of healing, the author weaves threads of traditional Ojibwa beliefs and practices that we hear from the mouths of community Elders. Mr. Old Indian, for instance, speaks of honouring the sun every morning. Ol' Jim teaches Danny the use of tobacco as an offering to the spirit world. One stormy winter night, when he finds himself stranded on a trail, Danny notices that wolves are actually taking care of him; had they not been howling, his friends would not have found him. The next day, Danny thanks the spirit of the wolves with tobacco. In this way he learns, if gradually, to be at peace with his surroundings and thus with himself. This is the best shield from abuse. Later, he learns that the community did, in fact, protect him from his father by talking the man into making changes to his life. In this way, he is able to meet his son again and start life anew. At their meeting, father informs son that his mother died of cancer. Then he promises that he will resume his duties as a responsible father. They will go back to the land where life is balanced and peaceful. When Danny accidentally shoots his father – in a hunting culture, every house has a gun – the man is paralyzed. So as the years pass, it is Danny's turn to take care of him.

This novel addresses the subject of father-son relationships. In too many cases, they are a battlefield of misunderstanding, friction, and rage. The novel also addresses the subject of exile. What makes this story distinctly Ojibwa is that, when things go wrong – in this case, the premature death of Danny's mother causes her husband to fall to pieces – the entire community inherits the parental responsibility that has been jeopardized. It is not uncommon, for instance, for people to take in and raise children who are not their own. Grandparents, in particular, are known for this – the instances of grandparents raising their children's children are legion. And those children, in turn, learn the value of contributing to a family unit that is not necessarily biologically theirs. They are frequently happier living in such circumstances than they would be living with their own parents. So it is with Danny. Redemption from pain is found in the community and in the land.

Weesquachak

RUBY SLIPPERJACK

Ojibwa from Whitewater Lake First Nation and Thunder Bay, ON
Published in 2005

Chanine is busy growing up, and growing up very happily, in a traditional
Ojibwa family in the lake-rich forests north of Thunder Bay. Her name is
an Ojibwa spin on the English name "Janine," abridged to "Channy." In her
late teens, Channy leaves that environment to find her place in the city of
Thunder Bay. Here her family and its culture are no longer present, and
she has to carve out a new way of living. In doing so, she reinvents the
Indigenous world as it was known up to that point in her people's history.

     Like so many young Indigenous people from the north in the middle
of the twentieth century, Channy is born on "the land." In a paradise of
forests and lakes and rivers with drinkable water and breathable air, animals such as bears and wolves are her family's companions. Though her
family has a house on the reserve some hundred kilometres south of their
hunting and trapping territory, they live a nomadic lifestyle. They travel
by canoe and dogsled, returning to that house only on occasions such as
Christmas. In her childhood, brothers and sisters and friends and Elders
and sometime boyfriends and the various members of their isolated First
Nation constitute a colourful community. Later on, when she has to go
school on the reserve, her family's lifestyle starts turning sedentary. Still,
by and large, all is cocooned and cozy. When Channy reaches adolescence,
however, she has to go to high school in Nipigon, a town of five thousand
people halfway to Thunder Bay. This is where she starts learning the lifestyle and mental attitude of non-Indigenous people. After high school,
she looks for employment farther afield. At first, it is in Sioux Lookout, a
railway town situated some two hundred kilometres away. Here, she starts
having boyfriends in earnest. One man, Fred, comes from her village. He
claims that their parents promised them to each other at birth. This is a
handy tool for courting her, but she finds him aggressive. When she moves

to Thunder Bay to advance her skills as an office worker and expand her horizons, Fred follows. And though other suitors come calling, including a white guy named Stuart, she leans in Fred's favour. Their relationship, however, is far from peaceful. In fact, when he gets her pregnant, he abandons her to drink. Left alone in their cabin in the forest, she miscarries. He crawls back a humbled man, though more fights follow. At one point, murder even comes into the picture. A friend of Fred's is implicated in the incident, and Fred gets caught in the intrigue. Still, after such traumas, Channy's relationship with Fred survives and they get married.

When Indigenous people make the journey Channy does in this story, it transforms them from green-bush Indians to modern young urbanites. In writing about the experience, the author maps out for others born in such circumstances a way to succeed in an environment that, at first, has no place for them. By the time the novel is finished, Channy does indeed have a place. Like all those other successful Indigenous people, she has created it from nothing. By sheer force of will, she has banished disempowerment. And always, her culture's Trickster – in this case Weesquachak (Wesakechak in Cree) – hovers in the background as a guiding spirit.

Keeper'n Me

RICHARD WAGAMESE

Ojibwa from Wabaseemoong First Nation, ON, and Kamloops, BC

Published in 1994

Taken from his parents by the Children's Aid Society at age three years, Garnet Raven spends two decades drifting about without an identity. In his twenties, he decides to go back to reclaim his roots in northwestern Ontario. This novel details from the ages of three to twenty-five his adventures in the great white world, some good, some not.

Garnet comes from White Dog, an Indian reserve just north of Kenora in northwestern Ontario near the Manitoba border. He spends his childhood and youth being shuffled from one foster home to another in small-town southern Ontario, an environment foreign to the land he comes from. He suffers through racist taunts at various schools. It doesn't help that he is always the only Indigenous child in the crowds of white children. Through such experiences, Garnet begins to consider himself not quite human. He wonders why, until he sees himself in the Indigenous people on the city streets – drunks, beggars, untouchables. He avoids them. When he reaches his twenties and starts hanging out in Toronto's bars, he encounters a kind African-Canadian family that takes him in. For the first time, he has a sense of belonging. From them, Garnet learns two things: to love their music and to dress like the Four Tops in concert. So high are his platform shoes that people get vertigo just from looking at him. Still, this doesn't stop him from understanding that these are not "his people." He also has his downfall with drugs in those bars. After getting set up by a pusher, he ends up doing jail time for trafficking. Then one day, Garnet decides to go north to White Dog to meet his family. When they laugh at him for his "clown-like" getup, he goes back to his "Native look." But then he learns something about his father that floors him. Distraught at his inability to keep his family together and confounded by a system – the child welfare system – that he did not understand, his father had killed himself. Still, all this time, Garnet's grandfather had been a keeper of the drum and a member of the Midewiwin Society. Deceased when Garnet was a child, he had left behind a protegé named Keeper who, in turn, takes on Garnet as his protegé, teaching him, among other lessons, the principles of kindness.

One fallout of Indigenous people's great migration to cities in the 1960s is that the lost urban Indigenous practically became a national symbol, like the beaver on the nickel. Keeper and Garnet and, through them, the author, extend a lesson to that lost Indigenous person: you can always return home and reconnect with your blood and, thus, reconnect with your balance. In this sense, this novel is a prayer, one that wishes health and wholeness for the lost urban Indigenous. The medicine people of Garnet's nation teach him to pray out their hurt. Neither rage or violence, after all, will heal it. Only reconnection with one's roots and celebration of one's community will.

A Quality of Light

RICHARD WAGAMESE

Ojibwa from Wabaseemoong First Nation, ON, and Kamloops, BC
Published in 1997

Adopted at birth by white people, Joshua Kane grapples with problems common for an Ojibwa growing up in a white rural environment in the late 1950s. He encounters racism in school as elsewhere. Then he strikes up a friendship with a poor white boy whose interest in "Indians" fires in Joshua a desire to explore his own Indigenous roots. In young adulthood, he moves as a pastor to a reserve and, from there on, makes it his life's work to reconcile the two halves of himself, the white and the Indigenous. The novel may address the subject of friendship between whites and Indians. On another level, however, it is about the reconciliation of races as seen through the eyes of an Indigenous boy and, later, man.

Joshua is fortunate enough to be adopted into the home of a kind and loving couple named Ezra and Martha Kane. Owners of a farm just outside the southwestern Ontario town of Mildmay, they provide Joshua with a stable environment. Though they are religious, their Presbyterian faith is solid enough that they have no reason to pass judgment on other forms of spirituality. With this as his base, Joshua starts school in town and there he encounters racism. As the only kid in town whose skin is not white, he becomes the target of taunts and it is well-nigh impossible for him to strike up friendships. Fortunately, he finds one in a poor white boy named Johnny Gebhardt. Johnny's fascination with North American "Indians" helps him adjust. Slowly, Joshua and Johnny come to understand that the world was born of "a quality of light" that is venerated by all religious and spiritual practices. In young adulthood, Joshua studies theology and becomes a pastor right there in Mildmay. But because of his interest in his Indigenous identity, in no small part due to Johnny's influence, he relocates to the Ojibwa reserve of Cape Croker on Georgian Bay. Here he applies lessons he has learned from his adoptive parents as well as from

Johnny – he uses his faith in the Christian god in tandem with respect for the Ojibwa religion to carve out a spiritual bridge between the two cultures.

It is almost as though Johnny is the one who gives voice to Joshua's feelings of rage and impotence. Or at least, he opens the way to their resolution. With an astute understanding of politics, Johnny enumerates for Joshua the effects of the residential school system, the American Indian Movement, and conflicts such as that at Oka, Quebec, in the summer of 1990. Johnny's premature death, however, leaves Joshua to struggle on alone in their shared vision. For the road to the banishment of such rages, ultimately, is up to his people and not to people like Johnny, kind as he may have been. Joshua's ability to find a middle way between the two cultures becomes redemption enough, at least for now. As with many books in this survey, defining the problem of colonization is one step taken in the right direction. It is possible, so many authors seem to suggest, to live in Canada with one foot standing in each of two cultures, cultures that, in the past, had appeared impossible to reconcile. And Joshua Kane is proof of that.

Dream Wheels

RICHARD WAGAMESE

Ojibwa from Wabaseemoong First Nation, ON, and Kamloops, BC
Published in 2006

An upcoming star of the rodeo, Joe Willie Wolfchild, then just in his twenties, falls off a bull. The accident ends his bull-riding career. Three generations of his family, at the heart of whose world is the rodeo, pull together to help him through his crisis. This is a story of family love and solidarity.

Joe Willie is on the point of becoming the world champion in bull riding when he takes a spill that maims him. Knowing he will never ride again, he sinks into depression. His parents and grandparents try to help him out of it but to no avail. Meanwhile in a nearby city, a teenage boy named Aiden Hartley is jailed for bungling a holdup. Knowing only a troubled neighbourhood and a troubled family life, he gets help from a kind policeman. When Aiden's time in jail is up, the cop pulls strings to have him hired at a ranch whose owners he knows; he hopes the change of scenery will straighten him out. To help restore their damaged relationship, his mother, Claire – who was abandoned by Aiden's father when she was pregnant with him – goes to the ranch with Aiden. As it turns out, the family enterprise belongs to the Wolfchilds. Guided by the strength and Indigenous spirituality of Joe Willie's mother and grandmother, the ex-bull rider and the street kid go through a period of painful transition. Their physical, emotional, and psychological healing is mirrored in their progress on the repair of an old pickup truck. Having a flair for mechanics, Aiden shows Joe Willie how to restore it. And Joe Willie, for his part, gives Aiden bull-riding lessons. The truck has served generations of the Wolfchilds to convey them and their animals from rodeo to rodeo. It is thus a symbol of their lives as ranchers, of their solidarity as a rodeo family, and of their dreams. At first, Joe Willie and Aiden don't get along. Both are too angry, one at the loss of a dream, the other at the circumstances of his birth. Gradually, however, they bond.

This helps them reconnect with a world that has changed irrevocably for each. At the end, by the grace of Joe Willie and his dream, Aiden replaces him on the bull as, by the grace of Aiden, Joe Willie gives his family back its "dream wheels."

Though they live in a thoroughly modern world, the Wolfchilds have not forgotten their people's spiritual traditions. The power of dreams, thirteen as a magic number, and the bear as a possessor of medicine, all have a place in their lives. In search of the strength to survive his trauma, Joe Willie, for instance, climbs a mountain in a vision quest and there, in the night, meets a bear who speaks to him. Courage born out of the strength of people who are grounded in their relationships with each other and with greater powers keeps the wheel of the Wolfchild family's life turning. They live on the rodeo circuit not for the glory that it brings, but as humble thanks for their contact with the land that nurtured that rodeo. To have the courage to take the "Red Road," as the Wolfchilds do, is one answer to the struggle of Indigenous people to overcome disempowerment, says this novel. And to marry land is another.

Ragged Company
RICHARD WAGAMESE

Ojibwa from Wabaseemoong First Nation, ON, and Kamloops, BC
Published in 2008

Through the years, four street people – three white males and an Ojibwa woman – have bonded to the point where they are inseparable. One day, one of them finds a half package of cigarettes on the sidewalk. Inside is tucked a lottery ticket with a value of thirteen and a half million dollars. This book tells the story of how the money changes their lives.

One winter, a cold spell forces the four "rounders" (street slang for "street people") into cinemas. Now all in their sixties, they live by their nicknames of Digger, Double Dick, Timber, and One for the Dead. Their real names are lost to tragedy of one sort or other. Digger was once an operator of Ferris wheels. Double Dick once killed an infant nephew in an accident of unspeakable horror. Timber was once a talented woodcarver who lost his wife to brain damage caused by a drunken driver. One for the Dead lost her entire family in youth to successive deaths, none pretty, one a suicide. And total renouncement of the "Square John" (normal) world is the only way the four can deal with their traumas. On repeated visits to one cinema or other, they keep meeting a retired Square John journalist named Granite who is obsessed by movies. Granite befriends them, thus becoming their only connection to the world of "humans." When Digger finds the lottery ticket and claims the winnings, he has no desire to join the Square John world and so shares his lottery money with his friends. One by one, the movies they watch unlock dreams that have lain buried in their psyches for decades. Suddenly, they can face their demons. Timber is inspired to "go home" by seeing *E.T.*, home being Vancouver where he will try to reconnect with his long-lost wife. As she is still in a state of memory loss and an invalid – and remarried, for this is some thirty years *after* her accident – he ends up giving her his part of the winnings. This way, she can be taken care of for life, which frees him to establish a woodcarving business.

The movie *Ironweed*, which is about street people, inspires Double Dick to try to face the fact that he killed his infant nephew. Finding that he cannot, he drinks himself to death in a five-star hotel room. One for the Dead buys a house that can serve street people as refuge though she herself returns to the street to be with them. And all along, Granite, and two other Square Johns who join him en route, is there to help negotiate the legalities that come with wealth. The narrative is interspersed by internal dialogue that, we learn, transpired between One for the Dead and the deceased Double Dick. All four heroes are in touch with the dead.

This is a novel is about the affirmation of spirit in the face of a world too much taken by matters of the flesh. Even in the face of great privation, these characters remain more joyful than people in the "normal" world. Their bodies may be sick, but their spirits dance. At first glance, they may be losers, but looking deeper, they are not. In fact, if anyone is lost, it is the Square Johns.

Traplines

EDEN ROBINSON

Haisla from Kitamaat Village, BC

Published in 1996

These four short stories each depict an Indigenous family on Canada's Northwest Coast dealing with family disorder of one kind or other. The stories are dark, sinister, even horrific. Evil lurks inside them, just as it does, it must be said, in stories of all world cultures.

In "Traplines," the parents of a high school boy have been rendered dysfunctional by alcohol. Will's father physically abuses his older brother, Eric, who in turns takes it out on Will. His rages fuelled by drugs, Eric is so vicious that Will regularly flees home. Sensing problems and impressed by a story Will has written on the subject of halibut fishing, Will's English teacher and her husband propose to take him in and nurture his talent. But to avoid his friends' teasing for his association with a teacher, Will desists. He thus jeopardizes his chance at a better life. The idea of hitchhiking to Vancouver with friends, all equally dysfunctional, appeals to him. This is only fancy, however, for he remains imprisoned in his life. "Dogs in Winter" depicts Lisa, a suicidal teenager whose mother is a serial killer. Lisa is haunted by the memory of her mother taking her on a hunting trip where Lisa shot a moose; the sight and scent of blood now makes her sick. "Contact Sports" tackles the subject of psychological torture. Tom lives with a single mother who can't make ends meet. The reason, sadly, is a partying lifestyle. Enriched by an inheritance whose source is kept murky but might be cocaine, a cousin named Jeremy moves in with them. He will support them, with a proviso – Tom must agree to play Jeremy's psychological toy. Jeremy gets rid of Tom's clothes, for instance, replacing them instead with brand-name gear, and forces a haircut on him. When Tom's mother's boyfriend, "Uncle Richard," beats Tom and Jeremy defends him, the author leaves the question hanging – is Jeremy doing it out of love for his cousin, or is he doing it so he can hold even more power over him?

When Tom retaliates, Jeremy's derangement reaches a climax – should Tom thwart him again, he will do something to his mother that Tom will regret. In "Queen of the North," Adelaine, a beautiful Haisla girl with a tough edge, is smitten by her boyfriend, Jimmy. Unlike the rough boys she knows, Jimmy is soft-spoken, even if he is an athlete who has just left a life of competitive swimming. At the same time, Adelaine is haunted by past child sexual abuse at the hands of her mother's boyfriend, Josh. It is hinted that this behaviour might stem from Josh's past at residential school. Just as Adelaine is working up the courage to confess her story to Jimmy, he finds out on his own. Some days later, as Jimmy boards Josh's boat, the *Queen of the North*, to go fishing, Adelaine stands there knowing that he will wreak vengeance on Josh.

All of these people are damaged individuals from the word go. Still, confronting such realities by writing them down is a necessary part of the process of expiation, of vomiting out the bile. If there is a problem, you talk it through. This type of writing is therapy, a way of healing the illness.

Monkey Beach

EDEN ROBINSON

Haisla from Kitamaat Village, BC

Published in 2000

A young Haisla woman named Lisa Hill goes in search of a cherished younger brother who has been lost at sea in a boating mishap. On that search, her internal musings take her on a journey through the history of her family and the land that surrounds them. Key to this history is the family's transformation from traditional Haisla living off the sea to a family living a bourgeois lifestyle on a contemporary West Coast First Nation.

Lisa and her hyperactive younger brother, Jimmy, are growing up in Kitamaat, a Haisla fishing village on British Columbia's North Coast. We watch them as children playing in this paradise of mountains and ocean. They splash in its waters, romp on its beaches, have close encounters with the mythical creatures that haunt it. In school, they have their tussles with the usual bullies and with cousins whose parents, all related, are entangled in the usual family politics. Having sent her children, Lisa's Aunt Trudy and Uncle Mick, to residential school to shield them from her abusive marriage, Ma-ma-oo finds herself dealing with the fallout. For Aunt Trudy, it is drink and destructive relationships with men. For Uncle Mick, it is involvement with militant and dangerous Indigenous organizations such as the American Indian Movement. However he is now home from the "wars." Relatively comfortable First Nations families still struggle with the impact of colonialism. Later, as young adolescents, brother and sister have their first encounters with members of the opposite sex. In Jimmy's case, it is a stunner named Adelaine Jones. Then, forced by an injury to abandon his dream of becoming an Olympic swimmer, Jimmy goes off with a family friend in a commercial fishing boat, a seiner named *Queen of the North*. After a storm hits, the boat goes missing. Lisa searches for him in a state of prolonged anxiety filled with dreams. The search is interwoven not only with memories of their childhood but also with signs of the *b'gwus*.* The most poignant, and last, of the memories is of Jimmy diving off a boat he shares with his sister on an idyllic summer day and swimming underwater with a pod of orcas. Seeing his fractured image embraced by swirling water, Lisa feels that her love for him, at that moment, is complete. That makes his loss just days later doubly unbearable.

Lisa comes from a culture where women are born with the ability to see into the spirit world – her grandmother, Ma-ma-oo, her mother, Gladys, and Lisa herself all have this gift. Her sightings, or near-sightings, of the *b'gwus** bear this out. The oolichan is another creature that holds a place of honour in her people's lives; its grease anchors their cooking. It is their lifeblood. Even water is a force to be communed with. The land bristles with magic. Here is an instance of a literature, and a novel in particular, in which a mythology as ancient as that of classical Greece threads its way through the lives of a people. That mythology shapes those lives; that is to say, it acts in collusion with the land and the community to save the people from destruction by the forces of colonization.

---

* Known in English as the sasquatch, the *b'gwus* is a giant hairy creature that has lived and interacted with the Haisla for generations.

Medicine River

THOMAS KING

Cherokee from Sacramento, CA, and Guelph, ON

Published in 1989

Like a fly in a spider's web, photographer Will Horse Capture finds himself hopelessly entangled in the idiosyncrasies of Medicine River, a part-white, part-Blackfoot community in southern Alberta. Its landscape is as magical as it is powerful. The coulees* ripple their way to the mountains. The community, too, reflects this magic. Its cartoon-like character, of course, has its roots in the Blackfoot language. With family names like Horse Capture, Bigbear, Blue Horn, Oldcrow, and Heavyman, how could it not come across like a Bugs Bunny movie? And we see it all through the eyes, and the camera, of Will Horse Capture.

Will's best friend, Harlen Bigbear, is a trickster figure who drags Will along on his madcap adventures. A meddler who only means well, he feels the need to kick up dust in a small town where nothing ever happens. For example, he coaches the local basketball team. When Harlen recruits Will, Will pleads lack of talent. The team, in any case, is forever losing games. Why? Because they play hungover after every first-night win during play-for-money tournaments out on the road. Joyce Blue Horn commissions Will to shoot a family portrait. Will agrees and, before you know it, five dozen members of the Blue Horn family have squished their way into his tiny studio, all wanting coffee and wondering what's taking so long. Then there is the medicine woman, Martha Oldcrow, who lives out by Rolling Fish Coulee; the once proud but now purposeless David Plume, veteran of the American Indian Movement and the occupation of Wounded Knee in South Dakota; and a host of others just as wacky and off-kilter. And each has a story. Still, despite this pastiche of hijinks, the author doesn't shrink from the problems that gnaw at the soul of Medicine River. A source of heartache for Will, for instance, is that he never knew his father, a wandering white rodeo bronco rider who, though he wrote letters to Will's mom,

Rose, never came to see her. This explains Will's mistrust of marriage; when his lover, Louise Heavyman, pleads her case, he cannot commit. And it also explains his willingness to "lend" himself as a father to this woman's fatherless baby. Will's consciousness of family comes from two painful incidents: his absence at his own mother's deathbed and the presence at that bed of his estranged brother, James. Now a world traveller, James, like their father, never comes home to visit. Will is left with the community of Medicine River as his only family.

Like Indigenous communities across our country, the town of Medicine River is a crying clown. This portrait of a late-twentieth-century Indigenous community in the midst of a white community is slapstick with a sad underbelly. As a social document, the novel is important in the sense that "this is where we are as a people in the last two decades of the twentieth century. We are surviving, clumsily perhaps, but we are surviving." What pulls us through every time is the humour that underpins our languages. If smallpox and alcohol came near to exterminating us, then laughter is the medicine that will pull us past our status as losers.

---

* The coulees of southern Alberta are treeless, grass-covered land formations, expansive knolls in effect, that alternate with hollows, or small valleys, they swoop up and then dive down and swoop up and dive down. The waves of an ocean would make for a reasonable facsimile. From the eternal flatness that is the western prairie to the awesome majesty that is the Rocky Mountains, the coulees constitute a dramatic transitional topography. Best seen at dusk on a cloudless summer evening with the mountains silhouetted by the setting sun in the distance, they are breathtaking.

Green Grass, Running Water

THOMAS KING

Cherokee from Sacramento, CA, and Guelph, ON

Published in 1993

A flood of Biblical proportions is triggered by a group of mythological characters. With echoes of the Great Flood, the first big difference is that, this being Blackfoot country in southern Alberta, the Blackfoot trickster, Coyote, retells it. Unfortunately, he bungles it. This is the story of the chaos he creates as the story leads, mess by mess, to the betterment of Indigenous people and of the world. En route, characters from various mythologies are roped into the plot.

Four grandmothers from Cherokee oral tradition are telling the story of Creation and of the Great Flood to Coyote. When he then clumsily retells the story, he creates chaos in real (as opposed to mythological) time. The four Elders are, in fact, four old Indigenous men who have escaped from a psychiatric hospital in Florida. For camouflage, they have donned the identities of characters from American fiction which, after all, is another level of mythology. In this spirit, the Lone Ranger, Ishmael (from Herman Melville's *Moby-Dick*), Robinson Crusoe, and Hawkeye (from James Fenimore Cooper's *The Last of the Mohicans*) travel to the southern Alberta town of Blossom. Their objective? To "fix the world." Central to the challenges that confound the Blackfoot people there is a hotly contested dam. It would change the course and levels of the water, with obvious consequences. Particularly under threat is Eli Standing Alone's cabin which stands at the centre of the vaunted spillway. A house he inherited from his late mother, it represents family tradition. Consequently, he has launched a claim against the dam's legality, much to the ire of the dam's investors. Because he is a lawyer representing the dam's controlling interests, the lawsuit includes Charlie Looking Bear. In only one example of the rifts that split their community, Charlie happens to be Eli's nephew. As the plot thickens, so does the traditional Blackfoot ceremony of the Sun

Dance. At the climax, Coyote's singing and dancing sets off an earthquake that causes the dam to break. The resulting flood destroys Eli's house but returns the waterway to its natural course. Ironically the breaking of the dam and the erasure of the Standing Alone family's ancestral home results in the reunion of a family formerly divided by rancorous conflict. The grandmothers have managed to "fix the world," if only a small part of it and in a completely unexpected way.

Taking up the colonizer's sacred cows, the author throws them into a bowl with Indigenous mythology and mixes merrily away. Biblical myth, non-Indigenous folk myth, literary myth, and late-twentieth-century Indigenous reality all get hopelessly entangled in the novel's plot that, with Coyote as puppet master, leaves us no choice but to laugh. The final tally? The victimizer has turned into victim, the butt of the joke. The official story, of course, is that the colonizer rendered the west habitable by humans. Unfortunately, in order to do so, it steamrollered a people who had been there for centuries. Now the people who were squashed have come forward to recreate that history. The author's way of dealing with victimhood is to poke fun at the victimizer.

One Good Story, That One

THOMAS KING

Cherokee from Sacramento, CA, and Guelph, ON

Published in 1993

Though these ten short stories cover various subjects, Trickster mythology holds them together. And because most of the stories take place in southern Alberta, this Trickster is Coyote. Even if Coyote is not actually present in every story, it is Coyote's energy that gives them their character and rhythm. Despite Coyote's all-out eccentric, the stories betray, in one form or other, a dark underbelly of rage and sadness.

In the first story, some ordinary Blackfoot men are sitting around one hot summer day shooting the breeze. Into their fractured dialogue creeps the story of how Coyote created the universe (the "when" doesn't matter). Coyote being a Trickster of the twentieth century, grocery stores and televisions somehow end up on the list of beings – deer, moon, dog – being created. And when it comes to meeting "Ah-damn" and "Evening" in their garden, Coyote talks at them in a voice as loud as Harley James's, a local character on the Blackfoot reserve who is forever getting drunk and beating his wife. Or would the men listening to the Trickster story rather hear about "Billy Frank and the dead-river pig"? Somehow the Garden of Eden and the Blackfoot reserve get hopelessly entangled in the reader's mind, thanks to the insane Coyote. In the second story, a local museum develops a problem with totem poles that gargle then chant then grunt, shout, sing, and just generally create an unholy racket. Try as they might, museum authorities can't solve the problem. In another story, a big Indian stands in the middle of a white man's cornfield intoning the words, "If you build it, they will come." No matter what the farmer does, he can't get rid of him, for it turns out that he is a spirit. In another, a white community in California mounts a pageant to mark the town's centennial. For historical veracity, the pageant will need Indians to massacre the white people. Which is how the Indians of the nearby reservation end up getting hired for the job. Problem one: Indigenous men in modern times all have brush cuts. Problem two: wigs in town are in short supply. The solution? They wear black yarn to approximate the period's braided wigs. Then there is the story where Coyote creates Christopher Columbus from thin air. Columbus didn't find the Indians, says the author. They were never lost.

In the stories where the Trickster is present, if not actually the central character, the writer uses a kind of pidgin, deliberately bad English in an attempt to capture the cartoonish nature of the Blackfoot language, surely one of the funniest languages on Earth (Cree being a close second). That's the first stumbling block an Indigenous writer encounters when trying to tell a Trickster story in English – the language is just too serious. The second stumbling block? The problem of gender. How to make sense of it in a language where the concept doesn't exist. Coyote in these stories bounces merrily from one gender to the other without rhyme or reason. The writer, in other words, is using Trickster-generated, absurdist humour as a salve to heal the wounds of displacement that Indigenous people have been subjected to.

Truth and Bright Water

THOMAS KING

Cherokee from Sacramento, CA, and Guelph, ON

Published in 1999

Two teenage Blackfoot boys live on facing sides of the Canada–U.S. border, Tecumseh in the white town of Truth, Montana, and his best friend and cousin, Lum, on the Blackfoot reserve of Bright Water, Alberta. The communities are divided by the Shield River, a split that hints at the boys' fractured lives. A dark undercurrent, in fact, will drive one to suicide.

Bright Water is preparing for its Indian Days which feature a foot race that Lum dreams of winning. The first time we see him, he is practising for it. But he sports a black eye, a warning that all is not right in his life. That evening, Lum and Tecumseh witness an event that turns out to be a premonition. From a distance, they see a woman throwing objects from a suitcase and then throwing herself off a promontory that overlooks the Shield River. In their scramble to save her from the current – a rescue that comes to naught – Tecumseh's dog finds a human skull. This skull, which the boys hang on to, propels the narrative. A cast of characters crowds its way in. Tecumseh's mother, who owns Truth's hair salon and dreams of being an actress. Lucy Rabbit, who works at the band health centre in Bright Water but comes in weekly to have her haired bleached like Marilyn's. The sisters Lucille and Theresa Rain, who run a gift shop in Bright Water. Gabriel Tucker, Miles Deardorff, Skee Gardipeau, Tecumseh's globe-trotting Aunt Cassie, the eccentric, fun-loving Monroe Swimmer. A visual artist originally from the reserve who has enjoyed an international career as an art restorer, Monroe has just moved back. Tecumseh gets a job as his assistant. Once a "friend" of Tecumseh's mother, it is hinted that he might be his father. And then there are the brothers Elvin and Franklin. The former, a carpenter in Truth, is Tecumseh's father. The latter, Chief of Bright Water, is Lum's. Neither has lived with his wife for years. In fact, Franklin tells people that his wife is dead. Our heroes, then, are products of dysfunctional marriages.

And Lum, we learn, is being abused by his father – due to a leg injury his father inflicts, he has to forgo his cherished race. Crushed, Lum throws himself from the bridge that connects Truth with Bright Water, an eerie fulfillment of the earlier premonition. In a tricksterish twist, the woman who threw the suitcase off the cliff turns out to have been none other than Monroe Swimmer wearing a wig. The suitcase containing human skulls he has stolen from museums over the years, he was simply performing an interment ceremony for their deceased Indigenous owners.

Yes, people's lives are weighted down by heartache. But barring the odd case, Lum's being one, they don't let it drown them. They are too busy celebrating the laughter that anchors their spirit. Phrases in the novel such as "everywhere the air is warm and sweet" say it all – these people love their land and their land loves them. Tecumseh, we can be sure, will survive.

A Short History of Indians in Canada

THOMAS KING

Cherokee from Sacramento, CA, and Guelph, ON
Published in 2005

These twenty short stories assume, in turn, the forms of domestic drama, romantic comedy, slapstick, cartoon hijinks, revisionist Trickster mythology, even revisionist Christian mythology. In fact, the two mythologies will sometimes collide and mingle in an utterly original manner. The results are often surreal. Still, underneath that exuberant, ultra-witty – some might even say flippant – surface simmer certain truths about Indigenous-white relations that, in reality, are not all that funny.

In the first story, Indians fly like geese in the air above downtown Toronto. Unfortunately, they keep crashing into the skyscrapers. As this happens only at night, the street cleaners who come by at that hour have become so used to the phenomenon that they identify the Indians by tribe as they pick them up either dead or simply stunned. In the second story, a married non-Indigenous couple from an affluent enclave collects Indians as a hobby. At first, we believe that these Indians are mere figurines. But then the writer's weaving of magical realism into his craft takes us to a different place – they may actually be human. We never do find out, however, for at story's end, they all disappear. "Stolen," says the husband. "Wandered off on their own," says his wife. The next story, though it takes a dramatic turn, is given buoyancy by the fanciful imagination of a four-year-old boy. Of the many games he plays, or tries to play, with his single mother, the most poignant is the one where he insists that he be born again from her "'gina." All while the mother tries to convince his absent father, on the telephone, to come home for Christmas. Then there is the one where a white baby is put up as a bingo prize on an Indian reserve. As chance would have it, and due to a mix-up, a truck is also up for the winning that night. Woven into the patchwork of dialogue among the various kooky characters in this vignette is the notion that, if white people have the right and ability to raise Indian babies, then why not the other way around? In yet another story, the Blackfoot trickster, Coyote – for the Indigenous community depicted in these stories is evidently Blackfoot – enters a house and has tea with its owner, himself a Blackfoot. As he drinks, he reads a newspaper and, bingo, gets a job. One thing leads to another and, the next thing you know, he has a truck that talks back at him. Shortly thereafter, even the paper talks. Later, Coyote combs the countryside confiscating enemy aliens. In another story, Jesus appears at a band council meeting where his apostles are the councillors and Mary is the secretary who gives him the job of photocopying the meeting's agenda. Themes and characters from the TV show *Star Trek* get interwoven into the Indian Act, a white town gets invaded by wild animals, and more than one broken marriage is depicted, sadly and realistically.

If disempowerment appears in these stories, it is to be found in the people caught in these marriages and, worse, in the children. Disempowerment at the hands of the white man is evident as well, but only in traces. And the rage, in any case, is diffused with humour. To understand how this mechanism works, you would have to know Blackfoot humour or even better, speak the language. Laughter, after all, is the best remedy for all ills.

Sage

CYNDY BASKIN

Mi'kmaq from Toronto, ON

Published in 1999

Three women from families damaged by alcohol struggle as adults to over-come the fallout of their childhood trauma. Determined to construct lives radically different from those they knew as children, each woman builds her spiritual strength through relationships, therapy, and reaffirmation of Indigenous culture. The novel celebrates the courage it takes to surmount such suffering.

Nancy Boudreaux is Métis and lives in Toronto. Michelle Cook is white and lives in Vancouver. Karen Paul, who is Indigenous and lives in Cookstown, is the only one of the three to have stayed in the town just north of Toronto where the three childhood friends grew up. Now they have reunited at Nancy's Toronto apartment to sift through their lives and try to put to rest the fears that have plagued them for decades. Karen, at one point, had moved with her three-year-old daughter, Danielle, to the house of an Indigenous Elder named Annie Mason to seek counselling. Her objective was to reconnect with her Indigenous roots, knowing that they had been shattered by the violence of her childhood. Her husband, Mark, threatens to sue her for child custody. Though he, too, has alcohol problems that make him violent, he claims that the fact that he is white and she Indigenous will clinch the case for him. Michelle has been addicted to cocaine, heroin, and vodka for years, the result of her own childhood scarred by dysfunction. As the story progresses, we see Michelle struggle with all her might to defeat these addictions. She sees a therapist named Cathy Robinson and leans on a friend named Jeannie she meets at Nar-cotics Anonymous. Nancy, too, has sought assistance with an Indigenous alcohol counsellor, James Batoche, while she studies at the University of Regina. At the healing centre that he runs, she meets people who come from backgrounds similar to hers and takes strength and hope from them.

We see her deal with her shame over being half Indigenous, with racism, with the effects of residential schools, with her guilt over loving a white man, and with the loss of a brother to early suicide. At the end, Karen receives her Indigenous name – Spirit-in-the-Light – from the Indigenous women's circle run by Annie Mason, thus finding herself. Michelle kicks her drug habit. And Nancy puts her deceased brother's spirit to rest with a feast for the dead. Not only does she graduate with a degree in creative writing, she also ends up teaching in that faculty. Back at Nancy's apartment, the three women celebrate their victory not with glasses of wine but with cups of coffee.

These women have been hurt, of that there is no doubt. Still, that circumstance doesn't consign them to inactivity. We see them struggle mightily to confront their demons. By seeking help in friendship and Indigenous spirituality, they quench their rage. They might not quite reconnect with their birth families, but they reaffirm their sisterhood; *that* is their family. And that is how they get over their pain and embark on a new life, one we know will be filled with confidence, health, happiness, and personal fulfillment. If these are admirable women, then the author is even more so for having written their story.

Red Rooms

CHERIE DIMALINE

Métis from Georgian Bay Métis Community and Toronto, ON

Published in 2007

Five lives transpire in the five rooms of a low-class hotel in a city that could be Vancouver. Because several Indigenous organizations have offices nearby, the hotel is frequented by Indigenous people. All five lives described are therefore Indigenous. And because she finds her work so tedious, the cleaning lady who works there – a young Indigenous woman named Naomi – lives inside her imagination. In that space, she grafts fictional lives onto the rooms' occupants. Their stories are told from Naomi's perspective. For her, the process is therapeutic – it makes life bearable.

In each of the first two chapters, or rooms, Naomi finds a dead body. The first is of a john who has just bought a prostitute whose room this is. After the sex, the john falls asleep, at which point Naomi projects an inner life onto the prostitute. Enraged at the abusive way these johns have always treated her and enraged, in a larger sense, at the way society always treats women, this hooker leaves the room to go for a walk. On that walk, she has intense internal dialogues with her aunts, her grandmother, her dead brother, people she sees fleetingly on the street and in a bar where she stops for a drink. Weaving in and out of the room where she envisions the naked john still sleeping, these voices become a kind of ghostly Muzak that floats its way up and down the hallways, in a sense, the hallways of Naomi's mind. When the prostitute comes back to that first room, she finds her client dead from a beating. By whom it is not stated, but one of the women Naomi has just seen on her walk has more than likely arranged the killing. So, at least, it is hinted. The body in the second room is that of a drug addict suffering from cancer who has died from a self-inflicted overdose. Just thirty-two, he is Indigenous and gay and apparently, for the evidence is there, had a fetish for women's purses. Finding a collection in his room, Naomi grafts a colourful life onto him. The third chapter springs from a photograph that Naomi finds in the third room. This time, she projects a life onto the man who took it. The fourth room is rented regularly by a man as a meeting place with his mistress; Naomi's imagination enters the life of the mistress. In the last room, Naomi finds a diary and enters the life of Natalie Greenwood, a successful Indigenous businesswoman. Natalie, in her turn, has just found a diary in her (higher-class) hotel room and enters the life of a powwow dancer, the girl who wrote it.

All cleverly connected, the novel's chapters feature three women and two men, one gay, one straight (the photographer). The hooker starts her story as loser but it is her john, white, straight, and American, who ends up as such. The mistress, too, is a loser, though mostly to her self-doubt. Only the businesswoman is portrayed as strong. The gay man dies of cancer and drug addiction caused by his victimized status, mostly for not being straight in a straight world. And the photographer produces a series of photographs from across North America and Africa that eventually make their way around the world. Their aim? To show the beauty of a downtrodden people. Through this medium, they end up as winners.

Deadly Loyalties

JENNIFER STORM

Ojibwa from Winnipeg, MB, and Couchiching First Nation, ON

Published in 2007

The Indigenous youth of Winnipeg have lost their direction. Kids as young as ten join gangs that roam the streets, committing one crime after another. All come from families scarred by marital dysfunction, alcohol, drugs and, in some cases, suicide. The heroine, Blaise Evans, is no different. A mere fourteen when she gets sucked into this maelstrom, she reels from one unhealthy situation to another until she hits rock bottom. Left with no choice, she returns to the single mother she had fled. This novel addresses the problem of Indigenous youth gangs in Winnipeg from the perspective of one who has been there.

Blaise is out of touch with who she is – a young Métis woman. As an only child abandoned by her father when she was ten, she lives with her mother. This mother, however, brings men home with such a high rate of turnover that Blaise never gets a chance to bond with one as a father figure. To make matters worse, her mother's poverty forces them to move from one dive to another until they reach the city core, a neighbourhood that is a snake pit of violence. Her best friend from high school, a boy named Sheldon, gets shot. The killers are a gang known as The Reds, only one of many. Blaise quits school, flees home, and falls in with a rival Indigenous gang. From sheer peer pressure, she starts shoplifting and robbing so she can eat. The only thing that matters is the next party where alcohol and drugs are the rite of passage, for to shield themselves from a reality that is just too painful, these young people with no past and no future seek oblivion there. Even the love between them, sexual or otherwise, is fleeting and meaningless. Try as they might to reach out to each other, that effort is aborted by the fact that none of them was raised with love. Apart from Blaise's mother, we scarcely see the parents; for the reader, as for the kids, the parents do not exist. If they do, their progeny have nothing but contempt for them. Finally, however, three incidents force Blaise to see the light. One is of closure – paying Sheldon's grave, she weeps profoundly, becoming, at that moment, a human with feelings. The second is when she sneaks by her mother's house and finds a note in the mailbox telling her that her mother misses her. And the third is when another young man, one in her gang whom she was starting to bond with, gets shot and almost dies.

Paralyzed by rage, these kids are in pain, but at whom are they enraged? At their parents, their community, their race and, ultimately, at life for having put them where they find themselves. Still, two elements shine a ray of hope, faint as it is, on all this confusion. The first is that the members of the gang do stick together. They are loyal to one another; they are in the end their own community. And the second is Blaise's love for her mother and her mother's love for her. When Blaise does get home at novel's end, she reclaims the homework assignment that she had abandoned on the floor of her bedroom. The paper's title? "My Life as a Movie." There is, after all, a future for at least one young Indigenous woman.

Billy Tinker

HAROLD JOHNSON

Métis from Montreal Lake First Nation and La Ronge, SK

Published in 2001

By a twist of fate, a young Cree truck driver named Billy Tinker ends up working for a mining company in northern Saskatchewan. Glad to have employment so he can pay for his truck, he encounters inner conflict when he realizes that the company, at the same time as it is paying him, is actually about to destroy the land of his ancestors. To resolve his dilemma, he finds guidance in his people's spiritual traditions.

The northern third of Canada is vast beyond reckoning. To be a long-distance truck driver in such a setting is unlike driving in the south with its jam-packed freeways and cheek-by-jowl megacities. In the north, you might not see a soul over an eighteen-hour drive. For huge areas there are no highways, just temporary winter roads winding through snow-covered forests and traversing forty-kilometre-long lakes frozen more than a metre thick. Add the fact that you are alone, dead tired, and navigating through darkness, and you can begin to understand how one might start having visions; in the deserts of North Africa, they call them mirages. At the novel's opening, in any case, Billy Tinker is driving a truck that is pulling a trailer on which sits a "60,000-pound D7 caterpillar bulldozer." En route to a site being cleared for a mine in far north Saskatchewan, Billy is alone. And dead tired. Which is when the Little People* appear to him. At this point in the tale, he doesn't know why; he is just mystified, unsure he is seeing them. They disappear. He arrives at his destination. The spring thaw is early, and Billy is stuck; he can't drive back south until freeze-up in the fall. So he ends up working for the mining company as a "dozer" operator. He spars with his workmates who are a mixture of Cree, French, and English – the usual hijinks and conflicts. Only when he gets time off do we see him in his hometown of Lac La Ronge, which he travels to by float plane. Here he meets his trapper brother, Grant, and his old Uncle Zack, a medicine man. In this uncle's sweat lodge, Billy sheds his pent-up anger so he can see unimpeded. Back at the mine site, the foreman leaves on a break and Billy ends up getting hired on as "acting foreman." This is when he locks horns with the on-site engineer. If this man and the mine investors have their way, they will turn northern Saskatchewan into a uranium-based version of northern Alberta's tar sands. And then our hero encounters the Little People again: he comes across their miniature sweat lodge in the nearby forest. That night, in a dream, one asks him, "Why are you breaking my house?" Not much later, he learns that the arrogant engineer's drilling operations have all come to naught. And the mine site is shut.

Caught as he and his people are in the world of modern technology and finance, Billy Tinker feels powerless. Wonder of wonders, however, the Little People and his uncle's sweat lodge save him. Our spiritual traditions, this novella's writer is suggesting, will save us from subjugation. These are the forces that will help us get over our bitterness so we can start rebuilding.

---

* Known as Memekwesiwak in Cree, Memequasit in Ojibwa, they are, literally, tiny, little people the size of dwarfs. Or five-year-old children. Central characters in these people's mythologies, in effect they are extensions of the power of the natural world. As such, they appear to traverse, with complete freedom, the border between reality and dream, just as angels do in Christian mythology. The Little People appear to humans when the moment is propitious, such as in the case of the hero in this story, Billy Tinker.

From **Oral** to **Written**

Charlie Muskrat

HAROLD JOHNSON

Métis from Montreal Lake First Nation and La Ronge, SK
Published in 2008

A Cree man from northern Saskatchewan named Charlie Muskrat goes
on a road trip. But the drive ends up being much more. It straddles the
worlds of memory, fiction, myth, and even reality – the author himself
appears at one point in the story to coax on its writing. As for myth, the
hero's invisible-yet-visible travelling companion turns out to be none other
than the Trickster known in Cree as Wesakechak. He is invisible because
he comes to Charlie from the world of dreams, at the same time as he is
visible because he inhabits the bodies of the hitchhikers Charlie picks up
all of whom bear a name similar to "Wesakechak" but thinly disguised as
something else. In this way, Wesakechak serves as a guardian angel, if a dotty
one, keeping watch over his "brother." The chapters on Charlie's journey
are intercut with chapters on Wesakechak's own adventures each one of
which echoes, shapes, and tints the emotional trajectory of Charlie's spirit.

 Charlie and his wife are at home awaiting the visit of his wife's younger
sister, Thelma. They are running low on moose and Thelma, says the wife,
likes moose. There is no question: Charlie has to go hunting. With a rifle
under his seat, Charlie takes off in his truck. The first hitchhiker he picks
up is named Wesley Jack. In a hint that this passenger is no ordinary man,
it seems that Mr. Jack is along for the ride just to make sure that Charlie
is fine. Then comes a chapter where Wesakechak scales ancient Greece's
Mount Olympus to spar with the gods Adonis and Hermes. They speak
of death. As the job of the Greek trickster god, Hermes, was to lead the
dead to the gates of Hades, this is an augury of where Wesakechak will take
Charlie by novel's end. The next hitchhiker, Winston Zack, is here to check
on Charlie's spiritual condition as viewed through the prism of religion.
Johnny Cash singing gospel on the hitchhiker's ambulant CD collection
serves as a test. Next, Wesakechak encounters the Greek philosophers

Socrates and Plato. Later will come the Muses, Jesus, Raven, and even golfers on a kind of heavenly golf course, a play on the ill-fated golf course at Oka, Quebec. As these encounters unfold, Charlie gets sidetracked from his original objective of going moose hunting. In fact, before we know it, he has arrived in Prince Albert, then Saskatoon, then Thunder Bay, Ottawa, Trenton and, finally, Toronto. Charlie may or may not have fetal alcohol syndrome, which may or may not explain his forgetfulness, which may or may not explain the fact that it takes him thirty tries to get to his wife's name, Mary. Still, the bag of pebbles he wears around his neck from the start serves as a charm that will see him through, grace of his "brother," Wesakechak. At one point, these pebbles transform into diamonds, at another, into bubbles of memory.

An artful interweaving of reality and myth, truth and fiction, this novella is a high-wire act on a razor-fine line. There is no pain here, and thus no rage against it. It is simply a rollicking adventure held up to the light by the buoyant, joyful cosmology that lies at the root of Indigenous language and thinking.

Porcupines and China Dolls

ROBERT ARTHUR ALEXIE

Gwich'in* from Fort McPherson and Inuvik, NWT

Published in 2002

This novel addresses the subject of Indian residential schools. James Nathan and Jake Noland, both Gwich'in and forty-three years old, are still struggling to come to terms with the experiences they had there. Forced removal from their parents at age six and the sexual abuse they suffered at the hands of an unscrupulous supervisor have taken their toll. Still, as the novel progresses, family members, friends, lovers, and even the land help them surmount and confront their fears.

Our two heroes are living in their home community of Helena, Northwest Territories, some distance north of the school they had been taken to. Their parents died while they were away and they feel rootless. Night after night, they drink themselves into oblivion, stumble from one sexually dysfunctional relationship to another, and fight off nightmares about their childhood. When they hear about the suicide of a fellow residential school survivor in their community, they attempt it themselves. To these men, life is not worth living. One day, the community's chief, a residential school survivor himself, sets up a healing workshop with the help of an Elder. At this workshop, James and Jake are able, at last, to scream out their fury. Having thus been given the power to love, they connect with two other survivors. Jake marries the woman he loves and they have a baby, the symbol, as always, of rebirth. Through the course of the novel, a wolf keeps appearing. A kind of guardian spirit who keeps watch over the men, he eventually gives his life so that they can keep theirs. At the end, James, "Porcupine," is able at last to say to Louise, his love since their school days and his "China Doll": "I love you." The first trauma they had submitted to as children entering that school was haircuts, brush cuts for the boys so that they looked like porcupines, page boys for the girls so that they looked like China dolls. Like Samson in the Bible, this loss of hair had sapped them of their strength, which is how they had lost control over their destinies and of their bodies, their sexual identities.

The fallout of the Indian residential school system has been much documented: family units torn asunder, parental skills lost to the generation who were taken from their parents as children, loss of language and of traditional skills such as hunting and fishing, inability to bond with others, resulting in dysfunctional marriages, shame, and self-loathing that find their expression in substance abuse and, too often, suicide. The heroes of this novel have both undergone this experience. One can sense the writer's sadness at being unable to write his story in his own language. He keeps leaning on the phrase "she said 'in the language'" when speaking of the Elders, thus betraying the fact that he is going through a process of simultaneous translation from Dene to English. Spiritual and physical colonization, and rage against it, live at the root of this novel. And this rage – against the church and the government – results in rage not only at one's own community but, worse, at one's self. By novel's end, however, through the grace of the Elder and of the land in the form of the wolf, that rage dissipates and love re-emerges.

---

* As with the Dene Tha, the Tlicho, the Chipewyan, and others, Gwich'in is another Dene nation whose people, like these others, live in the Northwest Territories. As a Dene people, theirs, too, is an Athapaskan language, different yet similar, similar yet different.

Final Season

WAYNE ARTHURSON

Métis from Norway House and Edmonton, AB

Published in 2002

Albert Apetagon, a Cree man from the Norway House First Nation in north-central Manitoba, defies the law and his own self doubts to honour the wish of a dying friend. In the process of the author's telling his story, we get a portrait of two Cree communities living out their lives at the northern extremity of Manitoba's immense Lake Winnipeg at the end of the twentieth century. Their names? Norway House and Grand Rapids. We see them fish commercially, work on the local hydro project that threatens their land, and immerse themselves in relationships with their families, friends, social traditions, culture, and land.

Barry Fency is dying of cancer. But he doesn't want to die in a hospital or even at home. He wants to die in the lake that has nurtured him from birth. Accordingly, he has asked his friend Albert to release his body into the lake before he dies. In other words, he is asking his best friend to commit euthanasia, to engage, in effect, in an act of murder. While Albert used to work with Barry on the lake's cargo barges, he has long left the job for commercial fishing. Through the course of the novel, he searches his conscience and his relationships for the wisdom and courage to honour his friend's wish. In a flashback, he falls in love with his wife, Elaine. We never see his four adult sons. But we do see him deal with his daughter, Jessica, who works for the hydro company that plans to augment the damming of the Saskatchewan River where it flows into the lake. The mouth of the river not far from their home, this will obviously affect their lives. He deals with his brother, Leo, a reformed alcoholic who has become a United Church minister. Leo's wife, Bernice, is also dying of cancer. Not only that but he has also lost his only son in his mid-teens; the boy fled his family because, at the time, alcohol was destroying it. Albert struggles with his and Barry's former co-workers. They, too, know what Albert is about to do, which means that he is in their power. He deals with Norma Mason, a local waitress, and with Jerry Johnson, a local gambling addict with whom, at one point, he plays the slot machines. Forest fires, the fish in the lake, the people young and old in the two towns in question, all form a part of the spiritual tapestry that is Albert's life. And through it all resonates "the act." This he finally fulfills when Barry's twenty-two-year-old son gives him his blessing. Late one evening, he and this boy take the ailing body out in a boat. And giving his friend one final puff on his beloved cigarette, Albert Apetagon lets Barry Fency's body slide into the waters of their cherished Lake Winnipeg.

What distinguishes this novel is the way in which it weaves the lives of all these sufferers into that of the one central sufferer. In doing so, it renders that life multi-dimensional, so that Albert becomes a kind of Everyman. In the face of everything working against him, he lives out his fate. And we are left with the image of a man reconnecting with the waters that made him, as at birth, through the dying body of a loved one. Reconnection with nature is a final victory over one's status as suffering human.

Fall from Grace

WAYNE ARTHURSON

Métis from Norway House and Edmonton, AB

Published in 2011

Leo Desroches is on the mend from a fall from grace. Having lost it all to a gambling addiction – a wife, children, a career – he is back on his feet. Back at work as a reporter for Edmonton's biggest daily, he is sent to cover the murder of an Indigenous prostitute. Half Cree himself, he identifies with the victim. In his zeal to solve her murder, he enmeshes himself in events that lead him to an unlikely source of this and similar murders. Against all odds and at risk of his own life, he solves the case. This novel is a murder mystery with a social conscience.

The body of Indigenous prostitute Grace Cardinal has just been found in a field on the outskirts of Edmonton. Having recently recovered from a life of destitution, Leo arrives to report on the incident. Because his ethnicity matches that of the victim, he gets special access to the scene from the police detective in charge. Unfortunately, in his reportage, he rubs the detective the wrong way. This, in turn, gets his employer, the city's major newspaper, into trouble. He comes close to losing his job again, a loss which would lead to life back on the street. His co-workers take sides. Larry Maurizio, the managing editor, is for him. Seeing his commitment to the case, Maurizio gives Leo the Indigenous issues portfolio whereupon Leo has to search through the city's Indigenous community for clues to the murder. He meets the victim's foster mother. He interviews the victim's friend, another prostitute. Resenting what he interprets to be his interference, the friend's pimp beats Leo. He interviews the city's most respected criminologist who convinces him that Ms. Cardinal's case is only one of several. That means that Leo is on the path of a serial killer. He mistakes a Cree man named Frances Alexandra for the killer, only to discover that Frances, too, has lost a niece to a similar incident. We see Leo in his tormented life of solitude and self-doubt, still fighting an urge to rob banks for petty cash, resisting casinos, aching from the loss of his children to his ex-wife. At one point, he participates in a sweat lodge, which brings him nothing. Then he meets a retired police detective who gives him a file. The document sheds light on information so damning that the newspaper could get sued over it. In a flashback, Leo is a child at a school for "army brats" in Germany. Already, he is bullied by his schoolmates, just as he will be later in his life by his wife, his co-workers, adversaries, the Edmonton police. He even comes close to being killed by a tasering he gets from undercover cops – someone out there does *not* want him to dig up the truth. Until, overcoming all these challenges, these hurts and traumas, he forges ahead and comes up with the most astonishing of finds – the serial killer has been in the midst of the community all along.

The half-Cree protagonist begins a victim, and almost remains one. Still, by dint of persistent effort, he rises from the ashes of his pathetic life. He finds the murderer, confronts him and, making it look like a suicide, kills him. Leo Desroches, Cree journalist and amateur detective, ends up a winner.

Motorcycles and Sweetgrass

DREW HAYDEN TAYLOR

Ojibwa from Curve Lake First Nation, ON

Published in 2010

Virgil is thirteen. His widowed mother, Maggie, is chief of the Otter Lake First Nation. One summer day, his grandmother – Maggie's mother – is lying on her deathbed when out of the blue, a tall, blond, white stranger roars into town on an Indian Chief–brand motorcycle. He pulls up to the house and walks into the old woman's bedroom. Kneeling at her bedside, he whispers to her. Gathered around her to hear her last words, the numerous members of her family are astonished. None of them have ever seen the man.

Unfortunately for them, he stays. And causes havoc, especially with the chief, an attractive woman of thirty-five. She falls for him. Her main bugbear as chief is a piece of land that abuts the reserve that is being sold back to it. Which is why she has to face an army of people – bureaucrats, lawyers, her own people – each of whom feels they have the right to decide, for her, what to do with it once it is acquired. Only Virgil and his "weird" Uncle Wayne (one of Maggie's many brothers) wise up to the fact that the stranger could be dangerous. For one thing, he keeps changing his name; John was just the first. Wayne and Virgil spend the entire book trying to unmask him. Their objective is to save their sister and mother from the man. Then the stranger clinches the argument over the land in question with a trick. He steals bones from a museum in a nearby city and buries them there. This allows him to convince everyone that the piece of land cannot be developed because it is an ancient burial ground. When he confesses this bit of trickery to Maggie, she flies into a rage and expels him. That's when we learn the truth about the stranger – that he is Nanabush, the Ojibwa trickster. Having appeared on the reserve as a white motorcyclist, he has come to say goodbye to Lillian, Maggie, and Wayne's mother and Virgil's grandmother. Why the old woman? Because she is the last person in the community to believe in his existence.

All of this makes us realize that, even if these Indigenous people are modern and practically white, they are still Indigenous. They may speak English, watch TV, drive automobiles – we did none of these when I was growing up in far northern Canada – but they are still *here*. This novel addresses the fact that, no matter how modern the world is that has come to surround us Indigenous people, no matter how much we have come to absorb its thoughts and feelings, our mythology still functions at some level inside our souls, inside our spirits. Our gods are still alive. On the surface this story may be a merry romp, but in its own quiet way, it speaks volumes about the indestructibility of spirit and the triumph over colonization.

Le bras coupé

BERNARD ASSINIWI

Cree-Algonquin-Métis from Montreal, QC

Published in 1976

The first novel by an Indigenous writer ever to be published in Quebec, this book relates the story of Minji-mendam, an Algonquin man of the late nineteenth century. He lives in the Gatineau, that region of Quebec just across the river from Ottawa, before, of course, Ottawa and Gatineau became what we know them as today. One fateful night in this lumber town, six drunk white men gang up on him and cut off his right arm ("bras coupé" means "cut arm" in French). Minji-mendam vows revenge. Even if he knows it will cost him his life, he will get these men. And he does.

As the traders and lumbermen arrive in ever-growing numbers, the traditional hunting and trapping territory of the region's original inhabitants is being razed. Their animals are being driven away; their livelihood is being destroyed. To add insult to injury, the new arrivals are imposing laws that forbid Indigenous people from fishing their own lakes, trapping, and hunting their own territory. Large tracts of land are fenced off as private property. This land now belongs to the white man, not to the Indigenous people whose ties to it go back millennia. Their "grocery store" is disappearing, the "store shelves" are empty, and they have nothing to eat or to feed their children. Even as Indigenous fur trappers are forced to trap territory ever farther afield, they are being used as virtual slave labour by the big trading companies. They have no rights. So Minji-mendam becomes a sort of Indigenous Everyman, serving as a symbol for the spiritual state of Indigenous society. His wife, a kind of Mother Earth figure, has been killed by a logging truck. He has lost her just as his people are losing their land, their mother figure. And losing an arm is perhaps the final loss of a soul overcome by circumstance, by encroaching technology. What more can he lose? Blinded by rage at his double-cursed life, he becomes a "mad-trapper," hiding in the forest that surrounds the village. From there, he stalks these men and kills them one after the other.

The fact that Minji-mendam refuses to give in to his misfortune is in and of itself an act of hope. Asserting his presence by killing his oppressor, brutal as the act may be, is one irrefutable way of saying that Indigenous people will not be driven away. We will not die; we will not disappear. Whether you like it or not, we are here to stay. The story may, indeed, be about the tormented, the subjugated, the humiliated. But this does not mean that we accept such a status. Quite to the contrary, Minji-mendam makes the colonizer cower with terror inside his stores, his trading posts, his homes, on the streets. He turns the tables. Revenge, we are told, is not the way to go; in good Christian society, the act is forbidden. But to what other method does the tormented have recourse in order to reverse his situation? He fights back and dies. He defeats that torment and, in his so doing, so have his people.

La saga des Béothuks

BERNARD ASSINIWI

Cree-Algonquin-Métis from Montreal, QC

Published in 1996

This historical novel relates the story of the Beothuks, the Indigenous people of Newfoundland, and how they disappeared with the arrival of Europeans. At the beginning, they live in harmony with their beautiful island as they have for eons. They also live in clans as hunters and gatherers. Around the year 1000, the first Europeans arrive. Fortunately, they are few in number and do not stay, at least for the most part. After 1500, however, the next wave arrives in somewhat larger numbers. And stays. As the decades progress, their numbers mount so that, by 1829, they have become so overwhelming that the Indigenous inhabitants are wiped off the map.

At the beginning, Anin, a youth of the Addaboutik branch of the Beothuks, is circling by birchbark *tapatook* the land known to his people simply as *L'Île des hommes rouges* (The island of the red man). He is on his vision quest, his passage to manhood. Up to that moment, none among his people has ever laid eyes on a European. The only *étrangers* (foreigners) they have seen thus far are the Ashwan (Inuit), the Sho-Undamungs (Innu of Labrador), and the Shanungs (Mi'kmaq of Cape Breton Island), and those but rarely. At one point on his voyage, Anin meets and takes to wife a young Beothuk woman named Woasut. But then he encounters some Vikings and Scots. He defends himself by killing a few, taking three captive, and chasing the rest back to their homeland. Two of the captives being women, a Scot and a Viking, he takes them both to wife and things settle down. They have children, Anin becomes chief of the nation, and he ages until, one day, he drifts away in his *tapatook* to die in anonymity. He leaves his legend as the greatest leader the Beothuks have known. The next generation assumes his mantle and the story continues. Some four centuries later, the English arrive, followed not long thereafter by the French. Already, warfare with the newcomers is common and disease proliferates. By the third part of the novel, which details what happened to the island now known as Newfoundland from the seventeenth to the nineteenth centuries, the Beothuks and their land have been so reduced by disease and warfare that they no longer have clans. Social breakdown devastates them until they are but forty in number, then twenty, then ten, then three, then one. The young woman named Shanawdithit dies of tuberculosis in captivity in St. John's on June 5, 1829, the last of her people.

At first, the Beothuks feel the peace of mind and soul that Anin experiences most of the time. Then come the explorers, followed by the settlers, followed by the diseases. Now we see the humiliation the people experience as they try to repel the aggressors. Of course, all is in vain. These *Bouguishiman* (*les blancs*) are just too numerous and better armed. One thing that is never evident, however, is Beothuk anger directed at Beothuk. Their colonization, after all, takes all their wind out. Like Shanawdithit at the end, they leave it to *Kobshuneesamut* (God) to have the world remember that they once existed and that they will never be forgotten.

Ourse bleue

VIRGINIA PÉSÉMAPÉO BORDELEAU

Cree and Métis from Abitibi-Témiscamingue and Val d'Or, QC

Published in 2007

Four full decades before this story, Victoria's Great-Uncle George has disappeared while out on his trapline in northern Quebec. The event has never been explained, his remains never found. Powerful dreams involving an *Ourse bleue* (a blue female bear) inform Victoria that it is she who has to solve the mystery. As Victoria's spirit form, the bear guides the young Cree woman on a vision quest of sorts. At first, Victoria resists the gift of shamanism that she was born with. Eventually, however – and with the help of a number of people and circumstances – she gives in. In doing so, she accepts the responsibility.

Accompanied by her husband, a white man named Daniel, Victoria embarks on a road trip. She drives from her home in Abitibi-Témiscamingue north to Waskaganish, an Indigenous community on the Quebec side of James Bay. The journey is intercut by flashbacks to her childhood, which was as happy as it was painful. Her parents were survivors of an Indian residential school; one side effect was her mother's alcoholism. Her people's incremental loss of their hunting, trapping, and fishing territory to *les blancs* (the white man) is already hurting. But the lumber industry and, even more dramatically, a dam Hydro-Québec plans to erect on two of their rivers is even worse. Missionaries have always demonized people like Victoria, whose shamanistic powers have rooted Indigenous communities. As Victoria and Daniel penetrate ever deeper north, they meet characters who are, for the most part, relatives Victoria has not seen in years. Person by person, they help her uncover the mystery. Stanley Domind, who works in genealogy at a local museum, turns out, for example, to be Great-Uncle George's grandson and thus Victoria's cousin. He warns her that she must work quickly for the area where the man disappeared will soon be under-water, thanks to Hydro-Québec. Halfway through the quest, Daniel is hit by a truck. Widowed, grief-stricken, and thus doubly vulnerable, Victoria soldiers on alone, until shamanistic practitioners Humbert Mistenapeo and Malcolm and Patricia Kanatawet convince her that she is "one of them." Before she joins them, however, she must first find compassion inside herself. Her begrudging acceptance of this guidance gives her the strength to complete her mission. More importantly, it also gains her entry into the circle of medicine people. Only at the end does she find out where this compassion has come from – the dead. Through her late husband's papers, she learns that he was having affairs with other women, all friends of hers, during their marriage. Still in mourning, she not only pardons them all, she also continues to love them.

The Cree language resonates throughout these pages. In a sense, even though it comes out in French, the novel is written in Cree. The Indigenous people portrayed are not enraged by colonization so much as they are beleaguered by it. Victoria does her best to help them heal. Her quest to lay her great-uncle's spirit to rest is a metaphor for this healing. That she finds within herself the wisdom to love under any circumstances earns her her status as medicine woman. And that is the victory over colonization.

Le mutilateur

JULIAN MAHIKAN

Atikamekw* from Obedjiwan First Nation (Mauricie), Montreal, QC
Published in 2008

A murder mystery with overtones of the supernatural, this is a tale of a serial killer on the loose. Neither the killer nor any element in the story, however, has to do with the writer's Atikamekw culture, northern Quebec, or even Canada. Pure fiction, it is set instead in, of all places, San Francisco, California.

A literary agent reads from a manuscript delivered by a client, a writer named James Andrews. Mr. Andrews, it seems, has just been committed to a mental institution for schizophrenia and "acts of horror." Then the story reverts to a time before that manuscript was written. James Andrews, a San Francisco writer, comes from a comfortable, white middle-class family, lives with a woman in a fabulous house and, at age twenty-five, has just been successful with his first novel, a thriller. He is stuck, however, for material for his second novel, and his publishing house is after him for it. Then something happens to yank him out of his bourgeois comfort. A serial killer is on the loose. Already on his fifteenth victim, he not only kills them, he also mutilates their bodies in a manner so inhuman that only a Loup-Garou (a kind of werewolf) could have done it. Or so it is hinted as the book progresses. Prone since childhood to fits of schizophrenia in which he is accosted by visions of the Loup-Garou, James learns of the murders from the media. But then he gets a letter from the serial killer himself. Going by the name of Robert Anderson, the man pleads with him to come and save him. For it is not he who is committing the murders, he explains, but a spirit who has come to possess him – again, shades of the Loup-Garou. The killer leaves James directives. All this fodder he so desperately needs for his second novel, James starts tape-recording everything that happens next. He plans to turn it into the novel he is contracted to deliver in mere months. As the plot thickens, so does his novel's plot. The murders mount.

James's hallucinations intensify. The killer is captured, jailed, and tried; other characters are caught in the accumulating web of events. Among them is a painter named Mully Iseroof, an occasional clandestine sex partner whom James inadvertently impregnates. James traces the killer's coded directions to a hospital and then to an orphanage where he discovers that he himself is the killer's son, adopted out at birth. To kill the strain of Loup-Garou insanity that taints his bloodline – that is, to prevent future murders – he decides he has to kill himself and his newborn just as his father is being executed by electric chair. And the tale comes to a spectacular finish on the city's fabled Golden Gate Bridge.

There is not a shade of victimhood or rage in this novel. Nor is there a trace of any Indigenous language, least of all the writer's native Atikamekw. In fact, the sole Indigenous elements are the myth of the Loup-Garou and, almost in passing, the fact that James's biological mother, who died in childbirth, is Navajo. Aside from that, it is just a good, old-fashioned thriller with elements of the supernatural. This, one surmises, is the writer's way of dealing with his and his people's victimhood – to just laugh it off and spin a good yarn. His objective? To entertain his readership. Which he does. In spades.

---

* Atikamekw is yet another branch of the thirty or so Algonquian-speaking nations that people large parts of Canada as well as the northeast United States, in states like Maine, for instance, and as far west as Wisconsin. Located in north-central Quebec just northwest of Lac St. Jean, they are closely related, on the one side, to the Cree of James Bay and, on the other, the Innu north of Lac St. Jean and up toward Labrador and the north shore of the St. Lawrence River. As for the name, it is derived from the words, *atik* ("caribou") and *ameek* ("of the water"). So that what *Atikamek* ends up meaning is "caribou of the water," which is what we – that is, including us Cree of northern Manitoba and northern Saskatchewan – call "whitefish." Of all the fish that populate northern freshwater lakes and rivers, whitefish are as numerous in that water as caribou are on land. Which is why both are staples of our diet, the food we eat most often. A delicious fish, we, too – that is, us Cree – could easily have been called "the people of the whitefish." Which is what, in essence, the tribal name, *Atikamekw*, means, with, that is, the *w* tagged on at the end for reasons of dialect.

DRAMA

Coyote City

DANIEL DAVID MOSES

Delaware* from Six Nations First Nation, Toronto, and Kingston, ON

First produced in 1988

This play transposes the myth of Orpheus and Eurydice from its ancient Greek setting to one that is Indigenous, contemporary, and Canadian. In the Greek myth, the musician Orpheus travels to the land of the dead in an attempt to bring his lover, Eurydice, back to the land of the living. With his lyre, he lulls the realm's king and queen, Hades and Persephone, into agreeing to her release. On one condition. Unfortunately, on the journey back up, Orpheus fails to honour that condition and thus loses his beloved, for good this time. In the author's take on what has, over time, become a story packed with universal resonance, he transforms Six Nations reserve in southwestern Ontario into the land of the living and the city of Toronto into the land of the dead. And he reverses the genders.

Living on the reserve with her widowed mother, Martha, and younger sister, Boo, Lena gets a phone call in the middle of the night. It is her Cree boyfriend, Johnny, asking her to meet him at the Toronto bar where they used to hang out. The trouble is that Johnny is dead. In deep mourning and thus vulnerable to bouts of irrational behaviour, Lena agrees to Johnny's request and prepares for her departure. Horrified, her mother pleads with her not to listen to ghosts. Siding with their mother, Boo joins in the argument; she is nursing an unrequited love for this same Johnny. In a panic, Martha calls her minister on the reserve, Thomas, for help. Before you know it, Thomas, a reformed alcoholic, has given Lena a ride to the city some two hours away. Walking down a street, Lena and Thomas meet an Indigenous hooker named Clarisse who, like Charon in Greek myth, ferries the two living people to the land of the dead, the Silver Dollar. A well-known Indigenous bar, this is where Johnny met his end, stabbed to death in a drunken brawl some six months earlier. Having pursued Lena and Thomas by bus, Martha and Boo show up at the bar. And there, amid much confusion, Lena and Boo see Johnny. But he sees Boo only and then disappears, faded into air for all one knows, leaving Lena hanging in limbo. And who ends up in hell but Thomas. Having seduced the reformed alcoholic into his first drink in years, Clarisse, the Charon of Toronto, has successfully ferried him from the land of the living to the land of the dead.

In technique as in vision, this play betrays a certain sophistication that lifts its material above an Indigenous-literature "ghetto." The Indigenous elements are there, but only as context, a clear sign that Indigenous writers, by this time in their literary development, have begun moving beyond Indigenous-specific themes to themes more universal. In this case, the writer's source material is a literature that has served as the basis for virtually all of European writing, much as its language, Greek, has served as base for virtually all European languages. Race doesn't matter here. What does is the characters' portrayal as not just cardboard cut-out Indians but as fully fleshed-out human beings with classical resonance. In this writer's agenda, the time to wail about one's status as "suffering Indian" is past. It is time to move on and just be human.

———————————

* The Delaware nation has a history that is long and circuitous. First, the name was slapped on them by the British. Their original name for themselves, in their own tongue, was Lenni-Lenape. A name that means, "Original People," they have been called "the Grandfather Nation" in the sense that theirs is the oldest and thus the original of all the Algonquian family of languages. As with Latin in Europe, it thus gave birth to some two dozen languages, among them Cree, Ojibwa, Mi'kmaq, and Blackfoot. Geographically, they originate in what would later become such American states as Delaware, New Jersey, and New York, including the storied island of Manhattan. From there, it's the usual story of decimation by disease and repeated displacement. Until one branch ended up in what was then referred to as "Indian Territory" (later Oklahoma) together with another more than a hundred displaced Indigenous nations from the east. A second branch ended up in Canada, specifically in southern Ontario. Siding with the British in the American War of Independence, this branch of the Delaware nation was given asylum by them and their allies, the Six Nations. Which is how one-third of this splinter group ended up being given land on the banks of the Grand River by its occupants, the Iroquoian people of the Six Nations. As such, therefore, they constitute a kind of "Seventh Nation." (The other two thirds of this group that came to Canada constitute the modern First Nations of Muncey and Moraviantown, both just west of London, Ontario.)

From **Oral** to **Written**

Big Buck City

DANIEL DAVID MOSES

Delaware from Six Nations First Nation, Toronto, and Kingston, ON

First produced in 1991

A sequel to the author's previous play, *Coyote City*, this one takes place at the Toronto home of Barbara and Jack Buck, sister and brother-in-law of Martha Fisher, the mother from the first play. It tells the story of an Indigenous family dealing with the realities of urban life, a social phenomenon that was largely unknown in the first half of the twentieth century.

It is Christmas Eve and Barbara and Jack are preparing for Santa's arrival. They are also dealing with a whole slew of problems: the potential purchase of a new condominium and the mortgage that comes with it, the bank, a dinner reservation at a fancy restaurant, problems with the plumbing, Barbara's inability to have a baby at her age, bills from her gynecologist, an Indigenous preacher woman who keeps knocking at their door in search of "Martha." And unwanted, ostensibly insane relatives visiting from the reserve who claim a near-encounter with, of all things, a ghost. The relatives are Martha, Lena, and Boo from *Coyote City*, the ghost of Johnny at the Silver Dollar. Clarisse, the Indigenous hooker from the earlier play, meanwhile, has converted and taken over from Thomas, the preacher who fell from grace. In this role, she is guiding Lena through a pregnancy that is fraught with danger because, for one thing, the baby's father might be a ghost. Clarisse's job? To tell Martha that the baby is imminent, which is why she is knocking at the Bucks' door – she knows Martha is there. For their part, the Bucks think the preacher is after their charity again, so they won't let her in. The traumatized Martha has locked herself in an upstairs bedroom, forcing Barbara and Jack into basement quarters. Meanwhile, a street urchin named Ricky Raccoon breaks into the Bucks' house, climbs into Jack's Santa Claus outfit, and wreaks havoc. The hijinks are numerous, the doors fly open and shut, even the plumbing screams and yells. Until Lena gives birth in the upstairs bedroom, which her mother still refuses to leave; in fact, we never see Martha *or* her grandchild. All we know is that he is the "Christmas present" Martha's sister, Barbara, has dreamt of for years.

A madcap comedy that betrays all the features of farce and slapstick, this play shows an Indigenous family living off reserve and removed from the natural environment on which Indigenous culture is based. Hints of the culture – in the person of the tricksterish Ricky Raccoon – may still play a small part in their ethnic identity; their blood certainly does, but they live in the modern urban world. Indigenous people's winning the right to vote in federal elections in 1960 was what made that difference. With this victory over colonization, they were free to leave the reserve and move to the city. Some were more successful than others, of course, just like some white people are more successful than others at living in cities. But that's par for the course. In portraying the successful ones, this play is a valuable social document.

Almighty Voice and His Wife

DANIEL DAVID MOSES

Delaware from Six Nations First Nation, Toronto, and Kingston, ON

First produced in 1992

Almighty Voice shoots a farmer's steer and is imprisoned, escapes but gets shot while fleeing, and dies, still only in his twenties. The play's two acts are played by just two performers, Almighty Voice and his wife, White Girl. The first act presents a poetic portrait of the two while the man is still alive. They deal with their relationship as a young married couple, only to be interrupted by the mishap. They struggle with the upshot as best they can but fail. When the man dies, the woman gives birth to their first child. The second act takes place in the afterlife. It is presented as an "Indian Medicine Show," which, in essence, is an Indigenous take on the travelling minstrel show. An entertainment popular in nineteenth-century America, minstrel shows featured white actors in black face. Here, with the Indigenous actors playing in white face, the play presents Indigenous life as a circus-like cabaret.

　　As the play begins, Almighty Voice courts a thirteen-year-old Cree girl named White Girl. She plays coy but finally relents. They marry and try to have children. As a student educated in the Indian residential school system, she has been affected by Catholicism. This element causes tension in their marriage as the man follows Cree spirituality. Their ongoing debate is interrupted by his shooting of the steer. Now fugitives, they consider running away to hide somewhere. If he is to be taken to prison, as he expects, then she will go with him, she says. He disagrees. Later, he escapes from jail and flees, which is when he gets shot and dies, without knowing that his young wife is pregnant. The sequence ends with her appearing with the infant over his body. The second act plays in direct contrast to the first. Now both in white face, Almighty Voice plays his own ghost while White Girl plays what the author calls the Interlocutor, a combination of emcee, circus barker, and Mountie. They run through all the racist stereotypes in which Indigenous people have been portrayed in the popular media. Resonating loudly are riffs on the cigar-store Indian, the noble savage who thrills European audiences with feats of derring-do (à la Buffalo Bill and his Wild West show), the Hollywood Indian who sings like Eddy Nelson, the Indian on horseback bow-and-arrowing heroic General Custer–era soldiers, and so on. At one point, the ghost even turns the tables and forces the Interlocutor to play the Indian Princess.

This play is a fictive account of an incident in the life of a young Cree man in late nineteenth-century Saskatchewan, an incident that has fired the Indigenous imagination ever since. In fact, there are those who say that this was the last armed Indigenous resistance in Canada's history. But the point here is the abuse that the Indigenous spirit has been subjected to over the decades by popular culture. In the first act, the spiritual beliefs of Indigenous people are subtly contrasted with White Girl's obsession with the white man's God – for instance, the waxing and waning of the moon play subtly against her constant harping on this God's "all-seeing" glass eye (that is, his binoculars). But in the second act, the portrayal of the blasphemy is over the top and, ultimately, obscene. Which is why it has to be funny. The author's proffered panacea to subjugation? Farce, humour, all-out laughter.

The Bootlegger Blues

DREW HAYDEN TAYLOR

Ojibwa from Curve Lake First Nation, ON

First produced in 1990

This play is the first of four the author collectively entitles the Blues Quartet. Their aim? To celebrate Indigenous humour. The author's position is that too many writers, Indigenous and non-Indigenous, have a tendency to cast Indigenous people in a negative light, that they harp on their problems with alcohol abuse and general dysfunction. With these four plays, he has decided to do the reverse – portray them as positive and functional. And funny. In this play, Martha is a fifty-eight-year-old Ojibwa woman living on a typical Ojibwa reserve in central Ontario. One day, she finds herself with 143 cases of beer, the result of a church fundraiser gone wrong. For a good Christian woman who has never touched a drop of alcohol in her life, this is too much. One farcical situation leads to another until she hits El Dorado – she becomes the reserve's most successful bootlegger ever.

As the play opens, Martha, the mother of Marianne and Blue, is in the middle of cooking for a church fundraiser at a powwow. Having bowed to advice from her eccentric sister, Marjorie, that Indians need beer to go with their meals, Martha has gone out and bought 143 cases. When this sister's theory turns out wrong – folks don't drink at a powwow, not with the drum around – Martha is outraged. Now she finds herself stuck with all this beer, and the question is what to do with it. Interwoven into this main plot are the normal clown-like shenanigans that plague all reserves. Marianne, who works at the band office, is fretting because she has just destroyed the band manager's computer and must replace it by nine the next morning. This situation can jeopardize the job her common-law husband, David, has there. Blue is attracted to a new arrival on the rez, a winsome twenty-two-year-old named Angie. Not knowing reserves, she is all hot-to-trot to learn all about them and Blue gladly takes on the assignment, at least until he learns, from Martha, that Angie is actually his cousin. Marianne, meanwhile, takes a shine to Noble, a handsome young powwow dancer from "out of town." This causes even more tension in Marianne's relationship with David. In fact, toward play's end, she threatens to leave him. All this activity, and more, swirls around Martha. For one thing, she has to move fast to keep their hands off her beer. And since her sister, Marjorie, has removed the little yellow stickers needed to return the cases, she can't take them back. Then Marianne and Blue jokingly suggest that she bootleg them. Amazingly, she takes the bait. But having no experience in the business, she starts putting signs up in public places announcing her sales. Her son, Andrew, who works in law enforcement, freaks out. The situation gets increasingly farcical until Martha manages to sell all her beer. And she is so inspired by the experience that, happening to lay eyes on a field of marijuana, she gets an idea – to the dismay of all present.

None of the people portrayed here are "suffering Indians." The author prefers to flout that stereotype – with glee. According to him, Indigenous people are too busy having a good time to sit around wallowing in self-pity. This is farce, pure and simple. Celebration over the subjugation with which Indigenous people are too often painted is the point here. Humour – laughter – *is* Indigenous people. It is their character, their culture, their soul, says the author with this play.

From **Oral** to **Written**

The Baby Blues

DREW HAYDEN TAYLOR

Ojibwa from Curve Lake First Nation, ON

First produced in 1995

The second of four plays collectively titled the Blues Quartet is a sequel to *The Bootlegger Blues*, in this play, a man reconnects with a daughter he never knew existed. In the process, he also reconnects with the father he never knew existed. And his journey from ignorance to enlightenment is a roller-coaster ride of hijinks, hilarity, and farcical coincidence.

An aging Ojibwa fancy dancer* named Noble has come from his reserve up north to dance at a powwow. At this powwow, which takes place on an Ojibwa reserve in central Ontario, he encounters sundry characters. Among them is Summer, a young non-Indigenous woman who is taking Indigenous Studies at the local university. Her objective is to recover the drop of Indigenous blood that she claims to have inherited. Skunk is a young Indigenous man who, like Noble, has come to participate in the dancing contests. Noble engages him in a bet to see who can win the top prize at fancy dancing. Amos, a Mohawk Elder, goes from powwow to powwow with his food kiosk. From there he sells, among other self-invented products, fortune scones.† Jenny, an Ojibwa woman from that reserve, works with the powwow committee to ensure the campsite is run properly. Jenny's daughter, Pashik, has one desire: to go and dance someday in Connecticut where the biggest powwow in the world is held every summer. The characters get entangled in knots, all of which are hilarious. The biggest knot is the one where the not-a-care-in-the-world Noble discovers that Pashik is his daughter, the product of one night's indiscretion with a woman at that same powwow some two decades previous. That woman, of course, was Jenny, the campground custodian, who now forces Noble to avow his paternity. She goes so far as to disconnect the wiring in his truck and block the one access road to the reserve until he pays the forty-thousand-some dollars in "absconded" child support payments she says he owes her. In the end, Noble makes peace with her and their daughter – to the latter's utmost delight, he will take her to that Connecticut powwow. The icing on the cake? His discovery that Amos is his father. Noble, too, was the product of one night's indiscretion, this one some four decades previous between the Mohawk kiosk owner and Noble's mother.

Like *The Bootlegger Blues*, this play refuses to engage with a stereotype of Indigenous self-pity. The central character, Noble, for instance, is every bit the image of the hapless old fool in European farce or the British dancehall, both forms of theatre that can trace their origins to the medieval clown show and *commedia dell'arte*. In fact, Noble is an echo of the classic target of parody, the clown, Pierrot. The author draws on the deep well of humour that is the essence of the Indigenous character and culture.

---

* Known as fancy dancers, they are the most colourful of all. The feathers on their bustles, headpieces, and leggings in combinations of the most spectacular colours imaginable – luminescent orange, luminescent green, fuchsia, you name it – theirs is the liveliest of all these dances. Accompanied by robust, virile drumbeats, wild jumping and leaping and twirling make them a blinding swirl of colour. In the context of this play, a male dancer in his thirties who insists on continuing to be a fancy dancer is already too old to be one; he is "over the hill," a "has-been."

† A scone (pronounced as in "gone") is a kind of Indigenous bread. Fried like a doughnut but without the hole and the sugar, it can also be described as bannock, though the latter is generally baked. Still, "fried bannock" is an acceptable term in some Indigenous nations, keeping in mind that we are speaking English here as opposed to Ojibwa, Cree, or any other language from which comes the idea. In my language (Cree), we call it "*eesaa-saapis-kisoot paagwee-siganis*," which translates literally as "fried bannock," the suffix, "is," merely transforming the noun, "bannock," into "small bannock" (bannock is generally large, say, the size of a pie; scones are much smaller, say, the size of a tart). As to "fortune scones," it is pure invention on the part of Amos – and via Amos, of course, the author – a tricksterish take on the idea of the Chinese "fortune cookie." If you bite into one of Amos's scones, you will find inside it a tiny piece of paper, as in fortune cookies, on which is typed a short sentence that tells you your future, all in the spirit of fun.

From **Oral** to **Written**

The Buz'Gem Blues

DREW HAYDEN TAYLOR

Ojibwa from Curve Lake First Nation, ON

First produced in 2001

The third of the author's four Blues Quartet plays, this one is set at a university in southern Ontario where an Indigenous Elders' conference is taking place and looks at stereotypes about Elders. Far from a hackneyed reverential take on the subject, the play presents elderly Natives as fun-loving people. They engage in hijinks. They laugh a lot. They even fall in love. That is to say, this is the closest these four plays get to a genuine romantic comedy.

Two Ojibwa women, Marianne and her mother, Martha, attend, at Marianne's insistence, an Elders' conference at a fictional Canadian university. Here, they meet and get entangled with some colourful characters. A white anthropologist known, tongue in cheek, as Professor Thomas Savage has come to this conference to do research for an academic paper on the sexual habits of Canada's Aboriginals. A young Indigenous man who calls himself The Warrior Who Never Sleeps has come to reclaim not only his own identity but also Indigenous identity in general. Feeling that too much damage has been done by the forces of cultural genocide, he intends to act on the matter. Later in the play, he reveals himself as Cree. Then there is the Mohawk, a sixty-something widower named Amos. As cook for the conference participants, he is expanding his culinary artistry to include what could be referred to as "nouveau Aboriginal" – western sandwiches made with turtle eggs, for example. And there to assist him in his kitchen and with this "research" is a young non-Indigenous woman whose real name is Agnes Ducharme. She, however, calls herself Summer. Claiming one-sixty-fourth Mohawk ethnicity, she is there to reclaim that doubtful fraction. These characters spend most of their time evading the clutches of the overzealous anthropologist who wants to interview them all for his paper – with hilarious results. In the process, they also get entangled with each other. Several issues are touched on, including the conflict between the

Drama

Christian and traditional elements in Indigenous society. There is also the rivalry between the various Indigenous nations, in this case, Ojibwa, Cree, and Mohawk. And there is Indigenous people's "traditional" relationship with a canned pâté known as Spam. As in all good comedies, the characters pair up at the end, Summer with The Warrior, Martha with Amos. And Marianne with, of all people, Professor Savage. It is, moreover, hinted that he will soon be moving to the rez. "Buz'gem," after all, means "boyfriend" or "girlfriend" in Ojibwa, as Summer, of all people, explains at one point.

This being a farce, and a hysterical one at that, there are no tormented souls here. Too busy having a lark, the characters have no time for such negativity. Indeed humour, in this author's approach, is the best medicine for neutralizing the long-term effects of colonization. And one would be hard put to disagree with his theory.

The Berlin Blues

DREW HAYDEN TAYLOR

Ojibwa from Curve Lake First Nation, ON

First produced in 2007

This is the fourth and final play of the Blues Quartet. In this instalment, two German tourists arrive on the Otter Lake Indian Reserve with an amazing offer. As economic development for what they see as a poor, disadvantaged people, they intend to transform the village into a theme park called Ojibway World. This way, they think, they will help the residents become economically self-sufficient, perhaps even wealthy. The greater part of the community reacts with enthusiasm. A small part does not. Finding the idea horrifying, they throw a monkey wrench into the works, thus making for a very funny story.

Andrew Kakina, Angie White, Donalda Kokoko, and Fabian Noah (a.k.a. Trailer), Ojibwa all, are living in a state of relative peace on their reserve somewhere in central Ontario. They have their problems, but no more than bedevil any other village of a similar size, white or Indigenous. Andrew, the band's police officer, gets engaged to Angie. Sometime country musician and general-good-time trailer resident Trailer tries to woo Donalda, the economic development officer at the local band office, without much luck. In from Germany come Birgit Heinz and Reinhart Reinholz, with great plans to turn the reserve into an Ojibwa theme park much like Disney World or Canada's Wonderland. They envision a Medicine Ferris Wheel, a Turtle Island Aquarium, the Whiskeyjack Pub, and a hotel called the Haida-Way. People will get rich; people will be happy. Donalda, Andrew, and Trailer get sucked into the vortex. Angie resists. Her position is that her people are selling their culture – their souls – to the devil. The pro-theme-park and anti-theme-park contingents come to a stalemate. Andrew has to arrest Angie, his bride-to-be, and throw her in jail (albeit in the most comfortable cell). Ever the performer, Trailer gets ready to mount the biggest show of his life, a musical version of the movie *Dances with Wolves*. Unfortunately, he gets carried away with his planning; the 160-some buffalo that he has succeeded in finding for the stampede scene do just that – they stampede (offstage, it goes without saying!). And all hell breaks loose. The result? The Germans have no choice but to move on to another reserve to rekindle their dream. There they will construct the Mohawk Mini-Golf and Marineworld.

Throughout this quartet of plays, the author gleefully flouts the stereotype-become-convention of Indigenous people as losers. These Indigenous people are too busy having a good time to wallow in self-pity. And, need it be said again, the Indigenous languages of North America are, so far as I know, among the funniest on Earth. One mere syllable and you're already laughing, from the gut.

Someday

DREW HAYDEN TAYLOR

Ojibwa from Curve Lake First Nation, ON

First produced in 1991

This play is the first of a trilogy. Together, the plays paint a portrait of the Wabung family of the Otter Lake Indian Reserve and their misadventure with the Sixties Scoop, a program instituted by the government of Canada in the early 1960s wherein Indigenous children were taken from their homes and put in white foster homes to, ostensibly, get a better upbringing. Many children were not even a year old. The mother in this story, Anne Wabung, lost a child to this process and hasn't seen her since. Until one snowy pre-Christmas morning thirty-five years later. Now an adult, the lost child appears at her doorstep. The chickens have come home to roost and the family must confront a period of their past that has been too painful to face.

It is the week before Christmas 1991 on the Otter Lake Indian Reserve some two hours east of Toronto. Anne Wabung, an Ojibwa widow in her mid-fifties, is living a perfectly ordinary life with her second daughter, Barb. Barb's boyfriend, Rodney, is shovelling snow in the driveway. Like any other family, they are preparing for Christmas when, suddenly, Anne wins the lottery – five million dollars. The question of what to do with it looms large. Her first idea is to hire a lawyer to help her find her elder daughter, Grace, whom she had lost to the Children's Aid Society at age two months. Unfortunately, as a lottery winner, she must face the media, so her image and story appear across the country. This includes London, Ontario, two hours southwest of Toronto, where Grace now lives. And, lo and behold, Grace reads the story. With help from the Department of Indian and Northern Affairs, she traces her parentage – and shows up at her birth mother's doorstep. The truth comes out. Anne's late husband, Frank, had joined the army out of economic necessity. Anne, therefore, was left alone to fend for herself, though she did receive financial support from the absent Frank. That was not enough to keep the government at bay – they took her baby. For her part, Grace Wabung is now Janice Wirth, an affluent entertainment lawyer. Having had a privileged upbringing, she finds herself unwilling to forgo the comfort and security she has found in London. To go back to an Indian reserve is too much for her. She leaves. When Rodney, on the driveway that he has just finished shovelling, asks if she will ever come back, Janice – she insists on being called Janice, not Grace – says offhandedly, "Oh, someday, I suppose."

This is the tragedy of the Sixties Scoop. Parents lost their babies, babies lost their parents, and siblings lost siblings. Even when they had the freedom, as full-grown adults, to go back to their birth homes, many found themselves unable to forsake the comfort, security, and often affluence that they had grown used to. The comparative poverty they saw in the reserve house was undesirable. As Janice/Grace does, they turned their backs on their blood heritage and became strangers in their own land. Taken on bureaucratic whim, they drifted away, leaving their birth families with gaping holes that can never be refilled. There is no rising above such a tragedy here; it is just there.

Only Drunks and Children Tell the Truth

DREW HAYDEN TAYLOR

Ojibwa from Curve Lake First Nation, ON

First produced in 1996

This is the second instalment in the trilogy that began with *Someday*. It continues the struggle of Janice Wirth to confront a past marked indelibly by the Sixties Scoop. Born Grace Wabung on the Otter Lake Indian Reserve two hundred kilometres east of Toronto, she was taken from her Ojibwa family and raised by a non-Indigenous family in London, Ontario, two hundred kilometres southwest of Toronto. Janice is at this point thirty-six years old and a successful entertainment lawyer living in Toronto.

Janice's sister by birth, Barb Wabung, along with Barb's boyfriend, Rodney, and Rodney's brother, Tonto, have just arrived in Toronto from their home in Otter Lake. They have come to inform Janice that Janice and Barb's birth mother, Anne, has just died. They want her to come "home" so that she can say a proper goodbye to the mother she never knew. Janice resists. Isn't it too late? She no longer belongs there. She never did. She belongs at her condo and her life in Toronto. Supported by the two men, Barb counters that Anne, their deceased mother, would have been happy if she were to do such a thing. The loss of her baby all those years ago inflicted a wound that had festered all her life. It would also do Janice good. Barb argues that if Janice doesn't know who she is now or where she is going with her life, then knowing where she came from will help her find that direction. Janice relents. And the second act takes place on the reserve. Among other things, Janice learns that the legendary aviator, Amelia Earhart, has been hiding out on the Otter Lake Indian Reserve since her disappearance a half century earlier. In that time, she has become more Ojibwa and more a part of the Wabung family than Janice. Amelia even speaks the language, which Janice doesn't. In fact, Amelia was Anne's best friend and is Janice's godmother. Fuelled by alcohol, with which Barb plies her, Janice agrees to go to the cemetery. Here, she is left alone to commune with her mother's spirit. She apologizes for the time she met her five months previously, but fled. It was not in loathing of Anne that she fled, she explains, but in terror of herself. And finally, she admits her love not with words but with a gesture.

One point that is certain in this story is that Janice/Grace is a tormented soul. If she was one at birth, she remains one as an adult. If she has been sweeping the pain of her exile under the carpet, only members of her blood family can help her sweep it back out. At the end, she plants a daisy at her mother's grave, signalling the start of that healing. This small gesture is an act of reclamation of her soul which is so needed in a tale of pain so deep, so extended.

400 Kilometres

DREW HAYDEN TAYLOR

Ojibwa from Curve Lake First Nation, ON

First produced in 1999

The final instalment in the trilogy begun with *Someday* and *Only Drunks and Children Tell the Truth*, this play continues the story of Janice Wirth and her struggle to confront a past marked by the Sixties Scoop. Janice, born Grace Wabung on the Otter Lake Indian Reserve, was taken at birth from her Ojibwa family and raised by a non-Indigenous family in London, Ontario, four hundred kilometres away. There, in London, she finds herself in a quandary.

Now thirty-seven, Janice is a successful entertainment lawyer in Toronto. She arrives in London for an impromptu visit with her adoptive family, having just found out that she is pregnant. The father is a man whom she had met on her birth mother's reserve on a visit the purpose of which was to reconnect with her birth family. That project, however, has met with only partial success. Still, a "white girl" is about to give birth to an Indigenous baby. This unforeseen development has plunged Janice into a state of turmoil. A second reason for coming to London is that she has been driven to do so by her birth mother. In dreams that are haunting her, her birth mother, Anne Wabung, is pregnant with Janice. In successive episodes, she tells Janice the circumstances of her conception, her birth, and her abduction during the Sixties Scoop. Back in the security and comfort of the house where she was raised by the kind, albeit non-Indigenous Wirth couple, Janice, in turn, is paid a surprise visit by one Eli Albert Hunter, a.k.a. Tonto, father of the child she carries. And here is launched a spirited debate on the pros and cons of cross-cultural adoption. Would Janice's child be better raised in an Indigenous environment such as his parents' reserve? Or would the child do better growing up in a comfortable, white, middle-class environment such as the one offered by his mother's adoptive parents?

Janice/Grace is certainly a casualty, a sacrifice in the name of empire and blatant colonization. The aim of the Scoop, after all, was to turn Indigenous children into white people. If she was a casualty at birth, then she remains one as an adult – she is incapable of letting the past go. Utterly confused, Janice gives in at last to Tonto's interpretation of her dreams. According to him, Anne's spirit has been laid to rest by the re-establishment of the sacred circle of grandmother, mother, and child. In completing that circle with *her* child, Janice/Grace will have "come home." Casualty she will be no longer.

Diary of a Crazy Boy

JOHN MCLEOD

Ojibwa from Mississaugas of the New Credit First Nation, Hagersville, ON

First produced in 1990

A fifteen-year-old Ojibwa boy named Darrel is being treated for paranoid schizophrenia at an urban psychiatric hospital. In this setting, he grapples with the mundane reality of doctors, nurses, and family, all of whom mean well for him but, try as they might, can't see into his world. On another level, he deals with his dreams, his subconscious. This is where figures from Ojibwa mythology emerge. A mythology that has its roots in the primeval forests of North America intertwines with modern-day urban reality. The result? A new kind of Indigenous storytelling – urban Indigenous mythology.

On the day-to-day level, Darrel deals with hospital staff whom he sees as boring adults riddled with hypocrisy. The male nurse, for instance, is a closet drunk; the hospital director an evil shaman disguised as a doctor who wants Darrel's spirit. Finding nothing in common with them, Darrel cannot communicate with them and has no wish to. When his parents come for a visit, he deals with them. But his condition remains stubbornly beyond their comprehension and these adults, too – like the hospital staff – are stymied in their efforts to communicate with him. Most importantly, Darrel deals with his own fractured identity. In a very private world well-hidden from "normal people" – and the evil doctor – Darrel lives with three realities from "the other side." First is his deceased grandfather who appears as a ghost at those moments when Darrel most needs protection from the second reality – a menacing, wordless presence the author simply calls The Lurker. In effect an extension of the evil shaman's spirit, this monster seeks to devour Darrel's soul. The third is a strange, naked boy whom his grandfather sends him when times call for it. Propelling himself with cartwheels only, rather than walking, the Spirit Boy comes to Darrel when he is most lonely and scared and his mind is playing tricks on him. Through the course of their many lively nocturnal philosophical discussions, this Spirit Boy serves as a kind of mirror image to Darrel. He is a doppelgänger through whom Darrel is able to analyze himself to answer the question: What is the place of an Ojibwa Indian boy in the twentieth century?

The Spirit Boy is, in reality, a member of the Memegwesi, the Little People of Ojibwa mythology. (In the production of this play that I co-directed, he looked like a troll.) Such figures come from a time when nature was still animate, when it still had a soul, that is, before humankind was evicted from it in that fabled story of the serpent talking to a woman in a certain garden. So, this play says, what Indigenous people must do to heal themselves of their trampled-on status – and of their rage at it – is to return to their sacred stories and reconnect with nature. Sacred stories take us back, in effect, to the "garden." This is what Darrel does when, at play's end, he divests himself of the evil shaman's power by connecting with the Spirit Boy and leaving the hospital. Now whole, now of a piece, Darrel is no longer used, no longer trampled on.

Sixty Below

PATTI FLATHER AND LEONARD LINKLATER

Non-Indigenous from Vancouver, BC, Inuvik, NWT, and Whitehorse, YT,
and Gwich'in from Vuntut Gwich'in First Nation and Whitehorse, YT

First produced in 1993

Caught in the web of the northern lights, six characters will be released
only when they lay bare the lie that torments them all. Young and Gwich'in,
they may live in modern-day Whitehorse, but their dream world is filled
with the mythology and spirits of their people. Central to the premise is
the Gwich'in myth that the souls of people are trapped in the northern
lights when they die deaths that were inconclusive. As Rosie in the play
puts it, "They have unfinished business."

It is the eve of the first anniversary of the death of a young Gwich'in
man named Johnnie. Husband of Ruth, brother of Rosie, and best friend
of Henry (and Dave and Big Joe), Johnnie died by suicide. Henry has
just been released from a prison in southern British Columbia. His wife,
Rosie, has missed him terribly during his nine-month absence. Still, with
plans for her future, she used the time to get her high school diploma as
an adult. For the moment, however, she works as a barmaid at the Sixty
Below. Into this bar walk Dave and Big Joe. They, like the other characters,
are from Old Crow, a legendary and much-loved Loucheux village eight
hundred kilometres north of Whitehorse. They insist that their old friend
Henry – Dave's cousin – celebrate his freedom with a drink. As drinking
is what sent Henry to jail in the first place – and alcohol abuse is a strong
undercurrent in this story – this is a bad idea. Through their banter, we
learn that Big Joe feels that he owes his life to the deceased Johnnie who
once risked his life to save Big Joe from drowning. At the same time, he is
depressed because his wife, Lorraine, has left him and taken her children
with her to Vancouver. Meanwhile, Johnnie's widow, Ruth, Rosie's best
friend and sister-in-law, suspects that her husband's death wasn't a suicide
but was caused, instead, by Henry in a fit of jealousy. Until we learn that a

rumour is what drove Johnnie to suicide. What rumour? That the last of Johnnie and Ruth's three children is actually Henry's and not Johnnie's. This is what traps the spirit of Johnnie in the northern lights. Only when Henry himself verges on suicide is Ruth forced to forgive him – she admits that her husband's death was indeed a suicide. Thus Johnnie's spirit is liberated. As, in a sense, are the spirits of the others.

This play portrays a culture in which four worlds co-exist: the land of the living, the land of dream (characters are haunted by dreams of Johnnie), the land of myth (characters cite ancient Dene myths that reflect their own story), and the land of the dead. In this last case, Johnnie keeps appearing from his place on "the other side" to manipulate the behaviour of the living characters. The story is modern but the spirits who live around and inside its six characters are as ancient as the Earth. Like puppet masters, they control and shape human lives. Still, all six characters are hurting. And until the truth comes out, the northern lights are the force that keeps them trapped inside that hurt. Trust, in other words, is a healing agent for the hurts that haunts us, all of us, Gwich'in or not.

fareWel

IAN ROSS

Métis from McCreary and Winnipeg, MB

First produced in 1996

As is the case on most reserves in Canada, the sad fact here is that welfare is the people's bread and butter. There is no industry, no economy, no ambition, just stasis. The Indian Act's creation of the reserve system has ensured this. In such a void, the welfare cheque becomes a kind of "Godot." And as in Beckett, the existential question festers: When will it come? The people wait. And wait and wait, imprisoned in a bubble where time has no shape. Like mice in a lab, they run the wheel of non-existence, never arriving. Even the fractured spelling of the word "welfare" in the title indicates a life out of synch with reality. In this twisted mirror, the concept of "well fare/well-being" is distorted to become "farewell/goodbye." In such a world, in other words, life is not worth living. This is a nihilist piece masquerading as farce.

On the Partridge Crop Reserve, the band is broke, the chief is back in Las Vegas, and the Natives are restless. Gas-sniffer Melvin McKay begs his fellow denizens in this no man's land for five dollars to buy his next hit of gas. One leg bitten by a dog, tooth aching, tongue burnt, Sheldon Traverse (a.k.a. Nigger) has been through the mill. Coming from a wake for a man named Angus – the only time he gets to eat, he says – he just wants a "cigrette." Starving, Phyllis Bruce's (offstage) children are bouncing their ball against the wall of the church. The only thing Phyllis can think about is her fear of dying. Rachel Traverse, too, wants a cigarette. But at the same time, she is salvaging the deceased Angus's powwow dancing outfit which the Christian Phyllis scoffs at as heathen. When she and Rachel make cigarettes from scavenged butts, Phyllis stops Rachel from using pages of the Bible to roll them in. Robert Traverse, who owns a new truck and is the only one on the reserve with employment, owns a plumbing service but spends his time fighting off people after his money. The owner of a pawn shop, Teddy Sinclair, dreams of being chief. He clinches it when, in a mock vote, he elects himself. Once chief, Teddy starts to battle the soul-destroying rot of "fareWel." He plans a casino and preaches self-government. When another person dies, Melvin wants his job at the band office. This he can't have, says the new chief, because he is "Bill C-31."* Instead Melvin will manage the casino, Nigger the "fareWel." The voice of reason, Robert announces that they are not a beaten nation; they just got tricked. For that's what welfare is – a trick. Later, when Teddy exposes Rachel as a former hooker, Rachel exposes him as a former john. The Christian Robert butts heads with the traditionalist Teddy. And it goes on.

A cartoon-like quality informs these characters; they inhabit an absurdist world. Smaller plots weave their way through, but the undercurrent is always the rift between the Christians and the traditionalists, that is, those who still practise the old Indigenous religion. The rift this causes in Indigenous communities across the country lies at the root of the stasis, the author implies. And that stasis is subjugation. It is no accident that the play opens and closes in front of a church where two kinds of music, Indigenous and Christian, vie for ascendancy. The ending is left inconclusive. Who will win? Or better, when will God arrive? No one knows, least of all the characters.

---

* Bill C-31, enacted in 1985, gave the status Indigenous woman the right to keep her status when she married a white man or a non-status Indian as did her children. According to information available in the text of the play, Melvin's mother had married a white man and thus lost her status as did her children. Since 1985, however, she has gained it back as have her children. And it is such people – that is those children and those children's children – who are named after the new law's designation: Bill C-31. Which is why Teddy "accuses" Melvin of being a "Bill C-31."

The Strength of Indian Women
VERA MANUEL

Secwepemc*-Ktunaxa from Neskonlith (Kamloops) First Nation and Vancouver, BC

First produced in 1992

Four female survivors of the Indian residential school system are preparing for a coming-of-age ceremony. The honoree is to be a young granddaughter of one of the women. As they work, they talk through, and rage at, an experience that may have been lived a half century earlier but still burns inside them as an explosive issue.

As Sousette, an Elder of seventy, prepares her thirteen-year-old granddaughter, Suzie, for her coming-of-age feast, Sousette brings out two objects. One is a faded old photo of herself with her classmates posing in front of St. Eugene's (Catholic) Residential School when they were children. The other is the dress she wore for her own such ceremony, the hide of which came from a deer that her grandfather had brought down. The dress, therefore, that Suzie is to wear for her big day is packed with meaning. Other women keep dropping by to help (or just get in the way). The first is Eva, mother to Suzie and daughter to Sousette, who admits that she herself had no coming-of-age ceremony because her mother, Sousette, didn't encourage it. Anything "Indian" was forbidden at the residential school, and to this day, Sousette is scared of "Indian things." Three other women, Lucy, Agnes, and Mariah, friends and contemporaries of Sousette, enter one by one. While preparing for Suzie's feast, they intermittently examine the old school photo, and the ties and conflicts among them are revealed to have roots in their common experience at that institution. Those experiences are horrific, so bad that Mariah still can't sleep, and though Sousette offers Indian medicine to help, even after all these years, the medicine is refused for fear of offending the Catholic Church. Lucy lives with ongoing abuse, it is hinted, because she may have been impregnated by the principal of the school, a priest named Father Leblanc. We are never told what happened to the baby, but Lucy's husband, out of irrational jealousy, still beats her brutally. The litany of wrongs goes on from there. Lucy and Agnes ran away from the school and were whipped when they were caught. Later in life, Agnes and her friend Annie ended up as hookers in Vancouver's Downtown Eastside until Annie met a bad trick – and was never seen again. At one point, Eva explodes with the accusation that her mother, Sousette, has always beaten her, as she was beaten at residential school. Mariah admits that she was eyewitness to a nun killing a girl by throwing her down a concrete staircase. She also saw a baby being born to a girl barely in her teens. The baby was buried, together with untold others, in a plot behind the school building. Sousette, too, had been raped by Father Leblanc, and so on. Finally, the preparations are ready. Grimly, the women dress Suzie in her ceremonial garb, which includes newly beaded moccasins. And this new-generation "Indian woman" is ready to take control of her life on her own terms.

The victimhood and rage in this story are extreme. They couldn't get any uglier or more filled with evil. The only way to exorcise themselves of it is for the women to scream it out and then bless themselves in a ceremony that comes from the heart of their own culture. One can only hope that the second generation after that damage, in the person of Suzie, will finally expiate that rage and victimhood.

---

* Formerly known as Shuswap, "Secwepemc" means "people" in the language.

Moonlodge
MARGO KANE

Cree-Saulteaux from Edmonton, AB, and Vancouver, BC

First produced in 1991

The subject of this play is the Sixties Scoop. When Agnes's father is arrested, all five of his children, including Agnes, are scooped up by child-welfare authorities. In this one-woman play, a single actor plays all the characters that make their appearance, though Agnes, of course, predominates. From the time she is "orphaned," Agnes is moved from one foster home to another. Finally, as an adult, she finds refuge in the moonlodge which is not so much a physical place as it is a circle, invisible yet "real," where Indigenous women sit in their "moon time." Here they support each other with song and story, with hugging and prayer.

Having essentially been abducted from her poor yet supportive blood family, Agnes is disoriented and maladjusted. Uprooted from a culture that is based on nature, she can't find her place in urban environments. Mainstream images of "Walt Disney Indians" and an ideal of womanhood fabricated by Hollywood still flourish in this new world. As she emerges from childhood, Agnes attempts to ground herself in one relationship after another. One example is a woman she calls "Aunt Sophie," a kind foster parent in one of the many adoptive homes Agnes flits through. None of the relationships work. And when they do, something happens to sabotage them. There is the Brownies club where she plays a tom-tom-banging, chicken-feathered, *ersatz* Pocahontas when really she "just wanted to go to Brownies"; a motorcyclist who rapes her; and powwow dancers who fail to live up to her expectations of what "real Indians" should be. And all through this voyage of self-discovery, Agnes carries a suitcase that serves as metaphor for her absence of rootedness. It represents the chasm of emptiness that haunts her, the longing for home and family. One of the few props in a play devoid of stage set, this suitcase accompanies Agnes to the end until, in a gesture laden with symbolism, she places it behind her.

A bittersweet sadness haunts this story, one that threatens to explode with rage at certain moments. When she is raped by her motorcyclist "friend," for instance, she asks why Indigenous women have always been considered such easy sexual prey by non-Indigenous men. In another instance, she asks mockingly: why, in mainstream imagery, are Indigenous people somehow more palatable as cartoon characters than as human beings? In this way, she steps to the edge of emotional violence, only to save herself with a joyful self-parody that charms as it amuses. The comic interlude of her Brownie performances is a prime example. We, too, come close to screaming with her at her status of perpetual loser. Still, this is only because we know that she will survive. She overcomes her downtrodden status, in other words, by never taking herself too seriously. Only after the balm of humour has cleansed her is she ready to enter the moonlodge where she celebrates her life with a circle of her blood kin. She does this with a final gesture – a soundless word escapes her mouth that gives the illusion of floating up in a shaft of vapour, first out of the moonlodge through its smoke hole, then skyward. In that shaft, we see the poison that has maimed her spirit leave her body.

Annie Mae's Movement

YVETTE NOLAN

Métis from Prince Albert, SK, Winnipeg, MB, Whitehorse, YT, and Toronto, ON, etc.
First produced in 1998

Anna Mae Aquash, a Mi'kmaq woman born on mainland Nova Scotia's
Shubenacadie First Nation, was found dead in February 1976 under circumstances that remained inconclusive. Entangled in the tense, some
might say lethal, relationship between the American Indian Movement
and the Federal Bureau of Investigation, she had been shot execution-style.
In depicting the final three years of her short life, the play examines the
series of events that lead up to its end.

   When we first see her, Anna Mae is crawling, then walking, down a
metaphorical river of blood. As she does, she laments the fate of Aboriginal people who have come to be perceived by the authorities as threats
and are thus "disappeared." Then it is 1973 and she is working at a survival
school in Boston.* One of several founded by AIM, the school's purpose
is to counter the dropout rate among Indigenous youth. A student named
Lawrence enters to inform her that the Rugaru† has been seen on the
Lakota Reservation of Pine Ridge, South Dakota, where AIM and the
FBI are still at loggerheads over AIM's occupation two years previous of
the nearby town of Wounded Knee. Anna Mae responds that education,
not superstition, will solve their people's problems. This position does not
preclude her own rage at her people's lot in life. It is a feeling, however, that
she gives vent to only in private. Next, she locks horns with her second
husband, Nogeeshik, who wants to go to Pine Ridge to help with the
cause. He asks her to go with him. Torn between the roles of warrior and
mother – her young daughters live with their father and his new wife – she
goes. Next thing you know, she is working for the movement out of AIM's
head office in Minneapolis. At one point, she is sent to Los Angeles to help
set up a West Coast office. Here she exposes a man named Doug as an FBI
informer – the government, knowing AIM is armed and fearing links with

terrorist groups in other countries, has been watching. Though suspicion is rife that he was framed, an AIM leader has killed two FBI agents. Anna Mae is thought to have heard the man's avowal of the deed. In December 1975, she disappears. Two months later, her body will be found in a ditch on Pine Ridge land, with her hands missing, cut off by police to be sent to Washington for fingerprinting.

The writer gives us a look into the soul of a woman in deep spiritual crisis – a girl from a reserve in Canada steps naively into a web of intrigue that eventually kills her. In the tension between motherhood and commitment to her people, she is torn in two like a little paper doll. If politics are the gasoline, then the match that sets fire to it is Indian medicine. Married to Nogeeshik "under the pipe,"‡ Anna Mae fears that, in violating her relationship with him by having an affair with a co-worker, she has violated that medicine. Somehow, the threads of medicine and arms get entangled in her life, and no one can undo the knots. She ends up the ultimate victim. The Rugaru comes to get her. Ironically, in dying, she helps her people take one more step forward in their struggle to vanquish their victimhood. As she says at the end, "You can kill me, but my sisters live…"

---

* For those Indigenous nations whose ancestral territory straddles the Canada–U.S. border, there *is* no border. So the lives of Blackfoot straddle the Alberta–Montana border, those of the Sioux – that is, the Dakota, Lakota, etc. – straddle the Manitoba–North Dakota border, those of the Ojibwa straddle the border between Ontario and Minnesota–Michigan, and those of the Mohawk straddle Ontario–New York. It is only natural, then that the lives of such Atlantic Indigenous Peoples as the Mi'kmaq and the Malecite will spill over from Nova Scotia and New Brunswick into such states as Maine, New Hampshire, and Massachusetts. Hence, Anna Mae's Nova Scotia–Boston connection.

† This is a western variation – or pronunciation if you will – of the eastern Loup-Garou. It took a mere generation or two, and a few thousand kilometres, to transform the *l* of "loup" to an *r, ergo,* "ru" (pronounced "roo") in Michiff, the Métis language which is an artful melding of French and Cree.

‡ In the wedding ritual "under the pipe," an Elder places a blanket over the shoulders of the bride and groom, who each place their hands on a peace pipe so that four hands are joined in holding the pipe.

From **Oral** to **Written**

Job's Wife
or The Delivery of Grace

YVETTE NOLAN

Métis from Prince Albert, SK, Winnipeg, MB, Whitehorse, YT, and Toronto, ON, etc.
First produced in 1992

Pregnant by an Indigenous man, a young non-Indigenous woman named Grace finds herself in a quandary. All the forces around her warn against having such a mixed-race child. Alone in her bedroom – though actually in her dreams – she struggles with the question: Should she or should she not? Three manifestations of *deus ex machina* heighten her anguish – and ultimately, help her solve it. First, the fetus of the child is present, right there in the room, dangling in the air from a hanging chair and addressing her at certain key moments with cries and babbles. Second, God appears to her in the form of Josh, a large Indigenous man. And third, all male parts in the play are played by the actor who plays Josh, a technique that further intensifies Grace's dilemma. These voices are her conscience; God is talking to her.

Josh steers Grace through the people and institutions that have shaped her life – her doctor, parents, boyfriend (the child's father), priest, and finally, herself. Her doctor hints at what he calls a "threatened abortion," that is, a possible miscarriage. This only serves to deepen Grace's crisis; the child, after all, is alive right there before her, babbling at her from its hanging chair. As she comes from a white, middle-class, Catholic background, her parents will be against the pregnancy. She has not yet had the courage to tell her mother. Grace's father warns that her mother's reaction will be that the child's father is "the kind of person [her] mother is used to helping with her church group." He suggests adoption. She refuses. Abortion has also crossed her mind, if only through God (that is, her conscience) who tells her the fetus is damaged. The priest, however, forbids abortion, suggesting, in its place, immediate marriage. But her boyfriend, Paul, is noncommittal. Never having wanted a child in the first place, he insinuates that Grace tricked him into the situation by a "sin of omission," as Grace calls it; according to Paul, she lied to him. Josh, for his part, is averse to the term "religion." He chooses, instead, to intervene "non-denominationally." By introducing Grace to the spiritual realm in which her baby lives, he teaches her that she must learn to take responsibility for her choices, including her "sin of omission." Fortunately, as the play's subtitle indicates, it is Grace herself who is delivered at the end of her pregnancy. In the Bible, Job's wife crumbles under the tests of faith, including the loss of her children, that are forced on her by a patriarchal God and a patriarchal husband. In this play, Grace faces the same sort of trial. The difference is that her God is Indigenous, meaning more lenient, less judgmental. And her own name is Grace.

The play's theme is moral duty. Grace, a white girl, is about to have an "Indian baby." All the forces around her warn against having it, but she wants to anyway because she recognizes, after tortured soul-searching, that her final responsibility is to the child, not to herself. This is why the God she speaks to is not a white Christian one but an Indigenous one. Her Indigeneity, such as it is, will not be silenced. She will fight subjugation tooth and nail. And for this, we applaud, admire, and love her.

Wawatay

PENNY GUMMERSON

Métis from Flin Flon, MB, and Vancouver, BC

First produced in 2002

A Métis family grapples with the question of racial identity in a white, racist environment. For decades, the lid on this question has been kept shut by the father, thus locking the family in a kind of limbo. Now the mother lies dying and the time of reckoning has come; the truth must out. And so it does, with results that are as surprising as they are spectacular. The first act takes place at the hospital and the second in the family home, both in Flin Flon, a northern Manitoba mining town.

Nominally white, the Lafontaine family is made up of Frank; his wife, Lois; and their four adult children. Frank is a retired miner and reformed alcoholic who was abusive to his wife and children for much of their lives. Mary, the eldest, dreamt of joining a convent but now hides her bitterness at her childlessness by fanatically embracing Catholicism. Billyjoe (BJ) has rejected urban living and gone back to the land. A rising hockey star in his youth and now, like his father, a reformed alcoholic, he lives in the bush not far from town, hunting and trapping. The next in line, Junior, just moved back to Flin Flon from Winnipeg, is a successful businessman, whose success is marred by booze. And Jaz, the baby, is a visual artist based in Vancouver. Away for a decade, she once, as a child, heard a secret from their mother to the effect that their father hides a ghost. The only one of the siblings to know this, she is thus as fanatical about Indigenous spirituality as Mary is about Catholicism. Like puppies, they jockey for position at their mother's bedside before she dies. The three elder siblings despise Jaz's posturings. "Spirit shit," Junior calls it. The boys hold Mary's brand of "holiness" in equal contempt. Junior, who drinks all the way through, spits on Alcoholics Anonymous of which BJ is a member. The fact that Junior was their father's favourite incites BJ into a fit of violence. He unleashes jealousy pent up for years. Mary, meanwhile, harbours resentments about

Jaz's status as "mommy's little girl." At the end, Mary tries to get a priest to come and perform last rites on their dying mother even as Jaz performs a smudging ceremony on her. At which point, the barren Mary accuses Jaz of being a murderess – she knows about the abortion Jaz had. Once their mother, Lois, is gone, they read her letter. In it, she exposes Frank's secret – they are Indigenous. His father was white but his mother was Cree. Frank breaks down. He tells his children that he hid his Indigenous ancestry to spare them racism. With Jaz's aid, he conducts one last healing circle, in fluent Cree, to honour his wife's spirit which floats off to join the Wawatay, the northern lights.

Indigenous families who move off-reserve to seek a better life in white towns or cities are – more so in the 1960s than today – almost always forced into the predicament of the Lafontaine family. And almost all respond in like fashion – they try their best to hide their Indigeneity. Stifling the language is but one symptom. A parent's instinct to shield their children from unwanted pain is just too great. Sooner or later, however, it is up to the children to deal with the truth in adulthood. And such is the case for the writer of this play. She dispels her torment by saying, "Enough is enough." The more Indigenous writers who confront such issues head-on, the weaker that pain and the stronger the healing will be.

Lady of Silences

FLOYD FAVEL

Cree from Poundmaker (Cut Knife) First Nation, SK

First produced in 1993

The playwright takes a European drama – *The Blacks* by Jean Genet – and reworks it to recount an Indigenous tale relating a crime of passion. Three young Cree women have just killed a young non-Indigenous woman out of jealousy. Her crime? Having a sexual relationship with a Cree, a man they consider to be theirs. If all three have loved him, they still do. One of them, in fact, is pregnant with his child. The man flees. He runs back to the memory of the murdered girl, who, of course, was his lover. In doing so, he is actually running away from his culture, his people, and ultimately himself, for he hates his Creeness. Meanwhile, a detective, also Cree, tries to get the man and the women to admit to their act, for they all, to his mind, are responsible. At the conclusion, the four perpetrators remain imprisoned in a kind of purgatory – with no resolution and thus no exit.

Just emerging from a sleep induced by heavy drinking, Village, a Cree man, wakes up on the borderline between reality and dream. The reality is Earth, a downtown bar in some unnamed western city; the dream is purgatory. Above him stands Belmondo, who, in Village's miasma, drifts in and out of his divine and human identities. On the human level, he is a detective; on the divine, a half god / half devil who manipulates human behaviour. Belmondo informs Village that he is in purgatory and that the only way out is an act of penance. That penance? To perform a show every day for eternity in which he re-enacts the murder. If he is convincing, he will go to heaven. If not, he will go to hell. His sin? To desire a white woman. The three Cree women enter discussing the murder they have just committed. Now also trapped in purgatory, they, too, must do the penance and re-enact their crime every day for eternity. If Village's sin was lust, theirs was hate, hate based on jealousy. In the play within a play, the girl who plays the victim reveals that she herself has always wanted to be white. Village admits to the same feeling, though with greater urgency. Over the story of the murder is superimposed the larger canvas of Indigenous history at the time of the invasion of Canada's west. On this level, people fight on horseback, white kills Indian, Indian kills white. Also resonating, if very briefly, is another larger picture – if the Indigenous people in the play are caught between their Indigeneity and their desire to be white, then the detective/deity is caught between himself as good or as evil.

This play is an allegory. As such, it interweaves reality with dream, history with myth, truth with fiction. It addresses in terms of subject, on one level, race and racism. On a deeper level, however, it addresses self-identity. Do Indigenous people hate themselves? the author asks. (In this larger picture, Village's real sin is self-hatred.) Do they hate their Indigeneity? Are they their own worst victimizers? The author leaves the questions hanging, which, of course, is what purgatory is about – in purgatory, there are no answers. It remains for us, as individuals, as a community, and as a race – here on Earth, in real time – to find them.

Princess Pocahontas and the Blue Spots

MONIQUE MOJICA

Kuna-Rappahannock from New York City and Toronto, ON

First produced in 1990

A woman searches for her place in a world she feels she has lost to the forces of colonization. The colonizer came to her homeland and, over the course of five hundred years, evicted her from it. In evicting her physically, the author suggests, the colonizer banished her from her own body. Her soul left her body, her spirit her soul. "Nowhere to set my feet, nowhere to stand," says a character at one point. This play is written as if we are watching Alice falling down the rabbit hole. On the journey, she is accosted by image after image of Indigenous stereotypes that have been foisted on her by the popular media, white historians, and the European perspective over the centuries. And not only does she see them, she wears them. She plays out their lives as, in a sense, they play out hers. Two performers, an actor and an actor/musician, play the multitude of characters who inhabit the text.

Standing for the moon and a woman's cycle, a series of thirteen "transformations" play themselves out. They go as follows: a contestant in an Indigenous beauty pageant, this modern Indigenous woman is on "a journey to recover the history of her grandmothers as a tool toward her own healing." Malinche, the Nahuatl (Aztec) woman who betrayed her own people by helping Spanish conquistador, Hernán Cortés, conquer them. The mythic Pocahontas in her three incarnations of Matoaka (her real name), Lady Rebecca (the name she was given when she went to England and died there), and the Mohawk princess. The Indigenous goddess in at least three incarnations, including the Queche Woman of the Puna and the virgin (who, of course, recalls Catholicism's Virgin Mary). Three faces of the Cree and Métis women who helped early fur traders "conquer" Canada's north. The classic Cigar Store Squaw. And a spirit animal. The actor/musician, meanwhile, plays the following: The host at the beauty pageant. "The Blue Spots," who back up Pocahontas when she sings. A contemporary woman who accompanies the aforementioned modern Indigenous woman on her journey. The troubadour in an Elizabethan court when Pocahontas arrives. A man who incarnates the husband, the lover, the friend, and the brother of the modern Indigenous woman. And a Spirit Sister to this woman. This performer even plays a ceremony – the personification of a puberty ritual. And last, she plays the musical instruments that provide the soundscape.

Drama and farce, melodrama and operetta, pageant and cabaret, myth and history, past and present, North and South America. All are mixed into a stew that foams, bubbles, and sizzles to produce this parody of, and all-out attack on, the "official story" of the arrival of so-called white civilization in the Americas. Once all these "rages" have been given their due, however, what we arrive at is a celebration of Indigenous women as the "hoop of the nation." The play, after all, may begin with dislocation and wallow in torment, but in doing so, it throws "a lifeline across the generations" so that it becomes a call to arms. Enough of subjugation, the author submits, just vomit it out and "wake up! There's work to be done! / We're here."

The Unnatural and Accidental Women

MARIE CLEMENTS

Métis from Vancouver, BC

First produced in 2000

Indigenous women are being murdered in Vancouver's Downtown Eastside. A race- and gender-biased justice system refuses to recognize the crimes for what they are – cold-blooded killings committed by the same man using the same brutal method. With evidence of foul play ruled out, the deaths are classified as "unnatural and accidental." Dreamscape, nightmare, traditional Indigenous legend, slapstick comedy, tone poem, Christian mythology, performance art, sound-and-light show – all are used in a tapestry of immense complexity. Its underpinning structure is threefold: abstract collage, quest narrative, and revenge tragedy.

Trees are being felled by white, male loggers in a forest. As they are dragged to logging trucks, the logs leave "skid roads" on the ground. Their wood becomes buildings and furniture in bars on "skid row" in Vancouver's Downtown Eastside. In these bars, and in the two-bit hotels that house them, live a chorus of the lost. Most from Canada's Indigenous, and female, community, all are in search of something or someone. Rebecca is looking for her mother who abandoned her as a child for the streets of Vancouver. Street-named Aunt Shadie, she died some years previous on skid row, an early victim to a barber who has since enticed many an Indigenous woman to her death with a drink and the words "Down the hatch, baby." Mavis is trying to connect, by telephone, with a friend, then a former lover, then a sister. But she is so far removed from their realities that she never reaches them. In truth, they are alive, she dead. Valerie misses her two young sons so desperately that she speaks to her bedroom dresser. In her "dream state" of death, the dresser drawers speak back in the boys' voices. Verna has just bought her young son a toy plane for his birthday. The gift never reaches him, because she is dead. Meanwhile, three young women live trapped inside the mirror at the killer's barber shop. Ghosts, they float in and out of the other women's fields of vision. And Rose works as a telephone operator trying to connect all these fractured voices with each other. She never succeeds, however, because she is trying to connect the voices of the dead with those of the living. And she herself is dead. Through it all, the women keep getting waylaid by men who echo the loggers who opened the play; if they were felling trees then, now they are felling Indigenous women. Certainly the barber has taken down more than one. Until finally, Rebecca reconnects with her dead mother in the form of a braid of her hair. One of many braids the barber keeps in a cupboard at his shop, each belongs to a woman he has killed. With the help of the ghosts of all these dead, Rebecca slits his throat.

Peopled by corpses, this play is macabre. Still, three elements keep it afloat. One is the humour in the women's banter. The other is the fluidity of the poetic language and imagery. At the end, for example, the women sit down to a distaff version of the Last Supper, their murmuring voices the moan of the trees in the forest at the play's opening. Which brings us to the final element to lift the play beyond the darkness of death. Even in death, the author posits, we as a people cannot be beaten. Our dead are still here among us, laughing and partying.

Burning Vision

MARIE CLEMENTS

Métis from Vancouver, BC

First produced in 2002

It is the 1930s and uranium is being mined on Great Bear Lake in Canada's Northwest Territories. The people these mines most come to affect are, of course, the Dene Tha (Slavey) whose homeland this is. Because of the mineral's radioactivity, it brings death by cancer on an unheard-of scale. On this tragedy is overlaid the story of the Japanese who also die in great numbers – this mineral is the key ingredient in the bombs that destroy Hiroshima and Nagasaki. Poetic language, the layering of time zones, the superimposition of worlds both living and not, abstract ideas personified, and the interweaving of images and sounds as in a nightmare, all come into play in the telling of this tale.

     The bomb drops on Hiroshima. Then the story reverts to a time before the mineral was discovered in the Earth's crust under the lake. Personified by a Slavey boy, the mineral fears its discovery and its inevitable result. Then Rose appears. The daughter of a Hudson's Bay store owner, she is making bread for the men who work on the barge that transports the substance up the river. Next, two brothers are prospecting for the ore; all they care about is the money it will bring for it is rich, apparently, in a substance that can cure cancer. An old Dene woman who lost her husband to the cancer caused by the mineral appears next. As it turns out, he was one of the many Slavey who carried it, in sacks, from the mines to the barges. She talks to him as if he were alive; by play's end, the man will talk to her from "the other side." The brother prospectors are now on the point of discovery. Meanwhile in Japan, a man named Koji is fishing just before the bomb is dropped. By play's end, he, too, will be talking from the land of the dead while his grandmother waits for him by a certain cherry tree. A painter works at a place where women paint the hands of clocks with radium so they will glow in the dark; she, too, is a ghost. Then there is Fat

Man. Named after the bomb that was dropped on Nagasaki, he is actually an American bomb test dummy who, as the bombs draw closer, becomes increasingly human. Tokyo Rose, the Japanese propaganda radio personality who aired coded "Zero Hour" broadcasts during the war, ignites the sexual fantasies of American servicemen. An old Slavey man from the nineteenth century foresees all this death. The voices of Slavey on community radio call for loved ones they lost to the cancer. And we learn that the wind has blown the substance in powder form everywhere – into children's sand-boxes, onto plants eaten by caribou, into drinking water, onto the flour for Rose's bread. At the end, the caribou of Canada and the cherry blossoms of Japan lament all this death.

The play pulls at the heartstrings for the leitmotif is death. Death and lies. Eldorado Mines has told the miners that they are digging for a substance that can cure cancer when, in fact, the cancer-causing substance is being used to make deadly weapons. One motif plays off the other taking us on a roller-coaster ride of emotions. The languages alone – English, Slavey, and Japanese – demand that this play be not just seen but also heard. The story of the subjugation, humiliation, and murder – need it be said – of entire nations is present. But if the rising above the story makes itself apparent, it is only in the fact that the lie has been exposed by at least one writer. So far.

Copper Thunderbird

MARIE CLEMENTS

Métis from Vancouver, BC

First produced in 2007

From where does the vision of Ojibwa visual artist Norval Morrisseau come? asks this play. And then proceeds to give us the answer. In a play therefore more visual than textual, the play presents a series of images that lull the viewer into a dream state. The truism that plays are meant not to be read but to be seen could not be more applicable. In comparison to the images, the text is mere map. Hence the sound bites of sorts, as opposed to fully realized scenes where characters engage in linear dialogue. If these images lull the viewer into a dream state, then that's where they come from: the dream state of their creator. And if that is the case, then they come from the dream world of his people, the Ojibwa of northwestern Ontario. And they come from the dream world of that landscape, insofar as a landscape can dream, a concept that is contained in the very structure of the Ojibwa language itself. And if that landscape is rich beyond compare, then that dreamscape, too, is incomparably rich.

An older Morrisseau is floundering at a flophouse in Vancouver's Downtown Eastside. Reduced to selling his paintings on the street to fund his drinking, he wrestles with the ghosts of his tortured past. He tries to rid himself of them but they rebuff him; he wants to die but they won't let him. Now a boy of six, he draws in the sand on the shore of the lake where he was born. No sooner does he make his drawings than the waves erase them (as, indeed, they will erase him at his life's end). Already at age six, however, he feels the pull between his spiritual roots and what is to come – commercial success, worldwide celebrity. He might or might not be eaten by the bear that his grandfather has sent into his dreams. "You should be scared," the artist says to his six-year-old self. "Big city visions are sniffing you …" When the boy's older alter ego tells him not to look, he does anyway. Which is why Norval blames him (that is, himself) for what happens to him in later life. Later, he engages in even more anguished wrangling with his self as young man. He deals with self-doubt and jealousy, with figures such as his auntie (terrifying authority personified), with his wives and his agent, with cities like Toronto, Los Angeles, and Paris, with men like Einstein and Picasso. Turtles, serpents, and the Thunderbird all come to play a role, much as the bear did. Drifting in and out of his dream world (and therefore his paintings), they all affect his psychology in one way or other. They all lead him somewhere, even to shamanhood. At the height of his nightmare, his people accuse him of selling their sacred stories while, at the same time, money rains down on him. The inner conflict drives him to drink, to near insanity.

In this story, the hero appears as a Holy Trinity: Grand Shaman as God the Father, Artist as God the Son, Thunderbird as God the Holy Ghost. God himself, in other words, as colonized, as beaten into submission, the sickness internalized. Still, as Picasso says to Morrisseau at the end, again in his dream world: "When I gave spirits form, I became independent and yet connected to something more." By the grace of his self-inflicted, internalized status as colonized, the artist, indeed, ends the arc of his life "connected to something more" – the lake he came from.

Please Do Not Touch the Indians

JOSEPH A. DANDURAND

Kwantlen from Kwantlen (Fort Langley) First Nation and Vancouver, BC

First produced in 1998

What is myth? this play asks. Where does it come from? How is it made and why? And why do we need it? The author works with three myths: the wooden Indian; the Trickster in his or her incarnation as Coyote, Raven, and Wolf; and the tourist. He starts with their myth, jumps back to their genesis, and then traces their growth so that, by the end, we do understand where their myths come from, how and why they were made, and what purpose they serve.

Two wooden Indians sit outside a gift shop. The male wears a sign around his neck that says, "Please do not touch the Indians." A tourist is taking a photograph of them, a photograph for which they play dead. To themselves, however, they are alive. The tourist disappears (French for now, he will later be English, then German, a Mountie, a bratty child, a U.S. cavalry officer, a priest, and finally, an ordinary modern man). Now alone, the wooden Indians each gives a monologue. Wooden Woman speaks of a human couple she once knew, Charlie and Betty Ketchup, which tells us that she, too, was once human. Wooden Man speaks of a vision in which he is paddling home with a boatful of fish who beg him to throw them back into the water. From the shore, Coyote and Raven follow him hoping for handouts, only to watch Wooden Man throw his catch into the river. Sister Coyote enters and, in a monologue, speaks of a freak show where she saw a two-headed baby. Then she and Wooden Man play with a baseball, Coyote claiming that she was once a great baseball player. Having just picked apples from the garbage, Brother Raven enters and reads a story about the time the person who wrote the story fell in love with a salmon that rebuffed him, which is why this person will not eat salmon. Then Wooden Woman and Brother Raven play marbles. It seems that the latter has a marble with magic powers which the former will take for herself at scene's end, though not before she has told him the story of her fall from a cherry tree. Then Wooden Man tells of the time he was carried off by his boat and met Mister Wolf who ate all his fish. Mister Wolf gives a monologue on clocks. Mister Wolf, Brother Raven, and Wooden Man play marbles. During their game, Mister Wolf speaks of the time he won a horse at cards, Wooden Man tells of being bitten by a dog and Brother Raven tells of being bitten by a snake. Later, Sister Coyote claims she has a brother with magic powers who can control the movement of marbles. This hodgepodge of monologue, dialogue, and trialogue builds up to the point where the wooden Indians' people are massacred by the U.S. Cavalry, Sister Coyote and Brother Raven are sexually abused at a residential school and hang themselves, and Mister Wolf hangs himself in prison. And it is only then that they turn into the mythical characters that are now part of the popular imagination.

We watch confused, then amused, and then horrified by the purposeful destruction the colonizing process wreaks on people. The writer rages at its all-out aggression. But this rage and aggression are transcended by harking back to, or even harnessing, the comic way these mythical characters began their lives. For even in death, they are still funny.

From **Oral** to **Written**

Tales of an Urban Indian

DARRELL DENNIS

Secwepemc from Secwepemc (Shuswap) First Nation and Vancouver, BC

First produced in 2003

This play traces twenty-two years in the life of a Secwepemc man. From his birth on the Kamloops Indian Reserve across from the city of Kamloops to his mid-twenties in Vancouver, one actor plays fifty-four roles. By play's end, we get an idea of what it means to be a young Indigenous man in western Canada in the late twentieth century. As he says in the play's opening monologue, his is a generation of "Indian" for whom living on the land the traditional way in the language of the people is a thing of the past. The image of the tomahawk-brandishing Indian in buckskin and braids has long been transplanted by the street-savvy big city Indian who watches television, speaks English only, and snorts cocaine. The tale heralds the generation of Indigenous people that has stepped into the age of the Internet. Cyberspace for him will be the new battleground.

Simon is born an only child to an unwed teenage girl and a residential school survivor who abandons them when he is three. Simon thus lives out the first years of his childhood with this mother, Tina, and her mother, Josie, a woman who will be a lifelong spirit guide. When he is seven, his grandmother, Josie, gives him a vial containing soil from his birthplace. She tells him that with it, he will never forget that he has a home. Then he is wrenched from his home by the granola-crunching, hyper-politically correct white boyfriend his mother has hooked up with. With them he ends up in Vancouver. When the relationship fails, Simon and his mother are back on the reserve. At the reserve elementary school, a bully spreads the rumour that Simon is gay. Fortunately, his friends stick with him while he finds a girlfriend to prove his maleness. But he loses two gay friends to homophobia. His grandmother tells him that gays were once a normal part of the community while another Elder states that they deserved to die. Which is when Simon learns the difference between a person who is an Elder and one who is just old. At junior high in the nearby town, he encounters racism but learns to roll with the punches. Having arrived at puberty, he begins exploring sex and alcohol. Rebuffed by a white girl, he goes celibate until his late teens. Alcohol, however, becomes a problem. In fact, he loses his best friend to it. By age fifteen, he is on his own in Vancouver, discovering what it means to be an urban Indian with heroes like Buffy Sainte-Marie, Robbie Robertson, the warriors at Oka, and the characters in the TV series *North of 60*. He slides into drug and alcohol addiction on the city's notorious Hastings Street. At one point, he sinks so low that a cockroach and a bank machine are his only friends. At age twenty-two and unemployable, he ends up in rehab. And it is only the vial of soil that brings him back.

For all the squalor it touches on, this play's tone is surprisingly upbeat. It is one streetwise, funky, space-age Indigenous boy we have here. At the beginning, we get the impression that the reserve is a cage from which the narrator as a wild bird struggles for release. But the city that he flies to turns out to be another kind of cage, a cage of the spirit. It is only by going back to his roots – and his grandmother's words – that he finally finds freedom from the pain that he was born to.

The Trickster of Third Avenue East

DARRELL DENNIS

Secwepemc from Secwepemc (Shuswap) First Nation and Vancouver, BC

First produced in 2000

A young Indigenous couple lives in Vancouver as struggling artists. Rudderless, they can only tread water with a growing frustration that threatens to sink them into oblivion. Until a spirit guide of sorts enters their world in the form of a Trickster. Once they have this being as an anchor, the going gets easier. The Trickster teaches them that, even though life is confusing as hell, you have to roll with the punches. Maybe you'll win, maybe you won't, but the trick is to never give up. And the Trickster, of course, teaches his lesson.

  Mary and Roger have moved to the city from a fictional First Nation called Wolves Lake somewhere in southern British Columbia. She is an aspiring actress who left her job as a receptionist at her reserve's band office to come to live with Roger. An aspiring writer, Roger left his job as a reporter for the reserve's newspaper. In their early twenties, they can't make a go of it. Mary works as a waitress at a restaurant supporting Roger who lives at home grappling with writer's block. Their financial straits have forced them into a cramped one-bedroom apartment on Hastings Street in the Downtown Eastside. Surrounded by hookers, johns, and drug addicts, they have no employment of the kind they dream they'll find. So they spend their days bickering about their relationship. Should they stay together, or should they separate? If they choose the former, their careers are going nowhere; they might do better if they choose the latter. In the middle of their quarrel, Mary reveals that she is pregnant with their baby. Just then, she gets a call from her agent – the first in months – telling her she has been offered a role in a TV series. This throws her into a quandary. Which to choose? Baby or career? Abortion is a real possibility, when in from nowhere comes a man whom neither has ever seen but who knows every detail of their lives. He offers them money that, he says, is their portion of the collective payment the reserve is receiving from their sale of land to a logging company. Perceiving him as a hoax, they try to throw him out. In the tussle, the mystery man reveals that he is more than three hundred years old and has an ex-wife. And magical powers, such as willing doors to move by themselves. Not to mention raising people from the dead, for at one point, he has Roger receiving a phone call from his dead mother. One things leads to another until Roger pushes Mary in such a way that it ends her pregnancy. And she walks out.

This is one scarred couple. Roger's drunken father killed his wife and then killed himself when Roger was a child. Mary's father raped her in front of her mother when she was a child. Now caught between motherhood and a career, Mary is on the point of exploding. In the midst of an impossible situation, it is the presence of the couple's ancient sacred mythology, in the person of the Trickster, that helps them find a way forward. If anything will save their anguished people, the author suggests, it is the people's spiritual heritage.

Where the Blood Mixes

KEVIN LORING

Nlaka'pamux (Thompson) First Nation from Lytton and Vancouver, BC
First produced in 2008

Years after the fact, three residential school survivors are still struggling with the aftermath of their experience. Now middle-age and sunk into the mire of alcoholism, a Nlaka'pamux man named Floyd Couteaux is unable to come to terms with the scars of that period. Two hurts he chafes at in particular: a wife, also a survivor, whom he lost to suicide some two decades previous, and their daughter. Unable to deal with the death, Floyd had lost the girl, then still a toddler, to adoption. But now that daughter, Christine, has come back to ask her father questions. Clustered around Floyd are his best friend, Mooch, and Mooch's wife, June, also survivors. All as George, the white bartender, plies the men with the alcohol they so need to drown out their pain.

Floyd sits in George's bar. In an alcohol-induced dream state, he hears Christine's voice. Filtering in from his subconscious, it is actually the land that is calling, the one he was torn from as a child to go to that school. When George wakes him, Floyd resumes what he was doing before he passed out, buying pull-tab tickets to meet his bar tab. Mooch enters, his face punched up by his wife. Floyd and Mooch spar about who will buy the next round. George quotes from a paper about Indian residential schools and the settlement money survivors can get from the government – the greater the abuse, the larger the sum. But the claimant has to talk about it. When Floyd claims that Mooch had it worse than he did, Floyd and George ask Mooch if he will talk about it. Mooch pretends to be busy with his own pull-tab tickets but, clearly, he is troubled. The next day, Floyd and Mooch are at the river fishing for sturgeon. Again, the river-in-the-person-of-Christine calls out to Floyd. Just as all those children lost their parents to those schools, as Floyd did the day he was taken to the school, so did Christine lose her parents in her childhood. The wound is so gaping that the river itself – his lifeblood, where it mixes – might as well have been ripped from its mother, the land. Floyd informs Mooch that Christine, now a young woman, is coming home. Floyd is haunted by visions of his wife leaving their child with him as her body is swept off by the waters; that river and that land plead with Floyd to come back to them. He can't. His emotional paralysis won't let him. When Mooch broaches the subject of the school, he shuts down. Christine arrives. She confronts Floyd, but he can't face her. She is the past that killed him. Christine has to go to June to learn what happened: that her mother jumped from that bridge due to the abuse she suffered at that school. It is only with huge pain that Floyd is finally able to embrace his daughter.

The after-effects of the abuse suffered at residential school are still too much for too many people. The damage cuts so deep that it not only eats like a cancer at the first generation but also seeps into the second, as it does in Christine's case. It is only through Indigenous writers writing it out time and again that the wound will heal. And heal to the point where survivors will be reconnected to the roots they were torn from and thus be victims no longer.

Son of Ayash

JIM MORRIS

Oji-Cree from Kitchenuhmaykoosib Inninuwug (Big Trout Lake)
First Nation and Thunder Bay, ON

First produced in 1982

This play sets into modern drama what is probably the most ancient and beloved of Cree-Ojibwa myths. If the Greeks have their *Odyssey*, the Babylonians their *Gilgamesh*, and the Celts their *Cuchulain*, then the Cree-Ojibwa people of northwestern Ontario have their *Son of Ayash*. That is to say, the story fits neatly into the form of classical hero epic. First, the protagonist is half human and half divine which is the classical definition of the term "hero." Second, the hero goes off on an epic voyage of self-discovery. And finally, on this voyage, he encounters monsters of one kind or other, confronts them, and defeats them, thus fulfilling his god-like destiny.

In this hero myth, a young Cree-Ojibwa man who is known simply as the Son of Ayash gets into trouble with his father. The father's vengeful second wife, that is – the boy's stepmother – lies to her husband. She tells him that their son has tried to have sex with her. In retaliation for this alleged affront, the old man, Ayash, banishes his son. Before he sets off, the young man receives three magic objects from his blood mother, Ayash's first wife: a spear, an axe, and a white fox pelt. Thus armed, the young man sets off on an epic voyage where, like Homer's Ulysses, he encounters monsters and slays them. The first is a man who preys on passing strangers by inviting them into his tent for supper and then poisoning them with the pus that fills his eternally ulcerous legs. Then he meets two crow-like sisters who, like Scylla and Charybdis in *the Odyssey*, kill travellers who pass between them. In this case, they stab travellers to death with the lethal bone-spikes that protrude from their elbows. Then there are two women whose vaginas are lined with teeth. And so on. The Son of Ayash, however, defeats them one after the other with strength, intelligence, and his magic weapons. Whereupon he is ready to come home not only a man transformed by experience but also a hero, a victor.

The story goes back to the beginnings of Indigenous racial memory in North America. If one definition of "myth" is "a story that comes to a people from 'time immemorial,'" then this is the Cree-Ojibwa people's *foundational story*. If another definition of myth is "the book wherein are contained the sacred stories of a people," then *Son of Ayash* has huge implications for Indigenous people as a reclamation of national heritage. And if a third definition, particularly useful for our purposes here, is "that which defines the collective subconscious of a people, a culture," then this story maps out, in the collective Cree-Ojibwa dream world, the epic voyage that we all start taking at birth. We encounter our nightmares one after the other, nightmares that incapacitate us, threaten to destroy us, enrage us. But we eventually defeat them with wily invention, with strength of character, with hope, and with certain magic weaponry given us at birth. Thus do we win for ourselves the right to celebrate our status as heroes within our communities, to find ourselves as beings who are, indeed, half human and half god. God is in us all, religions proclaim. And this, in the end, is the centre of rootedness, of self-knowledge, of happiness, of health.

Le porteur des peines du monde

YVES SIOUI DURAND

Wendat* from Wendake First Nation and Montreal, QC

First produced in 1983

In the author's words, this play is "an act of re-appropriation of Indigenous spirituality as imaginative territory intact and whole." More ritual-drama than actual play, seven scenes make up its structure: the portage ("the bearing"), the funeral march, the wolf financier, the circle of fire/hell, the spirit (or the master of the caribou), the dance of the serpent (or the road of stars), and the dance of the eagle (or the birth of day with its sky, Earth, four directions, and centre of the universe). Caught between the trauma of dispossession and the necessity of recovering their culture, the characters invoke, admonish, dream, and suffer not so much through words as through the media of movement, lights, and sound. Thus, at play's end, ritual, drum, and dream are the means by which they re-emerge from the ashes of their death.

The Bearer of the Pain of the World (for whom the play is named) is the sun: "old...and tired of bearing the world on his back." In the first scene, he goes into the centre of the world to divest himself of his burden and address human beings (the audience). He notices the sadness of Indigenous people and the decrepitude of Mother Earth. The next two scenes portray the death of the nations and the agony their territory is suffering as a result. A young Indigenous person sows his cornhusk doll in the entrails of the Earth. "How many of our children die like that?" And then a wolf, wealthy conqueror of the American west, starts howling, hunting Indigenous people. Suddenly, the vision of the bearer illuminates the landscape: "I see in...the moon, the tents lost and torn..." The reign of the white man now establishing itself in the form of money, a shower of garbage inundates the planet and the "four extremities of the universe... melt." So the bearer sets aflame the circle that imprisons him and unveils the contents of the bundle on his back. It is his death. Ashamed of his gesture, he gets drunk. In the fifth scene, the master of the caribou emerges from the dream world to remind Indigenous people that they are hunters. The circle of the flames of hell is alcohol and resignation. One must recover the power of the hunter: "don't drink anymore, the Earth is dying…" To bring about the necessary renaissance, a new journey starts. In the sixth scene, the bearer carries his death on his back and returns to life, light, and liberty. In the last, he places his mummy on a pyre and sets it on fire, at which death changes to an ember that turns into light: "A young eagle dances… symbolizes the white light of day reborn… The Native chants and the drum resounds. The eagle alights… crosses space… then disappears in a crash of thunder and lightning. Only the ashes of the dead flicker in… the ember that is the sun."

This voice minces no words – in French, English, or Innu – in addressing the issue of colonization. It is an angry voice. The white man has stolen our land, it says, and with it our soul. As a result, we are dying. So if we are not to die, we must recover that soul. And the only way this will happen is for us to dig to the root of our collective dream life where the nerve has been severed and reconnect it. The ascending eagle opens the way to such healing because, in all Indigenous culture, the eagle is celebration. The eagle is the spirit of the people.

---

* In the languages of the colonizers, that is, the French and the English, the term was "Huron." In the language of the people to whom it applies, the term is "Wendat" which means "people" in the Wendat language. As to "Wendake" (pronounced "Wen-da-keh") the French named the settlement on which they put their Indigenous hosts "le Village Huron." Now, of course, it has reverted to its original name, "Wendake," which means, in Wendat, "where live the Wendat."

From **Oral** to **Written**

Atiskenandahate

Voyage au pays des morts

YVES SIOUI DURAND

Wendat from Wendake First Nation and Montreal, QC

First produced in 1988

Atiskenandahate (Voyage to the land of the dead) is a sequel of sorts to the author's earlier *Le porteur des peines du monde*. Again, he conceives of the play, told as much with movement, sound, and lights as it is with words, more as ritual-drama than as play. This time, he delves into ancestral memory to address not only human beings but also figures from myth. Preceded by a prologue where the Indigenous people of today sit around a fire recalling life before the Europeans' arrival, the ritual-drama plays out in four tableaux: the river of blood, the desert of shade, the mountain of bones, and the last migration.

In the prologue, the Elders recount their myths, of creation and others, and recall wars, famines, and illnesses. Some worry about what they will become: "Our land is…ruined…you have taken our children…our souls…" Then the story begins. Siblings Sun and Moon teeter between the truth of conquest and the world of mythology. Feeling unworthy and then jealous, Sun kills Moon, a young Indigenous woman who can no longer endure alcohol and the degradation of her people. The spirit of the river of blood abducts Moon's body and carries it off to the land of the dead. Then Sun decides he must get his sister back. First, however, he must overcome the power of mythic figures such as the vulture (the master of shadows), the Windigo/Atshen (guardian of the land of the dead), Bear (the image of death), and Sagodywe'hgo'wa (the master of illness and death). Helped by the Deyu'kiyo'wedja'nia (four figures in dark masks), Sun eventually succeeds. Whereupon the messenger (a fifth masked figure, this one in a white mask) comes bearing Moon back to the land of the living. Ecstatic, Sun and Moon reunite.

Mohawk, Innu, and the writer's native Wendat are used in certain passages, particularly when characters affirm their identity. The social and religious practices of both Algonquian and Iroquoian peoples, too, are juxtaposed. But when they testify to the ravages of dispossession, the characters change to French, English, and Spanish. Tableaux two and three, for example, reproduce Spanish text to denounce the genocide of Indigenous women and children by the Mexican cavalry. The voice at this point is particularly angry: "I have seen men kill women, slash their throats, rape them…" As with the first play, the structure corresponds to the Indigenous vision of the universe: the circle, the seasons, the four directions, the sky, the Earth, the centre of the universe, in brief, nature. Even the number of scenes and of actors correspond to certain sacred numbers. Still, the final tableau speaks of hope: Indigenous people have recovered their memory, they have faced their past, and they have survived. "Here lies hope…of a…rebirth which will perpetuate our identity…" "This Native ritual-theatre," the author has said, "is our memory buried beneath the yoke of humiliation." With these two plays, he has contributed to the unearthing of that memory. Thus has he helped his people heal themselves so that they now have a future when, as recently as forty years ago, the Wendat were considered a dying people.

La conquête de Mexico

Adaptation dramatique du Codex de Florence

YVES SIOUI DURAND

Wendat from Wendake First Nation and Montreal, QC

First produced in 1991

Another play as ritual-drama, this one tells of Aztec emperor Montezuma's encounter with Spanish conquistador Hernán Cortés in 1521. The work is based on documents unearthed at the library of Florence, Italy, after being lost for three hundred years. Referred to as the Codex of Florence, these documents contain eyewitness accounts of the tragedy as told to and then transcribed by a Franciscan friar named Bernardino de Sahagún. Also transcribed are descriptions of the Aztecs' system of spiritual beliefs. The narrative is predictable: the people live in peace, the conquerors arrive, that peace is gone. Not that the Indigenous of what today is known as Mexico lived perfect lives, as can be attested by the behaviour of their gods but, at least, they were masters of their own fate. By the time the Spaniards are done with them, they are no longer masters of their own fate. In fact, within decades, the destruction manifests itself tsunami-like across all three Americas. At the end, the survivors who remain are powerless, though the prologue at least hints at a renaissance.

In 1987, a Mexican guide is taking tourists through the modern metropolis of Mexico City. He points out the sites where Aztec temples once stood, long since supplanted by Catholic cathedrals. The cathedrals were built with stones that once were the walls of those temples. The guide then time-travels, taking his clients – that is, us – to pre-1520s Central America. And far from a simple world it is. Gods and goddesses interact with humans in ways that are seldom kind or peaceful. In fact, in a ritual that may bring to mind the Christian sacrament of communion, human sacrifice is practised. The emperor, Montezuma, addresses his people, exhorting them to ritual of one kind or another. Insofar as he serves as intermediary between humanity and the gods, the people consider him divine himself. We see a spiritual life in full bloom. Unfortunately, as early as ten years beforehand, the omens have started appearing – a flame lights the sky, a house bursts into flame, a temple is hit by lightning in broad daylight. And in the perpetual entanglement between gods and men, two signal events predict the outcome. The first is that Quetzalcóatl, the serpent god and a sort of right-hand man to Montezuma, gets tricked into making love to his own daughter who is then sacrificed. Such acts result in his exile; he vows revenge. The second is that, in a spate of sibling rivalry, the Sun god, Huitzilopochtli, kills his sister, the Moon goddess, Coyolxauhqui. And the two foreshadowed events are as follows: when Cortés arrives, the Aztecs mistake him for Quetzalcoatl returned for his rights. And the Christian monotheism that Cortés brings supplants Aztec polytheism – out go the goddesses who had shared the planet with their male counterparts. Thus is the soul of a people destroyed.

As in ritual, the lines are declaimed, often chanted, to the audience, in French, English, Spanish, and Nahau (an Aztec dialect), the words in the last two languages taken from the Codex of Florence itself. Masked figures populate the stage. Scenes of destruction, on levels both divine and human, are played out one after the other. Little in the way of healing or overcoming that destruction is evident. Only in the prologue – about the regeneration of the Earth and the turning of the wheel – is hope of any kind touched upon.

POETRY

The Collected Writings of Louis Riel / Les écrits complets de Louis Riel

Vol. 4, Poetry / *Poésie*

LOUIS RIEL

(Volume edited by Glen Campbell, collection edited by George F.G. Stanley)

Métis from St. Boniface (Winnipeg), MB

Published in 1985

This is a compilation of poetry by Louis Riel, the Métis leader. Whether as hobby or as therapy when times were hard, the fact is that Riel did write poetry and his poetic voice calls for recognition. The poems cover the twenty-seven years from his youth on the Red River to his death in 1885, hanged for treason at age forty-one. In between flow his years as a student in Montreal, leading his people in their first rebellion in 1870 against the Government of Canada, as a patient at a mental asylum in Quebec, a convalescent in New England, a political exile in North Dakota, Minnesota, and Montana and, finally, his last months in Saskatchewan leading his people in their second uprising. The works include fables, songs, love poems, conversational poems that address friend and foe, confessional poems in which he talks to himself, poems that express his political frustrations and his spiritual convictions. Of these 159 poems, 141 are written in his mother tongue of French, seventeen in English, and one in Latin.

The opening fables use animals to illustrate human behaviour. As in Aesop's fables, most work as allegories. "Le Lion Mourant" represents French King Louis XIV in all his excesses, excesses that Riel criticizes. A cat-and-mouse fable has the former standing for English Canada, the latter for French. A fable of the fox and the dog warns against avarice. His love poetry is filled with yearning. Its objects are the off-limits (for reasons of race) Marie-Julie Guernon in Montreal; Evalina Barnabe in Keeseville, New York; and finally, the woman whom he marries in Montana, Marguerite

Monet dit Bellehumeur. In his conversational poems, he says goodbye to his student friends in Montreal, talks to fellow fugitive Ambroise Lepine, blasts drunks like Joseph Parisien and even, at the end, addresses his prison guards. Most arresting are his political and religious poems. In the first, he strikes out at anglophone antagonists who seek to destroy him, at George-Étienne Cartier, a fellow francophone in Ottawa, whom he believed betrayed his dream of creating a French-speaking nation in the west, and Prime Minister John A. Macdonald and his hated English Canada. In the religious poems, he praises all that is Catholic. In fact, he goes so far as to equate his archbishop to Alexander the Great and to plead with the Holy Family for help. At one point, he exhibits signs of messianic delusion and, by the end of his life, he sees the afterlife he is destined for in days.

The emotions run the gamut from love to hate. They express the anguish of a hunted man, the nostalgia of one cut off from his homeland, of one who loves, who thanks, who despairs. They outline the inner workings of a soul in the grip of a mighty vision beset by monsters while, over it all, flies the flag of Métis nationalism, pride in Indigenous roots, and undying love for the land. For that the man merits thanks from those of us who, after a pause of one hundred years, have followed in his footsteps. As we, too, sing our people out of the subjugation to which they were relegated, we stand on Riel's shoulders. With pride.

Flint and Feather

The Complete Poems

E. PAULINE JOHNSON (Tekahionwake)

Mohawk-English from Six Nations of the Grand River First Nation, ON

Published in 1912

The bulk of this poet's work celebrates the natural beauty that is Canada although it also touches on other subject matter such as the Dreyfus affair and British royalty. So awesome is Canada's beauty, the poet repeatedly states, so immense and breathtaking, that it takes on divine proportions. Johnson may have been born a British subject to an English mother – in her day, all Canadians were considered British subjects – but she was also, on her father's side, a Mohawk. And it is the roots from the latter that so infuse her thinking. She may have been raised a Christian, moreover, for she occasionally mentions the religion, but she venerates the god that is nature. If her blood is half Indigenous and half English, then so is her spirit. And to illustrate the point, she observes in one poem that she knows immutably there, beneath that church spire with its crucifix, rests a "great unseen." But then she quickly parallels the image with one of an altar. Christian and Indigenous spiritual beliefs, in other words, have begun to cross-breed.

Once this overarching theme of nature-as-God has been introduced, it infuses every poem. It propels her spirit, her thinking, her very body. Eventually, it takes her clear across the country, a crossing that takes on the resonance of a pilgrimage. At each "shrine" that she encounters, she finds special in some way places that most people would consider pedestrian. To each she utters a prayer of thanks, of praise, of veneration: Golden, Lillooet, and Vancouver in British Columbia; Sault Ste. Marie in Ontario; St. Andrews in New Brunswick; Lake Erie; the Sleeping Giant in Thunder Bay, Ontario; the Qu'Appelle Valley in southern Saskatchewan; Brandon in Manitoba; Halifax; the Crow's Nest Pass; Calgary. And if nature-as-religion is the fuel that propels her spiritually, two conveyances, in particular, propel her physically: the Canadian Pacific Railway (which she also praises) and her ever-present canoe and paddle. She loves water, the play of sunlight on it, its music: to her, the rhythm of water is as elemental a force as amniotic fluid. In poems outside this vortex, she expresses a yearning for the land of her maternal ancestors. It is quickly followed with her preference for Canada, but as a footnote, she does retain a loyalty to the former.

Pauline Johnson's writing comes to us in the trappings of nineteenth-century English romantic poetry. Once the contemporary reader gets beyond that, however, one encounters a sincere soul who bears an undying love for her land and her people, and takes immense pride in her Indigenous identity. Still, because the writing is so very British, one wonders how the poet would have expressed these same ideas in Mohawk, a language she apparently spoke with equal fluency. As for the effects of colonization, there are some poems, though not many, that speak of the Indian as having had his land stolen from under his feet by the immigrant. A poem titled "The Cattle Thief" is one instance. Still, such traces of anger are few; the greater bulk of this collection is a hymn to the land and to the Indigenous spirit. The land is beautiful, therefore we as Indigenous people are beautiful.

Indians Don't Cry

GEORGE KENNY

Ojibwa from Lac Seul First Nation, ON

Published in 1977

This collection of poems and short stories examines the transition of a people from one way of life to another. The first way is the age-old nomadic lifestyle of hunting, fishing, and trapping in a natural environment, with Ojibwa as the lingua franca. The second is that of the white man, with modern technology, cities, a cash economy, and the English language. The bridge that connects them is residential school, for better or for worse. Children who went to these schools learned many things, not least employability in the white man's world. But in the process, they lost their culture, families, communities, and often their language. This book gives the reader an inside look into the what and how of this transition.

Now only performed for tourists, the rain dance has lost the meaning the author relates in the first poem, "Rain Dance." In "Rubbie at Central Park," Indigenous people wrenched from their roots in the northern forests people the parks of cities such as Winnipeg, drowning their pain in bottles of rubbing alcohol mixed with Fanta. In the first – and title – story, an Ojibwa father in Lac Seul has to watch his children being flown to residential school near Sioux Lookout, some hundred kilometres to the east. During the ten months of their absence, he and his wife slide into the nightmare of alcohol addiction. The wife, in particular, is hit hard. She goes so far – it is hinted – as to sell her body to white men for drinks. In another story, an American woman comes north to work for a Pentecostal mission on a reserve and gets emotionally involved with a young Ojibwa man. To her horror, he is killed in a barroom fight. In another story, a young Ojibwa man awaits the arrival, by bush plane, of a flame only to find that she has gotten pregnant "down south." Several poems and stories weave their way around young Indigenous people being sent to residential school, then on to high school and college even farther south. In the fallout, they lose their traditional skills such as hunting and fishing and are drawn, instead, to modern city ways. And suddenly, they find themselves inhabiting a spiritual and emotional no man's land. But then there is the story of the Ojibwa high school student who races for his people. And wins not only the race but also the girl. Other entries touch on death and supernatural phenomena surrounding it, racism, and love.

The bulk of this collection centres on young Indigenous people uncomfortably straddling two worlds. Even the English used here reads like someone trying on a new but ill-fitting suit. So while the old generation is being eaten away by alcohol, despair, and displacement, the "transitional" generation soldiers on trying to hold things together. The odds, of course, are immense. Still, we can't help thinking – if they pull through, hanging on to just enough of the old ways, such as the language, then that much more hope remains for the next generation. The grandparents of this third generation were the sacrificial lambs at the altar of colonization, their parents less so. But they themselves will not be. It is the second, transitional generation that is paving the way.

Voices in the Waterfall

BETH CUTHAND

Cree from Lac La Ronge, SK

Published in 1989

This collection of poems takes us on a journey through the heart of a young Cree woman who lived in northern Saskatchewan in the late twentieth century. And a jumbled heart it is, one filled with pain, marital dysfunction, racist victimization, and drink and drugs. But there is also love and fun and laughter. Through it all, she carries her race on her heart like a medal – where it goes, she goes, where it has gone, she has gone. Come hell or high water, she will not leave her Cree identity nor forsake it.

In the opening poem, "In the Firelight," she describes her life as a single mother who wonders if she will ever again be held by a man. For now, however, she clings to hope in simple pleasures such as "more time to read." In "Married Man," she expresses contempt for those who victimize women. The fake holy man, a phenomenon that, sadly, infects her culture, fares no better. "Shake'n bake medicine men," she calls such people. And then there is the "Zen Indian" who surfaces in all the right places at all the right times. Until the cold of winter comes and it's "time to find a filly / with a job" and "not too many kids." Then again, not all men betray such traits. There are those who are the genuine article, such as the old man who says that "knowledge comes in many ways" in a "half-remembered dream," for instance, that leads to "voices in a waterfall." In "Seven Songs for Uncle Louis," as she calls Riel, she invests seven characters with the voices of, in order, Riel at prayer ever doubtful of his relationship with God; his betrothed, Evelina Barnabe; the dreaded Orangemen; the English (for whom Métis and Indigenous people are savages); his friend and colleague Gabriel Dumont; the Cree chief, Sailing Horse, who describes Riel in the Métis's last battle with the English as Joan of Arc; and, finally, former Canadian prime minister Brian Mulroney, to whom she says, "don't harbour your delusions ..." Seven poems entitled "Horse Dance to Emerald Mountain" ring out a paean to the beauty of her land. At the end, the mountain turns out to be a metaphor for her centredness in and with the land. The Earth/Sky trilogy speaks of the complexity of this relationship. In "Dancing with Rex," she finds, thank God, love in a man. "Four Songs for the Fifth Generation" is a history of the poet's family in which she laments the passing of the buffalo and the old ways. She reminds us, however, that the depression was harder on white settlers because, unlike the Indigenous, they had cut down the trees to establish farms while Indigenous people still had game and fish to live on. Then she speaks of the coming of the vote for Indigenous people in 1960 and the social upheaval it spawned. Mass migration to "a town with sidewalks" was the least of it. In "She Ties Her Bandana," she remembers "mothers in the bars and children / eating ... chips in the lobby" and her teenage sister overdosing, thanks to her pimp. Saved from suicide by her grandfather, the poet dons her own bandana and soldiers on "like all the widows before her." And she ends by asking a friend, "Were you there" when all this and more happened? But then it "rained / and the land was green."

Again, it is land and community that enable this writer to help her people overcome their downtrodden status and thus find redemption.

Delicate Bodies

DANIEL DAVID MOSES

Delaware from Six Nations First Nation, Toronto, and Kingston, ON

Published in 1980

In this, his first book of poetry, Moses dons the English language like one would a new piece of clothing. Like most contemporary Indigenous writers, he may not speak his own native tongue. But far from hampering his use of English, it fuels it. His English has a kick that would not be there if Delaware, in this case, didn't simmer at the bottom of his ancestral memory. As Stó:lō writer Lee Maracle once said, by the grace of this memory, we still "dream" in the language, still feel and imagine in it. Which is why, as with Secwepemc poet Garry Gottfriedson, this writer's poetry has that extra layer of "Indian" refinement. A virtuosic leap of faith, the challenge of using the colonizer's language may be scary, but that's precisely what makes the experience so thrilling—and these poems show it. The poet can't get enough, on the one hand, of the experience of language attempting to define nature and, on the other hand, of nature as too rich for language to define. The effort amounts to a delicate game of tag between the two disparate forces.

Of a blackbird in flight, the poet writes that his "banded wing made the perfect / lure, the gay colour a hook / ... a blushing / wash." Who but a poet would imagine colour as a hook? Seeing geese in flight, it is "as if / waves floated them south." In the lines "a dust coloured for a while like a barn / swallow's breast and then like the river," the colour of dust, which is static, is defined by natural forces that are dynamic; that is, the swallow and the river. Of the movements of a heron's wing, he writes, "ultimate flowers / are rooted in delicate bodies." It is true that the body of a heron, its wings in particular, is as delicate as a petal. The human body, itself a natural wonder, is also ardently described: in the line, "as the breath rains / ... touching / off a shivering," the language itself becomes the "shivering." To name another wonder of nature, light is a sensate being; its tint after rain "inhabits the movement." And human kidneys "threaten to pop / through our back like raw / little wings." Of a dying friend, he wonders where in the progress of death he is by saying, "did we share / that laugh or did your / ... squint see my mouth as / a blank?" And of his grandmother's body, just laid to rest in its grave, he writes: "now in the soil / she's becoming slowly / like water, growing cool / and clear as an under / ground river." And the snow, "that slow celestial / beast repeats the breathy word: *Yes. Yes. Yes.*" Even time has a tangible presence; of a man walking along the Niagara Escarpment, he writes: "this man ... / has stepped into / the signal moment he wants / to remember always."

Far from being threatened by nature-as-foe, as is seen in much non-Indigenous writing, the poet is connected to it as a child would be to his mother. Nature, to him, is a silken fabric that he wraps himself in. Without saying it – and without even knowing where he is going, his journey is that instinctual – his position is that the mastery of the white man's language is one great, and humble, step in the direction of aligning oneself with nature, as opposed to remaining its subject, its frightened servant.

The White Line

DANIEL DAVID MOSES

Delaware from Six Nations First Nation, Toronto, and Kingston, ON

Published in 1990

In this, the poet's second volume, Moses celebrates the relationship his culture has had with the natural world since time immemorial. In the context of this relationship, nature is a living being with a consciousness that is every bit as active, intelligent, sensate – and valid – as that of humanity. Human life has no place above nature, nor does nature have a place above human life; they are partners in a game filled with magic, much of it invisible to the prosaic human eye. Indeed, in this collection, nature and humanity are intertwined in a subtle-as-gossamer, never-ending game of hide-and-seek. The tone is playful, joyful, gentle, loving, and finally, mystical. This is Emerson with a sense of humour, the sense of humour in which all Indigenous languages are rooted, by the grace of a central mythic figure known as the Trickster.

 The list of natural beings that breathe, speak, watch, laugh, and play silly games with human skin, hearts, and blood is long. The author, for instance, wishes that worms would share with him the secret of their ability to breathe underground; that way, they could share their hopes. The field "flares up in stars" which, it turns out, are dandelions; poppies "mouth a cry perpetually." Day has a home "the size of a fist" inside its chest, "trees fall in love," night "stares even as it slumbers," stone and fire have a love affair that ends in "a cool and perfect divorce." On an airplane in which the author is travelling, the wind "stares in through the portholes / trying to catch the movie." His own relationship with the sky, at one point, is angry and jealous; he worries that it is so stupid that it won't see when he's dead, but then realizes that it is, in fact, full of remorse. Hands are wiser than the people who own them. Corn in a field has a gripping relationship with its life and its incipient conclusion, only to catch a glimpse, at the end, of hope for renewal – in light. And so goes a roller-coaster ride of images, textures, and feelings – human and natural emotions as a falling series of dominoes, one toppling the other toppling the other, until the poem as form is the last to topple. Language, in other words, is a spiral of thought into which it spins its lure until that lure nudges at your ear. That's the only way this act of verbal gymnastics can be described, an act through which the natural world seethes with intelligent life.

Indigenous cosmology is known for its closeness with nature. It is living inside the natural world as opposed to outside, as does European thought with its central narrative of eviction from a garden. Indigenous languages, of course, function best to express such a principle. Regretfully, the poet has to use English, not least for the simple reason that that is the language of the public he is addressing. Still, considering that the tongue is so ill-suited to such aesthetic constructions, he does it and does it well. Even though it is expressed in a foreign language, ancient Indigenous wisdom informs and infuses these poems; the poet does his ancestors proud. From a certain perspective, we may be the downtrodden, he suggests, but from the perspective of this wisdom, we are triumphant.

Lnu and Indians We're Called

RITA JOE

Mi'kmaq from Eskasoni First Nation, NS

Published in 1991

This Mi'kmaq woman reminds the non-Indigenous community of the contribution Indigenous people have made to the province (Nova Scotia) and asks them for due respect. At the same time, she encourages her own people to think constructively about reclaiming their place in Canadian society with all the rights and privileges that such a status entails. Last, she stresses such a meeting of minds and hearts as being of particular importance on the eve of the five hundredth anniversary of Columbus's arrival in the Americas.

"I want to cry but that is not our way," she begins, reflecting on all that her people have lost since that fateful arrival. ("My country does not recognize me ..." she will write later.) She then explains away Columbus's arrival as accident – "the man kept losing his way." It was not his fault, in other words, that he ended up causing the avalanche of Europeans that followed. Next come the "long robes," the missionaries, and the beginning of the end of Indigenous religion. Or so it was thought because, in "showing the wrong we didn't know existed" – that is, the concept of original sin, and so on – what they did was force Indigenous religion underground. Hope still glimmers. "The path is still in existence," the dignity still there, disconnection from the garden of nature still not part of her people's phil-osophy. And her yearning to share such truths with white people jumps out in lines such as "I want to teach you about me ..." and later, "Trying to touch your heart, please listen!" "The offered hand is still in place," after all; she wishes to make no enemies. Which doesn't prevent her from expressing her anger, if in flashes – "I am down but not done." The reason for such brevity of expression is that "beautiful words became [her] tool" to deal with such negativity, as is her people's mythology – "Klu'skap [the Mi'kmaq trickster] ... will return someday." Of the coming together of

Christianity and the sweat lodge, she exults, "I love you, my Great Brave," the Brave being the Christian God. Of Christ's grandmother, she writes, "beautiful St. Ann we love / our *kijinu'* in the sky" (*kijinu* means grandmother in Mi'kmaq). And of Christ as infant, she writes, "He is our babe as surely as he is native." Armed with such meditations, she sings at the end, "We are the country's symbol."

"Unforgettable is love ..." "There is good ..." "Thank you my country for accepting my salutation ..." These poems are peppered with such lines. It is therefore hard to deny that this writer desires to help construct as beautiful a country as possible out of the many peoples who have come to call it their home. Still, she can't resist one little poke at her white "friends" in her own gentle and tricksterish way *and* in Mi'kmaq: only if they express their love for her people in her language will they know her nation. The book's title, after all, is part Mi'kmaq; others may have dumped the name "Indian" on us but we, in our own language, call ourselves *Lnu* (human). That is what she is saying with that title. Love, in this writer's thinking, is the only remedy powerful enough to counteract the ulcer of colonization.

Wiles of Girlhood

JOANNE ARNOTT

Métis from Winnipeg and Vancouver

Published in 1991

This poet voices her concerns as a woman who straddles two races, as a mother beleaguered by poverty, by childhood family violence, by parental sexual abuse and its long-term consequences. In her hands, the English language is a weapon with which she slices through emotions. The blood spurts out, the nerves are exposed, the viscera glisten.

When we first encounter the narrator of these poems, she is a girl of eleven with a "pain-hollowed face" walking down a street. Her thoughts are tipped into action by the random observations of a child: garbage strewn, the clothes she wears and that get comments, two dogs fighting, tasting the rain, and wanting to fly on a shaft of wind. At night, she sees phantoms in a corner of her room and hears "angry voices" coming from what is likely a room downstairs. Indeed, in the kitchen, she sees her father throwing her little brother and sister against a wall. Back in bed, a ghost comes in and tries to suffocate her older sister; as a child, she doesn't get the import but it is rape, likely by their father. "This was a very evil spirit," she writes, and "though it left," she fears that it will come back to haunt her. Ruminating on the same kind of rape performed on her in the poem "Absences," she feels "cold drafts creeping / through my breasts …" In "flatland summer," she meditates on the fact of her existence: "the echoes of the silence / running soft and low within / her empty head …" She writes of fear that wages "war inside her." She writes of travel, of landscapes passing like wheels turning, "rocks and hills, rocks and trees …" Gripped by the madness that is her life, she flees for safety to a woman's shelter, though "there is pain there, / here, / inside …" In "William's Wake," she sings the song of the battered wife as if chanting a nursery rhyme, "William full of wonder / pockets full of thunder / tears the world asunder …" As a wounded individual in search of a place where she will not be hurt again, she practises stillness until she is "blue / inside my face." Even bus drivers and factory workers she passes persecute her gently with their voices. Fortunately, "the rain, the earth, the fire of me / are cleansing." In the section titled "Crowning Sequence," she turns to energies more proactive. In place of reacting to hurt and trauma, she fights back. She revels in the fact of womanhood, "nuzzling my way through … / the pores of your flesh …" And she spits at the forces that have threatened to undo her: "why should I forgive?" For the act of giving birth is "the place / where the rage came through …" Of being battered by a man, she grits her teeth, "I will struggle, you down … / i will name you" (note the lowercase *I*). Still angry at her father, she threatens to shoot him down like a dog. And sitting on a park bench still tingling from the childhood trauma, her body claims its space: "this is all mine."

The rage is palpable, the fact of torment indelible; it almost makes your eyes sting to read about it. But the fact that she screams it out is therapeutic. When one vomits, after all, one feels better. And though they are small and few, there are enough rays of hope to inform us that this poet did make it through her trauma, long enough, at least, to write about it. And, indeed, she has since written more.

Beneath the Naked Sun

CONNIE FIFE

Cree from Saskatchewan and Winnipeg

Published in 1992

Victimhood has been imposed first on Indigenous people, then on Indigenous women, then on Indigenous lesbians, according to this author. Indigenous and lesbian herself, Fife feels disempowered, robbed of her right to live a fully human life with rights and dignity equal to those of the colonizer and of men, the forces she identifies as the two main causes of her disempowerment.

Any number of poems from this collection of forty-seven can be cited as a catalogue of the indignities that are an Indigenous woman's lot in a male-dominated society. She doesn't have the right to commune with nature in the form of mountains, sunlight, and wind. It has been taken from her. She doesn't have the right to walk the streets at night. That, too, has been taken from her. She talks about a man who has "reconstructed" her bones, that is, committed an act of violence on her. Given such aggression, why should she not be allowed to express love as she prefers, with another woman? She talks about forced relocation, about her children's hair being cut (a reference to the residential school system), death by AIDS, rape by members of her own family, death that was meant for her but that she somehow evaded. Using words like "narrow," "abrasions," "stench," and "pus," she expresses her loathing for the foreign way of looking at the world that has been forced on her. In other poems, terms like "forced assimilation" and reference to loss of (Indigenous) language jump out. In one poem, being a "brown Indian lesbian" is crime enough to have one thrown in jail. There are more encounters with police ("How to be caged and never know it"). There are references to Oka, a symbol of police brutality against Indigenous people, and Helen Betty Osborne, the Cree girl who, in November 1971, was abducted and raped by a group of white men. As the collection progresses, words like "resistance," "perseverance," "determination," and "strong" appear with increasing frequency, particularly in those poems where she turns away from men and seeks comfort in the arms of other women. Love for another woman, she finds to her blissful relief, is so much more empowering than rage against the violence committed on women by men or by a patriarchal culture. Reject the patriarchy, these poem seem to say; it is killing us. Embrace in its place the matriarchy. That is the only way we will survive. As she says in "Sunset," "loss of language implies firstly then ensures secondly certain death."

This collection is written in English because, as the author states, her own Indigenous language was taken from her a long time ago. Which doesn't lessen the beauty and power of the English that she uses. In rejecting men and turning instead to women, she turns her back on God and embraces the Goddess. In hearing, at the end, the line, "I place my head gently between your breasts," one hears, "I place my head gently between the breasts of my mother, the Earth." It is no coincidence that the last poem in the collection is titled "Reconciliation," for in that word, we hear celebration.

My Heart Is a Stray Bullet

KATERI AKIWENZIE-DAMM

Ojibwa from Chippewas of Nawash First Nation at Neyaashiinigmiing (Cape Croker), ON

Published in 1993

The poet addresses herself to friends and loved ones in a confessional manner, that is, with intimacy, affection, love. Still, some poems go beyond personal relationship. Some, for example, address themselves to her own self, to the universe, history, God, even toward the end, to the Maori of New Zealand, a people with whom she identifies. A few poems address the public. And then there are some, again few, that are just narrative, though the story being told is short. The collection is divided into four sections: "wilderness," "i witness," "what the earth might say," and "desire."

In "wilderness poem #1," she speaks to a lover, equating her love with the nature that surrounds her; "through this wilderness that is my love ..." The next poem addresses "woman" as a collectivity that is to be admired because woman is ancient while the writer is young. In another, her identity merges with that of a sturgeon – she is nature, nature she. She wages war with a lover in a manner where her love for her daughter – their daughter? it is not specified – gives her the strength to withstand his emotional assaults. In "words for winter," her relationship with her lover – the same? another? – are couched in terms more pacific ("the connection between love and life / tonight is tenuous"). In "my secret tongue and ears," she is ready to "stand naked in a December snow" to understand what the rain is saying. "Stray Bullets" speaks out at the powers that unleashed Oka – the bullets that stand for her heart go nowhere. To begin the second section, a confrontational relationship with a lover is couched in the language of a court case. Next, she establishes her identity: "part cowboy, part Indian." Here we catch a hint of insecurity about her status as a "mixed blood," a sentiment that deepens in the next poem. She admits that she finds herself under attack by those – Indigenous and not – who tell her that she is not Indigenous enough, because she doesn't look the part. As a city resident, she finds herself losing "track of the land." In the third section, she pleads with us to listen to nature "like a true human." She admits that her father's death has given her voice added strength. She pays tribute to her two grandmothers, one Indigenous, one white, though she rues the fact that she did not take the time to know them better. The poem "river song" sounds almost ecclesiastical in its homage to life and humble thanks for it. The final section is mostly love poems. One example: "the craft of devotion / is the passion of saints idiots lovers ..." Even Nanabush, the Ojibwa trickster, appears toward the end to, in a sense, bless that lust. The collection tapers off with the author's ode to her love for the Maori. And it ends with hope – "rain on fertile soil ..."

What is striking about this collection is the beauty of the language, its lyricism, its rhythm and punch. This writer finds that her sole weapon against the ravages of colonization is the colonizer's language: English, that most intelligent, but unfunny, of languages.

Wolf and Shadows

DUNCAN MERCREDI

Cree from Misipawistik First Nation (Grand Rapids) and Winnipeg, MB

Published in 1995

Having left his home and moved some four hundred kilometres south to Winnipeg, the poet finds himself unhappily caught between two worlds. The first is Indigenous, connected to the land and to nature. The other is not ("white man loses his way in a circle"). Coming as it does from parts "not here," that other world has unleashed forces – industry, pollution, the city – that have thrown the land and its inhabitants into an imbalance and created the type of schizophrenia with which the poet grapples. The "wolf" of the title is the land, the "shadow" the city, the point being that a wolf living in a city would be an anomaly, a tragedy. So it is with Indigenous people, says the poet with just that title alone. Thus he addresses the question that lies at the root of so much Indigenous writing of the decades we are examining.

"What are you becoming brown warrior," the collection opens by questioning identity, "after you lost the trail on city streets ..." The trails of his youth now soulless concrete, the city's back alleys become a dirge to which the collection dances. On them, a friend "used to roll drunks for a living" while another walks down them "tripping over bodies wasted on city life." The title of one poem, "Prairie City Lost," speaks for itself; its streets once host to thundering buffalo, it is now a wasteland where robins cough diesel. The spectre of racism – "mister gary he lights the match that burns the cross" – only serves to intensify the poet's disorientation. His despair is so deep that, at one point, he lashes out at his own people: "fake" Indians who wear all the "trimmings" only to use them to hurt others. Still, he finds beauty, if in odd places, such as between beer bottles on barroom tables. Then the subject of priest-to-child sexual abuse rears its head: "trying to reach the child inside, that god and his servant touched." A line such as "your sons have discarded the leather and tobacco, trading them for a bible and collar" drives that nail even deeper. In a larger arc, it was the Indigenous goddess whose trust was taken. But then the poet pulls himself from the abyss with lines such as "spirit dancers, turning the pain to light" and "see there a sign made by a wolf," only to have the debate come back at him when Jesus comes down "to listen to the wolf sing" and finds him dying. At which point, the poet cries out to a bird, "Oh cardinal ... why have I forgotten your message." He has dreams where "eagle will fly, and I will too." And when he looks north, the city sky fades behind him. Looking to the future, though, he says of the next generation, "they gonna take us places we never dreamed ..."

The poet's incessant sense of imprisonment in his urban setting is palpable. He hates the concrete, the straight lines, the air. His yearning for nature is constant, even when his despair is at its bleakest. Without that circle that is his culture, he implies, he wouldn't live. It makes you wonder why he doesn't go home. Maybe he will in his next book; maybe, once he is older, he will come to terms with these dark forces. One thing that is certain is that this book's subject is disempowerment. The rage is in your face; you can't miss it. If there is hope, it is only a glimmer.

At Geronimo's Grave

ARMAND GARNET RUFFO

Ojibwa from Sagamok Ojibwa and Chapleau Fox
Lake First Nations and Kingston, ON

Published in 2001

Using as its springboard the life of nineteenth-century Apache chief Geronimo, this collection of poems takes on Indigenous history as its subject matter. To this end, it intersperses snapshots of the chief's life with those of the poet's. Two time zones thus intersect. Or, as the book's cover puts it, a double exposure results. The difference is that one experience described was visceral, the other an event more abstract. Still, the author's point is that what happened to Geronimo a century ago is not that different from what is happening to Indigenous people today. And to prove his thesis, the poet goes to the chief's grave to pay him homage.

Opening with a prayer, he asks, "From where does the Power / come?" and answers: "in a moment of desert twilight." Before Christianity arrived in the great chief's homeland (the southwest United States), the religion he espoused was based on nature; the planet was the goddess, not the wasteland it would become. Whereupon the author shifts to the personal. In saying of his lover "you fell out of the sky / of my world, dove overboard, / and came up with a piece of soil," he recreates his own personal universe, a universe that seems every bit as huge as the real one. Gods speak here, in other words, so that when the line "the land ... will have the last word" appears, it might as well be intoned by a pre-Christian deity. The poet then writes of his parents in terms free of poetry. Of a family fishing trip with his parents on which his mother caught a huge pike, he writes: "He warned her if she kept it / she would carry it herself." Of a cousin, he writes, "nobody can call moose like Doug," of an aunt, she doesn't recall "any hugs" at the residential school she went to. Such incursions into his own life are followed on their heels by references to Geronimo, sometimes as addresses to the old chief himself: "What did you feel / when they made their promises?" Whereupon the narrative slips back into the personal – his deceased mother's voice "is still here inside me." Then there are lines – "an eagle chief / dividing the darkness / into birth / destruction" being a perfect example of where the author and Geronimo meld into each other for a second. As in a double-exposure, we see them simultaneously. Still, the chief's life has been marked by suffering: "He remembers when they treated / his people to a gift / of piñon nuts / seasoned with strychnine." An Indigenous jazz singer in the 1940s, Louis Riel, alcoholism, love, Indigenous languages and their near extinction, the lumber industry raping Indigenous land, global warming, wife battery, period paintings of savage Indians abducting virginal white women, and the poet on his couch "armed" – like the Geronimo he is watching on TV – only with "quick-draw channel changer" all are thrown into a heady mix.

There are moments when we honestly forget who is speaking, the chief or the poet. So it is that we see Geronimo in love, fishing with his family, drinking in a bar, listening to jazz, and so on. Because time in Indigenous cosmology is circular, not linear, not only is he a metaphor for Indigenous history, he also continues to live among us. This time around, however, his message is one of hope. As the poet vows to the chief at book's end: "your spirit ... exists on the land, in the hills, grass, rock, soil, in the air itself." In other words, Indigenous people are here to stay. Try as you might, you can't get rid of us.

Bear Bones and Feathers

LOUISE BERNICE HALFE (Sky Dancer)

Cree from Saddle Lake First Nation, AB, and Saskatoon, SK

Published in 1994

In this collection, the poet takes elements as diverse as Cree mythology, black comedy, spirituality, and memory and puts them to work as healing agents. In her hands, they become salves she applies to the wounds that have been inflicted on her people by colonization. The mythology includes appearances by *pāhkahkos* (the flying skeleton), *Wisahkecahk* (Wesakechak, the trickster), and *wîhtikow* (the cannibal spirit), while the spirituality weaves its way through her memories of her grandparents, parents, siblings, lovers, husband, children, friends, and people she has met, most alive, some not.

As if summoning "helpers" to give her the strength to assault the aggressor, the poet affirms the oneness of her culture and nature. She sleeps with Sihkos (the weasel), sings with robin, weaves with spider. Her ancestors' bones are alive. The animals she eats – ducks, rabbits, fish – become an organic part of her. Veins, blood, and sky unite in one substance. *Pāhkahkos* is her dancing companion. Her grandmother is a "medicine bear" and a "healer of troubled spirits," her mother a rock. She pays tribute to the men in her life. Her father may have punched her mother ("She always wore ... a shiner") and lived on skid row, but that does not stop her from acknowledging his giving her life. She celebrates her body; describing her first period, she says of her hand that has touched her vagina: "My finger is an infant rabbit / slaughtered out of the mother's belly." Women encounter male aggression, as when one woman's corpse is found in a ditch ("men plastered to her mouth / belly and her spoon"). Which *still* doesn't stop the deceased from singing with the old woman who finds her body. Encounters with men, however, do not lack humour – one woman calls them "fucking men" while another taunts them: "Men / day hang dere balls / all over da place." Of residential school, she says, "The family not ever more," and of the sexual abuse in such institutions, "pain, pleasure, shame." She rails at the church ("priest said all us pagans / will go to hell") and the Pope, whom she has saying, "Too bad that rancid pig … came on your land." To which insult Sihkos crawls up the Wihtikow's anus to get to his heart ("Little brother travelled / up the dark passage / to the North"). Finally, however, after all this darkness, thunder and belly dance to nature.

Part lamentation, part protest song, part hymn of praise, these poems cover a huge emotional arc. From insects as tiny as ants to planets traversing space, it is as if the universe itself is the poet's body, and everything inside it, including the mythology and language that drive human life, her veins and blood. It is only with all these helpers that she is able to expel her people's disempowerment, so that they can heal. Without that language and mythology, the sense of humour and dignity of spirit that so marks them would not exist.

Blue Marrow

LOUISE BERNICE HALFE (Sky Dancer)

Cree from Saddle Lake First Nation, AB, and Saskatoon, SK

Published in 1998

The emotional territory these poems mine is that of the bones, the women's in particular, that have lain in the soil of Canada's western prairie for centuries. The voices of the poet's *ohkomuk* (grandmothers) – Adeline Cardinal, Emma Woods, Sara Cardinal, Bella Shirt, and others – resonate. They echo like gunshots. They share their wisdom from centuries past, a wisdom that, eerily, is as relevant today as it was back then. And the present-day *ootachimoo* (Keeper of Stories) orchestrates these voices, interweaving subtly into their music the voices of fur traders, priests, Métis, and others in the dramatic history of first contact between First Nations and Europeans in that part of the world.

To begin, the poet mixes ancient Cree story and language with Catholic prayer. The mesmeric cadence of those age-old prayers – the Hail Mary, for instance – is rendered more haunting, and thus more powerful, by the insertion of elements of the Cree language and Cree thinking. "*Askskiy* as it is in *kisik* ... " (On earth as it is in heaven ...) is a perfect example of this technique. For those who know Cree, not only does it give the prayer a whole new dimension, it also gives it a whole new relevance. It cuts into you. And the message that it sends is that this sacred communion between a soil and a people goes back before the arrival of the first missionary. Because where, in Christianity, women are excluded from contact with sacred powers except through a man, women in Cree culture were the keepers, the reciters, the custodians of those prayers. "Grandmothers hold me," the poet says at one point. "I must pass all that I possess, every morsel to my children. These small gifts." Another strong theme – and one found in many of the works celebrated here – is that of the intimate contact between nature and people. The Cree are not foes of nature. And nature is not their foe. The oneness of human bone, animal bone, and soil – "I hang onto this bone ... I am married to her garden of carrots and sweet corn heads" – is explicit. The relationship is tactile: soil is flesh, and flesh is soil is bone is marrow is water is soil.

One senses, woven ever so subtly into these poems, a silent rage at the men who came here to teach us that nature is dead, that worshipping a tree is an act that will send you straight to the tortures of hell and is tantamount to worshipping the devil. Because for Indigenous people, that is exactly what you are supposed to do: to worship that tree, that land, that nature, which very much has a soul, a living spirit. This wrath is directed, as well, at those lonely, womanless fur traders who used Indigenous women to slake their "thirst" and then dumped them, leaving behind a generation of Indians "with dirty blond hair." This weaving, however, is done with such intelligence, taste, and style that you don't see the rage. Rather what you see is the hope beyond that rage. You see a healing by prayer, a pagan celebration of a land – Saskatchewan, Alberta, Manitoba, Canada – that is, indeed, very beautiful.

The Crooked Good

LOUISE BERNICE HALFE (Sky Dancer)

Cree from Saddle Lake First Nation, AB, and Saskatoon, SK

Published in 2007

To depict her family, the poet interweaves myth with reality. The reality may be modern, but the myth harks back to a past so ancient that human memory becomes indistinguishable from biological memory. There are points when two time zones coexist within one sentence, or when characters address each other from opposite sides of a "wall" of time. And because the myth here is Cree, psychedelic beings such as *pāhkahkos* (the flying skeleton), *wîhtikow* (the cannibal spirit), and others surface at intervals to animate the human protagonists. In fact, two become major figures: Rib Woman and the Woman of the Rolling Head.* The first, her energy taken from the Biblical Eve, is a metaphor for the centre of womanhood; though she stays abstract, she wields great power. The second plays a similar but more dynamic role: she galvanizes action.

"The ancient roots that stem through our bodies," the poet, speaking as *e-kweskit* (turn-around woman), opens, thus asserting her presence in the narrative. But then she qualifies her humanness, "I am not a saint, I am a crooked good." She applies a "brush stroke" to her status as animal, as part of nature; describing herself and her siblings as children helping their father build a shack, she writes, "we squished mud between our toes … otters dripping …" Later, a boulder recognizes her. And a moose hide addresses her, "I want … beads. Up and down my torso." Like all families, hers knows darkness. She says of a sister, "No one knows Wapistikwan ["White-haired One," their father] dug into her diapers." Or alluding to sexual abuse encountered by a cleric at residential school, she writes, "Ospwakan on his knees by the toilet." Through the layers of time, *nohkomak* (my grandmothers) teach her to swim, "Dance this new language." When Rib Woman appears, the poet informs us that "the dreamers sat in the large roundness of Rib Woman" and "I, *e-kweskit*, am folded in Rib Woman." As to the Woman of the Rolling Head, "Rocks are her spine." She is "mounds of earth, standing wood." She "lived in the dark moon of aspin's den" ("aspin" is the poet's mother). "I saw myself butchered," the poet writes in another poem, "so I went to ... Rolling Head ... her skull ... the only safe place." As they "follow a SaskTel truck" down the highway, the poet and her husband digest Rib Woman's and Rolling Head's revelations. And the narrative closes with Rolling Head announcing, "I'm earth born each moon," by which time the line applies to the poet herself. By now, reality and myth have melded.

Insofar as the Woman of the Rolling Head is divine in resonance, the point here is that these people are human at the same time as they are animal and god – humanity, nature, and divinity are the original "holy trinity," the sacred circle that frames Indigenous cosmology. And if Rolling Head is the planet – the original mother goddess whose head rolls through the universe calling out the names of her children – us – then we are participants in a cosmic journey. These poems speak of a people whose lives on this land go back to the time of the birth of magic. In the end, they themselves are magic, they themselves are myth. And thereby the absence of subjugation, thereby the joy, the sense of rampant celebration.

---

* The myth of the Woman of the Rolling Head goes like this: somewhere up north, a hunter left his home every morning to go out hunting leaving behind his wife and children, two young boys. Once he was gone, the wife would give the boys chores to keep them busy while she herself went off into the forest to gather berries, herbs, whatever was needed. Or so she would explain to her charges for what she would do, in reality, was go to a glade hidden deep in the forest out of which protruded a certain stump. And there she would sit astride that stump drumming a beat upon its bark. Responding to this signal, snakes by the hundred would crawl out of the stump. And to these creatures the woman would give herself in love. And she would do this every morning until one day, suspecting something, her husband tracked her, saw what she was doing and, horrified, chopped off her head. The woman's body died but her head didn't. Enraged, it devoured the husband and then went rolling after the sons. The story continues with regional variants in the telling but, to this day, the head rolls through the forest, the fields, the night, outer space itself if need be, crying out the names of her fleeing children.

From **Oral** to **Written**

A Really Good Brown Girl

MARILYN DUMONT

Métis from Edmonton

Published in 1996

A descendant of legendary Métis rebel Gabriel Dumont, the poet addresses the issue of what it means to be a Métis woman in late-twentieth-century Canada. Racism exists and Indigenous people are too frequently its targets. At least, this is how "the other" looks at her and her people from the outside in. From the inside out, love, self-respect, and pride bloom. They radiate like ripples from the poet, to her family and community, to her people as a nation. What emerges is a definition of her people's place within the cultural mosaic that is Canada. Though it may not be one that is free of conflict, it is a place of honour and of comfort. And no one can take it from her or her from it.

As a call to arms of sorts, she starts with her parents and the solidity of identity she finds in their care: "their voices talking us to sleep / while our bellies rested in the meat days ahead." Next comes poverty and her self-consciousness about it. She describes, for example, her family living in a house that was dragged into town by a team of horses. The entire community gathered around to gawk in mockery. And then comes the racism. "Squawman: / a man who is seen with lives with laughs with / a squaw," is how she touches on her status as half white, half Indigenous. About her emerging sexuality as an Indigenous girl, she considers rape victim Helen Betty Osborne with words such as "townsfolk who believed native girls were easy." Still, her love for her family, her father in particular, is palpable, as when she wishes she could save the ailing man his earthly pain by helping him die: "I would open that gate if I could find it." Later, she addresses him, "I know / you'd rather be betting #3 and #7." Still, her delight in life's treasures glows: "I've seen this light before; / before I was born." And she, of course, is capable of romantic love. "I am parched / and you are water / and my eyes drink." As a woman, her feelings run deep: "fingers outstretched into the room save for ... our tender dangerous opening, woman's space." More abstract concepts are addressed in lines such as "these flat-footed fields and applauding leaves ... are my prayer" and "just bossy cedars, / obnoxious ornamentals, / maudlin vines and / roses that flaunt / their breasts over fences." As to the place of her people in Canada, she says to Sir John A. Macdonald, "we were railroaded / by some steel tracks that didn't last." She says to the priests, "I'm gonna throw-up / 3 years of communion hosts / from this *still unsaved soul.*" And to the English language, "Its / lily white words / its picket fence sentences / and manicured paragraphs." When love ends, she writes simply, "I hired two moving men and ... / relocated romance / myself." And finally, the clarion call to the Métis at book's end moves by its simplicity: "Danny come home / it's sunny / the ponies are frisky" and "I am, as you, made of water."

The poet may not feel good about being a member of the downtrodden – who would? – but her confidence in the value of her identity helps her quickly pull herself out of those negative feelings. What emerges is the quiet, humble ferocity of this woman's connection to the land on which she was born and grew up and the love she has for her people. She celebrates them. She celebrates her land. And in doing so, she celebrates herself.

From **Oral** to **Written**

That Tongued Belonging

MARILYN DUMONT

Métis from Edmonton

Published in 2007

In this volume, the poet touches on many subjects – language, aging, time, pollution, writing, memory, love. At its core, however, is an ode to the strength and resilience of Indigenous women. Since the arrival of Europeans in this part of the world, they have been through much. They have been the chattels of white fur traders who left their "real" wives in England. They have raised generations of children, many not their own. They have been the recipients of extreme violence, much of it attributable to racism. They have worked like slaves to hold their families and communities together, with or without their men. And not only have they survived, they have done it with humour.

The poet opens by invoking the languages of her ancestors. The language may be gone – she does not speak it, as is the case for so many others – but Cree "will always exist / on our cold side / and ache / like a phantom limb." That is what gives her the strength, or even the permission, to move on to the subject that really calls her. And indeed, in poem after poem, line after line, the central theme of Indigenous women resonates. Touching on the subject of the traders who used Indigenous women, she writes, "This is, for the wives ... who were not important enough to mention." Then she moves on to violence against Indigenous women. She mentions rape, a woman set on fire, the case of the pig farm in Coquitlam, British Columbia, where Indigenous women were butchered like hogs, one after the other. At the end of this litany, she encapsulates, "we breathe an air heavy with death song." Then, calling them "breed women," she thanks those who raised her. These were women, for example, who could step-dance all night "and still go to mass / the next morning" (for Métis women were always Catholic). She writes of her mother making a living in the drudgery of some camp kitchen while dreaming of "indoor plumbing, gas heating, and carpets." In another poem, her mother's purse serves "as a portable shrine to Ste. Anne" (mother of the Virgin Mary). She thanks her elder sister for teaching her "how to hit a baseball." She even, in a sense, thanks her body, her breasts in particular, with affectionate humour: "they don't get in the way when I do chin-ups." In other words, she is comfortable in her own skin. Of love, she writes, "I sense only the space between / our mouths," only to have that love turn sour: "let's not call it anything but / betrayal." Of memory, she writes, "this place we can mend ... over and over"; of time, "evening lists and folds, a fan / onto the glass plate / called water"; of pollution, "we trust the perch are not on fire"; and of cities, "a disaster of commerce and capital ..."

Indigenous women have always been the glue that has held the Indigenous nations together, she says. The odds against them have been overwhelming, but they have remain unbowed. Without them, where would we be? What quietly suffuses that tacit question – and its answer – is the joy that imbues the lives of these women. Defeat, even degradation, is indicated, but the women, and the poet herself, manage to rise above it and celebrate their lives and their womanhood.

The Gathering
Stones for the Medicine Wheel

GREGORY SCOFIELD

Métis from Maple Ridge and Vancouver, BC, Brandon, MB, and Sudbury, ON

Published in 1993

The poet takes the sacred teachings of the Medicine Wheel and applies their principles to life on the street, a life known by too many Indigenous people. The language of poetry is used as salve to heal wounds caused by the poverty, despair, and toxic abuse. His own life is used to tell the story of a people, their culture, their displacement, their disempowerment, and ultimately, their endurance. The language he uses may be chock full of bitterness. But it also has humour, pleasure, and love, for his people in particular. By book's end, he has built a bridge that ties the Métis world to the world of those who are not Métis. Or rather, of those who don't have the privilege of being Métis.

He opens with the being who stands at the heart of the Indigenous subconscious, the Trickster. He is described as capable of selling his spirit "for the real stuff," meaning alcohol, an act his people have engaged in too much already. One line of many that betrays this is, "I work damn hard for my / drinkin' money." Still, the consequences no matter, the party rages on. The humour is acid-laced – "Jigging til my moccasins blew a hole." Even the "royalty" of the Métis nation is living the street life, "her royal throne / Under the Georgia Viaduct." Because these are city Indians, uprooted from the land, "We might have moose / If we were bush Indians / But our appetite is city cuisine." And then there is the violence. "You got your street degree / Bashing in some squaw's face" and "She just lay there, convulsing under his boots" are two examples. Fortunately, the poet himself has street smarts, "survival poetry / Raw, unflinching / Watching your back in some skid row bar." He, for one, has been watching his back since childhood. He writes of his mother, "I tagged along / making sure she came home," because if he hadn't, she would have bought a bottle and never made it back. That's what happens when she loses him to a home for abandoned children. Of this home's proprietor, the author writes, "She couldn't break me like her other kids." With such sad tangents, he feels that he is losing his Métis culture. "I don't know how to promenade."* He hates his absent father, "Saying I should forget every fist, each hateful / mouthful is to say I deserved it all." But then comes the love and, always the rebel, gay love it is. A line such as "while the moon swells to twice its normal size" is one of several giveaways. Speaking of which, God himself comes looking for action – with children ("After the lights went out / God's hands went to work"). And lines such as "There is an emptiness / So vast my heart echoes" come surging like sobs. So then he tries to piece himself together. And with the help of four eagle feathers given him by an Elder, he eventually does. Hence his war cry: "I speak the language / Eat my bannock with lard."

And speak the language he does for Cree peppers this text. At the start, he loses himself to alcohol and the self-abuse that comes with such a lifestyle. Through it all, though, he somehow conjures up a fractured jig, the quintessential dance of the Métis nation. His people are still jigging, the difference being that their steps are informed now by pain. The Medicine Wheel, with its four stones of illumination, humility, honesty, and wisdom, is indeed doing its work.

---

* After the jig, the second most popular dance in the Métis community is the square dance. And in that dance, the most common move is known as the "promenade." Pronounced in English in this context – that is, its ending to rhyme with "maid" – it is actually a French word, in which case it is pronounced in such a way that its last syllable rhymes with "mad." Meaning "a walk" or "a stroll," it indicates a leisurely, joyful forward walking movement where the two partners walk the square of the square dance – which, at this point in the choreography, is more circle than square – with arms and hands interlaced one partner's with the other's. To go one step further in this explanation, promenades usually punctuate, at regular intervals, all the other moves of the dance, the "swing your partner round and round," for instance, or the "dive through," or the "do-si-do." French for "back-to-back," the "do," in that language, is spelled "dos" with the s silent, like most French words that end with s.

Native Canadiana

Songs from the Urban Rez

GREGORY SCOFIELD

Métis from Maple Ridge and Vancouver, BC, Brandon, MB, and Sudbury, ON

Published in 1996

In celebrating the life of the poet, these poems celebrate life. To do so, however, they must first address the darkness that has given that life its shape. To start with, the writer was born to a mother whose life was already broken. Victim to one abusive relationship after another, she barely manages to raise her one child. There are times, in fact, when she loses him to the authorities. By age fifteen, the boy is on his own, at which point the destruction begins in earnest: substance abuse, violence, promiscuous (and dangerous) sex, rage, all-out confusion. It's amazing that he does not kill himself. Instead, he writes it out.

He prefaces these songs with a word on his mother tongue, Cree, and how it, too, has gone through abuse. Threatened by drowning at the hands of English, "maybe" he writes, "the *pikiskwewina* [words] / got away from us." This is where his dirge gets its kick-start. He goes back to his early childhood ("I remember / Whitehorse / we lived in an old trailer"). From the start, he grew up fatherless ("In the dark / my mouth practiced / that word, dad"). And when a father figure does materialize in the form of a stepfather, the poet "[sings] down his thundering fists, / her muffled cries." By age sixteen, he has "overdosed / for the third time / unsuccessfully." Still, the violence that ensues somehow keeps him going: "Every blackened eye … was the silent warrior / guiding my pen"; his mother, after all, "keeps watch." And then there is the racism: "We spoked pretty broken / so when dey mimicked our dalk," it makes him wonder who he is and where he belongs. "I was convinced / God had yet to decide / what colour I'd be." But later he deduces he is half white, half Indigenous. "So we end up scrunched in between / Suffocating ourselves to act accordingly."

Then he discovers his sexuality. This section is one fun romp. ("Hey pretty buck, / Wanna come to my te-pee?") The Trickster guides him at every step, "he says you be da nicimos* / so he be charming up my backbone." Amid such promiscuity, thank God, there is real love: "if ever there is love / between men / I wish your eyes / endless moons." Then he takes us to the streets to meet his friends, the junkies, drunks, hookers, petty criminals, even murderers. The junkies "Hover around the needle van / Shrieking … / Their rez dog mumbo-jumbo." Death is a constant – "her body was found / wrapped in plastic / dumped / like rotten garbage." Still, amid such squalor, he is proud of who he is. "I got so much lower-class / I far surpass / their usual upper-class groan," he crows at one point. Finally one night, a grandfather works his medicine "in a dream" and saves him.

Rez life – that is, life on a reserve – has an unfortunate reputation for poverty and all the social problems that come with it. And when that life gets "translated" to an urban setting, the violence is that much more deadly, the squalor that much more vivid, the broken lives that much more broken. But that doesn't stop the poet from singing his song from that "urban rez." Far from it. In fact, not only does he refuse the status of martyr, he kicks sand in its face. As he says at book's end, "I might not be the best / indigenous poet / but hey, my English is lousy enough / to be honest."

---

* Pronounced "nee-chi-moos" with the short clipped *oo* on the "moos," as in "book" (as opposed to the longer double *oo* as in "loose"), *nicimos* is Cree for "my sweetheart" or "my lover." No more touching, more affectionate term of endearment exists in the language.

Love Medicine and One Song
Sâkihtowin-maskihkiy êkwa pêyak-nikamowin
GREGORY SCOFIELD

Métis from Maple Ridge and Vancouver, BC, Brandon, MB, and Sudbury, ON
Published in 1997

These poems address love in three of its forms: romantic, sexual, and spiritual. The poet explores each one from all possible angles. And he does it in Cree and English, languages he uses in an extravagant and virtuosic manner.

In the introduction, he writes, in Cree, "Hello, my relations. Today, I am going to talk about love," and then explains "love medicine" – what it is, and how it was used by the ancients. "It is not to be taken lightly for the consequences are great and, if used improperly, often fatal." Then he thanks these ancients and offers us *his* love medicine, these poems, taking care to warn us to use the medicine with care. And his medicine intoxicates. He starts off with his love for the Earth – "a sacred moon mother / birthing stars / for my dream path." In the madness of the love that is about to transpire, she keeps him rooted. Then he launches into the act, "turtle he is / slow, so slow / nuzzling and nipping," "our bed a swamp / we swim in," and "my mouth / the ancient canyon / where wild horses / gallop the sky." These are just three lines of many that capture the spectacle he paints. And that is just the first section, the one entitled "Earth and Textures." The urgency intensifies with the three sections that follow. All of the external organs of the human body – and some of the internal ones – come into play at one point or another. In a trice, they are transformed to receptacles, extensions, or metaphors for such magic substances as dreams, clouds, drums, weeds, and the sea ("my mouth is the sea / I have laid upon your chest"). When his love is away, he rails at the elements, including his "obstinate skin." And of his love, "you are the cruelest / of any silence – / the night is your hair, / the rain, your lips." Nature is, indeed, not only an active participant in the physical connection, it is also its lifeblood. "I love you. / ... and the geese / in all their unceasing chatter." Eyes are fireweed, sap from maples induced by dreams. So that by the time the writer's lover is present, "*piko kikway miyonakwan* (everything is beautiful)." But then he is away again and, not to be eclipsed, the Trickster bumbles in to incite implosion – "Coyote has torn her (the moon) to shreds, / dances wild from the blood of her / to the cracking of the trees, / the forest and my heart exploding." At the end, exhausted by the energy he has just expended, he says to his lover one final time: "*astam ota nicimos / otantayan* (come here, my lover, I am here)."

One must understand that, by this time in the life and work of an Indigenous writer – and this is the writer's sixth book – he has gone past the pain for which Indigenous life can be the calling card. Certainly, if we are to judge by his earlier collections, this writer's life has not been painless. But now it is as if he has had enough of moaning and groaning, though vomiting it out would be a fairer description of his work. There is nothing left to say. Now that his system is clean of the poison, he is ready to glory in the life, and the body, that was given him by the Earth as life-giver. And he thanks her. This collection is a prayer to nature. It is a reaffirmation of the biological reality that Christian missionary work tried so hard to raze from Indigenous cosmology.

I Knew Two Métis Women

GREGORY SCOFIELD

Métis from Maple Ridge and Vancouver, BC, Brandon, MB, and Sudbury, ON

Published in 1999

This a portrait of two Métis women living in Canada's west in the 1950s and 1960s. The author's mother and aunt, these women have been born into lives that are underprivileged, downtrodden, and powerless. They are poor, they are not white – they are victims. Still, none of this breaks their spirit and two forces see them through. The first is their sense of humour, their ability to laugh, to party. The other is country music which they love with all their hearts. In the end, these poems are about the healing power of art.

Dorothy Scofield and Georgina Houle Young come from poor backgrounds and continue to live in poor circumstances. They have no money. They bumble about from one cheap rented home to another. Their curtains are homemade, the linoleum is peeling off the floor, they wear Salvation Army clothes. And they lead a rough-and-tumble life: they love to drink, to smoke, to play bingo. Dorothy once beat up three women in a bar washroom. Aunty Georgina would beat up her husband; once she gave him a shiner the size of a plum. They have been abandoned with six-month-old babies by dysfunctional husbands. They have been called "fucking squaws" by white kids. They have been beaten to within an fraction of their lives by nuns at residential school. They have been told that their mother tongue is the language of Satan. They have been beaten by their men to the point where they couldn't even open their eyes. They have been raped. They have come near to being killed. By their men. Aunty's mother burnt to death in a house fire. The author's mother has tuberculosis and eventually dies of it. Remarkably, these women do not once complain. Instead, they pick up their guitars and sing: about loved relatives who have died, about long-lost lovers, to the waves, to the clouds, to the stars. They wail out their pain. Their love of life comes pouring through the words and melodies of all the old country songs. There are points where their guitars seem almost more human than their men. The deities of the religion they practise, which is pleasure, are the country stars of the 1940s and 1950s. "Their dueling guitars," the poet writes, "were the twelve strings I climbed to dreams on." And how he loves the way their lives are transformed into miracles by the magic of music, as we, the readers, sit and watch in amazement.

The Cree language breathes through these poems (though translation, of course, is provided), so much so that the reader feels that they were practically written in that language. In fact, some, like "Oh, Dat Agnes," are written in a sort of half-Cree / half–pidgin English. The women are victims from beginning to end. With that, there is no argument. But do they let it show? Hell, no. With their laughter and music, they are too busy celebrating life to even notice that pain so that, in the end, they win. White people are going to heaven, these poems suggest, where you can't even smoke cigarettes, let alone have sex; we're going to hell, where the party is.

From **Oral** to **Written**

Singing Home the Bones

GREGORY SCOFIELD

Métis from Maple Ridge and Vancouver, BC, Brandon, MB, and Sudbury, ON

Published in 2005

The poet addresses his family's history. Dividing its members into a triptych of "the Dead," "the Missing," and "the Living," he converses with them. The interchanges are, at times, declarations of love. At other times, they are castigations of their flaws, railings, tears of sorrow at their absences, tears of joy, of rage, of profound regret. They are confessions, questions, musings, acts of thanks and, their author being Indigenous, hoots of laughter. Through such means the author comes to terms with unresolved issues that were left hanging when these loved ones (and not-so-loved ones) died or went missing. And because much of that history is marked by pain – at this point in his life, the poet is thirty-nine years old – the conversations *are* catharsis.

First the dead. Of one great-grandmother, he asks about their (Cree) language, "if I take *ki-tâpiskanikan*,* / place it scolding on Portage and Main† / will all the dead Indians / rise up from the cracks, spit bullets / that made silent our talk?" He looks at the faded photograph of another great-grandmother and writes, "The dress that holds you together / is barely breathing." In the nineteenth century, the Hudson's Bay Company would send young men from Scotland to manage their trading posts in northern Canada. In many cases, these men would leave their "real" wives in England and take on as spouses Indigenous women who, in the men's journals, wouldn't even have names or, if they did, would have their Indigenous names replaced by English ones. To one of these "great-great-great-grandmothers," he says, the English husband "could have said, / ... my sweet prairie crocus, / *tapwe, mistahi ki-sâkihitin*!"‡ In another poem, he regrets that his star-crossed mother never had the chance, when she was alive, to tell him, "You are my miracle." Then the missing. Enraged, even now, by his absconded, partly Jewish father, he says to him, "the yellow leaves outside my window

/ thirty-nine years later / cling stubbornly to the trees, / to the sound / of your never-ending deportation." An aunt was once known by her white husband as "Punching Bag Woman." In a more universal context, he talks by "osmosis" to a "senorita" on the violence-wracked Mexico–U.S. border, telling her that many Indigenous women in Canada, too, have died violent deaths at the hands of white men – "two countries away / my own dark-skinned sisters / turn in a grave of silent rages." Toward the living, he expresses two extremes. One is his hate – "holding upright my vertebrae, / the long-ago weight / of my stepfather's fists" – and the other his love: "Three whole nights ... / I've eaten you. *peyakwâw,* / *nîswâw, nistwâw.*"§ By book's end, having expiated all this emotion, he is ready to enjoy looking at something as simple as someone dancing.

This family of lost souls has been much affected by violence, by hate, by huge misfortune. In bringing its members back to life like this, however – and much of it in Cree! – the poet has reclaimed its dignity and spirit. In doing so, he has honoured his own. This book is about art as healing. It is about "singing home the bones" and laying them to rest.

---

* *"ki-tâpiskanikan"* is Cree for "jawbone."

† For those not familiar with the city of Winnipeg, its epicentre is the spot where meet the streets known as Portage Avenue and Main Street.

‡ *"tapwe, mistahi ki-sâkihitin!"* is Cree for, "it's true, I love you very much!"

§ *"peyakwâw, / nîswâw, nistwâw"* is Cree for, "once, twice, thrice."

Looking into the Eyes of My Forgotten Dreams

JOSEPH A. DANDURAND

Kwantlen from Kwantlen (Fort Langley) First Nation and Vancouver, BC

Published in 1998

These twenty-four poems meditate on topics from mystical experience to suicide; to residential schools and their sexual abuse; to loss of land; to love romantic, familial, and fraternal; to ancestral spirits; to land. The collection is an elegy, as complex and jagged as it is lyrical, to the soul of a people before and after the arrival of Europeans in their part of the world. At certain points, the two eras fold imperceptibly into each other, and we can't tell where one ends and the other begins.

In the first poem, the poet marvels at the fleetingness of life and the smallness of his presence in the great scheme of things; watching him describe that smallness is like watching someone grasp at a mass of air – there is nothing there, and yet there is something. The second poem notes the coexistence of two time periods, one in which his ancestors "fish and laugh and hide from the spirits," the other in which the land they once occupied is no longer theirs and so they wish to live no longer. Two concepts also become one when human life merges with that of nature. In the third poem, for instance, the girl the poet loves becomes a bear; they have two daughters, a sun and a moon, and his soul soars accordingly. By contrast, however, the meeting of Indigenous and white in the person of the fort the latter erected was less attractive – "ever seen smallpox? ... not as pretty as wooden walls." In the poem that follows, the poet states that his eyes have never let go of that past. Some poems verge on the macabre, such as the one where two dead humans – ostensibly Indigenous, "hair ripped, skin broken, slashes, burns" – float above their world watching it disappear into the sand. Six poems, interspersed among the others, address residential schools – little boys lying in bed look out at the moon and think of their mothers in their distant homes dying of smallpox while a cleric manoeuvres his hand under their blankets. The language is handled in such a way that the cleric – a priest? a brother? – is never mentioned. In another of these school poems, a brother screams at a small child, "you are my gift from the lord," even as he forces himself on her. In "Feeding the Hungry," an island bristles with the magic of spirits – "you can hear their songs pounding in the trees." Still, alcohol abuse does not escape mention. Then there is the everyday; a phone just rings, and a good day comes to an end. On a closing note, the photographs that punctuate the text feature the poet's ancestors; their faces look so like the bark of trees, it is as if those trees were his ancestors.

The range is wide. Extreme beauty coexists with extreme ugliness, love with hate, tears with laughter, despair with triumph. Still, the poet's anger at his people's subjugation is handled with such intelligence that, far from recoiling, we are magnetically drawn to the imagery. That the writer is fettered by the chains of a language that is foreign to his spirit only sharpens the experience.

Glass Tepee

GARRY GOTTFRIEDSON

Secwepemc from Tk'emlúps (Kamloops) First Nation, BC

Published in 2002

Divided into three parts – Horsechild, Glass Tepee, and Reservation Dogs – this poetry collection addresses three aspects of Indigenous life. The first is the beauty that exists at the core of the Indigenous spirit. This beauty is given expression by the movement of a horse as it lives out the rhythm of the months and the seasons. (The writer, we might note, is a rancher.) The second is roots; the writer pays tribute to his race, to where he comes from physically and spiritually. This is where the age-old mythology of his people comes into play. The third is the dark side of Indigenous life – skid row; corrupt, leaderless communities; the havoc of organized religion; and the effects of the Indian Act.

We begin with a hymn to the beauty of the Indigenous spirit in the figure of a horse who makes love to, and is made love to by, the months and seasons of a calendar year. Difficult to grasp because his presence is so ethereal, the writer's beloved – this horse – is nature, god, love, life, all he holds sacred. The month of January, for instance, says to the horse, "I will be traveling / in the currents of your blood"; July, "I will cloak / your painted hide / with rain-dappled roses / & dew." Next we experience the poet's pride in and love for his roots. Sentences like "We have long lain / on the belly of our Mother / since the time we emerged / from nothing" marry those roots to the Earth as animate being. This is where the Trickster appears: "yesterday Koyoti sipped wine ... with a priest ... spoke of philosophers / like Plato ..." Later, the poet confesses that he once was told that Koyoti had fled south "never to return to Winter Dance / on the wall of my glass tepee." He refused to believe it. He makes fun of "wanna-beez," which is a back-handed way of saying he is proud of who he is. He writes of lively sexual encounters at powwows, of whimsical meetings on dance floors between "two spirits," of "hands reaching through the frozen earth / grabbing at Northern Lights." And though there are touches of pathos, joy and optimism predominate. It is only in the third section that anger and bitterness appear. Here the poet rails at Canada for what it has done to his people, blasts Indigenous life on skid row, spits at reservation life where "dogs piss on condemned houses ..." Seeing an absence of Indigenous leadership, he asks, "Where have our chiefs gone?" Organized religion leaves him seething. Of the Indian Act, he writes defiantly: "there is no white law accurate / enough to stop the law of nature." It all, however, ends with hope, if only as a glimmer: "we are jigging clones in glass tepees ... pointing bony fingers at dead boogey men."

The "glass tepee" is a metaphor for the modern Indian who no longer inhabits a buffalo-hide tepee but lives in a house with glass windows. And the fate of the "boogey man" – the white man – is a foregone conclusion. His spirit is dead, the Indian's is not.

Whiskey Bullets

Cowboy and Indian Heritage Poems

GARRY GOTTFRIEDSON

Secwepemc from Tk'emlúps (Kamloops) First Nation, BC

Published in 2006

Divided into four sections – Koyoti Indian, Copenhagen Cave, Whiskey Bullets, and Shadow Walk – this collection addresses the issue of living in two worlds, Indian and cowboy, in the ranching country that is the poet's home territory. By definition, these worlds are polar opposites – traditionally, cowboys and Indians killed each other. Is this Indian cowboy at war with himself? While there are poems that resonate with intense inner conflict, others pulsate with an even more intense inner beauty. So if the latter constitutes the writer's spiritual existence, which thrives on magic, then its physical counterpart is grounded in the culture of horses and rodeos, bars and whiskey-drinkers and, of course, the interloper. The image, after all, of "whiskey bullets" is a deadly one. The reader is taken to places cowboys don't normally inhabit, places where race and politics, gender and sexuality seethe electrically. To survive this volatile journey, the author resorts to his strong Indigenous heritage with its shape-shifting trickster, Koyoti. Shape-shifting – in the mental, emotional, and spiritual senses – is what one needs to successfully straddle a world so fractured.

The first poem, "in perfect English," (without even a capital *I*), opens "Koyoti commentaries stalk / TV cameras ..." Of bars, the poet writes, "Indians have come to know that / resilience is the size of a fist." Academics can dig forever into the meaning of the lines that fill these pages but, for this cowboy, "it is merely the moment / when the cattle-driver's love of writing / pours through the pen." On the other end of the spectrum, "cowboys never weaken, / they just grow thick skin." And there is magic: "Koyoti concocted magic ... / Thunder clapped in your womb / ... you became the life-giver, / I the receiver ..." Images of violence and love lock horns. "I am in love alone / filling my mouth / with whiskey bullets ..." Imagine a cowboy capable of expressing love, if an imperfect one: "I have seen your wishy-washy love / at work beneath that cowboy hat ..." And a line such as "Warm and salty / blood / passes twisted lips / to kiss historic wounds / reopened to air" expresses the lethal inner conflict at the heart of Indian cowboy country. The collection is filled with such jagged imagery.

The sentences connect one with the other, and then they don't but they do, if in a funky, off-kilter manner. English written as filtered through Secwepemc? Secwepemc being written through the webbing of English? The choice is the reader's, because the English is being reinvented to accommodate a magic that lives beyond its comprehension. One would need a book to explain the phenomenon. Suffice it to say that, in order for Indigenous people to overcome their colonized status, they will have to bend the dominant language to their own needs. This poet makes a valiant beginning here. May he continue.

Skin Like Mine

GARRY GOTTFRIEDSON

Secwepemc from Tk'emlúps (Kamloops) First Nation, BC

Published in 2010

Again, this volume of poems is divided in three – Skin Like Mine, Scalps and Derma, and Tender Terminology. The suite addresses what it means to be Indigenous in modern Canadian society, affording us a view of the internal workings of the mind and heart of a Secwepemc man living at the beginning of the twenty-first century. Anger, bitterness, and biting sarcasm inhabit its pages; the writing is certainly critical of certain forces the author sees at work around him. Still, these emotions are overshadowed by the evident love he has for his people, his land, and his horses – for it seems, according to the biographical information his poems provide, that he is a rancher, a man of the land.

His relationship to the Christian God comes through from the start as one of doubt: he speaks of Mary Magdalene handing him the hammer, to which God cries blood for both her and for him. Later, the poet will call himself a "born-again pagan." At Christmas, "the boy child readies himself to / make way for comedy" and cites "Coyote innovation fooling the master …" In contrast to this sarcasm is his closeness to nature. When, for example, the crow finds no roadkill, the author is almost apologetic. In lines such as "I scope corporate skulls out of control / stuffing my Mother full of defilement," he is angry at what industry has done to his land. Still, he remains unvanquished, saying, "I am a rock …" The dust of his grand-mothers, after all, "still blows between the barbs" (of the fences erected by the government to claim Indigenous land for whites) and he "cannot overlook / the blood my grandparents / left before me." While in Mexico, he expresses guilt about the region's Indigenous people being servile to whites – "ghosts … hide on Gringo Street / past dignity" – while he drinks beer like a white tourist. His senses, then, are that much more sensitive to the world's wonders, so much so that one sense, sight, exchanges places with another – "blue is the sound of the world." Lines such as "the crystal globe / beauty itself" and "the Milky Way quilts a moonless heaven" are simply his way of declaring his love for life. The collection bristles with such imagery. But sarcasm seeps in with lines such as "English is the first language in a multi-cultural society" and "we think / that Canadian history was not busy with murder." Drug use dismays him. As to politics, he says, "white man is all business / the Indian muddled – / combine the two and you have a lawyer." Mercifully, he ends with love for a character he names Horsechild. As cryptic as he evidently is beautiful, she remains a mystery (like all Indigenous languages, Secwepemc is genderless). Lines about and addressed to this character say it all: "marrow flames deep within bone / the skin flushes blood" and "no matter where you are, much-loved, / do not forget home." He/she, after all, will ensure that the salmon return so that "the mountains will forever be abundant."

It is a seesaw of emotions that we encounter here, a seesaw that ends, fortunately, with love. And with what shines through as potent as light: pride in one's skin ("like mine"). "I am … Secwepemc," he declares at a crucial point in his song, "like the land from which I come." If there is torment in this collection, it flickers briefly by comparison to what stays inviolate: triumph.

Songs to Kill a Wîhtikow

NEAL MCLEOD

Métis from James Smith First Nation, SK

Published in 2005

Its title may contain the name of a monster who eats human flesh, but its subject, ironically, is love. And that is the author's point – love as one's only weapon in the never-ending battle against life's negatives for which the *wîhtikow* is the ultimate metaphor. That negative may be sadness, loss of land or of a loved one, disorder of one kind or other, absence of truth or love or laughter. It could be anything that threatens one's physical, emotional, mental, or spiritual well-being. In the face, therefore, of hurt so imminent, the only antidote has to be the essence of positivity. And if anything is positivity incarnate, it is love.

The motifs of negative and positive thread their way through the collection. The former is a constant menace to the latter, though the positive emerges as victor. The poet pays homage to his forbears. Describing their adventures, his love is unmistakable. "They spoke sanctuaries into being," he says at one point, and later, of his grandfather, "Words came from him like water / formed from the shallow fog ..." He pays homage to his land, lamenting how it has changed for the worse; his love for it, again, is undeniable. "The retreat of the buffalo from the land ... a land polluted by new presence ..." Certainly the title "Urban Castration," makes its point succinctly. He pays homage to his friends, people he admires, the "Saulteaux Billy Jack," to name one, a world-weary soul who says little else beyond "I am so tired." He pays homage to his culture: "Wrap the open spaces / of revelation / with transparent tapestries ..." and "Light of land / clothed people / with *maskihkiy*, medicine ..." Even more notably, he pays homage to language, practically making love to both Cree and English: "No longer bound by pain / I felt myself fall from the sky / with words holding me ..." and "Words grew / like water droplets forming / with more words ..." And there is humour as when the bannock wagon is "a platform of desire /

an altar of illusion / a reserve within a reserve," "rez dogz boogie," and mourners play "Buck Owens' 'Act Naturally'" at a funeral. Still, what cuts most deeply and comes up most often is the author's desire for his lover's presence. When she is not there – or when he is not there with her – he palpably aches for her. "I kiss your eye lids / in the morning / to let the sun / back into the sky ..." and "I drink the sky from your lips ..." There are points where the words he uses to describe such feelings practically become sex organs. "We extend our words in divinity / as I collapse in your watery earth ..." But always, there is the monster, lurking, stalking, waiting for his moment to sink his teeth in. "*Wihtikow* teeth / could not find feast / in my flesh ..." "*Wihtikow* wanders / in the grey, concrete forest ..." But though the monster haunts, he does not conquer. Because love does.

Only love, the poet posits, can bring to fruition the redemption so needed by the damaged Indigenous spirit. The collection, finally, is about the resilience of the human spirit against powerful internal and external forces. The *wihtikow* may keep trying to reduce the poet to prey, but the poet confounds him. Too busy loving, he will not bend. Rather does he sing the monster to death.

Gabriel's Beach

NEAL MCLEOD

Métis from James Smith First Nation, SK
Published in 2008

This poetry collection states that if we as Indigenous people are going to heal ourselves of the ills that haunt us, then we must look to our ancestors to find that healing. To forget the past or sweep it under the rug would be our undoing. To the contrary, we must recognize it, come face to face with all its faults, disappointments, hurts, defeats. And its joys, its triumphs, its beauty. In order to survive as a people into the next generation, this writer posits, we must heed our ancestors' voices. We must learn from them and thank them.

As a Métis, the writer first invokes, if by association only, the name of one of the great fathers of all Métis, Gabriel Dumont, contemporary and brother-in-arms of Louis Riel. In fact, when we first pick up the book and find that its author is Métis, Gabriel Dumont is who we think it's about, and perhaps that is the intended effect. Such an association makes the collection ring with that much more power. Still, he writes here of another Gabriel, his *mosom* (grandfather), who, as a young man, served his country in the Second World War. In fact, the suggestion is that this second Gabriel, being a warrior, was likely named after the first, also a warrior. So just as the name resonates with the spirits of two different men, so does the "beach" in the title resonate with the spirits and the violence of two different beaches. One is in France where the author's *mosom* landed with his unit in 1944, the other is the "beach of his life," so to speak, here in Canada, on the prairies of Saskatchewan, the life that he came back to after the war and lived out to the end of his days. While in Europe fighting, where he lost many friends, the only thing that kept him going was his ancestors. The first was his mother, Cihcam, who was the niece of Atahkakohp (Starblanket), the great Cree chief. To the author's *mosom*, Cihcam is his blanket of stars. Her songs give form to the moments of his birth. She gave him life and language. To him, as to the author into whose body and dream world his spirit seeps, their bodies are tattooed with "land speak," *askiwewin*. Old stories give our bodies shape and guide the path of sound like trees guiding the wind. In poems like "Meditations on Paskwâw-Mostos Awâsis" (Buffalo child), the line between man and nature blurs; there are moments when we don't know whether the writer is writing about a human or a buffalo. And it doesn't really matter because the buffalo, a "child" – that is, a young buffalo – is his ancestor anyway. Same for Memekwesiwak, the Little People who are simply extensions of the natural world, freely traversing the border between reality and dream. As is typical of Indigenous literature, humanity and nature, far from being two separate entities, are one and the same.

Though this collection of poetry is written in English, the Cree language resonates throughout. And though the author recognizes the trauma colonization has caused his people, he refuses to give in to its onslaught. To him, the land and its people, guided by the spirit of their ancestors, will always have the final word. They will save us.

This Is a Small Northern Town

ROSANNA DEERCHILD

Cree from O-Pipon-Na-Piwan (South Indian Lake) First Nation and Winnipeg, MB
Published in 2008

On the surface, these poems are about growing up in Canada's north. The setting is a small mining town that is split down the middle by race, white and Indigenous. One could almost say that the twain never meet, but they do – by marriage. The author's Cree mother marries an itinerant white hunter from the south. As a result, the daughter grows up straddling the racial divide, a divide that harbours many secrets. This collection paints a portrait of a young Cree girl and the secret places inside her heart – and her town and culture – where she finds comfort, solace, and love.

As a waitress at a greasy spoon in town, the mother finds herself serving breakfast to a white hunter. He tells her that he has come north to hunt moose. When she tells him she is one,* they laugh. And fall in love. Later, the poet says of them, "his pale body / does not make her heart dance / but his promises do." Growing up in town away from the land of her ancestors, leather shoes hurt the poet's feet; they ache for moccasins. Here in this town, she says Indigenous "girls from good families dream of inco rich boyfriends." Meanwhile, the Elders of her people watch this mining company, Inco, the town's economic lifeblood, "take apart the earth" as their young people "get pissed drunk." Fortunately, with such pain always nearby, the poet has her siblings. She soothes one sister who has just been beaten by their father. Having snuck into her room, she "promises[s] to build her an ark," while her elder brother "takes the blame / even when i break mama's crystal vase" and another brother, this one hard of hearing, "takes radios apart / to solve the mystery" of sound. Her mother does beadwork – "flowers berries dancing vines / bloom from her fingers / a cree garden of eden" – while her father works as a garbage collector. In this role, he sees into people's lives from a distinct perspective: "saw your wife's clothes in the dump / did she leave you?" The wild outdoors gives the poet the solace she so needs; the wind says to her, "you are a seed / a sweet berry." Then along comes religion. Her mother having converted to her husband's Mormonism, she says to its penitents, if sarcastically, "my dear latter day saints / i love you with … / unquestioned devotion." Still, there is domestic violence: "daddy says cleanliness / is next to godliness / and makes sure mama / is as godly as possible." And there is drinking: "i know waylon / dolly[†] … / before jack and jill." There is troubled adolescence: "pretty girls puke on the cobble stone driveway." There is awakening sexuality – "martin is the new / allowance day addiction" (Martin's mother runs the local candy store) – and, with it, lurking sexual abuse. "I feel his blue eyes always watching," she writes of a man (her father?). Happily, there is also experimentation with another kind of love, as in when "me and lola hold hands at sleepovers."

No matter what happens, however, there is always love from her mother ("her fingers / read each scar / like Braille") and from her people. "I fed you sucker head soup," an uncle says to her when she and her mother visit their home reserve. She remembers. With such love hidden in her heart, there is no room for self-pity.

---

* "Moose" is a common family name on the South Indian Lake First Nation in northern Manitoba. In fact, the maiden name of the author's mother is "Moose," thus making the author herself a "half Moose."

† "Waylon/dolly" refers to the American stars of country music, Waylon Jennings and Dolly Parton. Country music has a special place in the heart of northern Canada. This is due to the arrival in the 1950s in that part of the world of the battery-operated transistor radio. In places so remote as the fish camps and trap lines which were our homes, virtually the only radio stations whose air waves could reach those tiny little boxes were located in, of all places, such American capitals of country music as Nashville, Tennessee, and Wheeling, West Virginia. And this at night only, this due to the idiosyncrasies that radio airwaves apparently are prone to, a mystery that flummoxes, to this day, all good northerners. When you throw in the added factor of our almost total unfamiliarity with the English language – or any other European tongue, for that matter – then our ignorance was total. Which didn't put a stop to our veneration of such stars of country as "kitty (wells)," "hank (williams)," "patsy (cline)," and a whole host of others ("waylon" and "dolly" came later). When the booze was flowing and the party was raging – which was not that often as liquor back then, like radio air waves, was just as inaccessible if not more so – they were deities worthy of worship at the same temple as Jesus.

From **Oral** to **Written**

Stone the Crow

CHRIS BOSE

Secwepemc from Tk'emlúps (Kamloops) First Nation, BC
Published in 2009

These poems plumb the depths of a young man's soul. And not just any youth but a Secwepemc youth. As with young men everywhere, this soul is not spared its fair share of questioning, confusion, pain, anger, despair, fear, even terror. Fortunately, there is also hope, love, defiance, yearning, anticipation. And there is excitement, at the experience of living and at the experience of love – love for one's lover, child, and nation, and most importantly, for oneself. This book will tell you what it's like to be a young Secwepemc man in Canada's west at the dawn of the twenty-first century – what it feels like, tastes like, looks like from the inside.

As many young people do, the author consumes alcohol, to name but one mind-altering substance, excessively. But one by-product of such behaviour, which we might think of as a good one, is that the experience in a sense supplants spiritual traditions erased from Indigenous life by the Christian missionizing effort. In the thirteenth poem, "Threat," the writer calls alcohol "the European vision quest." In that physical and emotional space where one's mind is altered – inebriation and its aftermath – there are echoes of such out-of-body experiences. To backtrack to the first poem, "Umbra" (shadow, in Latin), a sparrow at the writer's window transforms into a crow and then into an owl, an ill omen in Indigenous culture. Its meaning: the next few years of the young man's life will not be easy. And this proves true for he delves into the physical and spiritual anguish caused by drink. It is almost as if life on the streets of this country's cities – Vancouver, in this case – is a rite of passage that young Indigenous men must go through. Unfortunately, another by-product of the fish-out-of-water existence that is urban life for an Indigenous person is shame at being "Indian." This he says out loud. Fortunately, the shame is not permanent. His contempt for Christian missionizers is evident – a priest, for instance, "is not in touch with god." In "Lock up the Pills," the spectre of suicide rears its head. Fortunately, it merely indicates the extent of despair the writer is experiencing. Travelling helps him for, when he travels, he "sees people with dreams slip silently by." And this is where we see the first glimmer of hope. We also see hope in his memories of life on "the Rez." Then there is the love that, he discovers, is "the way out." It inspires defiance ("they cannot take you from me"), though love for his newborn softens the hardness. As for physical love, it thrills and empowers him. And that is the most lasting impression in this collection.

Without quite stating it, this writer implies that if there is an answer to our problems as Indigenous people, it rests in love. He says it simply, humbly, and honestly: the message comes from the heart. And he dredges it from the chaos with a mind that amasses clarity and strength as it hobbles along unbroken, unsilenced. Martyrdom crushed by love – imagine! Stone that crow, that bird of ill omen.

Being on the Moon

ANNHARTE (Marie Annharte Baker)

Anishinabe (Saulteaux Ojibwa) from Little Saskatchewan
First Nation and Winnipeg, MB

Published in 1990

This collection of poetry addresses the subject of Indigenous women and womanhood in modern-day Canada. Using the moon as running metaphor, the author goes through the phases – ups and downs, hurts and bitterness, joys and sorrows and, ultimately, soaring elation with great gobs of humour. It is a roller-coaster ride on a tide of words by a writer working in a language that is fundamentally not her own. Her use of language may be fluffy, but its simmering undercurrent is as hard as steel. The author packs a punch with a ball of cotton candy. And we are left appreciating the abiding endurance of Indigenous women.

In the first poem, "Lacey Moon," she pokes fun at white people – "immigrants" – and their finery as seen through the doilies that "guard" their furniture. Then she superimposes on that image patchwork snow in an unusually mild winter, betraying the "yellow piss" marks that stain their surface. In "Moon Bear," the language slides between the image of her "moon-time" and the rhythms of nature, for example, "little fishes" swimming. Whether these creatures are swimming in water or inside her "moon," that is, the fluid of her femaleness, we can't really tell. Or perhaps we can guess. In "Chasing Moon," a "baby moon swells" her sides and, with that "bump," promises her and her grandmother to "chase" her "clan." Evoking a beautiful young Indigenous woman, "Hooker Moon" bristles with danger and with hate for her "boozer," that is, her client. "Jumper Moon" slides almost imperceptibly in and out of time zones, so to speak. In the poet's time, she makes her way through grasses once haunted by buffalo. In the highway's time, she imagines a deer she's just seen smashed up against her windshield. Without pause or even punctuation, this image slides into one of Indigenous sisters in the glare of lights from a police car. And out of this bleeds the image of Indigenous girls "jumping over the moon …" Some poems have no moon in their title and simply speak. They speak, for instance, in the voice of rape victim Helen Betty Osborne in a tone that bites with hatred. As if to mock the English language, there is word play, as in "Good Moaning": "How I moan so but I am / not moaning so much as / I used to moan in times past / I moaned …" In "Raced Out to Write This Up," the hint of self-loathing (for her race) is expressed with humour laced with sarcasm: "I write about race … I know I am classy brassy crass ass / of a clash …" And in "His Kitchen," we learn that the poet and her father were abandoned by her mother and feel the consequent sadness that runs through her life.

This is social commentary masked as word game. The clever language cushions the impact of "Indian-ness as second-class citizenry in one's own country" and the rage that arises from such a status and it makes you laugh. The overall impression? A language that was never meant to express such emotions – that is, English – expresses them anyway. Or tries to. Which is why the poems feature jagged rhythms of words that normally don't go together and sometimes uncomfortable but always tricksterish juxtapositions.

Exercises in Lip Pointing*

ANNHARTE (Marie Annharte Baker)

Anishinabe (Saulteaux Ojibwa) from Little Saskatchewan
First Nation and Winnipeg, MB

Published in 2003

These poems address identity, community, race, and history. The most striking feature is their use of the English language. It is roped into service to articulate Indigenous images and ideas that would otherwise remain elusive and unexpressed. As with flashes of light, you can't quite put your finger on them; they appear, glint, and are gone, leaving you blinking. Did I just see that or did I not – that pinprick of light that sheds a fleeting insight into some aspect of life's mystery? In some cases, it is as if the author has taken the language, put its words, syllables, and the spaces between them into a box, shaken the box, and then turned it upside down to pour it out. And what we are left with is the contents fallen helter-skelter onto a page.

In "Auntie I Dream," the poet speaks through a series of fractured images of a cherished aunt who has just died. One moment, the aunt is a ghost standing on a road waving goodbye to her niece, the author. In the next, she is sitting on a case of beer with one arm around the author's father; this time, she lives in memory. In the next, she appears in a dream, cleaning fish on a sandy shore. With a coquettish play on the title of a Hollywood comedy (*Diamonds Are a Girl's Best Friend*), the poem describing her first experience with sex is titled "Cherries Could Be a Girl's Best." In "Four Directions After Her Life," images are juxtaposed to portray humour and sadness melding one into the other, in an inexplicable manner. Another example of this approach is "All-Star Mother Wrestling except one died before treatment was invented." In reading this line, we laugh and cry at the same time. This is a poem that bleeds subtly into prose. In "An Account of Tourist Terrorism," death is danced on again, so to speak, using pop-culture terminology such as "postcards," "artifacts," "souvenirs," and "plastic toma-hawks"; the grave might as well be a fairground as, indeed, many Indigenous burial grounds actually are. There is unmasked anger, as in "Woman Bath," where an Indigenous hooker is "found dead in a ditch." But the writer also flips back to frivolity, albeit acid-laced. The title poem, for instance, the clearest example of "words poured from a box," makes no sense – but then it does. Only to come out with "cowboy lines" – and hard ones at that – in "JJ Bang Bang:"[†] "I told you go back up north" (said ostensibly by a cop); there is raw hate here, in other words. Happily, Indigenous mythology in the guise of the Trickster (in "Even Raven Has Hang Lips") appears on the street to court the ambling author.

The poet's first book, *Being on the Moon,* employed fluffy, pop-culture language to mask the rock being thrown hard at its target. In this one, the language has hardened. It is much more aggressive in addressing the position of Indigenous people as undesirables in Canadian society. Angry at their reduction to the status of downtrodden, the author writes these poems as acts of rage against it.

---

* Indigenous people, the Cree especially, have always had a way of indicating a direction by pointing their lips mostly because, at least traditionally, their hands were busy pulling nets from the water, say, or butchering a moose, or kneading bannock dough, or sewing beads onto a moccasin.

† "JJ Bang Bang" is an oblique reference to the case of J.J. Harper (John Joseph Harper), a young Saulteaux man from the Island Lake First Nation in northeastern Manitoban. One winter night in 1977, he was shot and killed, mistakenly, by a white cop in Winnipeg. A racist motive was suspected but was never proven. The scandal the incident caused reached national proportions.

Andatha

ÉLÉONORE SIOUI

Wendat from Wendake First Nation, QC

Published in 1985

This collection of poetry celebrates the fact of being Indigenous. Divided into three sections, the first is an invocation to the Great Spirit, an acknowledgment of her guiding presence. It evokes a past of happiness and balance prior to the invader's dislocation of the Huron nation (now known as Wendat). It is a call to reunification, to the re-establishment of harmony, to a renaissance. The second section, about the coming of the colonizer, describes how Indigenous life was turned on its head. It focuses on the abuse of power. The third section contains love poems and nostalgic poems. It is about the life of a woman and a mother affected by people around her and the presence of nature.

The first section talks most directly about being Indigenous. It celebrates a past before the arrival of Europeans when Indigenous people lived in a state of balance and partnership with the land. In "Saconcheta, Venez au Festin" (Saconchta, come to the feast), for instance, we read, "the heart of the 'Amerindian,' embraces the essence, the tears, the smiles, the soul of Mother Earth, impregnated by the Sun ..." Some poems bring to mind traditional Wendat chanting, evoking the presence of the Great Spirit. "Seousquachi, Transcendant Unity" is one example. Another uses the refrain, "Manitou, Manitou, Manitou ..." as a mantra to connect the ideas it contains. The second section delves into starkly different emotional territory. It is harsh, abrasive, filled with anger and even hate. A passage that calls the colonizer "the acid man" addresses him in terms such as "we must turn you plastic ... divest you of your pills ..." Invoking the ravages of colonization in countries beyond Canada – Haiti and Cambodia are two – it asks the colonizer, "whose foot is it that has crushed the breath of the child?" The third section, in contrast, is like a river after the falls. The storm is over, the flow of the water returned to its former tranquility, although some poems – particularly those about the woman abandoned by her lover – betray echoes of the restlessness so evident in the second section. For instance, "I read, meditated, cried out, my memories, which stained my pillowcase, like a mouthful of sobs, to conceal your footprints …" Still, most evoke a quiet ebb and flow of love of one kind or other. For instance, "Oh, breeze of perfume and of silk, that embraces my body … as the sun penetrates my being … you drive my spirit towards ecstasy."

Elements of the Wendat language, now sadly gone, are used in certain passages showing a desire to revive it. But the text, for the most part, is written in French. The book starts with peace of mind and happiness, turns abruptly to hatred of the status to which this writer sees her people have been reduced, then comes back to peace. The middle section thus serves as kind of purging. Without it, the poet wouldn't have been able to come to terms with her anger and celebrate her Indigeneity. Much like we, as a people, must purge ourselves to find our way, our voice.

Aki

Pour le monde qui aime la terre

RICHARD KISTABISH (Ejinagosi)

Cree-Algonquin from Abitibiwinni First Nation and Val-d'Or, QC
Published in 1986

This volume of poetry (and some prose) is a plea to the author's people to get their act together to save themselves. Essays by Quebec's Indigenous people predate the appearance of their novels, poetry, and plays. Many denounce – as does this author – the people's dispossession. He may first evoke the beauty of the land he lives on – and for this he relies on the memory of his Elders – but the "misconduct" of industrialists and bureaucrats has left him angry. He employs different forms of writing – poetry, historical chronicles, naturalistic descriptions – to relay his message. *Aki* (Land) is divided into four sections: yesterday, "ghosts in the garden," today, and tomorrow. The "ghosts" are *"les Blancs"* (the white men) who have exploited his people's territory and resources.

He begins by recalling the values – generosity, mutual aid, sharing – that once united his people, a system of values that "les Blancs" have changed irrevocably. They imposed an economic system foreign to Indigenous people, introduced alcohol, and most damagingly, divided the people. Then he points out the important dates of the dispossession, from 1650 when the first French arrived in Algonquin territory in search of fur, to 1763 when the Royal Proclamation came into being, to 1850 when the timber industry came to Temiscamingue,* to 1900 when it came to neighbouring Abitibi,* to 1920 when the first gold mines were opened, to 1986 when the Algonquin people witnessed, powerless, the destruction of their territory. In the third part, the poet takes on the bureaucrats and "experts" who manipulated and isolated Indigenous people. "They have turned our eyes inside ..." The worst is that the Algonquins themselves have come to destroy each other through the new materialism: "One freezer is not enough. So two freezers. Full of meat dry sooner than you know it ... The more one gets, the unhappier one gets." The poet's cry of alarm shows that he is scared for his people. He exhorts them to shake off the yoke of the government. Indigenous people have to take their lives back into their own hands and decide their collective future for themselves. If they don't, he warns, they will lose everything. As with most Indigenous authors, his comparison of life before the arrival of Europeans to life after leads to the observation of two truths: the degradation of the land and Indigenous people's need to reclaim their autonomy. Included are the reflections of a politician – besides being a writer, he is a leader of the Council of Algonquins of Western Quebec – in which role he expresses a desire for Indigenous people to reclaim their Indigeneity. These reflections are brief, tightly phrased, even-tempered, but the voice is forceful.

For a little twenty-five-page volume, this book contains a lot of anger. That it is written in French and not the poet's native Algonquin might, one feels, be partly to blame. The Algonquin, in fact, strains for release. And considering the topic – the degradation of a people – such strong anger is no surprise. Still, the poet doesn't resolve that anger, not within himself, not anywhere. The times in which he is writing prevent that. All he can do is plead with his people to take action, to reclaim their lives, repair the broken circle, and re-establish the old values of respect for and harmony with the Earth.

---

* Temiscamingue and Abitibi are adjacent territories in northwestern Quebec. The former named after the long, narrow – and very beautiful – lake that separates the province of Quebec from the province of Ontario, the latter after the pulp-and-paper company that established itself in the area between the years 1850 and 1900, they border northeastern Ontario near Kirkland Lake. Not only have the two territories come to be known collectively as Abitibi-Temiscamingue, they form a region of the province apart from the rest, one that has come to have its own distinctive culture and history.

From **Oral** to **Written**

Broderies sur mocassins

CHARLES COOCOO

Atikamekw from Wemotaci First Nation, QC

Published in 1988

This book of poetry and essays glorifies life, childhood, and the regeneration of Mother Earth. The author uses the title of *Embroidery on Moccasins* as a kind of map to rediscover Indigenous spirituality and reconnect with his people's traditions. Containing several poems and five essays, the book is divided into the six great periods in a human life: creation, birth, childhood, maturity, tradition, and wisdom, all working together to shine a light on Atikamekw culture.

In the first part, the poet converses with the animals and rhapsodizes on the abundance of nature and the cycle of the seasons. He rejoices in the presence of God. "How good it is to cherish dawn, when life throbs to the rhythm of the Great Spirit." In the second, he likens the love of Mother Earth and the love of a mother for her children to the "murmur of the cosmos." This gift helps her to integrate herself into the precise laws of conception. The "hope chest" is prepared to receive the newborn. The continuation of the race thus assured, the drum lulls the newborn to sleep: "Drum, listen to me, promise me to support the sound of newborns. Stimulate the courage of our dear mid-wives." In the third part, the poet, in recalling the origin of the Indigenous cradleboard, exults in one of the great riches of Indigenous culture: children. In the fourth, "stillness in the contemplation of nature leads towards respect for creation." Maturity permits a person to become one with nature. The sacred Earth contains the Indigenous soul, giving it strength to live. The cycle of the seasons teaches patience. "Spring dries tears and the miracle materializes." The poet talks to the seasons: "Summer, where are you?" In the fifth part, he recalls his grandfather who would recount many memories. He also harks back to those who have marked his life, notably the medicine man and Macesk, a chief, who taught him the essentials. He knows that his people will survive only if the Earth survives. The fight for the timelessness of the culture implies respect for traditions: "The embroidery on moccasins is thought as poetry…" In the final part, prayers, chants, and rituals of purification maintain life; the Indigenous person follows his spiritual quest in accordance with the values of the Sacred Circle. "It was in this way that I started to hum the song, for the beavers … a new breath of life."

The author goes to the very source of his people's universe. He writes in the rhythm of the seasons and is inspired by tradition to explore nature and the Earth to their roots. The poems explain the immutable attachment of Indigenous people to the religion of the ancients and to the Great Spirit. The poet's spiritual vision embraces all components of the culture. Victimhood, it seems, holds no prominent place in his thinking; neither, consequently, does rage. He is too busy celebrating the positive aspects of his people's life: children, love, community, the Earth, and the Indigenous worldview, which is every bit as complex and beautiful as that of any other culture anywhere on the planet.

Poèmes rouges

JEAN SIOUI

Wendat from Wendake First Nation, QC

Published in 2004

Red Poems is about identity. It is about being Wendat. It is about being "red." And it asserts that redness on the land where the Wendat – the "red" people – live as they always have. We were here long before the white man got here and named this land "Quebec," proclaims the poet right off the bat. Due to disease and war brought over by this "visitor," we may be far fewer in number than we were when he first got here but we are still here and we are not going anywhere. After reading this collection, there is no doubt that there exists in Quebec today an Aboriginal nation whose presence should not be ignored, whose contribution to the history of that political identity has counted for something.

The collection comes in three colour-coded sections: Red, White, and Green. The first opens with a prayer that sings out the beauty of the land and the sacredness in which the Wendat people hold it. As it progresses, the poet's passion in singing out those praises builds. For the Wendat, the land has lungs. The dust that rises from its soil is the blood of the ancestors. The poet flies over that landscape not just like a bird but *as* one. In the wrinkles of today's old people, he reads the history of his nation. His roots on the land go deeper than the roots of trees; those trees themselves *are* his ancestors. If his world is a canoe being paddled inside his soul, then that soul is a lake, the lake before him his soul. The sky rains prophecies, his blood breathes culture; walking in nature, he is a pilgrim en route to a shrine – the forest. In the second section, the "white" has arrived. From that moment on, red must learn to live with white. Words like "evil" and "jealousy" and lines like "Unhappiness in the taverns of the white" begin to appear. The Indigenous language hides itself in a farewell letter, prophecies rot in urns, the sun loses its way. Still, this does not stop the poet from hoping for the best kind of relationship between the two races; we will not fear, he says at one point, we will live together. Then comes the section titled "Green" and a return to peace, though one transformed by experience. The trauma of first contact has abated but life is less innocent; it is mature somehow in a way that it wasn't before. Greed may have entered the picture but the poet still talks about the Great Tree of Peace. The water, however, has been lied to – that is, chlorinated – and the poet mourns its death. Like the railway, crucifixes now criss-cross the land. Even the animals have become mere trophies, stuffed and hung on the walls of houses and museums. If there is always a spring to make the red sun dance, he says in one breath, then there is always a Wendat evicted from his land, he says in the next. But then a ray of the moon "marches" on water for "one last kiss." And he concludes by wishing the next generation a long, good voyage, for indeed, it will be a long one.

In a land claim, Indigenous people resort to legal means to reclaim land that has been taken from them by illegal means; these poems might be called a "land claim of the spirit." Still, considering the disempowerment that that spirit has just been through, what surprises is how intact it still is, how strong, how passionate. And this collection celebrates that fact.

Le pas de l'Indien

Pensées Wendates

JEAN SIOUI

Wendat from Wendake First Nation, QC

Published in 1995

More a book of private reflections than a book of poems – indeed, the subtitle, after "The Step of the Indian," is "Wendat thoughts" – it takes us on a tour through a Wendat mind as its owner goes about the business of living. The land he lives on – urbanized Quebec at the turn of the twenty-first century – has, by comparison to the length of time the poet's people have lived there, only recently been settled by *le blanc* (the white man). The book, then, is a reassertion of the presence of the poet's people on that landscape, the pride that it takes in the fact, and the depth of the relationship. Telling them that they have no idea of the secrets and power inside that land, it defies all pretenders to that territory.

There are five sections: "The Roots of the Heart," "Day and Night," "The Forest, the Wind, the Rivers," "They Have Trapped You, My Father," and "Son of the Rising Sun." A line that represents the thrust of the first section is "Our roots are as solid as those of the tree anchored in the rock." Pearls of wisdom follow such as "The turtle, symbol of my nation, carries the planet on his back" and "You may lose your land but you keep your roots." Paramount is the belief that the Wendat race was created by a woman. The second section – "Day and Night" – speaks more about the Elders. The poet thanks them for what they have taught their descendants as in "From the wrinkles of the Elder streams a spring." In the section titled "The Forest, the Wind, the Rivers," the poet informs the newcomer that the land, too, has a language. "Enter the forest and you will come out humbled." Then he becomes openly defiant, with lines such as "My country ... bigger than a treaty, stronger than the law." Still, the line that sticks out is "An old tree fell but then re-took root; my people are like that." In the title "They Have

Trapped You, My Father," the poet goes one step further in his description of "the invasion." At one point, he writes "they put us on a reserve" when "In our time, we possessed natural rights, without reserve." That idea is echoed with the line "My father, one day, you were trapping; on another, you were trapped." *Le Blanc* constructs dams without concern for those who lived there, he says later, adding, "How can one believe that, in defying nature, one can hope for a better world." And he warns, "fear the day when you can no longer drink the water," which leads us to the last section, "Son of the Rising Sun." Here the defiance resurges: "The roots of my people are so deep that nothing can pull them out of the Earth." As in prayer, he chants, "I owe myself existence." Then he closes with another prayer, "At the end of my life, one should be able to say: he did something for his clan."

There is a sense of accomplishment here. Just by writing these words, the poet has applied a sheen of protection around his community, his people. It is as if, like a shaman of old, he has woven a magic circle of safety around its perimeters. Anger at the fact of degradation surfaces here and there, but the collection is, by and large, an act of defiance and of celebration.

L'avenir voit rouge

JEAN SIOUI

Wendat from Wendake First Nation, QC

Published in 2008

In tidbits as brief as haikus or Confucian adages, as well as in longer poems, this book affirms the presence of the poet's people in North America. In the face of the European colonizer's driving encroachment, islands of stillness pepper the text. Biting indictments of the interloper pop up now and then, as do admissions of social problems among his people, but they are not the norm. More typical are hymns of praise to the partnership with nature from which springs the hushed stillness that so anchors the poet's life and that of his people.

Far from disturbing him, the fact that he is different from the white man gives him strength. Images from nature – for example, "We would need snow to cover our differences; we would need the moon to polish our memories" – connect abstract concepts such as happiness and innocence to human life. In the face of the tacit tension between his people and the white man, he prays for all four races to become part of a circle. The river, after all, finds equilibrium at the heart of the rapids, he writes. The words of Elders may be softer than breezes but they are the antidote to the noise pollution that is television. When dreams die, mothers mourn. Winds are the words of spirits hinting that the patience of a people can heal the pain that death can bring. And eagles, as they are for all Indigenous people, are wisdom. There is whimsy, such as the poem that expresses a desire to be a little boy again so he can hang a rattle from the moon's crescent. He yearns for his ancestors. He laughs at the moose for its funny appearance, then confesses his love for it. Forces such as water and stories testify to the fact that his people are still alive. Beauty is in the eye of the beholder; *ergo*, frogs are beautiful. Sunlight talks to the writer. He walks with the wind. The berry-picker dances with that wind; there is no need to look at the thorns that pierce her fingers. Like the wolf, the Elders had the freedom of the land; their descendants, by comparison, are confined to plots. The importance of dreams in his culture forms an undercurrent throughout. For instance, he thanks all who have canoed these waters before him and left their dreams in their wake. An Elder enters the city with all the animals, an act for which he is referred to as a savage. While recognizing the social problems of his people – including gas-sniffing children – the poet still pays homage to the nature that formed them. In the wrinkles of an Elder is written the history of his people. All is disarray – concrete, pylons, city – but the land remains land in the eyes of the Wendat.

Social problems that point at victimhood make their appearance in this collection but only briefly. The author is far too busy loving his land and cherishing the relationship between nature and man that stands at the core of his people's cosmology. That is why, after all they've been through these past five centuries, they have survived. *L'avenir voit rouge* (The Future Sees Red), says the title of the book – and by "red," it means "Indians." And so it does.

Ou vont les vents …
Émergence, débacle, et mots de givre

CERCLE D'ÉCRITURE DE WENDAKE

Wendat from Wendake First Nation, QC

Published in 2005 and 2006

These two volumes of poetry are written by a group of Wendat writers based in Wendake, Quebec. The titles translate into English as "Where the Winds Go …" and "Emergence, Debacle, and Words of Frost." The two share one purpose – to train Indigenous writers to write non-fiction in French. The group is made up of fourteen people. The nation each comes from is unspecified but they are likely Wendat, although one writer may be Innu, for that language emerges in at least one poem. Beyond the craft of writing, the objective is to keep Wendat thinking alive through language thus apprising future generations, both Indigenous and non-Indigenous, of the existence, vitality, and importance of Wendat thinking and its place in Quebec history.

To this end, the writers tackle forms that are indigenous neither to their minds nor to their culture. Besides the poetry, there is prose and even haiku, that distinctly Japanese form of epigrammatic verse. And they tackle subjects as diverse as the writers are themselves. Forces of nature such as spring and fall, light and darkness, the sea, even love, are invested with human character. Though one might argue that it is the other way around – humans are invested with natural character. The border between human identity and its natural equivalent, in any case, is left hazy on purpose. The search for identity is touched on in at least two poems. Even science fiction makes an appearance serving as vehicle for an imagined suicidal leap into an abyss. In one poem, human lips, physical sensation, and death are equated. In a thrillingly virtuosic piece, they travel one orbit, one line of consciousness. In another poem, Buenos Aires, Argentina's fabled Plaza de Mayo* inspires a poet to sing out the praises of motherly love. In another, the desire to divest oneself of one's body and fly through words is, in a sense, achieved by just its mention. The wind as a loving guide and a voice of human spirit, grappling with time to hang on to life, the love for one's people through the wisdom of its Elders ("from his wrinkles flow a spring"), a call to arms ("be proud of who you are; don't let the city get you"), a celebration of the movement of time, anger at the constraints imposed by colonialism and the church, a prophecy on the building of the railway and how it will change Indigenous life, the sea as friend, conversations with the sun, the terrible struggle to exist – all, and more, are addressed. And often there is the word play, the near mocking of a language that is not indigenous to these writers.

Three impressions remained with me. The first was a desire to leave one's physical constraints and marry one's spirit. The other was that language – French, in this case – prevents one from doing so, resulting in a kind of rage. Which leads to the third impression – a bowing to nature which is infinitely more important than humans. There is a humility in Wendat culture that is not evident in non-Indigenous culture whose story of eviction from a garden is the debacle of yore. Nature, these writers scream, will not be silenced through a foreign, colonial language.

---

* The Plaza de Mayo is the Times Square – or Nathan Phillips Square – of Buenos Aires, the capital city of Argentina. An expansive square or "place" – *ergo* "plaza of May" in Spanish – with room for thousands, it faces Buenos Aires's Casa Rosada (Pink House), the city's equivalent of Washington's White House. The Plaza de Mayo is thus the place where all national demonstrations and protests take place. In the case of the Mothers of the Plaza de Mayo, it is the mothers who lost their children to what is called the Dirty War of 1976–1983 who hold these protests. The Dirty War was that period in that country's history when a brutal military dictatorship took over the country and terrorist tactics were employed to keep the people in line. The fallout was that as many as thirty thousand people – most of them between the ages of twenty and thirty, all of them leftists, artists, intellectuals, that is, the country's most talented, most intelligent – were "disappeared." That is to say, they were abducted from their homes by police with no warrant or warning, taken to centres of torture, and then killed. Some were even thrown, live, from planes, into the Rio de la Plata, the body of water on whose southern shore stands the city, their bodies never found, never recovered. And some thirty years later, the aging mothers of those victims still march every Thursday afternoon in the city's Plaza de Mayo demanding restitution and telling the world that such things should never again be allowed to happen.

From **Oral** to **Written**

Fou floue fléau

Nin tshishe ishkuess

MÉLINA VASSILIOU

Innu from Uashat-Maliotenam First Nation, QC
Published in 2008

With an Innu mother and a Greek father, this poet considers her dual heritage an asset. Using it as a tool, she tackles subjects as diverse as religion; spiritual and cultural confusion; pollution; the fight between good and evil; violence, emotional and otherwise; motherly love; happiness and unhappiness; Innu nationalism; and the search for identity. She delves into the darkness of her people's lives and souls and resurfaces, having found in those depths the roots of joy and empowerment. Through it all, we get a look into the mind of a young Indigenous woman living in northern Quebec where it abuts Labrador at the dawn of the twenty-first century. And in that picture, we get some insight into the emotional, psychological, and spiritual place her people inhabit today.

Religion being of central importance to this author, she opens with a prayer invoking God's help for her task of speaking for her people. Using the familiar *tu* as opposed to the more formal and therefore more distant *vous*, she asks God to drive away her doubts, of which she has many, and to illuminate the voyage she is about to embark on. At this point, we have the impression that the God she addresses is Christian for that part of the world was Christianized early in its colonial history. Later, she addresses the Indigenous equivalent – *"Deesse/Peste"* (Goddess/Pest, in French they rhyme) – though in negative terms, a sign of the extent to which the imposition of one spiritual system on another has wrought confusion. The land, for one, has been poisoned by toxins not of her people's making. Dislodged as a result, they need to re-anchor. The young are discontented. Bitterness, even rage, form an indelible part of their – and therefore her – thinking, and she gives vent to it. This allows her to take an enjoyment that borders on mockery in playing with French, a language that is not hers. A perfect illustration is the book's title – *Fou floue fléau*, literally, "Crazy Blur Scourge" – a nonsensical alliteration that works in French. Which doesn't stop her from using her native Innu when she most needs it – "*nin tshishe ishkuess*" (I am an Innu girl). In some poems, she rises to the challenge of winning at the game of life, which is where Innu nationalism emerges. In a call to arms – *foncer* – she exhorts fellow Innu, in effect, to take the bull by the horns. Still, if any force will get her people to the finish line, it will be the children. And writing.

This is a young writer trying out her wings for the first time. A mother at just nineteen, she is fuelled to write for her son and for her people. In fact, the child at one point assumes a kind of messianic stature – his generation will rescue the nation. The division of the forty poems in the collection into the title sections "When We Search for a Patch … Then We Are Lost," "*Artifice*," "*Affirmations Fragiles*," "*Foncer*," "Jeronimo" (her son's name), "Write," and "Send" says it well. This girl means business. The toxins she writes of may be industrial but their roots go deeper. The rest is mythology, theology, philosophy – disciplines for which she doesn't yet have the language. For the moment, she simply struggles in her own way with the tools she has against the colonized status that so haunts her people.

Batons à message

Tshissinuatshitakana

JOSÉPHINE BACON

Innu from Pessamit First Nation, QC

Published in 2009

As with so many of the works examined here, this volume defines the relationship between a land and a people. That land is the author's home territory on North Shore Quebec. An area much less developed, much less populated, and thus much more Indigenous, they call it, in French, *la Côte-Nord* (the North Shore). But it also includes the forest that spreads north from there to Labrador, the land where her people, the Innu, have, since time immemorial, lived out their winters as nomadic caribou hunters. They are an Algonquian people whose language springs from the same root as Cree and Ojibwa. Their word *Tshissinuatshitakana* (the book's Innu title) means two sticks of white pine that hunters would position in the snow to indicate their location or situation to other hunters. One position would indicate famine, another the presence of caribou. In this way, says the author, "trees talked before humans," meaning that, far from being inanimate, trees have souls. And the dream, both human and natural, is the carrier of codes from one time to another, from one generation to the next.

The author's Elders teach her that if she patiently looks at nature, she will see phenomena not otherwise visible, the "star of noon," to name one. Her felt-soft steps, she says in one poem, caress snow imbued by the sky with its own pale blue whiteness. The four winds are her sisters, as is the Earth, which not only lives inside her but dreams with her. The sea is a mother whose cradle of waves rocks her children to sleep. The author's back, she says in another poem, resembles a sacred mountain. Even her pain, when it enters the picture, bleeds not only into the Earth but also with the Earth. When the caribou desert her, she cries out to their king, *Papakassik*. The lake cries, too. When the trails of the ancestors are erased by progress, she feels lost and fears for her people. Christianity has made her *sédentaire,* that is, it has taken her nomadic nature from her; the Christian God has thus made her his slave. "Kill me," she cries out at one point, "if I don't respect the Earth." She argues with the river, accusing it of betrayal. A small island talks to her. The whale is her grandmother. The Trickster, in the guise of *car-cajou,* the wolverine, is the one who showed her people their ancient way of life. At one point, she explains that one's soul lives before one is born. And at the end, she writes, "dream, I saw you live before I lived you."

Each poem is written first in French, then in Innu. The nature-based, river-like gurgle of Innu makes the French sound clinical by comparison. The languages speak for themselves; Innu is *of* that land, French is not. Which brings us to the second notable feature about this collection – the unity of man and nature. The poet's steps don't cut or attack the snow, they caress it. The Earth dreams with her, not against her or apart from her; her father dances with the tundra, not on it or at it; nature dreams, just like humans do. Though pain is expressed, this collection comes out as not so much the wail of a martyr but as the cry of a celebrant. The poet exults in her people's connection to nature, a bond so ancient that it goes beyond the mists of time.

Eshi Uapataman Nukum

Comment je perçois la vie, grand-mère

RITA MESTOKOSHO

Innu from Ekuanitshit (Mingan) First Nation, QC

Published in 2010

How I See Life, Grandmother comes to us from a part of Quebec that the rest of Canada seldom hears of – the part that sprawls from the north coast of the St. Lawrence River some seven hundred kilometres northeast of Quebec City and straight north to Labrador. The poet thus explores the question of what it means to be Innu and a woman born in such a land in such a culture at such a time. To this end, she writes of love, hate, joy, sorrow, hurt, misery, anger, bitterness, destiny, beauty, memory, nostalgia, confusion, loneliness, despair, silence, hope, dreams, magic, dignity, wisdom. All these topics are addressed, in confessional mode, to her beloved, deceased grandmother.

The message her ancestors have given her, she begins, is for humankind to care for the Earth. When you are in pain, the ancestors advise, look to nature to ease that pain. Your life is a garden, the poet muses in another poem, so water the flowers with love, peace, and wisdom. There are two roads in the life of an Innu, she writes in another, one physical, one spiritual; when the two cross paths, true life has been realized. In fact, the coexistence of the physical world and that of the spirit is a leitmotif in the collection, as when, expressing her love for her deceased grandparents, she talks to them in "the great beyond." The poet drops many pearls of wisdom. One thirsts to keep on going when one is young; the question is, to where? One can choose to hate the enemy, but love will win. The "poet at liberty" will meet many challenges both sad and joyful. When she prays, she prays to the Earth. "Never let me forget the size of your love, God," she rhapsodizes, "and to share it with those around me." She learned how to listen by listening to the Earth's heart beating. Rain, earth, tears, dreams, sound, music, stars, sky – all gave her life, all gave her strength. When her children cry – for she is a mother – the best she can do is hope to appease whatever torments them. She prays to the "little light" to help her find true happiness. "If I must live like a white man," she says toward the end, in a vein of despair, "then I would like to die filled with suffering, like a true Innu." Happily, through memory and dreams, her grandparents give her the strength to go on living. "If I can't give you my love, *nukum* [my grandmother]," she ends, "then where will I cultivate it?"

The poet's mother tongue being Innu, her French merely adopted, she writes the first eight poems first in Innu, then in French. But the second set of twelve are in French only, presumably to reach a wider readership and remind it of the land's dire need for survival. The sound of Innu, after all, speaks of the attachment between land and people. Every vowel is a drop of blood that trickles through the veins of a land and of a people. This collection is a hymn, if at times a painful one, to her people's attachment beyond human memory to that land. The wail of the colonized is there, but what floats above it, through that love, is the cry, if not quite of the celebrant then at least of the hopeful.

Uashtessiu

Lumière d'automne

JEAN DÉSY AND RITA MESTOKOSHO

Non-Indigenous from Montreal and Innu from Ekuanitshit (Mingan) First Nation, QC
Published in 2010

This book of poetry (and some prose) is written by two poets, an Innu from North Shore Quebec and a francophone from Montreal. Their objective is to establish a rapport between two people who, though they have coexisted for four hundred years in that province, remain separated by language and culture. The effort, apparently, springs from one that resulted in the publication, two years earlier, of the collection of writings entitled *Aimititau! Parlons-nous!* (Let's Talk, in Innu and in French to appear later in this survey.) The credits for that first book were shared by the francophone and Indigenous communities of Quebec; the Indigenous part was actually made up of several communities, Innu, Atikamekw, and Wendat, to name just three. This time out, the Indigenous contribution is Innu exclusively. Having met at the launching of the first book (to which they both contributed), the poets correspond by email. They send each other poems and bits of prose written expressly for the present book. In these writings, they reach out to each other for a relationship of respectful equality, both for themselves and for their people.

The Innu, a woman, writes of the beauty of nature and how it cradles her. She dies, she says, in the arms of the moon. The francophone, a man, replies by saying how inspiring he finds her words. She urges him to navigate *"la grande rivière de la vie"* (the big river of life) with her, to let the language of poetry take its course. He writes of the happiness it brings him to know that writers are capable of bringing two worlds together. "Writing (after all) is a way of giving life sense and direction," he quotes Emily Dickinson. She promises they will go together "to the grotto." He is full of wonder at her joy at the fact of her existence. He doesn't know the seasons or the wind or the river, not like she does with her Native Innu, but *la parole* – the word – will guide their pen in its journey across the page as it expresses their union. Both are awestruck by the north's beauty. Wanting to heal the long history they have shared so uneasily, the francophone drowns himself in a swirl of poetic language hoping it will mend the damage. Guilt is evident in his writing, although his desire to heal is as well. She keeps going back to the sea and the forces of nature, forces her people have been bound to for eons. He can merely follow her to these places; he admires her Innu-ness and sometimes wishes to be an Innu himself. In fact, he mentions the fact that most Québécois have Indigenous blood in them. After a while, it is as though, through poetic language, the writers are physically connected in a "dance of life."

Though the collection is written mostly in French, the Innu poet sprinkles her text with Innu to the point where the francophone begins inserting such words inside his own writing. In fact, they share their book's title, *Light of Autumn*, in such a manner. If the Innu poet is cognizant of her people's status as victims now or in the past, she doesn't complain or scream out her pain. She is far too considerate. She merely continues her hymn to the north, the sea, the tundra, the winter, the snow, even the light, as the title says. One has to read between such lines of celebration to get the full message for, inside such language, she is asserting that Quebec's North Shore is her home.

NON-FICTION

The Traditional History and Characteristic Sketches of the Ojibway Nation

GEORGE COPWAY (Kahgegagahbowh)

Ojibwa from Trenton, Upper Canada, and Oka, QC

Published in 1851

The author was born in 1818 in Trenton, Ontario (then known simply as Upper Canada). As a Methodist missionary, he lived in many places including the United States but came home to die in Oka, Quebec, in 1869. A grab bag of forms – travelogue, history, and social commentary among them – this book tells the story of the Ojibwa nation from the early days of colonization to the late nineteenth century.

The book opens by delineating the nation's territory which encircles, for the most part, the Lakes Superior, Huron, and Michigan, and later adding the northern shores of Lakes Ontario and Erie. It describes this landscape's appearance – a great "confusion" of lakes, rivers, rock formations, mountains and cliffs, caverns, and forests of pine, maple, and oak and, as one goes northward, of birch, spruce, and tamarack. It describes the region's animal life – the elk, deer, rabbits, lynx, and marten, all of which provide the people with food, clothing, and shelter. Sports and games are described; lacrosse, for instance, is big. This reverie is broken as the book then takes us into the depths of the battles that rent this land with "war cries." The Sioux in the west were a threat; the Hurons and the Iroquois in the east were even more dangerous. For instance, if the Iroquois sided with the English in the never-ending rivalry with their foes, the French, then the Ojibwa sided with the French. Their land may have looked like paradise but paradise it wasn't. At one point, says the author, he counted twenty-nine battlegrounds on the shores of a river and the "country was covered with blood and ... mangled remains." We take a detour through the wonders of Ojibwa mythology. Stories of the Thunderbird figure large, as does the people's relationship to the heavens. But then we are pulled back into the ugly realities of colonization. Land was acquired by immigrants using unscrupulous means. Their plying of Indigenous people with liquor, for instance, resulted in many a family being destroyed, the culture a close second in the race toward destruction. The language is described: how it works, what it sounds like, what it expresses, and how it was preserved – in petroglyphs. Next comes the political structure followed on its heels by religious beliefs, including vision quests. The location of each Ojibwa community in southern Ontario is pinpointed with some historical background. And then comes the story of the people's conversion to Christianity followed by the arrival, each in their turn, of the "great" explorers; La Salle is only one of many. In the end, we get the sinking feeling that this beautiful land will not belong to the Ojibwa people for very much longer.

Copway was the first Indigenous writer ever to publish in Canada. Born to a converted family, he was fluent in English, which is why he wrote in the language. Nonetheless, his aim in writing was to help save his people from the all-out destruction that he foresaw. At one point, he even travelled to England to ask for protection from the whiskey traders. His cries, however, went unheeded. Scared as he may have been and worried sick for his people, all he could do was pray.

Here Are the News

EDITH JOSIE

Gwich'in (Loucheux) from Old Crow, YT
Published in 1966

This compilation of articles for the *Whitehorse Star*, Yukon territory's main newspaper, details daily life in the early 1960s in the hamlet of Old Crow, which sits on the banks of the Porcupine River some eight hundred kilometres north of Whitehorse. The news stories pivot around the village's main industries of fishing, hunting, and trapping and they are broken down by season, four stories for each of the two years chronicled. The characters – with the exception of the nurse, the clergy, the police, and the occasional fly-in doctor or government bureaucrat – are all Indigenous. With names such as Freddie Frost, Eliza Steamboat, and Ed Overshoe, they make for a colourful lot.

   In one news story, Mr. John Joe Kay catches four "minks" on his trapline just across the river from the village. For Old Crow, this is news. But then, so are the skiers – "four boys and three girls" – who are going to Whitehorse to race. Old Crow has no airport (or roads in at the time these news stories were written) so no scheduled flights serve it. The isolation is therefore, extreme. Planes land on pontoons in the river in summer and on skis in winter; they fly in from places such as Dawson City some four hundred kilometres south or Inuvik near the mouth of the Mackenzie River in the Northwest Territories. But their efforts are made sporadic by fickle weather. "Mail day," thus, is a big day in Old Crow. People go down just to see who is getting off that plane, or onto it. An ardent Anglican, the author comes home from a service one Good Friday "sure glad to hear everything about Jesus, what they did to Him ..." With her husband gone to Old Crow on business, Helen Charlie finds herself alone with the children at the family camp and, not far off, meets a bear; uncertain whether she has shot it dead, she refuses to go back to check. One news story reports that when the people are cooking a feast for the minister, "the sun is eclipse around 11 a.m." In another news report, the women's dog race is almost scuttled by the loss of the time sheet which kids have torn off a wall; luckily, someone recalls Clara Tizya winning. Peter Benjamin's house burns down so everyone pitches in to help him. In summer, the riverboat, *Brainstorm*, plies the waters of the Porcupine River from Dawson City; when it pulls up to the dock with provisions for the store, among other cargo, a virtual carnival breaks out. The caribou come and go; some get shot, some do not. Ditto for the ptarmigan. Births, deaths, floods, elections, Christmas, square dances, at least one murder, the court case that follows, and a flu epidemic, all are described. In a place so magical, even the vagaries of the climate merit reporting on the news.

The most notable feature about this collection is the language. English is far from this writer's mother tongue – Loucheux is, an Athapaskan language, closely related to Tlicho (Dogrib) and Dene Tha (Slavey). Unfortunately, the *Whitehorse Star* has an English readership so the author has to deliver accordingly, with predictably eccentric results. Imagine Margaret Atwood writing in Blackfoot or Michael Ondaatje in Mohawk – you would get the same wacky, tricksterish results. The last thing on your mind would be colonization. In fact, if anything is colonized here, it is, ironically enough, the English language.

The Unjust Society
The Tragedy of Canada's Indians

HAROLD CARDINAL

Cree from Sucker Creek First Nation, AB

Published in 1969

Canada's Indigenous people have been cheated, the author states bluntly. Right from the start, the colonizer marched in with his own definition, not in Cree, not in Mohawk, not in Blackfoot, but in English, of what an "Indian" is, where his land is, how he should relate to it, and what his rights are on it. The two documents that cast these concepts in stone are the British North America Act of 1867 and the Indian Act of 1876 followed by the treaties of which there are eleven. Wrapped inside this legislation lie the powers that govern the lives of Indigenous people from cradle to grave. And try as they might to have them interpreted into a language that they can understand, try as they might to have things altered to their own advantage, try as they might to voice their dissatisfaction at the terms legislated, Indigenous people have been ignored. With these documents, a "Buckskin Curtain" was raised that irrevocably separates Indigenous from white, says the author. The time has come for that curtain to be taken down.

    The Indigenous people of Canada had much to expect from the results of the federal election of June 1968. For an entire year, the new government spoke of what sounded like a revolutionary program in Indian affairs. This government (a Liberal one) made public its desire for dialogue with Canada's Indigenous people. It promised the involvement of Indigenous people themselves. It announced consultation meetings. The Indigenous people, for their part, prepared for change. They attended consultations in their provinces. They met in Ottawa in national assemblies all the while believing that the government was finally listening. In June 1969, however, the Minister of Indian and Northern Affairs announced a new policy. Known as the White Paper, it had been conceived by this government before any meetings had been held with Indigenous leaders. In this paper, the government made arbitrary projections for a people's future that only the government could make, prefacing its policy with the words "Indian people must be persuaded ..." This White Paper proposed to wipe out the Indian Act and advocated all-out assimilation for Indigenous people. All this *without* consultation. Asked why his people couldn't do a certain job, an Indigenous leader in the Northwest Territories once sagely answered, "They could, but they have been told for so long by the white man that they can't, that now they don't think they can."

All our lives we as Indigenous people have been told, over and over, that we are worthless, that our culture, our languages, and our spiritual beliefs are worthless. All our lives our destinies have been decided by others – missionaries, educators, social workers, bureaucrats, politicians. But the time has come, this author says, for an educated force of Indigenous people who know the rules and the languages – in this case, English and French in addition to their own Indigenous tongue – to step forward and take the reins of power. The time has arrived for them to change their lives for the better, to wrest them from the status of the perpetual victim that has been their lot for centuries. This book asks white Canadians to let Indigenous people face the future on their own terms, without interference.

Sacred Legends of the Sandy Lake Cree

CARL RAY and JAMES R. STEVENS

Cree from Sandy Lake First Nation and Thunder Bay, ON, and non-Indigenous

Published in 1971

This is a compilation of myths from the Sandy Lake Cree First Nation of northwestern Ontario. Told to Carl Ray by his Elders, they were then transcribed and translated into English. As a body of work, they cover pretty well the entire spectrum of mythology. Creation mythology, of course, is paramount. There are flood myths, hero myths, monster myths, Trickster myths, stories that describe the end of the world and its rebirth, and stories that explain the origins of objects, animals, and customs. The world they paint is psychedelic, visceral, and very funny.

The introduction gives some background on the place and people from which these myths come. Then they get under way: in the beginning, O-ma-ma-ma, the Earth mother, gives birth to the Thunderbirds who will protect the world's animals, then the frog who will lead the insects, then Wee-sa-kay-jac (Wesakechak in Cree), the Trickster who, in turn, will create humans. When a flood destroys the world, this clown-like character constructs a giant canoe to save all the animals. When the rain stops, he commands first the beaver, then the otter, and then the muskrat to dive into the depths to look for soil. Only the muskrat succeeds. Wee-sa-kay-jac's misadventures with the wolf, kingfisher, weasel, ducks, a water monster known as Mishipizhiw, humans, trees, and rocks give all these creatures the features they possess to this day. The legend behind the grey and red feathers on the kingfisher's throat, for instance, is related. Ditto for ducks waddling, ravens eating carrion, and so on. When he encounters siblings fighting over who will take the sun on its daily orbit, the Trickster resolves the problem by giving the boy jurisdiction over the sun, the girl over the moon, thus giving us day and night. Learning that the wolverine has eaten a child, Wee-sa-kay-jac punishes him by causing white hair in the shape of a child to grow on his back, a mark of shame he bears to this day. He tricks ten women into sex the description of which is outrageous. Stories contemporary Indigenous writers have turned into "high art" appear, of the Weetigo, for instance, or of the Woman of the Rolling Head, Paguck (the Flying Skeleton), the Son of Ayash, the Little People. In another series, a hero named Ja-Ka-Baysh gets trapped in the belly of a fish for days. Biblical – and universal – resonances abound.

The problem is language – just as Cree is not equipped to deal with space travel, English is not equipped to express such ideas. In European languages, based in cultures whose religions are monotheistic and identify pleasure as the reason for eviction from the garden, sex is dirty. In cultures based in pantheistic religions, of which Indigenous North America is one, no such story exists; the attitude to sex, and therefore to nature, differs diametrically and the language and traditional stories reflect this attitude. The Trickster is a clown and is here on this planet for a romp, not for repentance. That being said, these stories belong more in dream than in reality. We all dream of flying, of climbing into the skin of another person, of talking to animals and having them talk back. These myths thus paint the dream world of a people and a language whose contact with nature has not been severed. Nature has not enslaved them and neither have they enslaved nature. Humankind and nature are partners.

Defeathering the Indian

EMMA LAROQUE (LaRocque)

Métis from Saddle Lake First Nation, AB, and Winnipeg

Published in 1975

This book addresses the issue of the "Indian as victim" in the public mind: where did this image come from and how can its damage be corrected? It calls itself a handbook that is to be applied like a first-aid kit: first you wash the wound, then apply disinfectant, then a bandage, then antibiotics. These wounds, though, are not physical but emotional, mental, and spiritual. The handbook is meant for educators who have responsibility for the formation of young minds, if not entire nations.

Prior to the 1960s, Indigenous people were spoken of in only the past tense. Doomed to obsolescence, they were considered a dying race. Therefore no one listened to them – they weren't worth it. They had no vote, no voice. The image of the "Indian" was completely in the hands of white writers. According to British-Canadian writer John Richardson, who wrote such novels as *Wacousta* in the nineteenth century, we were cannibals. And the white writers who followed him only deepened that image – we wore feathers, brandished tomahawks, scalped white people, and our English was confined to grunts. We were poor, drunk, lazy. Then along came the White Paper of 1969 and the rapid and extreme reaction from the Indigenous community. In fact, it might be said that it served as a catalyst for Indigenous people to enter university and start writing. And in starting to write, they started changing this image. With chapter titles like "Heritage or Culture," "Stereotypes: Past and Present," and "The Media and the Indian" and section headings such as "Native people must define themselves," *Defeathering the Indian* encourages educators to assist in changing this image and it shows them how to do it. This is crucial when you consider that, as it says, "the majority of Canadians are excluded from educative exposure concerning Native people." Most Canadians know nothing about us, not our land, not our culture, not our languages; all they know is what they see in the media and in books and there is a wide gulf between that image and what we are. The time has come for us to change the image, to "defeather" ourselves.

Fortunately, the times are changing. As the author writes, "the responsible thing for educators to do now is to open their policies and their classrooms to Native people who are defining themselves." She qualifies the statement by adding, "there are encouraging indications that more educators are accepting this responsibility." Events couldn't have been more timely, for "Native people are in the painful process of developing their identity." In fact, the writer herself was a catalyst in the development of Indigenous education and, since she wrote this book, that movement has advanced considerably. This is a good thing, for, as she writes, "the Indian heritage has a lot to offer to the Canadian society." This book goes to the heart of the victimhood and rage that has been the lot of Indigenous people since the beginnings of colonization. The door it opens, however, lets in a ray – if not two or three, and strong ones at that – of hope and redemption from such harmful negativity.

Ojibway Heritage

BASIL JOHNSTON

Ojibwa from Chippewas of Nawash First Nation at
Neyaashiinigmiing (Cape Croker) and Toronto, ON

Published in 1976

This book describes "the ceremonies, the rituals, the songs, dances, prayers, and legends of the Ojibway people." It doesn't specify the time when these concepts existed undisturbed, but ostensibly, it would have been before colonization began in earnest. Much has since transpired. To cite one instance, the Ojibwa language is no longer spoken as widely. Fortunately, even if the Christianizing process has eroded them, traditional ideas still persist. This book describes the inner life of a people, the soul of a nation.

 It starts with the myths of creation. The universe with its celestial bodies, land forms, and bodies of water was created. The spirit beings that populate the dream world of the Ojibwa came into being followed by plant life, animals, and humankind. Whereupon follows a description of the Midewewin. In essence a training ground for medicine people, its base was plant life and its healing powers. Teachings on life and death are laid out. Next come the four stages of a person's life journey, the right and wrong way, the nature of visions, the four seasons, and so on. The author writes about ceremonies, songs, and dances, and concludes the section with a description of the various lesser beings in the Ojibwa dream world – gods and goddesses, if you will – their names, their histories, their roles, and their meaning. First was Nokomis, humanity's first mother, then Epingishmook, who was the spirit husband of the human woman, Winonah. As a result of her union with this spirit, Winonah gave birth to Mudjeekawis, Papeekawis, Chibiabos, and Nanabush. This last is, of course, the Ojibwa name of the Trickster, emissary between the Great Spirit and Earth. Mudjeekawis shared the guardianship of the mountains with his father. And because he travelled, he would bring back stories of other lands and people to the Ojibwa. Papeekawis was a patron of beauty.

Chibiabos was a musician who taught hunters to imitate the calls of birds and animals; a kind of muse, it was he who made the drums, flutes, and rattles with which the people made music. There was Windigo, the cannibal spirit who haunted the people in times of famine. There were the Maemaegawaesuk (Memegwisi) who were the Little People, manifestations of the sounds of nature, Makinak the turtle, and so on. As in ancient Greek mythology, all are described as engaging in hair-raising encounters with each other, with bears and other animals, in time with the seasons. The thing to remember, however, is that each being in the dream world is an extension of the power and magic of nature. These myths come to us from a time when nature and humankind were one.

The first thing a speaker of an Indigenous language notices about this book is the way the English language hampers it right from the start. For instance, Ojibwa has no gender, which automatically renders God's gender moot. In English, God is categorically male. Ojibwa mythology has been criminalized and gone into hiding, but the very fact that its description has been written down and published in this manner gives a glimmer of hope that it will not die. It will survive to be criminal no longer.

These Mountains Are Our Sacred Places

The Story of the Stoney People

CHIEF JOHN SNOW

Nakoda (Stoney) from Morley, AB

Published in 1977

Town and reserve at one and the same time, Morley sits between the city of Calgary and the foothills of the Rocky Mountains. As members of the Siouxan linguistic family, the Nakoda or Stoney people speak a language that is related to Lakota, Dakota, Assiniboine, and others whose communities straddle the southern extremity of Canada's three Prairie provinces and northwestern states such as Montana and Idaho. Though the author couches the narrative in the story of his life, it is really the story of his people. In this vein, he starts with their oral history, which goes back eons, and finishes at the year of the book's publication, which is 1977. We thus get a picture of the traumatic transformation the nation went through between the first treaty signing and the late twentieth century. The experience is a bit like being hurtled like a rock through a time warp of a thousand years.

The narrative opens with a portrait of the Stoney as a people in tune with land that has been theirs for thousands of years. Then come the Europeans. Among them, most sadly for the Stoney, are traders who stoke their commerce with vats of whiskey and unscrupulous land-grabbers who bring with them technologies and values – and diseases – the Stoney know nothing of. In the midst of the social problems these new presences set off, Indigenous people have to resort to the aid of missionaries and the North West Mounted Police. Sadly, many of the latter two, too, are dishonest. Next comes the period of the signing of treaties. This motif, dealt with in detail, weaves like a thread through the rest of the book. Misunderstandings and failure on the government's part to hold to the promises spelled out in these documents coupled with the immigrants' greed for the land are viewed from the Indigenous perspective – the Indigenous people see themselves as having been hoodwinked. By the 1950s, the treaties have been swept under the rug. The fourth part of the book brings us to 1969, a year of special significance to the Stoney people – they have been given self-government following the granting of citizenship to Indigenous people nationally. At this point biculturalism is introduced as a theme, for the author's people realize that their survival hangs in the balance – they have to combine the best of their values with those of the European. The loosening of ties to the Department of Indian and Northern Affairs plays a big part here. And the theme of religion enters in the final pages with a description of the Indian Ecumenical Conference that Morley hosts every summer. At this event, seven thousand Indigenous people from across North America come together to discuss and celebrate their spiritual heritage.

If spirituality is going to play a major part in the salvation of his people, the author implies, then education will be even more so important. In this regard, a phrase that jumps out is "the real obstacle to the continued success of the schooling of our children is not teaching them to read (a language that is not theirs) but making suitable reading matter available." If anything will help eradicate the collective subjugation that so haunts us as a people, it will be books like this one. For if spirituality anchors the writing, then writing spells education, and education is healing.

I Am Woman

A Native Perspective on Sociology and Feminism

LEE MARACLE

Stó:lō from North Vancouver, BC, and Toronto, ON

Published in 1988

In what, in effect, is a manifesto, the author sets out her position as an Indigenous woman living in "CanAmerica" in the second half of the twentieth century. Her perspective has been shaped by two main forces: racism and sexism, both rancid outgrowths of the colonialism that has made "CanAmerica" as we know it today. She puts forward a concise analysis of the effects these forces have had on her people and on their land. Powerlessness for women is the least of it, she states. Offering illustrations from her own life, she advances solutions that might be employed to address the barriers that have been erected.

Central to her argument is the fact that, before colonialization, traditional Indigenous life was matriarchal in structure. If women didn't exactly wield power over their men, they at least were equal. The forces that began arriving in North America from Europe in 1492 were patriarchal in structure. In such a construct, women had no place and, if they did, it was negligible. And if white women (as she calls them) sat at the bottom of the hierarchy of genders, then Indigenous women sat even lower. As she says in one vignette, if an Indigenous woman – back in the 1960s, we can assume – was seen at the checkout counter of a grocery store with a larger-than-usual pile of groceries, she was suspect. Did she have the money to pay for such "spoils," or did she not? Stares would pierce her back. In the most brutal example, girls of twelve and even three get raped by their fathers. Where does such behaviour come from? she asks, confounded. The answer: the patriarchy. Where does the poverty of the Indigenous nations, whether city or reserve, come from? From the patriarchy. Whence comes the corruption that so aggressively afflicts the Indigenous organizations that were put into effect in the 1960s? From the patriarchal governments and bureaucracies that fund them. To illustrate this point, she tells a story of crabs in the pail. The white crabs are fine; it is the Indigenous crabs who expend their energy preventing each other from crawling to freedom. When will the Indigenous nations find their way out of such confusion, such oppression? she cries out, enraged. Give the voice back to the women, she replies, and re-establish the matriarchy.

Colonization, the author admonishes, is the force that lies at the root of the disempowerment of Indigenous peoples. Such cries of rage may not bring down the walls but this book was an early entry in the history of Indigenous literature in Canada. In fact, it was a revolutionary one. Still, if you put enough such voices together over time, they collectively might accomplish the task. Who knows, with the dire predictions on the state of capitalism at the time of writing, the powers that be might have no choice but to give in to a radically different way of thinking. The effects of colonization that so infect us might then be laid to rest.

Write It on Your Heart
The Epic World of an Okanagan Storyteller

HARRY ROBINSON (compiled and edited by Wendy Wickwire)

Okanagan (Syilx) from Lower Similkameen First Nation, BC

Published in 1989

This book of non-fiction was narrated by an Okanagan Elder to a non-Indigenous woman from Vancouver who then compiled and edited the material. The stories cover the mythology and history of the people who have inhabited the Okanagan Valley and related regions since time immemorial. They thus span the time from when humanity and nature were so close as to be indistinguishable to the period when chronological time began making inroads. At one point in the narrative, precise dates enter when, before, they hadn't mattered. Abutting nations such as the Secwepemc and Nlaka'pamux (Thompson) make their appearance but most people depicted here are, like the author, Okanagan.

An all-powerful being whom the narrator calls, in English, God, creates the sun so that he can see, but then sees only water. In this water, he wills into being a tree, from which he plucks six leaves on which he places six men. Then he commands these men, each in turn, to dive to the bottom of that water to seek land. Only the youngest succeeds. From the speck of soil with which he surfaces, God creates Earth. Then Coyote, the Okanagan trickster, makes his appearance at a name-giving ceremony being held by the "Big Chief" (that is, God). Here he vies with eagle, cougar, and others for their names, but fails. Which is how he ends up with the name Coyote. He has confrontations with Owl, with Fox, where he and Fox leap entire continents, and with Eagle, where he ends up on the moon eons before Neil Armstrong and meets Spider, his wife, and a tree that becomes a man. There is a story in which Coyote challenges God to a contest as to who is older. His adventures, that is to say, are psychedelic. Images flow in and out of each other like oil.

An emerging division between human and animal is made clear. In one story, a man's life is saved by a grizzly, in another, by a wolverine. God tells an old woman and her grandson a prophecy to the effect that the white man is coming centuries before the event. Humans receive powers from certain animals and become healers. Then we slide into the epoch of recorded history which speaks of murders and punishment such as a man banished to England to work in a circus as a freak-show Indian.

Due to the sheer span of time that these stories cover, the narrator's memory seems to fade in and out. His numbers vary, for instance. The situation is not helped by his advanced age nor by the fact that he is using a language that is not his. One wonders what the result would have been if the editor had known Okanagan, the language in which the narrator's subconscious works and in which these stories originally functioned. At the beginning, the line between human and animal is muddy. In fact, Coyote himself shifts imperceptibly between the two states of being; that's how far back these stories go. In the "prehistoric" stories, we see Indigenous tormenting Indigenous, Indigenous tormenting animal, and vice versa. But it is only in the epoch of recorded history that we begin seeing Indigenous tormented by white. Still, the account is not one of rage against a conquering foe. Rather, the author simply offers an objective depiction of historic truth.

When the World Was New
Stories of the Sahtu Dene

GEORGE BLONDIN

Dene from Sahtu (Great Bear Lake) and Yellowknife, NWT

Published in 1990

The narrative opens with the ancient myths of the Sahtu Dene people of
Great Bear Lake telling of a time when humans and animals spoke one
language. It goes on to the warriors and the medicine heroes, a time of
magic when myth and life were indistinguishable. Then it talks of life on
the land as recounted by the author's grandfather. Then his father takes
over to tell of the arrival of the first white people in Sahtu and the opening
of the first mine. And it ends with the author's own stories of an era that
forces him to stop living on the land so that his children can go to the white
man's schools in the south to learn "the new way." At this point, the magic
of the past disappears. Born in 1922 in the region described, the author is
the last of a breed. He witnesses the caribou-hunting nomadic way of life
supplanted by a cash economy and modern technology. His parents spoke
Sahtu Dene only, his children English, he both languages. In this way is he
a bridger of two ways of life.

For those who have never seen it, the land written of here is unimagin-
able in its vastness. Great Bear Lake is greater in area than many a sea, the
Northwest Territories larger than all of western Europe – and this without
Nunavut. But imagine western Europe with the territory's population of
forty thousand instead of the half billion that it has. For generations that
go back millennia, the author's people lived on and with that land. With
its vast herds of caribou and unimaginably rich animal and plant life, its
thousands of lakes and rivers with water so pure you could drink from
them, nature was the people's garden, their supermarket. For exchange
with white traders who began arriving in the mid-twentieth century, the
people had mink, marten, fox, wolf, lynx, and ermine in limitless quantities.

Non-fiction

Few settlements existed because people were nomads, forever in pursuit of the animals as the seasons demanded, by dogsled in winter and canoe in summer. A distance of a hundred kilometres took three days to cover, depending on cargo and weather. Nature was not only ever-present, it was a character, a friend; even snowdrifts had a language. That's where the literary tradition of these people begins, in that ancient past when powerful medicine people spoke "raven," "moose," and "caribou." Some had the power to enter, in spirit, the bodies of these animals, a mystical power that came from the relationship between a land and a people. Picture an electrical cord connecting a man to the heartbeat of the planet. It was with this "charisma" that they summoned snowfalls, wind, caribou. Sadly, as "civilization" encroached, this power faded. Today, now that people live in cities such as Yellowknife and their children go to school in Vancouver, it hardly exists.

Though one wishes for Dene, this book is written in English. We watch a way of life come to an end and a new one arise from its ashes. Still, the author adapts. Where will the future take us? he asks. There is no raging against invaders, merely the description of an awesome land and an awesome culture. The land has a past, says the author, but it also has a future – "some Dene say the Earth is our body."

Stand Tall, My Son

GEORGE CLUTESI

Tseshaht (Nuu-chah-nulth) from Tseshaht First Nation, BC

Published in 1990

What fiction there is in this volume is based in reality. The principal character, a boy named Meek, is a thinly disguised rendering of the author himself. In telling the story of the boy, the narrator paints a portrait of Indigenous life as it was in his home territory in the first half of the twentieth century just before the arrival of the first Europeans. As in so many of the books profiled here, nature was very much a partner as opposed to a foe. With English yet to come, the language of the people was as yet intact. From this base, we watch Meek grow from age five to early adulthood, his parents and members of his extended family his guides at every step.

When first we meet him, the boy's father is taking him to a creek to watch the salmon scale the rapids to spawn. Salmon being the staple of his people's diet, the creature is in effect sacred. Its behaviour patterns in that water will thus lodge in the boy's memory and form a fundamental part of his spiritual identity. At the moment when he sees his first fin flashing among the foam and ripples, that seed is sown and a miracle transpires. The boy watches his father fish for salmon with his bare hands, another memory that will shape his life. Through it all, Meek's father explains the behaviour of fish, their migration patterns, their reproductive methods, and the different roles of the genders. As Meek learns, we learn. We learn about the powerful relationship the nation has with the ocean. We learn that bears are left-handed, raccoons dig for crabs at low tide, cranes warn other animals of imminent danger, and frogs summon spring with song. The seal hunt is explained as an "exchange of life" – the people must eat or they will perish. Meek learns about the movements of sun, moon, and stars, the rhythm of the months and the seasons, and gathering mussels. Nature is one act of magic after another. And at every turn, there is the Tseshaht language; virtually each plant and animal is named first in

Tseshaht, then in English. As a young adult, Meek learns what might be called his people's Ten Commandments though they actually number more than ten: "The more you give, the more you will get." "Ask not for wealth; wealth can destroy a man's soul." "Ask for a meek and generous nature." "Be compassionate." "Make time your companion." And more. Having learned these teachings, Meek is ready for adulthood.

This is a portrait of what was best about Indigenous life in one part of our country before the white man came. People had freedom of movement and useful employment, diseases such as tuberculosis had not yet decimated them, and the dead end of the reserve system had not yet been invented. Clutesi believes that, despite the problems that have come to besiege Indigenous people, their culture is fundamentally beautiful and holds much wisdom. As he writes in the group of essays that conclude the volume, "you come from a happy, singing people." Education in the white man's way, though, is key to helping the people survive. Celebrate what was there before our victimhood surfaced to kill us, says this Elder. And after reading how he has described it in this volume, we believe him.

Crazywater

Native Voices on Addiction and Recovery

BRIAN MARACLE

Mohawk from Six Nations First Nation, ON

Published in 1993

Through a series of interviews, the author dissects the relationship between Indigenous people and alcohol through the years. The interviewees are Indigenous people who live in communities, reserve and otherwise, across Canada and into Alaska. They are Cree, Ojibwa, Cayuga, Blackfoot, Assiniboine, Dene, Tlingit, Tsimshian, Nisga'a, and Inuit. They are young, old, male, female, and come from many walks of life. And their story is tragic. Broken bones, broken bodies, broken homes, broken families, broken lives. Death after death, spirits destroyed both in the individual and collective senses. The book tours us through some extreme illustrations of this disaster. At the end, it suggests solutions to a sickness that has come close to destroying an entire people.

Before first contact, Indigenous people lived on, with, and inside the land. Then came the Europeans. Their initial objective have may been quicker passage to the riches of the Orient but what they found instead was a land beautiful and rich beyond compare. So they wanted it. And to get it, they inflicted germ warfare on its people in the form of smallpox blankets. Within decades, they had killed millions. And as if that wasn't working fast enough, they inflicted a second kind of germ warfare: alcohol, a substance against which the Indigenous bloodstream, as with smallpox, had zero immunity. On top of that, the Government of Canada made two rules that doubled the impact of alcohol. First was that Indigenous people be shepherded onto plots of land, generally the least desirable, that would be called reserves. Second, that the people who lived on those reserves were prohibited access to alcohol. Thus was born the scourge of binge drinking. People would sneak off their reserves and into the nearest town with a bar or a liquor store, buy the alcohol, then down the entire bottle, practically in one gulp, before they got caught by the law and thrown in jail. Within no time, such drinking habits became legion. The result has been untold misery and the debasement of entire peoples and entire languages. In France, people have drunk wine for centuries as part of dinner or even breakfast. Two glasses in an hour suffice. In Canada, some Indigenous people drink two bottles of whiskey in one hour. And get sick. Their minds go crazy. They grab guns. They kill friends, brothers, wives. Child-welfare authorities would sweep into the picture, take all eight children, and the family was gone. And all of those eight children were born with fetal alcohol syndrome (FAS), as was the next generation and the next, before the illness was identified. There are schools today in northern Manitoba where 80 percent of the students are third-generation FAS.

"Progress must be made on self-government, land claims, and economic development," says this author, with studies to back him up. "There must be a cultural and spiritual revival in the Native community." In this book, Indigenous people are victims through and through. Such victimhood has never been seen ever before in the history of the world. Alcohol programs continue to help. But only efforts such as this book with its stories of healing and recovery can eradicate that victimhood in the long term. It will take a thousand books – but those books are being written as we speak.

Night Spirits

The Story of the Relocation of the Sayisi Dene

ILA BUSSIDOR and ÜSTÜN BILGEN-REINART

Dene from Sayisi Dene (Tadoule Lake) First Nation, MB, and non-Indigenous
Published in 1997

In 1956, the Government of Canada relocated an entire community of Dene
from their home in the boreal forest of north-central Manitoba to the town
of Churchill on Hudson Bay. Suddenly, they found themselves living beside
a cemetery on treeless* ground. Not only that but, for ten months of the
year, this wasteland is blasted by the wind of the Arctic Ocean. With no
trees they had no wood to heat their houses, whose walls were paper-thin
and uninsulated. In government-issue plywood shacks, they had no running
water. And because they could no longer hunt in the boreal forest, they
could no longer feed their dogs, which for eons, had been their sole means
of winter transport. So no transport and no food, for them or for their dogs.
As for shopping in Churchill some five miles away, lack of money made
it impossible. And when the purchase of alcohol by Canada's Indigenous
people was legalized in 1960, their doom was sealed. This book tells the
story of the three hundred people to whom this happened.

For generations, Athapaskan peoples roamed the vast territory that
straddles the three Prairie provinces and what, back in 1956, was still just
the Northwest Territories (as opposed to Nunavut). Forever in pursuit
of the great herds of caribou, the Sahtu Dene of Great Bear Lake, the
Tlicho (Dogrib) of Great Slave Lake, and the Dene of northern Alberta,
Saskatchewan, and Manitoba were nomads living in harmony with a
land blessed by riches beyond compare – thousands of lakes, to begin
with, and great herds of caribou whose flesh provided food, whose skins
provided shelter and clothing, and whose bones and antlers furnished
the tools of survival. Now all this was gone. In order to achieve better
administrative control over them, the government took that branch of

the Dene nation known today as the Sayisi from their paradise in north-central Manitoba, without their permission, and plunked them on land they knew nothing of. For a people whose spiritual beliefs hold the dead in fear and reverence, their placement beside a cemetery was an omen. And when the alcohol kicked in, their fate was sealed – husband killing wife, brother killing brother, child killing parent, one fatal house fire after another (many caused by arson), adolescent boys dressed in rags raping passed-out women. The town garbage dump the community's sole source of food. Abandoned newborns died of pneumonia on the floors of heatless shacks in minus 50-degree weather wearing nothing but urine-soaked diapers frozen ice-solid. The degradation was total. By the end of the nightmare some two decades later, one-third of the community was dead.

Victimhood of this magnitude is without precedent. Fortunately, there was hope – at the time of relocation, one family had remained at an encampment on a river some fifty miles inland from Churchill. Their contact with their people's old way of life remained intact. It is from here that the effort was launched, starting in 1969, to reverse the relocation. Thus was born Tadoule Lake, the Dene First Nation that sits at the heart of Manitoba's north-central interior. Halfway between Churchill and the Saskatchewan border, these people's original homeland now harbours an emerging educated generation. It bodes well for a future of strength and well-being, one where victimhood will be but a memory.

---

* Because of the nature of Canada's Arctic and Subarctic climate, the trees get shorter and shorter as you travel ever northward until you reach the barrens. A land of no trees, it is breathtaking in its vastness. The place where the forest and barrens meet is known as the treeline. Clearly visible in its demarcation, this line dips at a sweeping diagonal from the west, where it touches the Arctic Ocean, to the east, where it touches the south shore of Hudson Bay. By the time you reach northern Manitoba, the very northeastern tip of the province that includes the area in and around Churchill, the land is left treeless. Thus did the ancient home of the Sayisi Dene have trees, whereas their new home in Churchill had none.

From **Oral** to **Written**

A Recognition of Being
Reconstructing Native Womanhood

KIM ANDERSON

Cree and Métis from Ottawa, Guelph, and Brantford, ON

Published in 2000

If Indigenous women have had their dignity stripped by the forces of col-onization, says this book, then the time has come for them to reconstruct it. The time has come to reinstall themselves in the place of honour that was, at one point in their people's history, their birthright. With that honour, of course, came power. So if they have been disempowered, then they are in the process of re-empowering themselves. And to do so, certain measures must be taken. Which is this book's objective: to outline those measures and to document the manner in which they are being put into practice.

The work is based on interviews the author conducted with forty Indigenous women from forty different nations and communities across Canada. The voice of Native America is represented as well through cita-tions from well-known Indigenous women writers who live south of the border. The women speak of the abuse they have known since childhood due to being Indigenous and female. They speak of the status of women in their communities past, present, and future. Or at least of what they are confident will be their status in the not-too-distant future. Most describe and quote their mothers, grandmothers, and great-grandmothers as women who held the family and home together and so they gave their daughters the strength to confront the oppressor. Little is remembered of the era before first contact but what can be gleaned trickles through in stories of the way tasks were shared. Women went hunting while men stayed home to change the diapers, and grandmothers were frequently better shots than their husbands. According to the old teachings, the human body – certainly the female, certainly the womb – was a sacred vessel made dirty only when Christianity arrived. Girls' menstruation is a prime example. In the old

Non-fiction

way, it was a sacred time for which special rituals were held and girls were ushered into their time of power by the community. In contrast, girls who first experienced menstruation while away at residential school were often publicly humiliated for staining their underwear and sheets with blood. And because sex was declared dirty – the playground of Satan – its abuse followed naturally in the form of child molestation, rape, wife battery, and the ostracism of two-spirits.*

This book posits that the abuse of Indigenous women is unlike anything else. They have had to live with what must be the most degrading word in the English language: "squaw." When you consider that word is a perversion of what, at one time, was the most sacred term in the Cree and other Algonquian languages, *iskwew* (woman), then all the more reason for that abuse to be examined. All the more reason that it be taken apart and put back together in the way these women suggest. In a word, the phallic/straight-line superstructure of a patriarchal system bulldozed the yonic/circular superstructure of matriarchy. And it is that yonic – that is, womb-like – design that must be reconstructed and *is* being reconstructed by the extraordinary voices in this book. Out with the status of subjugation, they are saying, and back with our dignity, back with respect for our wombs, the source of life.

---

* In the circular/horizontal superstructure that is matriarchy, there is room for many genders, including, what we Indigenous people call, in English, the two-spirit people who are both male and female simultaneously. Men who have the souls of women and women who have the souls of men, they had a special place on the matriarchal circle of life. As healers, artists, magicians, visionaries, priests-of-a-sort, they were the people who added the colours of the rainbow to the black-and-white, violence-ridden, and very boring world of heterosexuality. And because Indigenous languages have no gender, God not only is female but assumes, on that circle, elements of the masculine as well. In the system that has room for two genders only – which is what the writer of *A Recognition of Being* is blasting – women are at the complete mercy of men. As for the two-spirits, not only were they straightjacketed with the disempowering terms of "homosexual" and "lesbian," among others, they were, through the course of much of European history, burnt at the stake. Which, of course, is from where comes the term "faggot" – they were "charcoals" that were used to light the fires that roasted women to death.

From **Oral** to **Written**

The Truth About Stories
A Native Narrative
THOMAS KING

Cherokee from Sacramento, CA, and Guelph, ON

Published in 2003

The Massey Lectures are sponsored annually by CBC Radio, House of Anansi Press, and Massey College at the University of Toronto. Their objective is to "to enable distinguished authorities to communicate the results of original study on subjects of contemporary interest." Thomas King's contribution to this lecture series consists of five interconnected talks that explore story and storytelling as forces that define human nature and human beings – in this case, Indigenous people. And not just Canada's but America's in general. (Born and raised in California, the man straddles both realities.)

Without stories, the author suggests, our lives would be nonexistent or formless as mud. The image projected by others writing about us Indigenous people would be erroneous, as indeed it almost always is. It would be askew, not quite the truth, or in too many cases, way off the mark. Indigenous representation is too often misinformed to the point where it is an outright lie. And it is too often manipulated to the point where even Indigenous people will believe information they read about themselves. Whatever the fallout, the author opens each of his lectures with a traditional story from his people's mythology. According to him, an oral storytelling tradition is no less worthy of being called a literary tradition. Stories are stories. In any case, he opens with the well-known (to us) creation myth that portrays the planet as being carried on the back of a turtle. Then he weaves his way through literature and history, religion and politics, popular culture and social protest, social commentary and autobiography and, armed with this arsenal, defines the continent's relationship with its original inhabitants. The Indian of fact, he states, bears little resemblance to the literary Indian, the dying Indian, the drunken Indian, all constructs so powerfully and often so destructively projected by white North America.

As a Cree who speaks my language with completely fluency, I can vouch for this. For instance, up to age fifty, I was convinced that I was a failure because that's how others writing about us presented us. That is their perspective. If they need to paint others in a less than complimentary light in order to validate their own existence, then God bless them. But there is another perspective. And according to this one – that is, *our* perspective – I am a raging success. I come, for one thing, from northern royalty. I play Rachmaninoff. I speak five languages; they speak one. Because of the stories woven by others, however, it took me half a century to dig out that truth. That's how stories can deform our souls to the point where we don't even recognize ourselves, to the point where we can end up as losers. God knows, stories have been known to kill. Ask Louis Riel. Ask six million Jews. But just imagine if Canada's history had been written in Cree. Imagine if those treaties had been written in Dene. The country's story would be different, as would those treaties, would they not? That, as this writer points out, is how powerful stories are.

Cree Narrative Memory
From Treaties to Contemporary Times

NEAL MCLEOD

Cree from James Smith First Nation and Regina, SK

Published in 2007

The subject of this book is memory as it animates, informs, and shapes human narrative, in this case, the narrative of the Cree of south-central Saskatchewan. The writer opens by citing Lakota writer Vine Deloria Jr.: while European memory is based on time, Indigenous memory is based on space. Space, of course, is land. But it is also sound, says this writer. If space includes the human body, which is a substance, then one extension of that body is the tongue, the organ that produces language. In this way, each syllable of Cree is a piece of space, space that has co-existed since time immemorial with the plains of south-central Saskatchewan. And it is through just such a prism that this writer tells the story of his people.

There was once a deer, the author begins, that was known for hearing great distances. But as the language of the land started changing – that is, as English started taking over – the deer disappeared; he no longer heard. As place names changed from Cree to English, so did people's. The language itself started changing; the old generation couldn't speak English, the new generation can't speak Cree. And because Cree was not written, everything was bound in memory. Contracts were verbal, so that even the meaning of signing was doubtful in meaning. Certain rocks were known as grandfathers who spoke to people and healed them. People talked to wind; wind talked to people. Like rocks, people were extensions of the Earth. Stallions emerged from lakes to mate with mares, thus creating a super-race of horses. As in King Arthur's time, characters in stories emerged from the mists. No one knew where they had come from; they were just *there.* The signing of treaties, imposition of the reserve system, residential schools, Christianization, decline of the fur trade, the economic shift from hunting to farming, urban migration, and the conflict between the modern and traditional worlds are all examples of "spatial exile," says the author. In at least one case, missionaries sank one of the "grandfather rocks" into a lake. Their reason? Because Christianization involved the erasing of Cree memory that had been etched into the landscape by sacred stones.

In order for that memory to be put back on track, the language must be revived, the author argues. Only by this means will reconnection with sacred places be realized. Two sentences resonate: "Their bodies become houses of ancient sound" and "Every time one word of an Indigenous language is spoken, we are resisting the destruction of our collective memory." *Mamaataawisiwin* – "tapping into the life force" – must be brought back, is the author's ardent cry. And with efforts such as this by articulate, well-educated young Cree, one has hope, one is optimistic that the Cree will make it.

The New Buffalo

The Struggle for Aboriginal Post-Secondary Education in Canada

BLAIR STONECHILD

Cree-Saulteaux from Muscowpetung First Nation, Regina, and Saskatoon, SK
Published in 2006

With its beginnings in the author's doctoral thesis, this volume's subject is post-secondary education for Aboriginal people in Canada. The book traces the development of this contentious issue from the first mention of a legal relationship between the country's Aboriginals and the British Crown in the Royal Proclamation of 1763, goes on to the British North America Act of 1867, the Indian Act of 1876, the various treaties and other less-known "agreements," before it arrives at the Royal Commission on Aboriginal Peoples established in 1991. A hybrid of history, analysis, and theory emerges. Whose responsibility is this education, the author ask, the federal government's, the province government's, the church's, or the people's? Who controls it, and how?

At first, the government's objective with these social contracts is simple: to make room for settlers, it must get land from Indigenous people. Nothing beyond that is of interest. Thanks to the chiefs who negotiate the treaties, however, the deals soon shift. Financial assistance with agriculture is the first promise added. Health care is next. Then comes education. The question that looms ever larger becomes, on what level? Primary, secondary, post-secondary? And where? On the reserves created by the Indian Act, in cities, in residential schools? The Indigenous, meanwhile, ask: with their land gone and the buffalo with it, what are they to eat? How are they to clothe and house themselves? At first, the help that is offered is minimal – this education will be at the primary and secondary levels only and be restricted to on-reserve. If post-secondary education is mentioned, it is with reference to loss of Indian status for any Aboriginal who graduates from university. Fortunately, a change of government in 1921 kills this bill before it gets enacted. Prior to the year 1870, in any case, three Indians are recorded as having acquired university degrees in all of Canada. The first three residential schools were built in 1879 in what would become the province of Saskatchewan, the policy there being to take Indian children from their homes and turn them white. To the few who made it through such a system, help was offered with post-secondary education on the basis of merit. In 1927, records state that 190 Indians were studying in high schools, business colleges, and other "advanced work," though we also find that few finished. In 1961, 60 Indians attended university. But it is only in the 1970s that these numbers truly start rising. In 1972, 800 Indians were going to college or university. In 1978, 2,606; in 1987, 13,196; in 1989, 18,535; in 1997, 27,000. From zero to 27,000 in thirty-six years? Not too shabby.

Due to pressure from key lobbyists such as the Assembly of First Nations, the Government of Canada begrudgingly increased its education funding. The numbers climbed. The creation of Indigenous Studies programs in Canadian universities only stoked the fire for curriculum development in such subjects as Indigenous religion, languages, history, and literature. The fights we face on the level of social, economic, and cultural development may still be daunting but we are winning if very slowly. And if there is a key, it is education. Education, indeed, is "the new buffalo," oppression's oppressor.

Loyal Till Death

Indians and the North-West Rebellion

BLAIR STONECHILD and BILL WAISER

Cree-Saulteaux from Muscowpetung First Nation, Regina,
and Saskatoon, SK, and non-Indigenous

Published in 1997

For more than a century, Canadians have been under the impression that the Riel rebellion of 1885 entailed an uprising of all Indigenous peoples in Canada's west. Any retribution that was subsequently foisted upon them by the Government of Canada was therefore justly deserved. Not so, says this book. The "Indians," as they were called at the time, had nothing to do with it. They remained loyal to the treaties they had signed in the years leading up to "the troubles." Treaty Six in particular, signed in 1876 and covering the area affected, is clear in its terms and conditions. Unlike the government, they did not break them. They thus did not earn their punishment. According to this book, the punishment brought down on them was a blatant miscarriage of justice masterminded by then prime minister John A. Macdonald. The book goes on to prove it with fact.

The Cree at the time, whose territory this book chronicles, were in crisis. The herds of buffalo that had once roamed the plains in the millions had dwindled to the point that the people faced starvation. For its part, the Government of Canada wanted their lands for settlement by white Europeans, and the stage was set for a confrontation. Treaties were struck whereby the government would acquire vast tracts of land, and Indigenous people were relegated to much smaller pieces of land called reserves. Certain "favours," moreover, would be given them as recompense, regular rations to tide them over lean winters, for instance, and tools to aid them in transforming their livelihood from hunting to agriculture. Chiefs such as Big Bear and Poundmaker, who wanted nothing but good for their people and who foresaw their future, accepted the terms, despite the fact that the documents were unilingual – in English, a language they neither spoke nor understood. The Métis, meanwhile, were being pushed off whatever land they had been able to scrounge up, mostly by squatting, to the point where outright rebellion was their only recourse. Newly enticed back to Canada from exile in Montana, Louis Riel mounted an "army" that, regretfully, was lacking in numbers – there simply were not enough Métis. He needed the Indians to bulk up the hustings. Citing their promises to "Our Great Mother" to keep the peace at whatever cost, the Indians refused. In the fallout, however, enough damage had been done to their reputation by the powers of the day for them to be implicated in "the treachery." Charges were trumped up, dishonesty was engaged in by the courts. The outcome? Louis Riel was not the only "rebel" to be hanged; eight others were executed, Cree who had had nothing to do with the rebellion. Not only that but a much greater number were sent to prison for years, their only crime maintaining their loyalty to Queen Victoria.

The story, of course, is complex and lengthy but the short of it is that the Indians were had. From the first, they were scapegoats. The long-term result? Saskatchewan today is a thriving province full of white people. Little do they know how much they owe to men such as Big Bear and Poundmaker. Only history in the form of books such as this will expose treachery so blatant, thus exonerating its silent heroes.

Solitary Raven
The Selected Writings

BILL REID (edited by Robert Bringhurst)

Haida from Victoria and Vancouver

Published in 2000

This book of non-fiction contains a collection of writings by Haida sculptor Bill Reid as compiled and edited by Vancouver-based poet Robert Bringhurst. Born in Victoria, British Columbia, to a non-Indigenous father and a Haida mother, Reid lived in many parts of Canada and even, at one point, in England but settled eventually in Vancouver. He started off working as a radio broadcaster before drifting slowly to his real interest which was jeweller making. This led him to his work as a carver/sculptor and restorer of the totem poles for which his mother's people, the Haida of Haida Gwaii, are world famous. Years of dedicated work, study, and discipline in the art form eventually earned Reid a reputation as one of the greatest artists Canada has ever produced. This book contains selections and excerpts from his lectures, speeches, book forewords, essays, newspaper articles, addresses for exhibitions, mini-biographies for exhibition catalogues, musings, meditations, and at least one eulogy.

Bill Reid was almost forty when he was asked to assist in the restoration of his first totem pole. Once he got involved, however, it became his life's work. Besides restoring them, he carved them himself, recreated the dugout canoes of his mother's people, and made sculptures and other artwork using the techniques found in those poles. In these writings, he muses on the mythology depicted in the carvings on the poles and boats of the Haida and their cousins, the Tlingit, Tsimshian, Kwakwaka'wakw (Kwakiutl), and Nuu-chah-nulth (Nootka). The Northwest Coast trickster, Raven, of course, figures largely. Negating the Bering Strait theory of Indigenous migration from Asia, Reid states bluntly that Raven found the people in a clamshell. The author lauds the cedar, the giant tree of the Northwest Coast, that has done so much for a people. In fact, the practice of building totem poles all started with the decoration of house beams made from the tree. He muses on the movements of the various Indigenous nations in that part of the world and their exchange of ideas and forms of expression. He writes about the smallpox epidemic of 1862 that decimated entire populations; the Haida alone lost nine-tenths of theirs and the survivors of that scourge still reel from the shock. He explains the technique involved in Haida art-making with its look as distinct as that of the ancient Egyptian culture that built the pyramids. He describes "formlines" and "ovoids," what they stand for, why those shapes and not any other, and how they constitute the genesis of all the elements of design in a painting or carving. Above all, however, he pleads for the preservation of Indigenous culture. He pleads to have its wisdom not destroyed but absorbed into the continent's thought and life so that we can all become not just displaced Europeans and displaced Aboriginals but true North Americans.

Subjugation is documented here in a way that hits the reader not as angry emotion but as scientific fact. The author being no complainer, he posits practical ideas for how the damage that has been inflicted can be set right. In fact, the restoration work Reid did on totem poles and on their artistic techniques and ideas serves as a perfect metaphor for what he did with Indigenous life here in Canada. He helped restore it to its former place of dignity.

Peace, Power, Righteousness

An Indigenous Manifesto

TAIAIAKE ALFRED

Mohawk from Kahnawake First Nation, QC, and Victoria, BC

Published in 1999

Are Canada's Indigenous citizens an independent people or are they not? If they are, to what extent are they independent? Or are they still, after all this time, wards of the government, of the Queen of England, still incapable of making decisions related to their own lives? What exactly is the definition of the term "colonialism" and where has it put Indigenous people, both in the past and today? This book takes us through an intensive exploration of these questions, questions rendered more complicated because they are couched in a language that our ancestors didn't understand.

The system foisted on us by the forces of European colonialism, says the author, is at odds with the system that was here before those forces arrived. That system had nature as its base. Built into the structure of our languages, nature had power over us and we were not so much to fear it as to respect it accordingly. Then along came this world view in which man has power over nature to the point where that nature counts for nothing and man assumes the right to vanquish and kill it. Divide and conquer is this new system's modus operandi. The result? The system has under its power, so to speak, both nature and the people who come from its womb. This book asks: how are we to reverse this situation? Can we do it using a legal system that is as complex as it is confusing for us? Expressed in a language that, by its very structure, dictates such hegemony? The task is so immense that it would take not only another century to accomplish it but also another language, an Indigenous language where man and nature have positions of equality on the circle of life. Patriarchy against matriarchy is the familiar dichotomy. When the circle of matriarchy bashes its head against the straight line of the patriarchy, when will the matriarchy give and the patriarchy take over? Stated in political terms, the reasoning is arduous, with harrowing twists and turns. Indeed, it looks impossible. Or maybe it's too late? Then there are all the smaller questions that stem from the overriding question: what is a leader? In one context, it means a virtual dictator, in the other, a servant to the people. What is the exact meaning of the term "sovereignty"? Ask that of a Dene Elder on Great Bear Lake in the Northwest Territories and all you would get would be a blank look.

There is so much work to be done by our newly educated, newly minted generation of thinkers, says this writer. Articulate in French, English, and at least one Indigenous language, the new generation has to find its way out of dependency on government handouts. We Indigenous people have to find our way out of being owned by the government and find our own voice and identity. If we are to dig ourselves forever out of the coffin of the colonized, then we have to master the white man's languages and ways of thinking. Now all we have to do is get to work – like this young man has.

A Concise History of Canada's First Nations

OLIVE PATRICIA DICKASON (Adapted by Moira Jean Calder)

Métis from Winnipeg and Ottawa, ON, and Sault
Ste. Marie, ON, and non-Indigenous

Published in 2006

This is a history of Canada's Indigenous peoples from prehistoric times to the present. Through archaeology, anthropology, biology, sociology, and political science, the author gives a sweeping picture of the Indigenous people of Canada of today, geographically, politically, and otherwise. Here we have the who, what, where, and why they are the way they are. The book investigates what makes Indigenous people distinct on the Canadian sociological landscape.

The story begins with the Ice Ages that transpired some seventy-five thousand to fifteen thousand years before the present. It was after this that human beings first migrated across an isthmus that then connected Asia to North America. At least, so goes one theory. The other is that sailing across the Pacific Ocean would have been a more practical means of travel than crossing an entire subcontinent on foot. However the movement came about, evidence is cited that the first habitation of humans at the tip of South America dates back to eleven thousand years ago. Subsequently, evidence of such habitation has been found scattered across all three Americas springing up at different times in different epochs. That habitation is then narrowed down to Canada. On the Prairies, the people hunted buffalo. On the Northwest Coast, they fished for salmon. In the east, they planted corn, squash, and beans. Starting with the Vikings around 1000 C.E., Europeans arrive, which is when the real troubles start. Smallpox epidemics are the least of it. The French and the English, transplanting old wars from Europe and vying for allies, spark hatred between the Huron and Algonquin peoples on the one hand and the Iroquois on the other. And the question of land entitlement is born. When the British defeat the French on the Atlantic coast in 1710, for instance, they push the Mi'kmaq and Maliseet aside, assuming that the French have extinguished Aboriginal title to the land. The pattern is repeated clear across the continent until, some three centuries later, Indigenous people end up with only small patches of useless land called Indian reserves. Penned in like animals, they don't even have the right to drink beer much less vote in federal elections (at least not until 1960, when this law changes). Laws such as the Royal Proclamation of 1763, the British North America Act of 1867, which created Canada, and the Indian Act of 1876 are foisted on them without their input. Deemed from the start an "inferior race," dying cultures that speak dying languages, they are deemed not even worth consulting about their own lives.

This book traces the deep roots of our debasement as a people. It goes on to cite the reaction of today's Aboriginals to such treatment, describing the way we have educated, organized, and armed ourselves, this time, with law books as tomahawks, and articulate politicians handling those weapons to nullify, clause by clause, edict by edict, our status as beggars in our own land. While much work remains, the twenty-first century awaits with its next generation of "warriors." And who knows what they'll do.

Taking Back Our Spirits
Indigenous Literature, Public Policy, and Healing

JO-ANN EPISKENEW

Métis from Winnipeg

Published in 2009

With the arrival and settlement on their land of Europeans, Indigenous people's losses began in earnest. First went their land, then their voice, then their power, then their languages, then their children. Every instance of dysfunction in Indigenous communities across this country today can be traced to this trauma, states the author. She then goes about giving evidence for her theory. By the middle of the book, Indigenous people are a complete nonentity on what was once their land. But then the author describes the emergence of the first generation of Indigenous people to have been educated in the white man's way. This generation has taken the oppressor's languages – French and English – to write out the trauma of displacement. In doing so, they provide a ray of hope for survival beyond the twenty-first century of a people that the colonizer had once assumed were a dying race.

When white people got here, begins the author, they considered themselves the superior race. Their technology, their military, their religion, and their numbers bolstered this theory, one that quickly established itself as myth. Then the author shows that, according to recent historical research, germs were the actual conquerors, smallpox, in particular. Disease not only decimated the armies that could have defended Indigenous land – that occupied by the Aztecs, for one – but it cleared the way for the settlement of the land by colonists. Unfortunately, not only did crops eventually flourish on those settlements but so did racism, another myth that wreaked havoc on the Indigenous spirit. The author cites policy after policy inculcated by white governments to further disarm Indigenous people. "Policies of devastation," she calls them. The "divide and conquer" dynamic effected by the Indian Act is one instance. This act gave the colonial government the power to decide who had "status" and who did not, who was Métis and who was not. As a result, Indigenous unity of any kind was nullified. Not to mention intermarriage between the divisions and what no man's land their offspring were consigned to. Policies that controlled Indigenous agriculture are another instance; the forces of imperialism decided to transform Indigenous people from hunters to farmers, without consulting the people affected. The white "farm instructor" became, in effect, the local dictator who decided the fates of his charges. Other policies controlled freedom of movement; laws relegated Indigenous people to small enclosures called Indian reserves. Now caged, in effect, they couldn't even leave without asking permission from a white bureaucrat. Fortunately, Indigenous writers started writing their stories in the late twentieth century: the author cites specific autobiographies, novels, and plays, of which Maria Campbell's *Halfbreed* is the most well known. What such works are doing, says the author, is rewriting the myth that is Canada.

Nothing is more effective than myth to cow the Indigenous person into submission, into a state of degradation. And raging against it has been their lot since Europeans first set foot on their extraordinary land. But *Taking Back Our Spirits.* The title says it all.

Qu'as-tu fait de mon pays?

AN ANTANE KAPESH (Anne André)

Innu from Uashat-Maliotenam First Nation and Schefferville, QC

Published in 1979

This book recounts the life of a young Innu man in the first half of the twentieth century. Never named, he starts life raised by his grandfather in a setting of well-being deep in the forest from where the author hails. Then the old man dies. This leaves the young man to take all the lessons he has learned from his Elder and apply them on his own. Not much later, the young man starts encountering *les blancs* – the white man – just then beginning to arrive in that part of the world. The story is about the impact these encounters, which increase in number, have on the young man and his people.

An old Innu man and his grandson live together in the forest of northern Quebec where it borders Labrador. And it is a good life. They fish, they hunt, they pick berries. Their land is rich and beautiful, and they have all they need to be healthy and happy. The grandfather takes pleasure in teaching the boy all the old skills. The boy responds in like manner so that, when the old man dies, the young man is ready for life. One night, he has a dream that turns out to be an omen: he dreams of meeting white people for the first time. As he has never seen them, he thinks they are *polichinelles*, a kind of marionette with a ghost-white face. Not long afterwards, the young man, indeed, does encounter his first *polichinelle*, a trader only recently arrived for reasons of commerce. He gives the boy a gun and a knife in return for furs. This first contact only slightly disturbs the boy's ancient way of life which is in balance with nature. But he soon has another encounter, this time with a priest. Again the effect on his life and lifestyle is not positive; he gains one religion but loses another. Then he meets a white doctor who gives him medicines that effectively nullify his relationship with natural healing agents such as herbs. He meets miners who, in building their mines, drive away animals the young man and his people have depended on for food and clothing since time immemorial. Then come the residential schools where young people's hair is sheared off and they are fed new food and given false teeth and glasses. Next come alcohol, the police, the courts. And at the end, ironically, come the film-makers to document a lifestyle that no longer exists. Even the land that the Innu have lived on for eons has been destroyed. The young man is furious.

The text is a translation into French from the original Innu, apparently the only language the author speaks. The story is one of advancing victimhood. At first, the Innu live a healthy lifestyle that is their own. Then as *les blancs* arrive in ever-greater numbers, their victimhood mushrooms until the Innu becomes a complete loser. And he is furious. He rages at fate; in fact, the book's title in English would be an outraged *What have you done to my land?* Even though the hero admits that life is changing, the story still ends by asking where and what next, for him and his people. In this book, in any case, there is no resolution, no getting over that victimhood, no celebration.

Histoire de la littérature amérindienne au Québec

Oralité et écriture

EDITED BY DIANE BOUDREAU

Non-Indigenous from Sherbrooke, QC

Published in 1993

This essay by a francophone woman from Sherbrooke, Quebec, analyzes the work of Indigenous writers writing in French. The writers whose work is cited are Innu, Cree, Algonquin, Atikamekw, Wendat (formerly known as Huron), and Métis, and this study traces this voice back some nine thousand years to the time when that land was first inhabited and oral storytelling flourished. It documents these peoples' first encounters with writing, via traders and missionaries, in the sixteenth century. Then it moves into the twentieth century when Indigenous people began to write themselves, if only in the form of essays and letters. As the 1970s dawned, Indigenous writers penned novels, poetry, drama, and other forms of writing in French. Why did they choose that point in time to start such writing? asks the book. Because of a document referred to as the White Paper. This was a law tabled by the Canadian government in 1969 that, if ratified, would have meant the assimilation of Canada's Indigenous people into the general population. The book launches into an analysis of selected novels, poetry, autobiographies, and essays published between 1971 and 1990, and concludes with a word on the future prospects of this new voice.

The book opens with the first methods of storytelling employed by Indigenous people – pictographs and drawings on birchbark and rock. When their oral storytelling develops, it is described as a mechanism to heal communities. Then comes the white man to show Indigenous people, among other things, the power of writing. Evidence is cited of Indigenous people as early as 1749 writing letters of protest to colonial authorities, though with the help of whites who translate their words into French or English. The missionaries invent alphabets to translate the Bible, liturgies, and hymn books so that Indigenous people can read for the first time. Then the schools educate sufficiently that Indigenous people have the language ability, as early as 1901, to write letters protesting land issues, in French, to newspapers. Until the White Paper hits in 1969 and the first wave of Quebec's Indigenous novelists, poets, and playwrights emerges to counter its stance. A 1971 work of short fiction entitled *Contes* (Tales) by Cree-Métis writer Bernard Assiniwi is only the first. In the next two decades, twenty-seven more works are published, the list ending with Métis-Abenaki singer-songwriter Sylvie Bernard's 1990 album of songs, *Marcher sur du verre* (Walking on glass). As to the future, the book predicts that Indigenous people will continue writing to remind the world that they, the first inhabitants of Quebec, are here to stay.

Though the bulk of this analysis and comment was written only in the late twentieth century, it harks back to the oral tradition once practised by the writers' ancestors. Still, its initial impulse was rage at a document that threatened to annihilate an identity, that threatened to eradicate an entire people. Certainly that anger is evident in the early work, much of which expresses, repeatedly, the factor of "being Indigenous" – "a literature of resistance," as the editor puts it. Still, this rage cools as the years progress and the writing becomes a simple celebration of "*Indianite*" (Indigeneity). Once deemed moribund, Indigenous languages begin re-emerging as languages of poetry and song.

Windigo et la naissance du monde

BERNARD ASSINIWI

Cree-Algonquin-Métis from Montreal

Published in 1998

These are myths selected from the oral traditions of Indigenous peoples representing all of Canada. On the Atlantic coast, the Mi'kmaq people tell their story of creation. The Algonquian peoples of Quebec – that is, the Innu, Cree, Atikamekw, Algonquin – tell their stories of the flood, the Trickster, and of other beings who inhabit the spirit world. Then come the creation and other stories of the Ojibwa and Iroquoian peoples of Ontario, the Cree of Manitoba and Saskatchewan, the Blackfoot of Alberta, and finally, the Gitxsan, the Tsimshian, and others of British Columbia. The result is a portrait-in-brief of the spiritual foundation on which Aboriginal thinking and life stands in Canada.

We learn that the Mi'kmaq value the number seven because, long before their land became the Atlantic provinces, they knew it as seven territories, each with its own clan. For them, creation happened in seven stages. First came the Creator who created the sun, then the shade, then the Earth, then Glooscap (the Mi'kmaq trickster) who came into being through a spark released by the sun. Then the Eagle arrives as a messenger from God to inform Glooscap that humanity is imminent and that it is from Glooscap that man will learn its role. Seventh comes humankind, springing from the same spark that birthed the Trickster. Seven women are followed by seven men. From them come the seven clans that today make up the Mi'kmaq nation. The Mi'kmaq, Algonquin, and Cree recount a tale of the Trickster (son and brother of the Creator), where he makes man's life a constant mishap steered by laughter. An Algonquin Elder tells the story of the flood as an animal, not human, event – it is the Trickster as Mista-Wabôs (the Giant Hare) who assembles the animals in his "ark of birchbark." We learn that the cannibal spirit, Windigo, eats people from the inside, thus manifesting guilt. In another story, the dog resents being ordered around by man and stops speaking "human." A tale from the Atikamekw of north-central Quebec tells of the boy who was raised by a bear, the reason these people revere the animal. An Algonquin tale features a water serpent that joins forces with a young woman to bring to the Iroquois the gift of corn. For the Iroquoian peoples, Creation transpired when a spirit woman fell from the sky onto the back of a turtle who, in time, became our planet. Then, as grandsons to this woman, male twins were born who, to this day, personify the eternal struggle between right and wrong. For the Cree, stories of Wesakechak, their trickster, are parables – animals and humans have access to God only through him. For Alberta's Siksikas (a branch of the Blackfoot), the world was made by an act of sex between two Tricksters, male and female. And so it goes…

What sets these stories apart as a genre are their sense of humour and the three-way partnership in their structure of humankind, divinity, and nature. Nowhere is this more evident than in the person of the Trickster, who is all three at once. One fact of note: there is no evidence in these narratives of eviction from a garden, so nature remains alive and humanity is still her partner, not her adversary. Colonial oppression does not inform these tales; neither does rage. These stories are celebrations of a fabulous and ancient literary tradition, one that says we are still in the land and the land still in us.

Ikwé

La femme algonquienne

BERNARD ASSINIWI

Cree-Algonquin-Métis from Montreal

Published in 1998

This book draws a portrait of womanhood from the Indigenous perspective. Gender roles are defined – the man hunts, the woman gives birth. The narrative moves on in history until, some nine chapters later, it arrives at modern times and addresses the question of Bill C-31. This is the law that, in 1985, returned to Indigenous women the right to retain their Indigenous status after marriage to non-Indigenous or non-status Indigenous men. Ultimately the book reasserts the contribution that Indigenous women have made to Indigenous history and life in Canada. All this through the prism of one community: Kitigan Zibi (Garden River), the Algonquin community in Quebec just north of Ottawa.

The objective is to correct wrong perceptions about Indigenous women that have lodged themselves in the public mind. She is a slave to man, goes the perception, meant to serve him. She is an instrument of pleasure, it goes on to say. Even her Indigenous name, "Ikwé," means "less important," states the author. The Indian Act of 1876 is the document that set in stone this onerous position. Then we are hit with the question: why has Indigenous woman always been perceived as playing second fiddle to Indigenous man? Has she not done her fair share? To answer that question, her role as life-giver earns merit as does her discovery of fire and her consequent role as the glue that holds the family and community together. She is portrayed with the specifics of giving birth, first in the home, then during migration (for her people, being hunters, are nomadic). Then she is shown discovering her own beauty through her reflection in a mirror (a subtle indication that colonization, in the form of a mirror, has arrived). She is shown, in the person of one young woman, of being as capable as

Non-fiction

the young men her age of the same feats of strength, speed, and courage, in war as in peace. She is shown, again through the person of one young woman, standing up to authority on the matter of arranged marriages, thus bettering the lives of all Indigenous women. And when unable to give birth due to "congenital malformation," she adopts and even starts a daycare centre of sorts, becoming, in this way, the "mother of many." Then we see the fictional Florence running afoul of the Indian Act by marrying an Irishman but then assisting in the fight to change that law; before she is finished, it will reinstall her Indigenous status. And last we see Sandrina marry a French Canadian, winning back her status through this change in the law, then running into complications – because her mother is white and her children's father is white, they are not recognized as Indigenous. So she moves back to the city to survive there as best she can.

In this account, Indigenous woman starts out as loser. But she slowly fights her way out of that status until she wins, at least for the most part. In the final chapter, for instance, Sandrina Balle de Plomb loses her fight when her children are not recognized as legally Indigenous. We sense, however, that, once she has moved back to the city where her husband comes from, she will exonerate herself; we don't know how, but we sense that she will win. This book, that is to say, is more positive than it is negative. Indigenous woman emerges not as loser, but as winner.

Littérature amérindienne du Québec

Écrits de langue français

EDITED BY MAURIZIO GATTI

Non-Indigenous from Quebec City

Published in 2004

This book of fiction and non-fiction contains thirty-one pieces of writing by twenty-nine Aboriginal Québécois writers. The difference between them and white Quebec writers, of course, is that their roots on that land go back millennia. Because of their history of colonization, however, they write in French. Some write, as well, in their Native Innu, Atikamekw, Algonquin, or Abenaquis, but French, for the most part, is their lingua franca, just as English is in the rest of Indigenous Canada. This collection, at any rate, features five categories of *écriture*: myths and legends, poetry, novels, plays, and non-fiction. The three novels and three plays are, of necessity, largely excerpted, but enough information is included in those excerpts to give their thrust.

The first section mixes ancient myth with modern-day Quebec reality. For instance, in one tale, Tshakapesh, the Trickster figure in that part of Indigenous Canada, gets caught between the *oui* and *non* camps in the Quebec sovereignty debate. The results are hilarious. Washing his hands of the matter, he exits the two camps leaving them to kill each other over the details. Animals talk, trees talk, the moon talks. Humans talk to animals, and vice versa. The land and the people are one, both equally alive, equally animate. It is in the poetry section that the love between a people and the land of their ancestors is expressed most succinctly and most beautifully. Natural forces such as sunlight, wind, and rain are prayers from the most profound part of a people's being; these forces come from within. The aroma of muskeg is palpable. The Earth breathes. The universe dances. In one poet's writing, one can hear echoes of William Blake's or Emily Dickinson's nature mysticism. There are some stories, especially in the non-fiction section, where horrifying events occur in the clash between modern technology and the old ways. For example, Inuit boys playing "dare" take turns inserting their heads inside microwave ovens, appliances that have just arrived and are thus not known in that part of the world. The results are gruesome. Residential schools, prison and the things that happen inside those prisons, and racism are all addressed.

Still, the feature that strikes one about this collection is its positive tone. This comes out especially in the way the Indigenous languages are mixed with the French: *Ni-wanshin, ni-madoune, Je suis perdu, je pleure* (I am lost, I cry) is but one example of many. Indigenous languages loom large in this writing. But make no mistake – the rage against colonization is here; it just doesn't take centre stage. What does is love, pride, and oneness. For these writers, theirs is a land not to be conquered and colonized, but to be thanked for having given them the life they know. These people are just too busy celebrating the positive things they have to waste time feeling downtrodden. In this spirit, one line rings out. After a wind tears down a cherished tree, the poet says of the shoots that spring up in its place, *Mon people est semblable. Je sais qu'il survira.* (My people are the same. I know they will survive.)

Aimititau! Parlons-nous!

EDITED BY LAURE MORALI

Non-Indigenous from Montreal

Published in 2008

The editor of this collection of correspondence immigrated from France to Montreal in early adulthood. Perturbed by the absence of communication between Quebec's francophone and Indigenous communities, she decided to do something about it. The result is this book, entitled *Let's Talk!* first in Innu, then in French. It contains the correspondence between thirteen francophone writers and fourteen Indigenous writers. The editor herself corresponds with two Indigenous writers, while a fifteenth pairing features an Innu-Wendake correspondence. Each pair of writers was assigned to write on subjects whose identifiers begin with a certain letter. The first pair thus writes on subjects whose first letter is C – *connâitre, creole, colonization, canot* (to know, creole, colonization, canoe), and so on. The second pair writes on subjects who first letter is E – *eau, enfance, écriture* (water, childhood, writing), Ekuanitshit (the name of an Innu village on the north shore of the St. Lawrence River). And so on...

We may forget that, even if there is a dearth of contact between white and Indigenous peoples, not only in Quebec but also across the country, there are still many people on both sides of the racial divide who care deeply about the other. There are white writers, for instance, who want to help see to it that the culture of their Indigenous colleagues is respected. And even if these non-Indigenous writers recognize – humbly, courageously – that they don't quite have the deep connection with the land espoused by the Indigenous people, even if they admit that they are scared of that connection, there is still a genuine desire for it. There is still in their hearts a heartfelt desire to love those rivers, those lakes, those forests, even the night and the very light of the sun. As for the Indigenous writers, they may recognize that their culture has been battered and put to the test, that they are hurting, that their culture is crying. But that doesn't stop them from trying their best to get beyond it. You can feel the effort. In so doing, they hark back to that ancient connection with the Earth which they know, instinctively, is still with them. And they try their utmost to share that wisdom with their new friends. "*Chère* Denise," Innu writer Rita Mestokosho counsels her non-Indigenous soulmate, "*la rivière, le fleuve,** *la mer, sont les signes vivants de la force du Grand Esprit* (Dear Denise, the river, the sea are living signs of the force, the power of the Great Spirit)." Don't be scared of that nature, these Indigenous writers seem to say to the new arrivals, she's not your enemy, she's your friend, your soulmate. In its purest form, such wisdom is so filled with joy that it all but leaps off the page. Lines like "*en moi, mon pays, éternel jardin*... (In me, my country, eternal garden ...)" are a perfect example.

The correspondence in this book is, of course, written in French. Still, the Indigenous writers, the Innu in particular, resort to their languages when they can (translating themselves into French as they go). And when they do appear, these language shine through like a beacon of hope. It is these writers' method of getting past the hurt and degradation that they so deeply recognize. That language is a song of triumph over that hurt, that degradation. It is a song of celebration.

---

* In French, there are two kinds of river as witness this sentence . "Une rivière" is feminine; see the article, "une," that precedes it. That kind of river must drain into a lake or other river, that is, another body of fresh water, in order to merit the article and therefore the gender. "Un fleuve," on the other hand, is masculine; see the article, "un," that precedes it. That kind of river must drain into a sea or an ocean, that is, a body of salt water, in order to merit the article and therefore the gender. Which is why and how we speakers of Indigenous languages which are genderless could never understand, as we still cannot, how one kind of river could be feminine and the other masculine when both are just rivers! The mystery, however, would require another complete book, and a thick one at that, to do it justice.

BIOGRAPHY and AUTOBIOGRAPHY

Life and Journals of Kah-ke-wa-quo-nā-by

(Rev. Peter Jones), Wesleyan Missionary

PETER JONES

Ojibwa-Scottish from Burlington Heights, Upper Canada·
Published in 1860

This diary is written by a half-Ojibwa / half-Scottish man born in Burlington Heights (now Hamilton, Ontario) in 1802. Raised biculturally, he went to a Christian church service at one point in his teens – and was smitten. From that moment on, he was convinced that Christianity was the only answer to his people's "pagan condition." By his late teens, he was at divinity school; by his early twenties, a Methodist minister. He became a missionary whose zeal took him from one end of the country to the other. Then still known as Upper Canada, it was actually just the region between the triangle formed by Ottawa, Kingston, and Windsor. In relating the story of his travels, Kah-ke-wa-quo-nā-by paints a portrait of Indigenous life as it was in that part of the world in the first half of the nineteenth century. Unfortunately, he is prejudiced against his own people for their backwardness. Still, he speaks their language with complete fluency, and this gives him, and the reader, an insight into the subject that is otherwise unavailable.

Like so many missionaries of the period, the author spends his time criss-crossing the country visiting one Indigenous community after another. To these "poor souls" he preaches the Bible; conducts prayer meetings; "exhorts" the masses to "the kingdom of heaven"; and baptizes the old, young, and middle-aged. He also teaches the English language, translating Bible passages and hymns from English to Ojibwa as he goes. He travels from Kingston to the Rice Lake area (around Peterborough) to the islands of Lake Simcoe and southward to York (now Toronto) then to Brantford and the Six Nations, where he really has to use his hard-won

English (for his knowledge of Indigenous languages stops at Mohawk). Then he moves on to the Muncies, Chippewas, and Oneidas just outside of London and thence on to Windsor, glorying in the number of baptisms he notches up at every stop. Unhappily for him, he meets opposition. The first wave is from the traditionalists who want to preserve their own age-old religious practices. The second is from two rival branches of Christianity, Anglican and Catholic, which he sees as "stealing" converts from his own Methodist faith. Third are the whiskey merchants who take advantage of the Indigenous people by turning them into alcoholics so the merchants can get their land. The madness caused by a substance to which they have no immunity is so destructive to families that the only solution, as the author sees it, is to turn these "drunks" into Christians and farmers. And once converted, they do settle down.

In all this activity, two things are certain: in giving his life to Jesus, the author gives his life to his people. His commitment to and his love for both are unshakable. Still, it is the peek into the lives of Indigenous people at this point in time – moreover, from the inside – that makes this book so valuable. Already, at this stage in the history of pre-Confederation Canada, Indigenous people were being taken advantage of by unscrupulous, land-desperate immigrants. Already, they were being used – as these journals are being written, Indigenous people were losing their land acre by acre to vice and trickery. The rage against such treatment was also already simmering. And simmer it would until the late twentieth century when the spark Kah-ke-wa-quo-nā-by may inadvertently have lit would explode into a full-scale literary movement.

Halfbreed

MARIA CAMPBELL

Métis from Nukeewin (Park Valley) and Saskatoon, SK
Published in 1973

This book tells the story of the life of a Métis woman born, raised, and living in western Canada in the second half of the twentieth century. She begins her account with the arrival a hundred years before of the first Europeans in her part of the world, touches on the North-West Rebellion of 1885, then skims through the next two generations until she arrives at her own. At this point, she delves into the circumstances of her birth, childhood, adolescence, and early adulthood. It is a tale of woe, with setbacks and tragedy at every turn. At times it looks like she won't make it. But make it she does, thanks to two factors. The first is the voice of her great-grandmother, a wise old half-Cree woman she calls Cheechum. The second is her people whom she still recognizes, beneath their sadness and flaws, as beautiful, as innately joyful.

The author's great-grandfather came from Scotland. Her great-grandmother, Cheechum, is niece to Gabriel Dumont, the popular folk hero who helped Louis Riel lead the second Métis rebellion. It is Cheechum who will be the author's spirit guide her whole life through. In Cheechum's day, Saskatchewan was still part of a huge expanse of land known as the Northwest Territories. So Europeans who came to settle it lived, like the Indigenous people, as squatters on land that had no government. Many also married Indigenous women. But as Canada expanded ever westward, establishing law and order as it went, these squatters lost land they had lived on for two generations in some cases. They got pushed ever farther west and north onto untillable land until they were reduced to penury. And that is the poverty the author is born into. Her mother dies when the author is still a girl. And because her father is always out trapping or looking for work to support his brood, he is rarely home. Thus, at age twelve, she becomes, in effect, single mother to her seven younger siblings, one of whom is just a baby. At one point, she and her eleven-year-old brother have to take the six smaller children, including the baby, to school with them, hide them in the bush behind the schoolhouse, and take turns pretending to go to the washroom so that they can check up on them. At age fifteen, in an effort to prevent the authorities from taking her siblings, she gets married. But her husband turns abusive and she loses the children anyway. He drags her to Vancouver where he abandons her. This forces her to work, for her survival, in the sex industry. She develops a drug problem and gets enmeshed in crime. After escaping, she drifts from one city to another, giving birth to four children along the way. Years later, a friend convinces her to go to an Alcoholics Anonymous meeting where she connects with Indigenous people who have started self-help organizations. The voice of Cheechum, now more than a hundred years old, rings through.

At first, the author flees her oppressed status. After much heartache, however, she learns to look it in the eye. And by the grace of her Cheechum, who is always there in spirit when she needs her, the author pulls through and thereby helps her people pull through as well. This book was the first in a series of stepping stones that a generation of Indigenous writers were able to build on so that, today, a small army of Indigenous writers are able to continue the work begun by this woman. That work? Defeating oppression.

My Name Is Masak

ALICE FRENCH

Inuit from Mackenzie Delta, NWT

Published in 1976

An Inuit woman is born in Canada's High Arctic, just north of the Mackenzie Delta. In 1930, the time spoken of here, this territory was still one vast expanse inhabited and seen only by its Indigenous peoples, the Inuit. The world of the white man was just starting to encroach. The change that world engenders, as seen through the eyes of an Inuit girl, is the subject here.

The heroine's father, Anisalouk, speaks Inuktitut and English. This, together with the fact that he has both an Inuit and an English name (Charlie Smith), are the first signs that change in the area is imminent. He has attained a level of education rarely seen among Indigenous people there in those days: grade ten from a white school in Alaska where he comes from. Masak herself, known as Alice in English, is born by midwife in a house on an island in the Arctic Ocean called Baillie some five hundred kilometres north and west of the mouth of the Mackenzie River, that is, in the Delta. That she was born in a house, not in a hospital or an igloo, is another sign that change has arrived. Disease is next. When Masak's mother develops tuberculosis, she is taken to a hospital in Aklavik, the largest town in the Delta (population six hundred) with the only hospital for thousands of kilometres. The nomadic lifestyle that hunting and trapping demands makes it next to impossible to raise children without marital support. His wife's hospitalization thus forces Masak's father to leave Masak and her younger brother at the residential school in Aklavik. And when the mother dies, he has no choice but to leave them there for three years running. In the summers, Masak and her brother, Danny, can't go home like the other children. They live out their lonely summer days at the school in huge, empty dormitories and dining rooms. This aside, day-to-day life during the school year at an Indian residential school is described. Like the other students, Masak learns reading, writing, and arithmetic. In the dormitory at day's end, they say their (Anglican) prayers and tell ghost stories. They engage in fire drills. On Saturdays, they snare rabbits in the surrounding bush, the meat from which they sell to the school kitchen for pocket money. At Christmas, they perform pageants. Another sign that change is inevitable: Masak meets Santa Claus for the first time. The cycle of the seasons on the Delta is described as is its bird life, wildlife, and plant life. Its mighty river that floods its banks come spring gets special mention. Finally, Masak's grandparents arrive to collect them for the summer. Their father has a new wife but Masak and her brother adapt. Now ten years old, she masters the skills expected of an Inuit girl her age: scraping caribou hides to make coats and mukluks, driving a dog team, helping at whale hunts, setting up tents in the summer, living on and with the land.

To this girl, the ups and downs of her young life are not nightmares. They are simply adventures some of which make her sad, some happy. What shines through is her love of the land. And what a land it is. At age fourteen, when she finally leaves school to go back to the land, she feels "like a bird flying home to the vast open tundra." Masak is no loser; she is a winner. As is the land that lives and breathes inside her.

The Restless Nomad

ALICE FRENCH

Inuit from Mackenzie Delta, NWT

Published in 1991

This book continues the narrative begun in the author's previous work, *My Name Is Masak.* That first volume described an Inuit childhood in Canada's Arctic; this one takes us into the child's teen years and early adulthood during a time of great change in the north after the Second World War. The author witnesses, first-hand, her beloved north making the transition from the "dog-team age" to the "mechanical age," a time in history when the dogsled is replaced by the airplane, the Inuktitut language by English. At the end, the author leaves not just the Arctic but also Canada for Europe. There she will live out her later years with her Irish husband, whom, by the way, she chose herself as opposed to having him "chosen" for her by her Elders, a custom practised by her people up to the time described here. Masak is to women's lib, it seems, as Rosa Parks was to buses.

Aged fourteen at the beginning of the story, our heroine is leaving the residential school in Aklavik forever. Her stay at the school – her home, in large part, for seven years – was forced by her mother's slow death from tuberculosis. Now she is going home to meet her new family, for her father has remarried and has had two more children during her absence. The first obstacle that she must surmount is language. Prolonged residence at the school has eroded her native Inupeak (as she calls her dialect of the Inuktitut language). Now she speaks English mostly, her new family, Inupeak. Then there are skills to be learned – driving a dog team, shooting a gun, handling an axe to chop trees for firewood, trapping and skinning muskrats, smoking duck meat, jigging for cod, living and moving with the seasons as her nomadic culture calls for. By dint of huge effort, however, and with relatives ribbing her initial clumsiness, she learns and earns her status as an Inuit woman. Still, Inuit womanhood itself is changing. Towns like Aklavik and Cambridge Bay have turned into boom towns and new ones like Inuvik have sprung up from nowhere. Traditional drum dances are still danced, but so are dances to popular music piped in from radio stations in the south. Myths of the Inuit are recounted, stories of goddesses who animate the ocean, for instance; still, they are being swept into oblivion by Christian beliefs. People are told that the dead no longer need hunting equipment and food like whale meat to travel to "heaven." Houses replace igloos. Distances once crossed by dog team over the course of days are now traversed by airplane within hours. Salaried work, family allowance, and welfare arrive to render the need for hunting and trapping redundant, and a sedentary life begins to replace a nomadic one. Families break up. Children lose their language. In the midst of it all, what can't be denied is that a white education is needed if Inuit culture is to survive beyond the twentieth century.

Masak embraces that knowledge. She ensures that her children get the best education available. She travels to Edmonton and Vancouver. She leaves her Inuit husband for an Irish one. She even moves to Ireland with him when the situation demands it. She is a pragmatist. For her, there is no sentimental hanging on to a past that exists no longer. Life must go on. And for her, it does. Most expressly, she is not a failure. She never was. She never will be.

I Am Nokomis, Too
The Biography of Verna Patronella Johnston

VERNA PATRONELLA JOHNSTON (with Rosamund M. Vanderburgh)

Ojibwa from Chippewas of Nawash First Nation at Neyaashiinigmiing
(Cape Croker) and Toronto, ON

Published in 1977

This is an as-told-to biography narrated by an Ojibwa woman and transcribed into print by a non-Indigenous academic. The account begins with background information on the narrator's branch of the Ojibwa nation and how it arrived in Ontario from the United States in the mid-nineteenth century. Then the narrator launches into the lives of her grandparents and her parents before arriving at her own. Here the bulk of the story takes place. Once she has raised her children to adulthood, she splits her life between Cape Croker on the Saugeen (Bruce) Peninsula and Toronto, some four hours south, though family remains central to her existence. Through this account, the reader gains insight into what it means to be an Ojibwa woman in southern Ontario in the late twentieth century.

The Ojibwa part of the narrator's blood comes from the state of Wisconsin. In 1833, the Treaty of Chicago ceded Potawatomi* lands in what was then known as the Illinois Territory to the United States. In the unrest that ensued, Indigenous people from that territory fled. Most went west but a small group ended up north of the border in what was to become the Cape Croker First Nation (now known as the Chippewas of Nawash First Nation at Neyaashiinigmiing). Among these latter were the Nadjiwons, the narrator's paternal ancestors who, by marriage, melded in with the area's original inhabitants, the Ojibwa. Her mother's people, however, come from England. When her Indigenous father married her English mother, the priest was unhappy not because of race but because of religion – the former was Catholic, the latter Protestant. That didn't stop her from raising her thirteen children as Catholics. The third of this brood, Verna Patronella Johnston, was born in 1909 and grew up in Cape Croker. Not quite having finished high school, she remembers, in particular, the negative portrayal of "Indians" in history books; correcting this image would become a lifelong mission. At sixteen, she marries an Ojibwa and within some years has five children. As she raises them, she leads a busy life as housewife and farmer. She grows vegetables, raises pigs and chickens, and makes her children's clothes. In a word, she pulls her weight in a marriage that becomes increasingly abusive. After nineteen years, she leaves it, whereupon her several sojourns in Toronto begin. The first is as cook, cashier, whatever she can find as a job. When she returns to Cape Croker, she runs a foster home for Indigenous children so that they won't be adopted out of their culture. Back in Toronto, she runs a boarding home for Indigenous people who are new to the city and, later, works as cook and housekeeper at a home for abused Indigenous women. Health problems force her to retire to Cape Croker.

In all of this, Johnston is motivated by love – of her family, of her people, of life in general. Her purpose is to help others. Despite limited resources, she manages to assist Indigenous people making the difficult transition from the traditional way of life to the ways of the city, of the white man, of the twentieth century. For her, they won't be victims, not as they were portrayed in the books she read all those years ago. In fact, in later life she lectures far and wide on the subject and, for her efforts, is recognized in 1976 as Indian Woman of the Year by the Native Women's Association of Canada.

---

* The Potawatomi nation constitutes one of the three nations (with the Odawa and the Ojibwa) known collectively as the Three Fires Confederacy. All belonging to the Algonquian family of languages and much unsettled by repeated forced migrations, these three nations represent the peoples whose traditional territory surrounds what is known today as Lake Michigan. In the unrest that was the American Revolution and its aftermath, the Odawa came to settle part of Manitoulin Island in Lake Huron and all of Walpole Island near Lake St. Clair. The Potawatomi, meanwhile, came to settle Big Bay on the Georgian Bay side of what is now known as the Saugeen (Bruce) Peninsula. With its modern-day city of Owen Sound close by, there lived on that spot already a small band of Ojibwa. And even this territory was to be reduced eventually by "the powers that were" to the much smaller Cape Croker of today – the "Indian reserve" Mrs. Johnston writes about in *I Am Nokomis, Too*.

From **Oral** to **Written**

Life Among the Qallunaat

MINI AODLA FREEMAN

Inuit from Nunaaluk (Cape Hope) Island in James Bay, QC

Published in 1978*

In relating the story of her life, the author tells that of the Inuit of Canada's eastern Arctic and the transformation they went through in the decades between 1940 and 1960. From the age of the dogsled and the whale hunt to the space age, the story is classically Indigenous Canadian, a genre in all but name, it could be said.

Born in 1936 on Cape Hope Island along the Quebec side of the James Bay coast – just inside what is now known as Nunavut – Freeman's is a nomadic family of hunters of seal, whale, and caribou. Already, however, the *Qallunaat* – the white man in the language of her people – has arrived, bringing with him tuberculosis. By the 1940s, the disease is raging its way across Canada's north. Her mother dies of it when the author is four and her paternal grandmother takes over her upbringing. Her childhood is idyllic – wandering by dogsled and boat up and down the coast from one camp to another with whales as her co-travellers. Her people are the southernmost branch of the Inuit nation. Their homeland thus abutting Cree territory, Cree becomes her second language. In fact, Freeman herself is one-quarter Cree. Then she is sent to a residential school in Moose Factory, Ontario, a town and reserve at the southern tip of the great bay. For a little girl of seven, this is so far south that it might as well be Venezuela. A seething hub of peoples and languages, it will eventually give her French and English as her third and fourth tongues. When the school year ends, she doesn't go home like all the other students but, instead, stays the summer, quite happily, in the empty school with a kind supervisor. She does, however, get to go home after her second year. After this, her grandmother keeps her home for a winter so that she can reconnect with her cultural roots, which she does with vigour. Then she is placed in another residential school, this time in Fort

George, north of her native Cape Hope Island. Here she continues to learn *Qallunaat* ways. After two more years, she stays home again, then goes back to finish grade eight, which is the highest grade level taught in the school. Following her schooling, she gets work at the local hospital as a kind of nurse-in-training until she herself contracts tuberculosis. She is sent first to the hospital in Moose Factory, then to the one in Hamilton, Ontario, where a surprising number of Inuit patients are, like her, quarantined. Now a young woman, she gets released, leaving behind her a glowing reputation as a volunteer translator between staff and patients. Which is how she gets work as a translator for the federal government in Ottawa. And there she arrives, fully transformed, if in appearance only, into a *Qallunaat* woman – *Qallunaat* clothes and heels have replaced her sealskin parka and footwear, a *Qallunaat* "pouf" her Inuit braids. And her repertoire of languages roundly impresses.

Though she has her days of weakness and crushing loneliness, not once does the author grumble about her lot in life. It doesn't cross her mind that she is a member of a disempowered race hard in the grip of change in a world hurtling toward self-destruction. She just lives her life from day to day with dogged determination and humble dignity, the only way, perhaps, to send victimhood and the rage it engenders into the garbage where it belongs.

---

* *Life Among the Qallunaat* was first published in 1978. Initially, however, it was suppressed. For some reason known only to it, the federal Department of Indian and Northern Affairs took more than half the print run, approximately 4,200 copies of what was already a limited edition, and locked them up in a basement room (possibly because the author criticizes Inuit relocation programs, suggests Carleigh Baker in the Winter 2015 issue of *Malahat Review*). And only in 2015 when the University of Manitoba Press republished it did this come to public knowledge.

Indian School Days

BASIL JOHNSTON

Ojibwa from Chippewas of Nawash First Nation at
Neyaashiinigmiing (Cape Croker) and Toronto, ON

Published in 1988

This book tells the story of an Ojibwa boy's attendance at an Indian residential school in the 1940s. He starts as a child of ten and ends as a young
man of eighteen. The author describes his arrival at the school, its daily
functioning, and the staff who run it. Most of them are clergy, some kind,
some not. He describes the bonds he forms with the students as replacing
the one with his family that his displacement deprived him of. Above all,
however, he describes the effect this education had on his physical, emotional, mental, and spiritual development.

The boys go to one school, the girls to another some distance away.
Siblings are thus separated; the author and his sister see each other perhaps
twice yearly. It is a regimented life with every minute accounted for: rise
at 6:15 a.m., mass at 6:45, breakfast at 7:30, chores at 8:05, class at 9:00,
lunch at noon, "sports, games, and/or rehearsals" at 12:30 p.m., class at
1:15, snacks at 4:15, more chores at 4:30, study period at 5:00, supper at
6:00, more "sports, games and/or rehearsals" at 6:30, more study at 7:00,
bedtime at 10:00 (or, for the younger children, at 8:30, with dormitories
divided by age). Each of those minutes is spent under the surveillance of
what appears to be a small army of priests and priests-in-training who each,
of course, have their own idiosyncrasies. Two, for instance, are subjected
to taunting because, as Germans, they are "enemies" (the Second World
War is in progress during part of the time the author lives at the school).
Another priest talks to the keys as he plays the piano. The chores the
boys are assigned take place in the tailor shop, shoe shop, or barn with its
cows and horses. Chickens, swine, sheep, plumbing, carpentry, janitorial
duty – all are tended to. Toilet cleaning is reserved as punishment for bad
behaviour. On time off such as weekends, the boys have adventures, many

ending hilariously. Projectile wars with rotten potatoes in the food cellar end when a priest is accidentally hit in the head. Attempts to escape end in debacles. A dock sinks from the weight of a roundup of heifers herded there by the boys and animals and herders are sucked into the river. Home-made football uniforms split during games. A confessor prefers three sins to seven because, apparently, he likes the number. And when most boys get to go home for summer, some thirty-five remain to spend the two months camping, hunting, and fishing off a nearby island.

Situated on the north shore of Lake Huron some two hundred kilometres west of Sudbury, Ontario, the school at Spanish was one of nearly 140 such institutions that were in place across Canada from the 1880s to the 1980s. With a combined enrolment of some 150,000 students, their purpose was to wipe out Indigenous identity and transform stone-age "savages" into good white citizens. Assimilation, in other words, was their *raison d'être*, put into effect by the Government of Canada through its Indian Act of 1876 and enforced by, in this case, the Roman Catholic Church. The author, however, kicks sand in assimilation's face. Despite all the negatives – the food, the language ban, the homesickness – he and his cohorts make the best of it. Far from being crushed by the system, the author comes out triumphant. Still proudly Ojibwa, he finishes as valedictorian of his graduating class.

Inside Out

An Autobiography by a Native Canadian

JAMES TYMAN

Métis from Regina, SK

Published in 1989

Born of a dysfunctional marriage, a Métis child is given up for adoption. From that start, it is a tale of not fitting in. Angry at not knowing his identity, he lashes out at adoptive parents, school personnel, police, prison workers, lawyers, judges, and society in general. It boils down to self-hatred. He was hated when he was born (or so he thinks), so how can he love himself? This is a story of slow death by suicide, a scream for help from an abandoned child. His enormous consumption of drugs and alcohol repeatedly brings him to the brink of self-annihilation. What will stop him? this book asks. And answers the question.

His first misfortune is to be born to a (white) father with a devastating alcohol problem. The author vaguely remembers being kicked unconscious by him when he was a tot. From that day on, the author believes that his father genuinely intended to kill him. At age four, his Cree mother gives him up for adoption. This brings him to his second trauma: why, rather than leaving such a man, did she abandon her child instead? The author's Cree roots are in Île-à-la-Crosse First Nation in northern Saskatchewan; the family that adopts him is, by contrast, white, middle class, and living in Fort Qu'Appelle. He is uprooted, in other words, from a northern forest environment and plunked into a southern urban one. Which is his third trauma, one that is central to the Indigenous experience in Canada. At such an age, he may not remember much of that forest environment or, for that matter, the Cree language, but there is ancestral memory. He is installed in his new home with a new name, something he learns only much later. He may have siblings his age but they are adoptive, not blood-related, and he knows it. Such love, he is convinced, just doesn't count. At the first school he goes to, he encounters racism; popular images of Indigenous people back in the 1960s were hardly positive. And his problems start. He gets involved with the wrong crowd. He plays hooky, which leads to one petty crime and brush with the law after another. Underage experimentation with alcohol and with soft drugs such as marijuana and prescription medication leads to more petty crime – breaking and entering, theft of money, alcohol, and cars, and wholesale destruction of property. By his mid-teens, he is a criminal, alcoholic, and drug addict. By the time he reaches legal adulthood, he is in and out of prison, fraternizing with dealers of hard drugs, pimps, hookers, and junkies, all, like him, unwanted as infants, unloved as children. Until, entirely by accident, he meets his biological mother in a bar in Saskatoon. She acknowledges him – and weeps.

There is something about the tear that crawls out from underneath the woman's sunglasses and down her cheek that shows her son that she still loves him. His ray of hope is *that* small. But it is what pulls him through and, with the support of a cherished girlfriend, sets him on a track leading away from drugs, alcohol, and crime, away from anger, away from victimhood. And toward love.

Bobbi Lee
Indian Rebel
LEE MARACLE

Stó:lō from North Vancouver, BC, and Toronto, ON

Published in 1990

Canadian society is hierarchical and patriarchal. Thus the top position goes, invariably, to the white male, and anyone else ends up voiceless and powerless. Bobbi Lee, Indigenous and female, discovers this obstacle early in life. Throughout her narrative, she struggles mightily to overcome it, encountering pain and confusion at every turn. Not finding solace in her own family or community, she crosses both her own country and others in search of enlightenment. How to give shape to a political consciousness that is still so confused is her first question. How best to express it, her second. She is born at the height of the baby boom and thus comes of age in the 1960s. This gives her journey a fertile background, a picturesque setting.

Bobbi Lee is born the fourth of eight children in a poor North Vancouver neighbourhood. Her mother is Métis from northern Alberta, her father a white boy from rural Saskatchewan. Both survivors of the Great Depression, their psyches and those of their progeny have the seeds of turbulence planted in them. Their marriage, to start with, is dysfunctional. He is never home, leaving his wife to function as a single mother with no means to feed or clothe her children. When he *is* home, drink-fuelled battles explode almost daily. By age nine, Bobbi Lee is helping to raise her younger siblings. She fights at school. She claims that her teachers and neighbours, all of them white, hate her for her colour. Still, this is nothing compared to the racism she sees when she is kicked out of home at sixteen and goes to California with a Mexican boyfriend. Later, she ends up in Toronto where, as a hippie, she dabbles in drugs and listens "to Bob Dylan music." When she returns to Vancouver, she drifts up to northern Alberta and back to Toronto, all along reeling from one confused relationship to another. Some are platonic, others sexual and, in later life especially, some are marital. She gets involved in anti-war demonstrations, rubs shoulders with "Trotskyists," clashes with "Nazis," helps draft dodgers, lives with a black guy. She discovers reading and encounters Malcolm X. She becomes involved in the Red Power movement. Marxist-Leninists, the Black Panthers, Mao, and proletarian revolution all haunt her emerging, if murky, political consciousness. She marries, gets pregnant, becomes a mother, gets divorced, remarries. Still, none of this stops her from helping organize occupations for lost Indian land, helping free friends jailed for such acts, and handing out leaflets at demonstrations.

Bobbi Lee looks out at the world of her people and sees that it needs changing. So, armed with whatever weapons she can get her hands on, she tries to help effect those changes. Against all odds, she succeeds. "Colonialism stole everything," Frantz Fanon's words loom large in Bobbi Lee's thinking, so "...let us demand reparation." This leading intellectual in the decolonization movement helped spawn an entire revolution. Fifty-some years after his death, the field is filled with such writing – young Indigenous people like the activist profiled here are negating the effects of that storied hierarchy, that hated patriarchy. If, at the start, she is the child of grievous misfortune, by the end, Bobbi Lee, Indian rebel, is an empowered advocate for her Indigenous community.

Grey Owl
The Mystery of Archie Belaney

ARMAND GARNET RUFFO

Ojibwa from Sagamok Ojibwa and Chapleau Fox
Lake First Nations and Kingston, ON

Published in 1996

This artful marriage of biography and poetry traces the life of Grey Owl, the notorious "Ojibwa" conservationist and writer of the early twentieth century. It starts with his birth in a town on the south coast of England in 1888 and ends with his death fifty years later in Prince Albert, Saskatchewan. During that time, he metamorphoses from the child of a working-class English family to an "Indian" trapper, nature guide, conservationist, and world-famous author whose works sing out the praises of Canada's natural wonders and Indigenous culture.

Archie Belaney was abandoned as a child by his parents and raised by two aunts. To while away his solitude, he would read everything he could about "red Indians" and sit on the cliffs looking out to sea, dreaming of Canada. By age eighteen, he had emigrated there. After a stint working at the Eaton's department store in Toronto and a detour as serviceman in the First World War, he ended up in the Lake Temagami area of northern Ontario, 150 kilometres north of North Bay, a region known for its lakes and forests. This was prime territory to master the skills he had come to learn – trapping, hunting, and fishing. Not only did he learn them from the Ojibwa whose land this was, he mastered their language. By the time he was in his mid-twenties, he was wearing more buckskin and feathers than the Indigenous people themselves. He drifted west and ended his days working as a conservationist in northern Saskatchewan's Prince Albert National Park. From the notebooks that he kept came five books that he published and that made him famous and rich. He did reading tours of England where three thousand people would fill a hall to hear him. He read to the rich and powerful, including King George VI, all while detractors trailed him. One night, a woman he had married during his stint in the war stood up in the audience and, flashing her wedding ring, called him a liar. It turned out that he had abandoned her and at least four others in England and in Canada, including many children. The more successful he became, the more he drank, to the point where alcohol all but destroyed him. All this while, in his books, readings, interviews, and films, he fought for the preservation of Canada's natural resources and defended the dignity of Indigenous people.

The author of this book was born and grew up in the area where the man, then in his twenties, made his transformation from Archie Belaney to Grey Owl. As a result, members of the author's family from his grandparents' generation knew him, making the author's knowledge of the man next to first-hand. He culls information from quotes by Grey Owl's schoolmates, wives, workmates, the Indigenous people he lived and worked with, bureaucrats, publishers, newspaper reporters who interviewed him, and even Prime Minister Mackenzie King, whom the subject once met to discuss the funding of a film. These vignettes, recast in poetic form, are interspersed with the author's own verse. Thus he creates a tapestry that gives the subject all the dimension needed for fair treatment. By the end, we are persuaded: the man was a fake, yes, but a glorious fake who did much to ameliorate the position in Canadian society of the people he so cared for, the country's Indigenous people.

Back on the Rez
Finding the Way Home
BRIAN MARACLE

Mohawk from Six Nations First Nation, ON

Published in 1996

To the general public, an Indian reserve is a cesspool of poverty and
hopelessness. Some of them are, this book admits, but not all. The common view has been transmitted to the public through the perspective of
white journalists who lack an insider's view. As a result, their reportage
is skewed. It is almost as if, the author posits gently, to make themselves
look good, they must make us Indigenous people look bad. This book sets
the record straight.

In today's slang, the term is "rez," short for "reserve." Of the some
3,100 "rezes" in Canada, Six Nations is the largest. With a registered population of more than 26,000 (the population of the average "rez" is more
like eight hundred), half are resident, with others scattered across Canada
and the United States. The author gives a history of the Mohawk people
who are but one of the Confederacy of six nations. The others are Cayuga,
Oneida, Onondaga, Seneca, and Tuscarora. An Iroquoian people whose
languages share the same linguistic root, the Mohawk migrated from what
is now western New York State into Ontario at the time of the American
War of Independence. They were rewarded by the Government of Canada
with a grant of land on the banks of the Grand River. Unfortunately, that
land decreased in size over the years, thanks to unscrupulous land specu-
lators. Compared to other "rezes," the level of acculturation is high since
the land lies in the midst of such urban centres as Brantford, Hamilton, St.
Catharines, Toronto, and even Buffalo. Only about five hundred people in
Canada speak Mohawk today, for instance, fewer Cayuga, though efforts
are being made to revive both. The author describes the conflict at the
heart of the community between the people of the longhouse – that is,

of the traditional religious system – and the band council. The former is based on the principles of matriarchy that go back eons; the latter is patriarchy that was forced on the people by the Government of Canada in 1924. He describes band council meetings and then does likewise for those of the Confederacy. He describes employment, education, cultural activities such as Bread and Cheese Day* held each spring, the Elders, and the ceremonies. He dissects the language. He describes his own struggles in getting back to the land, planting gardens, chopping wood, and making an old abandoned house livable again.

All in all, this is a positive portrayal by someone who knows and loves his people. Far from being a hopeless cesspool, Six Nations is a healthy, dynamic community; like all communities, it has its problems but it deals with them one day at a time. What is most telling about this account is the Onondaga prayer the author quotes at the end. In this prayer, the people thank nature – the birds, deer, corn, grass, water – for giving them the life they have. Christian cultures don't do that; they hold themselves above nature. The Mohawk people may have been colonized at one point in the past, but, like nature, they will be no longer. Like nature, they will survive.

---

* According to Maracle, Bread and Cheese Day, which takes place on Victoria Day each year, evolved from a celebration of the historic ties between the Six Nations and the British Crown during the American War of Independence and the War of 1812. Today the Grand Council of Six Nations continues a tradition begun by Queen Victoria, with gifts to members of the community, first of blankets and then of bread and cheese. Maracle writes that some years volunteers cut up and distribute 2,000 loaves of bread and 3,200 pounds of cheese.

Song of Rita Joe
Autobiography of a Mi'kmaq Poet

RITA JOE (with Lynn Henry)

Mi'kmaq from Eskasoni First Nation, NS

Published in 1996

Born in the village of Whycocomagh on Nova Scotia's Cape Breton Island, the author has lived much of her life on the nearby Eskasoni First Nation. Brief sojourns on other reserves and in towns and cities across Nova Scotia and beyond have also marked her. She describes her experience from birth to age sixty, giving us a look into life in the twentieth century first as a Mi'kmaq woman, then an Indigenous woman, then an Indigenous person of Atlantic Canada, then an Indigenous citizen of North America. At book's end, she pleads with the public for a better understanding of Indigenous people. As she says, so much of the injustice that has been done to us by the media is because that media doesn't know them; it doesn't, for instance, speak her language.

When the author is five, her mother dies. For the next seven years, she is placed in one foster home after another, some with relatives, some not, some with kindness, some without. Whatever the case, her itinerant labourer father keeps relocating her. When he hears, for instance, that his now seven-year-old has sunk into a bog (of her own doing) and no one has come to get her, he moves her to a new foster home. At nine, she finally gets to live with her father and his new wife and likes her, but he dies and her stepmother can't continue to look after her. In the next foster home, that of an older half-brother, she is taught to make alcohol so that, by age eleven, she is "the best under-age homebrew maker in Cumberland County." But when the drinking there gets to be too much, she writes to the Department of Indian and Northern Affairs for placement in a residential school. Staying at this school in Halifax for four years, she finds kindness and meanness in equal measure. At age sixteen, she leaves to take up menial jobs in town. By twenty, she has three children, all out of wedlock, all by different men, all given up for adoption. Shyly, she explains that the sudden freedom from the "military" strictures of the residential school were the cause of such "mistakes." When she moves to Boston to be with a brother, she meets the man she will marry and have eleven more children with. After the first child is born, they move back to Canada. In this marriage, however, she is beaten for years. At thirty, more to help her through the violence than for any other end, she starts writing. At this point, her children's schoolbooks alert her to the need for Indigenous people to rewrite Indigenous history. When she sends her first poem to a local paper, the reaction is encouraging. She also comes across evidence that her children are one-quarter Beothuk, grace of boat traffic between Nova Scotia and Newfoundland that goes back eons. Contrary to history as written by white people, this "extinct race" lives on in the blood and language of the Mi'kmaq nation. And the floodgates open.

The writer has a way of focusing only on the positive. She has a way of turning pain to joy, hatred to love. She says, for instance, that "bad things" did happen at the residential school, but so did "good things." There were good people who worked there, nuns, for instance, whom she still loves. At the end, as grandmother to scores of children, she reconnects with her spiritual roots. And even here she manages to find a balance between her Catholic upbringing and the way of the sweat lodge. Hers is the way of forgiving, of loving, and of healing.

Thunder Through My Veins
Memories of a Métis Childhood
GREGORY SCOFIELD

Métis from Maple Ridge and Vancouver, BC, Brandon, MB, and Sudbury, ON
Published in 1999

The author was born in southern British Columbia but grew up in small-town northern Manitoba, northern Saskatchewan, and Yukon. Gay and Indigenous in a world where both are anathema, he is from birth a target of hatred. Shame, self-loathing, self-abuse exacerbated by alcohol and drugs, sexual dysfunction, violence, lack of education and employment, poverty, rootlessness, despair, and attempted suicide dog him at every turn. How is he to dispel a darkness so all-encompassing? This book describes his struggle fairly and squarely.

On trial for fraud, the author's father has a heart attack in the witness box and gets rushed to the hospital where his son has just been born. Still there with her newborn, the mother sneaks him into her husband's ward so the father can see his son, if only briefly. Shortly thereafter, the man disappears, never to be seen or heard from again. That leaves both son and mother with a rootless life. Now on her own, the mother reconnects with a high school sweetheart and moves with him and her baby to another town in the province's southern interior. Towns in northern Manitoba, northern Saskatchewan, and Yukon quickly follow; by the time he is five, the author, an only child, has lived in five different places. When his mother is hospitalized for lupus misdiagnosed as mental illness, his stepfather leaves him in the care of foster homes. In one, he finds hate, in the other, love. So that, when he is transplanted yet again by this stepfather, the separation from his foster home is shattering. He ends up with relatives until his mother, released from hospital in Edmonton, comes to reclaim him. Weakened by years of electric shock treatment, she falls into a relationship with a man who beats her, with alcohol – and in her case, prescription drugs – fuelling the violence. At one point, the boy enters a treatment centre for disturbed youth in Vancouver where he is sexually abused. In his teens, he finds himself in the drug-, alcohol-, and prostitution-riddled streets of Vancouver's Downtown Eastside. He tries out one relationship after another, all in vain. In his twenties, he makes two suicide attempts. One relationship that does bear fruit is with a kindly Indigenous neighbour from his childhood, a woman he calls Aunt Georgie. She teaches him beadwork and Cree and opens the door to what he always suspected but was never told – he is part-Indigenous. He learns this from a distant relative. His family, as it turns out, has hidden this fact for the shame that it brings. This knowledge and the love he feels for his long-suffering mother give him the strength that he so needs to survive.

Reclamation of his Indigenous heritage – and, in this case, the Cree language – pulls the author out of the downtrodden state that society has locked him into. It is precisely the denial of bloodline that has made a living hell out of his and his mother's lives. Embracing that bloodline, it is the author's heartfelt belief, is the force that pieces one's soul back together. It puts the hope back into the author's spirit, the thunder of his ancestry back into his veins. And allows him to sing out with triumph at book's end.

For Joshua

An Ojibway Father Teaches His Son

RICHARD WAGAMESE

Ojibwa from Wabaseemoong First Nation, ON, and Kamloops, BC

Published in 2002

This book relates the author's life story, told to his son, recounting details of life as an Ojibwa man and as a victim of the Sixties Scoop. At the time of writing, the son is still a child and estranged, the product of a broken, too-brief marriage. The author's intention is that the boy will read these stories when he is older to understand the love and wisdom of a father he didn't know. The author alternates his life story with the interior journey of a vision quest that he undertakes as a grown man.

As a child of two, the author was taken from his home by the Children's Aid Society. He only learns about it when an elder sister tells him the story some two decades later when they have reconnected. He was then placed in a series of foster homes that took him ever further from the land of his birth, the garden that is northwestern Ontario. At thirteen, he landed at the opposite end of the province – in St. Catharines, just south of Toronto. These repeated displacements hammer into him the belief that he is unwanted. The farther east you go in Canada, it must be noted here, the less visible is its Indigenous population; to truly see it and to hear the languages, you must go west and north. So as the author sinks ever deeper into southern Ontario, he increasingly finds himself the only Indigenous kid in town. With multiculturalism in Canada nowhere near what it is today, he is mocked for his appearance. Still, through the difficult period of early high school, he succeeds in winning a girlfriend. She rejects him, however, when he doesn't measure up to her idea of "Indians" as she has read about them in books. Despite this setback, he manages to make a friend, another socially awkward teen the others call "Pizza Face" because of his acne scars. The author's home life becomes increasingly meaningless, and he starts running away for ever longer periods until, by the end of grade nine, his disappearance is permanent and his life on the streets begins in earnest. In back alleys, under bridges, in flophouses and jails, he drinks vast amounts of alcohol including, when the cash runs dry, such liquids as mouthwash, hairspray, and Lysol. For close to two decades, he reels out of control. His one island of calm is whatever library he can find in which to read books on every conceivable subject and listen to classical music. Until, at age thirty-two, he meets John, an Ojibwa man based in Calgary, who takes him under his wing and, among other things, shows him the ropes of a vision quest. This is the spiritual journey the author interweaves with the episodes of his tale of woe. And it is what puts him back on his feet to become, in time, the award-winning writer that he became.

Sad as it may sound, this is a classic tale of Indigenous life in Canada. Wagamese is far from being the only sacrifice to this kind of tragedy. It is almost as if life on the streets as a complete drunk is a rite of passage that we Indigenous men must all go through in order to earn our stripes. The author writes this letter to his unseen son so that he won't have to repeat the experience, so that he won't be the casualty that his father was, so that he will know that he is royalty in his own country and the custodian of its undoubted beauty.

Pimatisiwin, Walking in a Good Way

A Narrative Inquiry into Language as Identity

MARY ISABELLE YOUNG

Anishnabe Kwe from Bloodvein First Nation and Winnipeg, MB

Published in 2005

This book addresses the issue of language as identity. On the way, it touches on many subjects – Catholicism, residential schools, racism, land, community, Elders, Indigenous spirituality, urban migration. The bottom line, however, is the concept of Indigenous culture as "embedded in the language." Having made her point, the author's objective is to stress the relearning of Indigenous languages by Indigenous people. Only in this way, she argues, can they re-establish their Indigenous identity and establish that identity as an integral part of Canadian society.

She starts with her own *pimatisiwin* (life, in Cree). As a child, she leaves her family for a residential school. Here Catholic nuns deny her the use of her clothes and her language. Instead, she is to speak English only and wear a sort of uniform that makes her just one of many at a church- and government-run educational institution designed to erase Indigenous identity. Much later, as part of a research paper – this book is a published version of her master's thesis in Indigenous Studies – she takes on two case studies. One male, one female, both Indigenous, they talk about their relationships to their language from childhood. Their parents speak it, they don't. The author interviews these two people over seven months straddling the years 2002 and 2003. The result is a picture of three young Indigenous people – the two case studies and the author herself – from southern Manitoba whose parents were part of the great migration from reserve to city in the 1960s. Another kind of migration had just transpired – so many people fleeing war-torn Europe had just moved to western Canada that it doubled some cities' populations. Entire Indigenous families, as a result, were absorbed into this new social fabric. At least that was the case for southern Indians, for when this book was written, that social reality had not yet hit the north. The first thing that happened to these newly urban Indigenous families was loss of language. In order to avoid racist taunts from white children in the schoolyard, Indigenous children avoided speaking "Indian." Speaking English was the best way to blend in, to avoid getting hurt. Having lost their language, all three are now, as adults, struggling to relearn it. Having lost their identity, they are struggling to recover it through, precisely, that language. And to help them do this, they look to the Elders, the communities, and the land that their parents left behind. As a result, they recover their identities as Indigenous people, if only in part. In the end, the author proves her theory – that loss of language causes loss of identity.

Even though the case studies and the author struggle with English, Saulteaux* words pepper the text. It is as if these three people are caught between two languages neither of which completely serves them. The only solution, the author posits, is to look to the last generation of people who spoke them. So the book celebrates not so much the language as what's left of it. Still, even that little is triumph enough over the indignity of colonization.

---

* The traditional territory of the Ojibwa nation encircles, more or less, the Great Lakes of Huron, Michigan, and Superior, and the Saulteaux (pronounced "So-to" as in "photo") are a western extension of that nation. If anything, due to the fact that that part of the nation spills out onto the plains of southern Manitoba and Saskatchewan (and even American states such as Minnesota and North Dakota), they are a kind of "prairie" Ojibwa. Known as Chippewa in the United States, they are the same people, same nation, and they share the same basic language or, at least, a dialect of the same basic language.

Morningstar

A Warrior's Spirit

MORNINGSTAR MERCREDI

Métis from Fort Chipewyan and Fort McMurray, AB,
Uranium City, SK, and Edmonton, AB

Published in 2006

Jolene McCarty comes from a totally dysfunctional family. The father abandons his wife and seven young children, one still an infant. The mother prefers her abusive new boyfriend and alcohol to her own seven daughters. Jolene sees childhood sexual abuse; violence in the home, on the street, and in the bars; extreme poverty; alcoholism and drug abuse; racism; and life on the street. Still, she doesn't do what someone less strong would have done; she doesn't take her life. Instead, she perseveres. Tired of fleeing one nightmare after another, she turns her back on the street and starts attending sweat lodges, powwows, drum dances, and sun dances. She consults with Elders, medicine people, healers, and teachers. She educates herself about the history of her people and her language.

A five-year-old girl wearing only pyjamas is running barefoot one cold autumn evening down a main street in downtown Edmonton. She is on her way to a dive where she knows her mother is drinking. Finding her, she drags her back to the basement apartment where her six child sisters sit huddled, terrified of the babysitter who has been known to abuse them sexually. The mother, however, comes with "baggage" – a case of beer and a pack of strangers whose sole objective is to drink. From there on, it just gets worse. They lose that apartment and move to a worse one, this time with demons as neighbours. Heroin addicts, they beat their girlfriends for their welfare money, shoot up in front of Jolene and her sisters, and talk to them – mere tots all – in language rife with four-letter words and threats of murder. Through all this, the mother does nothing but continue drinking. She brings home her boyfriend at all hours of the day and night; he beats her senseless in front of the girls, just as their father had before him. At age nine, Jolene is raped by this boyfriend and by the time she is twelve, she is on the streets of Edmonton surviving on her fists, wits, and body. Even in high school, which she never finishes, she is forced to steal lunches from other students' lockers just so she can eat that day and not faint from malnutrition. When she isn't living on the streets, she is shunted about from one relative's house to another, from Edmonton to Fort McMurray to Fort Chipewyan to Uranium City (the last two both on northern Alberta's Lake Athabasca) and back to Edmonton. Her life is never stable, never centred. Somehow through it all, she gets married, has a son, gets divorced, and does some studying. Her parents both come from a mix of Dene, Cree, Anishnabe, even Mi'kmaq, in addition to French, Irish, and Scottish; Jolene McCarty is a true Métis. This is the culture she turns to in her mid-twenties to save herself from destruction. In her late twenties, she attends a sun dance. And here she gets her new name, Morningstar. She turns herself around and is enabled to help others as well.

There is huge pain in this autobiography, and much rage against the results of colonization. But she is angry at her people as well, her parents especially. Still, when she turns around to go back to the land on Lake Athabasca, and to the Elders, the healers, dances, and sacred stories, she sees hope. She emerges, at story's end, as Morningstar, a woman with "a warrior's spirit."

I've Been Shot At, What's Your Excuse?

Lessons from My Life

SHERRY LAWSON

Ojibwa from Rama Mnjikaning First Nation, ON

Published in 2007

In a series of vignettes, the author tells of her life as a girl on the Rama First Nation reserve. Located on the shores of central Ontario's Lake Couchiching, it sits right next to the city of Orillia, which is why a prominent thread in the narrative is the manner in which Indigenous people co-exist with non-Indigenous people. And why this is a portrait in miniature of Canada as a country where Indigenous people see poor white people arrive from Europe and come to reside among them, then push them aside. At least these Europeans didn't outright exterminate them, as the Spanish did in Argentina through that same era. So not only did the Ojibwa survive, they also did it with humour. This volume amply proves it.

Some vignettes are funny, some sad, some both, some bittersweet. In one, the author's father decides he wants to start a taxi business so he goes to the bank in nearby Orillia to ask for a loan. Even though he is one of the first Indigenous people in Canada to get a college education, a leery bank manager tells him that his signature alone will not suffice. He needs a second signee, preferably a man of influence. Luckily, the businessman-to-be plays poker and drinks with, of all people, the mayor of Orillia. When he comes back to the bank with His Worship's co-signature, the manager suddenly and unconvincingly explains that a second co-signature is obligatory. We never find out if the author's father bought his planned fleet of taxis; all we know is that we are laughing with him at the absurdity of the whole situation. In another tale, the author stays up late to watch her alcoholic father play poker with his cronies. A player cheats and an argument erupts. The author's father grabs a gun and shoots the cheater who is sitting right across the table from him. Unfortunately, the gunman's seven-year-old daughter – that is, the author – is also sitting there, right behind the cheater. The bullet misses its target and almost hits her. When the author is eight, her mother fails to come home from work one night in late August. The girl feels hurt because the plan was for them to go shopping in Orillia the next day for back-to-school clothes. When her alcoholic mother finally comes home the next morning after having partied the whole night through, she passes out. The girl has no choice: she takes some money from her mother's purse, hops the bus to Orillia, and shops for clothes, all by herself. She even has enough left at the end for a stop at a Chinese restaurant where, impressed, "Ting" serves her a favourite snack. Then there is the story in which, to solve the reserve's chronic state of unemployment, a local "visionary" suggests a casino and, two decades later, Casino Rama is a roaring success. The author's father is chief at one point, and to educate his little girl, he takes her to the odd band council meeting, which is where she learns that the Department of Indian and Northern Affairs owns her people. The tales tell of family and extended family. But more importantly, they sing of love.

The thing that impresses about these stories is how resilient the people are. With the modern world threatening to drown them, they are disempowered and plagued with problems; they are losers. But they have never forgotten their spiritual traditions. And not once have they forgotten how to laugh. Whatever the menace, they celebrate.

Don't Stand Too Close!
You Might Get Some on You
More Lessons from My Life

SHERRY LAWSON

Ojibwa from Rama Mnjikaning First Nation, ON

Published in 2008

As in Sherry Lawson's first book of stories, to which this is a sequel of sorts, vignettes give us an inside look at the life of a girl on an Ojibwa reserve in southern Ontario in the second half of the twentieth century. The stories paint a portrait of an Indigenous community coexisting, if uneasily, with non-Indigenous people of the small city, Orillia, that sits on the community's outskirts. How do the Indigenous survive the experience? With great gobs of humour. Humour is their genius, laughter their saviour.

In one story, asked to find a spirit name for the author's grandson, her brother entrusts the task to their ancestors, in the spirit of their deceased grandmother, to name but one, who come to her in dreams to offer their guidance. In another story, told in flashback to the author's birth, her parents argue over which church their child should be baptized in. Since they are unable to agree, the infant ends up with both Catholic and Protestant baptisms. The truth of the matter, however, is that the parents are neither; they are what the author calls "closet" traditionalists; that is, they follow the old Indigenous religion. Then there's the time when the author is nine years old and she goes with her father to a seed store in Orillia that a friend of his owns and runs. That the friend also happens to be her godfather and the mayor of Orillia doesn't hurt. While the two men play cards and drink in a back room, the little girl, on the mayor's request, staffs the store by herself. Driving her home at day's end, her father weaves "only once" over the white line in the middle of the road. And she is tired from her first day of "working in retail." When the author as a small child gets chicken pox, her mother takes her to the hospital where she works as a nurse and hides her in a secret room; she might lose her job for thwarting quarantine but she is determined to care for and cure her daughter. Kids from the Rama reserve keep falling victim to students and teachers at the school they attend in Orillia. But they always pull through. In Lawson's case, when a teacher tells her that she "will always be second best," she proves her wrong, four decades later, when she wins the title of "Orillia's Business Woman of the Year." At a powwow on Ontario's Manitoulin Island, she counsels a German tourist on the kind of paint he should colour his horse with; the truth is that horses are for Prairie Indians, not easterners like her which means, of course, that she knows nothing about them. In a moment of crisis, she is helped by strangers so she vows to help strangers for the rest of her life. Her mother parting her hair to braid it when she is ten years old is her life's happiest moment. Its unhappiest comes mere minutes later when she spies her mother sneaking a bottle of vodka from a cupboard and, thinking no one is watching, gulping a mouthful.

As with the previous collection, the stories here impress upon the reader how resilient the people are. With the clang and clamour of the modern world around them, they are plagued with problems. They are disempowered and victimized. But they have not forgotten their spiritual traditions or how to love, laugh, or cry. Come hell or high water, they know how to celebrate. And do.

Cries from a Métis Heart

LORRAINE MAYER

Métis from The Pas and Brandon, MB

Published in 2007

In an even mix of prose and poetry, this volume chronicles the life of a woman born to and raised under the roof of a mixed marriage. Her father white, her mother Indigenous, the author finds herself caught uncomfortably between two worlds, two ways of thinking. She also happens to be born in the 1950s in an era when Canada's immigration policy had not yet opened the doors to races and colours from six continents. So the racial divide is in your face, nowhere more so than in Canada's north. There was white and there was "Indian," and the two never met or mingled. She pays with pain and anguish for her life on that cutting edge.

The author gets straight to the point – Indigenous women in Canada's north, in those days especially, are looked at as objects of shame. It is not a source of pride to be an Indigenous woman. Not only does her mother, for instance, hide her bannock when people visit, she also wears white make-up to mask her darkness. Her daughter vows that she will never do so herself. To be part-Indian doesn't cut it either. From one side of the fence, Indigenous people mock her for being part-white, while from the other, white people ostracize her for being "Indian." And "Indian" is the word. "Native" came into the lexicon only later to soothe or mask the word's connotation of, as the author says, such slurs as "drunken Indian," "dirty squaw," and "easy and lazy." For the first part of her life, she meekly accepts the burden of such biracial oppression. Even her own family offers no support. An elder brother, for instance, beats her physically, leaving her with lifelong emotional scars. She weathers four wrecked marriages and as many children and, for this, rages at men and their treatment of women. Still, she picks up the pieces and soldiers on. Fraught with anxiety, she begins her journey to self-empowerment. She finishes high school. Against all odds, she goes on to study philosophy at university in the province's largest city. This small-town girl, in other words, comes out fighting. Not only that, but she goes on to get a doctorate from a university at the other end of the United States. As she leaves her community, a sister, having come to be proud of her if not genuinely amazed by her determination, asks her to use that education. Write something good about Indigenous people, she says, because, to paraphrase her, white people write nothing but bad things about us. And that, says the author, is the motivation behind this book.

"When our grandchildren want to enter the upper echelons of academia, we need people there who will guide them, offer support and show them it can be done," the author writes. "I have met (through their writings) many strong Aboriginal women and men who have unknowingly guided me through the years of loneliness and fear. They function as necessary role models to help me see past the institutions of bigotry. They helped me recognize that I am not alone and have never been alone. These courageous scholars provided the support that helped me regain my own sense of dignity and inspire me to pass on more than alienation to my children and grandchildren." Hear, hear!

Je suis une maudite sauvagesse
Eukuan nin matshimanitu innu-iskueu

AN ANTANE KAPESH (Anne André)

Innu from Uashat-Maliotenam First Nation and Schefferville, QC

Published in 1976

"I am a damned savage woman" is how the French title translates into English. The book laments the second-class status to which the author sees her people have been reduced in modern-day Quebec. Having started life as a nomad roaming *nutshimit* (the bush) with her extended family, Kapesh, an Elder, feels she has been "rounded up" and relocated by the Government of Canada. And now she lives *sédentarise* in Schefferville, Quebec, a mining town on the province's border with Labrador.

From this perspective, Kapesh traces the effects the encroachment of Europeans has had on her land, her people, her culture, and her language. The Europeans' sudden presence on her people's ancestral territory has restricted their movements; her people are no longer free to roam where they have roamed for generations. The construction of mines has chased away the animals that they depended on for food, clothing, tools, and shelter. The residential schools into which their children have been herded have eroded their language and, with it, their culture. Young people no longer know how to fish, hunt, and trap, let alone raise a family in the boreal forest. The game wardens who have come to regulate their hunting and fishing practices, the liquor merchants, the police, the court system, the housing program – read, the reserve system – foisted on them by the Department of Indian and Northern Affairs, all have done their part to reduce the people to an abject state. She feels these days like a trapped animal: "*Je sais bien qu'aujourd'hui il est très difficile de me montrer ma vie d'Indienne parce que ma culture n'existe plus … Quand j'y réfléchis, il n'y a que dans ma tête que je conserve ma vie d'autrefois.*" ("I know that today it is very difficult to show my Indian life because my culture exists no more. When

I think of it, it is just inside my head where that old life of mine still lives.")

This book is written simultaneously in Innu and French but one gets the impression that it was written first in Innu and then translated by the same author. This means the author did, at least, get to use her own language and not the colonizer's to tell her story. If Indigenous people are victims anywhere in the body of literature being assessed here, this book is where that victimhood stands most plainly articulated. Not a word is minced. Even the title expresses self-loathing. If readers find it a hard read because of the constant dirge that it spits out like venom, then they should take note. These are the words of an Elder who has been there, who has seen her culture go, in one generation, from one of tools of bone, sinew, and stone to one of computers. From that standpoint alone, therefore, it is a valuable document. And though there is not much evidence in these pages of getting past that victimhood, and even less hope, the fact that the book was written and published – *in Innu* – is reason enough for such hope. It provides a light at the end of the tunnel to which the next generation of Indigenous writers can turn with less fear and worry. And with more confidence.

L'Odawa Pontiac

L'amour et la guerre

BERNARD ASSINIWI

Cree-Algonquin-Métis from Montreal

Published in 1994

It is the mid-1700s and the French and the English are infiltrating North America as never before. With each set on establishing dominance, it is clear that, as in Europe, theirs will be a complex and violent rivalry. The continent will hang in the balance. At this juncture, the area of contention is the land lying south of the Great Lakes in the land of the Three Fires Confederacy. Other Algonquian nations figure but these – the Ojibwa, Odawa, and Potawatomi – are the principals. Born an Odawa in 1720, Pontiac walks into this hornets' nest. By his early thirties, he is a leader, allying his people with the French who got there first and on whom his people have become dependent, for arms not least. Unluckily for him, the English come to outnumber the French. Pontiac and his people get caught between the two superpowers. And pay dearly.

The biography starts with a battle between the French and the English and their Indigenous allies on the Monongahela River, a tributary of the Ohio. The prize is a fort that will later become the city of Pittsburgh. The English lose. Other battles follow, however, where they win with increasing frequency. At one point, Pontiac fights beside a commander named Montcalm who, promoted to general some five years later, will lead the French on the Plains of Abraham to a devastating loss at the hands of the English. Through it all, Pontiac works to unite the Indigenous nations in support of the French. So forceful is his personality, so far-seeing his vision, that he succeeds in uniting all the Algonquian nations south of the Great Lakes in a way that they have never been united before. (It is mostly Iroquoian peoples such as the Mohawks who side with the English.) Amid all this military activity, we see the man's human side. He encourages his people to learn French; in his view, education is the only way they will survive the onslaught. He loses his first wife and child to smallpox. He falls in love again, courts a French girl who rebuffs him, then finds another mate among his own people. Dealing with mutiny, he argues against those who try to convince him that they are fighting a losing battle and that they should, instead, join the English. He grapples with self-doubt. He mourns the thousands among his people who have died, or are dying, of smallpox. But even though he meets an ignoble end, stabbed in the back at age forty-nine by a member of the Peoria nation in Illinois, he is the crucible that comes extremely close to making North America a French-speaking continent.

This book may be written in French but the author has gone the distance to honour Chief Pontiac by including elements of his native tongue – the chapter headings, for instance, are in Odawa. In the history related, the Indigenous people of the Great Lakes region start off a dignified people. Then, through the course of the book, they are swallowed by a people more numerous, not to mention better armed. Even more devastating, however, is the onslaught of disease to which they had no immunity and which weakened them to the point that their land could be taken. This is how the modern-day cities of Pittsburgh, Detroit, Chicago, and others put down roots. Books like this show Indigenous people in a position of strength. Following their example, as descendants, we too can adapt to modern-day conditions and the march of history. And what will help us do that, as Chief Pontiac says here, is education.

Récits de Mathieu Mestokosho, chasseur Innu

MATHIEU MESTOKOSHO (edited by Serge Bouchard)

Innu from Mingan (Ekuantshit) First Nation, QC

Published in 2004

This autobiography consists of a verbal account narrated by an old Innu hunter to a French-Canadian anthropologist who then transcribed it. Because the culture it describes is nomadic, the story roams widely. The base community is Mingan, the reserve on the north shore of the Gulf of St. Lawrence from where the narrator hails, and the story covers territory from there north to Labrador. As the time is the first half of the twentieth century, electricity had not yet arrived so there was no television, radio, telephone, or computer. And no French language. Everything functioned in Innu and through natural means. Houses were lit by kerosene and oil lamp and heated by woodstoves, fish caught in rivers were cooked over campfires, canoe and dogsled were the only modes of travel, and women gave birth in tents pitched in snowbanks. Mathieu Mestokosho describes that lifestyle from first-hand experience.

He speaks enough about his father and grandfather to give an idea of the length of time that such a lifestyle has been lived in that part of the world. It is one of daily subsistence. In the summer, he paddles his canoe either with his wife and children, alone, or with a hunting partner, through the network of waterways that snake their way from the Gulf of St. Lawrence all the way into what is now known as Labrador. Along the way, he hunts moose, bear, rabbit, porcupine, ducks, and geese and fishes trout, whitefish, and pickerel; the land is so rich it virtually breathes. In winter, he traps otter, marten, mink, and beaver and follows in his dogsled the caribou that come thundering from the north in herds of thousands. He describes the way he hunts down, or traps, all these animals, how he and his wife dress and cook them, and how he and his family eat them. For instance, whatever people couldn't eat within the first few days of killing, they had to smoke for there was no refrigeration, at least not in summer. And, in any case, they lived in tents they erected one day and took down the next so they could move on to the next place for hunting or fishing. And depending on how the hunt had gone, or how the weather was going, they would camp at one place for a day or a week and there erect structures to smoke their meat or fish. All of this was accomplished with techniques distinct to the culture.

The original account was spoken in Innu then translated into French. So, although it is not written by the hunter himself, it is his story in his voice. More description of a lifestyle than actual story, it validates the existence of a narrative voice on that land long before the arrival of *les blancs*. The story it tells, moreover, is different in a major sense from that told by the mainstream literature that was to emerge in the province of Quebec. Where in the latter tradition, nature is a foe to be feared and conquered, here she is an ally, a family member. In the very structure of the narrator's language, nature has a soul, just like humankind. There is, then, no colonization in this narrative, only celebration of a beautiful, if harsh, lifestyle.

E9-422

Un Inuit, de la toundra à la guerre de Corée

EDDY WEETALTUK (in collaboration with Thibault Martin)

Inuit from Kuujjuaraapik and Umiujaq, QC

Published in 2009

Written with the collaboration of a francophone man named Thibault Martin, this book relates the life story of an Inuit man, Eddy Weetaltuk, who was born and raised in northern Quebec where it borders what today is known as Nunavut.* The author's home territory is difficult to pin down because, as with so many Indigenous peoples, his were nomads. The immense coasts of both James Bay and Hudson Bay, with all their islands, are their home. If, therefore, the people belong to no province or territory, the government has them registered as residents of a part-Cree, part-Inuit village on the Hudson Bay coast just north of James Bay on mainland Quebec. Known as Kuujjuarapik today (formerly Great Whale River), it is a mere stone's throw from Nunavut.

The story begins with the narrator's birth in the snow on an island in James Bay mere kilometres from mainland Quebec. At the time, the Government of Canada had a system in place, at least in Quebec, by which Inuit, then called Eskimos, were identified in official records by the letter *E* for Eskimo – as opposed to *I* for Indian. They were also identified by numbers, 9 (in this case) to identify the community and 422 (in the author's case) to identify the person. Even the village houses had these letters painted on them. Born one of twelve children, he describes the lifestyle in which he was raised: the seal hunts, the whale hunts, crossing the tundra in dogsleds, trapping for animals and then trading their furs at the nearest Hudson's Bay Company trading post, the family's sometimes near-death struggles with a harsh land and climate. Hunger if not near starvation haunts the people when the caribou don't come. He describes the arrival of competing Christian missionaries, in this case Anglican and Catholic. So fierce is their rivalry for souls that, when still a boy, he converts from Anglicanism to Catholicism.

This is how he ends up at a Catholic residential school where, among other things, he learns not only to speak French but also to garden. For an Inuit, this is an anomaly. Having grown up in a part-Inuit, part-Cree community and gone to school in English and then French, this multilingualism will serve him well when, in his late teens, he joins the Canadian Armed Forces and goes to Korea for the war there and, later, to Germany. His wartime adventures, particularly in Korea, are as harrowing as they are colourful. He lives as close to the gruesomeness of death as he does, when on furlough, with the pleasures of life, particularly the girls of Japan and what he considers to be their awesome wisdom in the art of sex. And generosity. Still, when he comes home, older and wiser for his experience, he laments the sorry state of the Inuit world. In the grip of social change beyond its control, the youth, in particular, are bedevilled by substance abuse, spiritual confusion, and emotional despair.

For all its ups and downs, the book is written with an infectious sense of joy and enthusiasm. The man so loves life that he seduces you with that love. As he says, hoping to teach by example he writes his story for the next generation of Inuit youth. "Go out in the world, open your mind, and open your heart," is his overall message. "Then bring that wisdom back to your people and help heal them of their status as victims."

---

* A little known fact: although, on maps, it looks like the body of water we call James Bay is shared equally by the provinces of Quebec and Ontario, it is actually part of Nunavut. At this point in its curve, the territory dips almost as far south as the town of Moosonee which lies, more or less, at the southern extremity of said bay. So as with my people who roamed at liberty in the territories known today as Manitoba, Saskatchewan, Nunavut, and the Northwest Territories – that is, without heeding borders – then so did Mr. Weetaltuk's roam indiscriminately the islands of James and Hudson's Bay off mainland Quebec and that mainland itself. In doing so, they wove their way, as we did, back and forth across a territory *and* a province without rhyme or reason; as in our case, what decided their route was not political jurisdiction but the animals they depended on for food and shelter. The other aspect of this particular geography is that, usually buffered by the Dene, this is the only region in Canada where the Inuit and Cree communities meet. Meaning to say that this is one of very few places on Earth where a child can grow up speaking both languages as, indeed, did Mr. Weetaltuk.

From **Oral** to **Written**

YOUNG PEOPLE'S
LITERATURE

The Curse of the Shaman

A Marble Island Story

MICHAEL KUSUGAK

Inuit from Naujaat (Repulse Bay) and Rankin Inlet, Nunavut

Published in 2006

Two Inuit families each give birth to a child, one male, one female. As was the custom in that culture before contact, boy and girl are destined from the cradle to be married in adulthood. At least the infant boy's father, The-man-with-no-eyebrows, makes that request from the girl's father, Paaliaq, who is a shaman. Not so much evil as ill-tempered when something irks him – for example, when his baby daughter will not stop crying – he refuses the request and, instead, curses the boy: when he is of age to be married, he will never again set foot on "this land." From then on, the boy, Wolverine, must live with this curse. Indeed, when he comes of age, he gets stuck on an island off the coast a distance from his home. Only the help of a friend saves him from exile.

We see the two children being born, each in turn, to ecstatic parents. Then we see the curse – in Inuit culture, the shaman has an animal assistant, a kind of guide who "carries" his spirit and brings to fruition his master's curses. In Paaliaq's case, this guide is a *siksik*, a lemming, an evil, weasel-like creature that will shadow Wolverine into adulthood. While this happens, we see the families living out traditions that go back eons. Theirs, after all, is a nomadic culture whose constant movements through an Arctic land are determined by the seasons. There is the season for whaling, for sealing, for hunting small game and caribou, for gatherings and celebration. The men build igloos, dogsleds, and kayaks; the women fashion clothing from sealskin and caribou. Children play tag and *aattaujaq* (toss-and-catch). Boy and girl grow up, sometimes together, sometimes apart, for as nomads, their families each have their territories for hunting. And myths come into play. Sedna, for instance, is an old woman who lives under the sea and whose severed fingers once turned into ocean creatures – seals, whales, and fish. Kiviuq is a young man who can paddle his kayak for days without getting tired. Always, however, the boy and girl are in training for adulthood in a land that, seen through their eyes, is unimaginably beautiful and vast. One day, the boy and his little sister find a baby owl with a broken wing. They heal and adopt him. Some years later, Wolverine gets stuck on Marble Island, up the coast. Each time he tries crossing in his kayak to get home, waves rise up to stop him. The curse is working; the *siksik* is happy. Until the owl with the mended wing, Ukpigjuag, starved from having been stuck with his friend on the preyless island for days, flies to the mainland and kills a lemming that happens to be *siksik*, the shaman's spirit guide. Thus he breaks the curse, and the boy is able to go back to his home and marry his love.

This illustrated children's novel is written in English, with some Inuktitut. As the story progresses, Wolverine starts melding into the land, so attuned to its rhythm that he becomes one with it. By the time he has his standoff with the curse – that is, when he is battling the waves trying to cross the channel – he enters the mythology, transforming into the mythic Kiviuq paddling his kayak for days and entering the soul of Sedna, the old woman under the sea, her long hair (the algae) embracing him. We see Inuit life at its most unsullied, that is to say. This is a portrait of a beautiful culture.

Dog Tracks

RUBY SLIPPERJACK

Ojibwa from Whitewater First Nation and Thunder Bay, ON

Published in 2008

A thirteen-year-old girl reconnects with her Ojibwa roots. As a child, Abby has been sent down to Nipigon, some hundred kilometres northeast of Thunder Bay, to live with her grandparents. When her grandfather dies, she is sent back to her blood family on the Bear Creek Reserve, so far north of Nipigon that the only way to get there is by bush plane. There she faces the challenge of relearning the "old ways," which she has lost while living in a "white town." Abby, however, quite enjoys the process. She learns to hunt, fish, trap, do beadwork, live in tents, make bannock, dry moose meat, cook over open fires, train sled dogs, paddle canoes, and best of all, she relearns her language.

Life's challenges for a thirteen-year-old girl may look minor to us, but to Abby, they are significant. The first one comes in the form of a younger brother nicknamed Blink, a brat she is forced to reconnect with. Blink does not appreciate being overshadowed by an elder sister he hardly knew existed. Abby, however, learns to live with and despite him. She makes friends and plans with the children of the small reserve and with the older people. One is Old Man Gish, who shows her how many houses the reserve has when, for a school project, she has to draw a map of the village. She makes friends with the chief of the reserve, who turns out to be a charming young woman named Chief Paulie. Abby becomes a crucial part of the plan that Chief Paulie and one of Abby's uncles, a bear of a man named Mad Dog, are hatching to establish a business. Aiming to make the community economically independent, their first project is to establish a tourist resort. The plan is marked by hilarious episodes, such as when young dogs being trained as sled dogs get out of control and almost kill the "fake tourists" being played by the chief and the local Anglican minister. Abby's father trains her puppy, Ki-Moot, to help him hunt ducks. Ducks, claims

Abby's father, are attracted only to dogs with beige fur. Unfortunately, all the beige dogs on the reserve are unavailable that day. The solution? He forces the very black Ki-Moot into his beige long johns and puts him to work. Ki-Moot runs back and forth on the shore in front of the ducks as they float and feed. And low and behold, they do come closer to shore. Unfortunately, Ki-Moot has an "accident" in the underwear. The father has no option but to abandon the garment there and then – after, of course, shooting the ducks. And the name of the bay from that day onward is Long John Bay. So go the stories. Even the blueberry-picking expeditions Abby takes with her mother and the reserve women are joyful events.

The Ojibwa language is spoken of because, of course, Abby, learns it as the story progresses, but that's as far as it goes. If disempowerment and suffering exist, Abby diffuses them with her gregarious, undefeatable, forever optimistic nature, a nature that is a treasure to witness. If Abby is about anything, it is hope. She is full of it, on every page, in every paragraph, and every word. This novel celebrates the most positive aspects Ojibwa culture and wisdom have to offer the world. It is a refreshing – and much-needed – voice in a library filled with dirges.

Will's Garden

LEE MARACLE

Stó:lō from North Vancouver, BC, and Toronto, ON

Published in 2002

A Stó:lō (Salish) youth prepares for and goes through his Becoming Man
ceremony. Before and after, he goes about living out his destiny as a young
man. He deals with his family, friends, and enemies. He comes to terms
with his sexuality, falls in love, participates in the life of his community,
and at the end, survives death. Through it all, we get an inside look at the
life and times of a Stó:lō family and community as it strives to preserve its
cultural identity despite the technological enticements of modern society,
which threaten to drown the traditional culture.

Will is a fifteen-year-old boy who lives with his family in the Kamloops area of south interior British Columbia. In his dreams, powers come
to him that exist beyond his waking life. Among them are his ancestors, a
land that is so present that it virtually talks, and beings from his people's
mythology. Principal among them is Raven, the West Coast trickster. They
inform him that they will guide him through the life-changing passage that
he is about to embark on. When he wakes up, his whole extended family is
preparing for his ceremony. The women are cooking, the men are making
wooden masks, and both men and women are beading blankets, capes, and
moccasins. In between, there are flashbacks in which Will, his siblings, and
his cousins caddy at a golf course and raise money to buy Will's first bicycle.
Later they ride their first roller coaster at the Pacific National Exhibition in
Vancouver and dig for clams on the mud flats of Vancouver Island. Then he
is in high school where he deals with the local bully and racist, the captain
of the football team. Will eventually turns him around to be his friend.
Will also has a gay friend, for whom he jeopardizes his own reputation as
straight. In another of Will's flashbacks, his grandfather is part of a work
gang laying out the first highway to cross the province. Young then, the
now-old man works with Chinese immigrants and Tsimshian people. To

find such employment, one Tsimshian has walked all the way from Prince Rupert on the North Coast to the south of the province. Again, and often throughout, the novel slips back to the motif of beadwork. Will is lovingly creating his on capes that will be used for dancing at his ceremony. The patterns he applies depict roses from his mother's garden and this is where the title image comes from. Then Will undergoes the ceremony, an event that includes a giveaway (a potlatch) and a sweat. In the midst of all this, he falls in love with a young woman named Lei-Lani. Like him, she is all of fifteen. He helps the community build a daycare centre, but then falls sick with a burst appendix. He ends up in hospital where he almost dies. Will's grandfather and ancestors appear and revive him.

All of these streams of Will's young life become like the beads he applies to his ceremonial capes. As with the rose patterns on those capes, they give that confused life form and meaning. Still, if there is one thread in that beadwork that is most significant, it is the women that surround him. He comes from and lives in a matriarchal society. If there is one force that will lift Indigenous people from their disempowered state, it is, as in Will's garden, the women.

My Name Is Seepeetza

SHIRLEY STERLING

Secwepemc from Kamloops, BC

Published in 1992

A young Secwepemc girl named Seepeetza is taken from her home and her family and placed in residential school. Describing her adventures at this school in this autobiography, she intercuts them with scenes of being with her family back home during summer holidays.

Seepeetza is twelve years old and in grade six at the Kalamak Indian Residential School. One hundred miles south of her family's ranch near a town called Firefly, it sits across the river from a fictitious small white city called Kalamak. Upon her arrival, the Irish nuns who run the school immediately cut her long hair. Then she is deloused and her clothes are taken and put "in storage" to be replaced by an institutional smock. She is beaten for the smallest of infractions, has scary encounters with a bully (Indigenous) named Edna, and is forbidden to speak her mother tongue. In fact, her Secwepemc name, Seepeetza, which means White Skin or Scared Hide, is replaced with the English name that was given her at her baptism. Now Martha Stone, she weathers these trials to the best of her ability, with some support from her siblings who also attend the school. There are some bright spots. Martha learns to write, falls in love with books at the school library, gets corralled into dancing in an Irish-dancing troupe that does local tours to thrilling acclaim. And although there are mean nuns, there also some kind ones. Sister Theo, the intermediate girls' supervisor, for instance, helps Martha's ambitious elder sister, Dorothy, engage in clandestine after-hours study. She finds her a flashlight so that she can study under her sheets without being seen by the wandering night watchman. The greater part of each chapter, which ostensibly takes place at the school, is usually eclipsed by euphoric memories of life on her family's ranch. Her love of horses, for instance, constitutes a vital part of her personal happiness. There is a bear cub they raise until he gets too big for the children's safety and a chicken that, unknowingly, hatches two ducklings among her brood and is greatly dismayed when they jump into a pond and swim merrily off. Seepeetza describes, with wistful sadness, her puppy love for a boy named Charlie. At age twelve, he drowns in a fishing accident on the river near their home, leaving her a "widow" of too tender years. Christmas and summer holidays punctuate each year. During those times she is able to engage in all-out enjoyment of the land that is her home – its wealth, its beauty, its comfort.

Through it all we see how the Indian residential school system affected the life and psychology of a girl of twelve. She is scared, she says, through most of the experience. But then she wonders why she looks so happy in pictures from the period. What is the source of that strength? What glue holds her soul together through those years when an entire system attempted to erase her identity? The force that saved her from a disempowered status is her land, her family, love. And her own joyful personality.

Girl Who Loved Her Horses

DREW HAYDEN TAYLOR

Ojibwa from Curve Lake First Nation, ON

Published in 2000

Eleven-year-old Danielle Fiddler is a loner. She has no friends; she barely talks. The only way she can communicate with the outside world is through her drawing. And not just any drawing, but drawings of one horse in particular. As life swirls around her for better or for worse, she escapes into the drawings of this beautiful horse that she, and only she, seems capable of making. In life, she is sad, scared, and barely functional. But inside the spirit of the horse, she is brave, daring, and magnificent.

In this stage play, Danielle is the only child of a dysfunctional mother who is prone to relationships with violent men. Her father is dead. And though we never see the offstage mother, it is evident that she mistreats her child and that alcohol abuse is a factor. No wonder, then, that her daughter has closed herself off. At school, the other kids mock Danielle for her strangeness. Her poverty also sets her apart. She lives, so to speak, on the wrong side of the tracks. She is a freak, an outcast. But when she draws, everyone takes notice. And when she touches the horse she has drawn, not only does she dance with him inside her spirit, she also flies off into a state of ecstasy. Success, however, has its downside. Her talent causes jealousy, in one boy in particular. When he challenges her to draw something other than this horse, she proves incapable – the dog she draws, by comparison, is, at best, an embarrassment – and the boy laughs in her face. And when another boy tries to touch her horse so that he, like Danielle, can dance with him, the horse disappears and so, in a sense, does his maker. No longer able to take life at home, Danielle at one point begs Shelley, another girl, to have her adopted into *her* home. But no one can effect such a move, not Shelley, not her mother, not the Children's Aid Society. And certainly not Danielle's mother. Until, sadly, this mother moves to Toronto, taking her daughter with her. And Danielle disappears, leaving behind only her drawing of the horse to keep haunting the other kids into adulthood.

From the start, Danielle is a victim of family dysfunction. Alcohol abuse is but one symptom of that dysfunction. Still, a woman's disempowered lot in the patriarchal structure that has been foisted on Indigenous society certainly appears to be the crux of the matter. If Danielle's mother is the primary victim of such disempowerment, then Danielle is a victim by association. And the only way out of it is her talent, her art. One senses, at play's end, that this talent eventually did save her, as her horse's continued reappearance in the lives of her childhood contemporaries appears to suggest. After viewing or reading this play, the image of a beautiful dancing horse is what stays with you. If anything will help Indigenous people surmount their victimhood, this image tells us, it is art. Art, the medicine that heals. Art, the grand celebration.

The Boy in the Treehouse
DREW HAYDEN TAYLOR

Ojibwa from Curve Lake First Nation, ON

Published in 2000

A half-breed ten-year-old named Simon Whitney attempts to uncover his Indigenous identity. As he was born and raised in a city far from the reserve that his mother comes from, he has no idea what his identity means. In protest, he has locked himself in the house that hangs from a tree in his family's suburban yard. There he plans a vision quest. But because he has read about such things only in books and has no one to guide him – his father is white and his Ojibwa mother deceased – he equips himself with a guidebook. When he is dissuaded by his father, Simon tells him that he is doing this to mark the first anniversary of his mother's death.

The father, of course, knows his first responsibility as a parent is to see to it that his son is fed. Submitting himself to the fast that a vision quest apparently requires would surely harm his son, the father believes, looking at the situation from a parent's perspective. Simon's reaction is that, even if his father has lived with an Indigenous woman for years, he knows nothing about being Indigenous, much less about vision quests. For the moment, his father relents and goes in to supper. Through the course of this play, a ten-year-old girl who has just moved into the neighbour-hood keeps visiting Simon. She does this by climbing to his treehouse by means of the tree next to it. Patty by name and decidedly non-Indigenous, this girl grills Simon about vision quests. What are they? What do they mean? Why is Simon pursuing one? What does it mean to Simon to be part-Indigenous? Simon skates through the answers as best he can. A kindly neighbour tries to get him to come down, as does a policeman. Even the local media, which has gotten hold of the stand-off, sends in a TV reporter and cameraman to ask Simon why he's doing this. Defending his Indigeneity, Simon lets slip his opinion that his British-Canadian father has no culture, a race-based judgment that forces him to bow to the fact that, being half white and half Indigenous, he has "the best of both worlds." Finally, upon receiving the father's urgent calls for help, Simon's uncle Clyde arrives from the reserve to advise his nephew that one doesn't honour someone's death, one honours their life. Simon starts to rethink things. When Patty, who has borrowed the vision quest guidebook from him, tells him that he is doing it all wrong – that he needs, for one thing, an Elder's supervision and that a vision quest is about others, not about oneself – he relents. His hunger from fasting, of course, has also done its trick. Once he is down from his tree, Simon learns from his father that his mother's middle name was Patricia. That's when he gets it – his mother, all along, was talking to him. Through Patty. He *did* have his vision.

The young boy, Simon, is a loser. Wounded by the loss of a mother at so young an age, he is hurting and needs sorely to re-anchor himself. Admirably, he has the wisdom to try, against all odds. Refusing to accept defeat, he keeps working at it until, finally, he gets beyond it. He is proactive. Connecting with community, with blood in the form of his mother's brother, Clyde, first gives him hope. Connecting with the spirit of his mother in the form of Patty clinches that hope. It turns his condition around so that he can, indeed, celebrate his Indigeneity and, by doing that, celebrate his life.

L'été de Takwakin

JACINTHE CONNOLLY

Innu from Mashteuiatsh First Nation, QC

Published in 2002

This novel for young readers is written by an Atikamekw woman from inland Quebec with the assistance of a committee made up of four women who are Atikamekw, Mi'kmaq, and Wendat. It recounts the tale of William, a nine-year-old Atikamekw boy on his annual summer visit to his mother's place of birth. The place is Wemotaci, an Atikamekw First Nation near the city of La Tuque. Living with his mother on the north shore of the St. Lawrence River some eight hundred kilometres to the north, he feels alienated; the white kids mock him for his Indigenous identity. But in Wemotaci, William comes alive as an Indigenous person. In fact, it is the only place in the world where he is known by his Indigenous name, Takwakin (Autumn in Atikamekw, Cree, and other Algonquian languages).

His *allophone* father having long disappeared, William is the only child of an Atikamekw woman who works as a cook at a summer fishing lodge on the north shore of the St. Lawrence River. This is why he has to take these annual summer trips to Wemotaci, his mother's home community, alone. Fortunately, his grandmother is always there to receive him, as are other members of her extended family. And through the summer described in the novel, Takwakin takes great joy in swimming with his cousins, picking blueberries with his uncle Roger and his children, and duck hunting. One day, he gets taken to his first powwow at which dancers from all over are present. And he meets a girl his age. A Mi'kmaq powwow dancer from the Gaspé region of the province, Mimiges (Butterfly, in Mi'kmaq) comes from a family of powwow singers and drummers. So who better to usher him into the ways of such celebrations? He watches the dancers but is too shy to dance himself. Mimiges's family feeds him and regales him with their stories. In between dances, she takes him on a tour of the crafts kiosks and their marvels. On the morning of the second day of the event, he takes her fishing with his uncle Roger, during which trip an eagle appears overhead. That same day he is coaxed into playing the drum with The White Stones, the members of which come from his new friend's family. The experience wows him; it connects him to himself in a way he has never felt before. At the end, Takwakin and Mimiges exchange gifts and promise to meet the following summer at a powwow her community is hosting, in Gaspé. Takwakin's granny closes the story with the sage words: "He who has friends is wealthy."

This, of course, is a children's book, but for the amount of Indigenous literature published out of Quebec up to this time, in a province where the Indigenous presence risks being rendered invisible by the francophone culture, singing out the praises of at least two Indigenous cultures, Atikamekw and Mi'kmaq, is significant. What stands out here is love, love for one's culture and for one's people. Indigenous people still live in Quebec, the author shows, and they may just have something valuable to offer to its people.

Hannenorak

JEAN SIOUI

Wendat from Wendake First Nation, QC

Published in 2004

These are creation stories masked as fictional short stories. In each, a Wendat boy named Hannenorak engages in an adventure with an animal. As the stories take place at a time before first contact, the boy lives in a longhouse with his family, a dwelling that is situated in a village surrounded by a forest seething with animals. Hannenorak is so close to nature, in fact, that he speaks the language of these creatures and they speak his.

In the first story, we learn that Grand Duc, the owl, didn't always have the round eyes he is known for. His eyes were once shaped like almonds. At that time, Grand Duc lived in the forest close to Hannenorak's village. Striking up a friendship, the bird taught the boy all kinds of things: the cries of animals, their food, their habits, names of plants and their medicinal properties, how to tell direction by the sun's position in the sky, and so on. They loved each other, so much so that Grand Duc wanted to keep watch over his friend day and night – but especially at night, as owls sleep during the day. Hannenorak slept in the Wendat longhouse, which has a hole in the roof for smoke to escape, and it is through this opening that Grand Duc watched over his friend. When smoke billowed, though, as it often did, Grand Duc saw nothing. Until one day, a woodpecker pecked a little hole in that roof right over the place where Hannenorak slept. Still, because the hole was so small, Grand Duc could use only one eye at a time. To see his friend properly, he had to open it very wide and press it right up against the hole. And over time, his eyes grew very large and very round. The second story tells of an unusual little bear named *Visage Rouge* (Red Face). While bears in the region had black or brown fur, his was red. One day, this unusual fur became very useful – the day Hannenorak got lost in the forest and no one could find him. *Visage Rouge* climbed a tree where the boy had stopped so that hunters out looking for him could see the cub's fur sparkle in the light from the sun or the moon, and thus find Hannenorak. There are stories of the world's only bald porcupine, the blind mole who could read the animal version of the Ten Commandments from a scroll of birchbark; though only with the help of a clever weasel, *Marie-Mielle* (Marie-Honey), the honeybee who cures children's noses of sores and bumps by deflating them with her benevolent sting; the beaver who rescues capsized canoeists; the muskrat who tricks children who fall asleep while fishing through holes bored in the ice ...

The purpose of these stories, of course, is to entertain. And that they do. But they also demonstrate the relationship between a land and the people who inhabit it. They demonstrate that these people saw no need whatsoever to exploit that land or to make money from it. Because they had no need to colonize nature, as it were, nature had no need to oppress or threaten them. A little simplistic, perhaps, but these are children's stories. And they capture a theme that underscores much of Indigenous literature.

Hannenorak et le vent

JEAN SIOUI

Wendat from Wendake First Nation, QC

Published in 2008

While its predecessor, *Hannenorak*, cast creation stories in the form of fiction, this collection of short stories lives more in the genre of hero myth. One day, in the Wendat village where Hannenorak lives with his family, the wind steals an infant. Spirited off to the sky, the "child of the wind" is never seen again. The village then has to live without infant or wind. In the discussion that ensues, human and animal communities engage as equals. The topic? Who among them will be able to bring back this wind. By the grace of the shaman, the chief, Hannenorak's father, and various animals, the candidate is found: Hannenorak, older now than in the earlier story. Unwillingly and against great odds, he sets off to fulfill his destiny.

When Sky Woman dreams that the wind has taken the infant known as the "child of the wind," the dream comes true and not even a breeze blows across the land. The clouds mourn the wind's absence. The leaves of trees droop sadly. Without warning, the lake freezes, because there are no waves. Even the hair of the beautiful Ondaacha, the chief's daughter, is stilled. In an effort to bring back the wind, the Carrier of the Pipe dances for two days around the sacred fire, but is unsuccessful. The shaman holds a meeting in the Shaking Tent. At the climax of his trance, the rope that extends across the tent miraculously weaves itself into braids. Emerging back to consciousness, the shaman announces that the person who can untie those braids will be the one who will bring back the wind. But he knows that no one will ever be able to do this, and if the rope is unwoven, he will lose his powers. Muskrat, the shaman's son, tries to imitate his father by holding a ceremony in the Shaking Tent but also fails. Meanwhile, Hannenorak is being taught by his grandfather, Habile-Chasseur, how to talk – and listen – to the animals and to nature, the wind, for instance. Hannenorak learns his lessons well. For now, however, there still is no wind.

The chief, Adario, is so desperate that he offers the hand of his daughter Ondaacha to whichever man in the village can bring back the wind. But even the desire of these young men has disappeared. Suddenly, the eagle swoops down, grabs the braided rope from the shaking tent, and transports it to Hannenorak. He tells him that destiny has chosen him – he will be the one to bring back the wind. How? asks Hannenorak. Consult your friends, the animals, answers the eagle. And so Hannenorak does, whereupon the animals – fox, bear, wolf, and so on – each offer their suggestions. The mole proposes to make a circle with a rope. Our culture, after all, is based on the circle, he says. Hannenorak heeds him. With this lasso, he ropes in the wind and brings it back to the village, together with the wind's child. Thus does he win the hand of Ondaacha. And all ends happily.

Two factors take pride of place here. One is, again, the partnership of man and nature. The other is the hero myth. The Greeks have theirs in Heracles and Odysseus, the Romans in Hercules and Ulysses, the Babylonians in Gilgamesh, the Germanic peoples in Thor. This book, based loosely, apparently, on an actual hero myth of the Wendat people, is one proof of many that the Indigenous people of North America, too, have their hero myths, another piece of evidence asserting that theirs, too, are genuine cultures.

Yawendara et la forêt des Têtes-Coupées

LOUIS-KARL PICARD-SIOUI

Wendat from Wendake First Nation, QC

Published in 2005

The father of a Wendat girl disappears. Yawendara, ten years old, goes off looking for him. With the help of her dog, Shiwou, her grandmother, and the animals of the forest in which she lives – and with much difficulty – she eventually finds him and brings him home. It is a magical coming-of-age, quest story that has great mythical resonance.

Yawendara lives with her family in a village in "*la forêt des Têtes-Coupées*" (the forest of the headless ones). This forest is a mythical place that existed before first contact in what is now the province of Quebec. Unfortunately, it has been taken over by an evil spirit named *Fils-d'Areskwe* (Son of Areskwe). Each autumn, Fils-d'Areskwe exacts human tribute from the village – he eats people. If he doesn't get them, he will destroy the village or maybe the entire forest. In fact, this is how Yawendara's mother and father both meet their end. And it is why she is now in the care of her grandmother. At harvest time, she goes into the forest to offer herself as tribute. Everyone, including the animals, is sick with worry. Fils-d'Areskwe and his horde of cannibals, the Têtes-Coupées, will surely eat her. One night in a dream, Yawendara comes upon a council of animals who are trying to figure out how to rid the forest of the headless ones. Led by *Petite-Tortue* (Little Tortoise), they have decided that *l'Homme Lumière* (Man of Light) is the only one who can vanquish Fils-d'Areskwe and thus return the forest to its natural state. But l'Homme Lumière has gone missing. No one can find him, not even after the council of animals sends first Deer then Bear then Wolf to go off and bring him back. Like l'Homme Lumière, all go missing. Finally, Yawendara herself is assigned by Petite-Tortue and the council to go out and find the three lost animals. After many wrong turns, Yawendara and her faithful dog, Shiwou, find them. And together, they find l'Homme Lumière, who gives Yawendara a magic kernel of corn that lights up with power when it is needed. Thus armed, they find the terrifying Fils-d'Areskwe. Yawendara confronts him. Boldly – though frightened half to death – she tells him that there will be no more human tribute. There is a terrible moment when Yawendara comes very close to losing her life. Fortunately, at the last second, she remembers to hold out the kernel of corn, which lights up magically. And wonder of wonders, Fils-d'Areskwe falls prostrate and reveals himself to be none other than Sastaretsi, Yawendara's father. It turns out that he had been cursed by an evil spirit to assume the shape of a monster and destroy the world.

What rage at colonization or disempowerment as there is in this novel is presented in the guise of a girl who is angry at the loss of her parents and her community. Far from letting this rage destroy her, however, she turns it to fuel. And with this fuel, she propels herself to action – she finds her father and heals her community. She acts against her disempowerment and transforms it to hope.

Natanis

CHRISTINE SIOUI WAWANOLOATH

Abenaki and Wendat from Wendake First Nation,
Odanak First Nation, and Montreal, QC

Published in 2005

Natanis, an Abenaki boy, lives in a village near the mouth of a river that much later will be called the St. Francis River. A tributary of the St. Lawrence River on its south side halfway between Montreal and Quebec City, it is where the Abenaki First Nation called Odanak stands today. Natanis meets the Megumowesos, the little magic people that populate his people's dream world. Known as Memegwesi in Ojibwa and similar names in other Algonquian nations, they are as real to Indigenous people as leprechauns are to the Irish, trolls to Scandinavians, elves to the Germans, fairies to the English, and angels to Christians. They exist "in reality" in the sense that they inhabit a society's collective subconscious which, of course, is where lives mythology.

One day, Natanis's best friend, a girl named Popokua (Cranberry, in Abenaki) falls ill with a fever. This leaves Natanis to play in the forest around their village alone, which makes him unhappy. Eventually, he lies down to rest and falls asleep. Some time later, he wakes up to the sound and sight of a little man the height of a corncob. The man complains that Natanis, in lying on his pipe and flute, has broken them. So he shrinks the boy to his size and takes him on the back of a turtle to the little man's village. Once there, Natanis's capturer gives him the materials to make a new pipe and flute. Natanis does. When he finishes, he meets the other village inhabitants, among them a boy named Kinus and his sister, Quasis. Taking a shine to him, Kinus and Quasis take him on a tour of the environs. They show him how to pick berries that are larger than they are, how to use mushrooms as cushions for pogo sticks, and so on. Along the way, they meet animals. At day's end, Natanis has to go back to his own village. He does this on the back of a crow, though not before receiving a little magic flute from Kinus and Quasis's mother, Mamijola. When he gets home, he takes a nap, from which he wakes back in his natural size. The only proof that he has been where he has been is the little magic flute. And this he gives to Popokua as a gift.

Again – as happens almost always in Indigenous literature, whether for children or adults – people and animals talk to each other. They talk to nature and nature talks to them. The partnership between man and nature is so pronounced, in fact, that the European language, French, in this case, gets in the way – because, precisely, that partnership cannot be expressed in any European language. Nonetheless, this is a fairy tale invented by the author based on certain elements of her people's age-old mythology. As with fairy tales in all cultures, it expresses the most beautiful part of a people's collective dream world. If *Alice in Wonderland*, for example, can become part of a culture's popular mythology, then why can't this novel, which, in a manner very similar, is set inside a dream?

Popokua

CHRISTINE SIOUI WAWANOLOATH

Abenaki and Wendat from Wendake First Nation,
Odanak First Nation, and Montreal, QC
Published in 2008

Popokua, the Abenaki girl who was friends with Natanis in this author's earlier book, makes friends in this story with a strange old man who shares his wisdom with her before he dies. The story is set in the same place and time, in a village near the mouth of a river in what today is the Abenaki First Nation called Odanak.

Crow and Pine Tree are talking to each other about their friendship. They also talk about the creatures, including humans, in the forest around them, over whom they have watched since time immemorial. Suddenly, one of them sees Popokua going off into the forest alone. The girl, an artist, is going off to collect clay and argillite for her pottery. En route, she talks to Crow, who is worried she might get lost. In spite of this concern, the bird can do nothing to prevent her getting waylaid by three Memegwesi, the little people of the Abenaki dream world. They lead her off to the isolated cabin of a monster – or what rumour has it is a monster. The "monster" is an old man named Odaskwin; legend has it that he has horns on his head and tree branches for arms. Because of his appearance, he was long ago evicted from the village and told never to return. Through the years, his myth has grown to the point where he really *is* a monster. If anything, the old man enjoys making himself look even scarier. Much to the surprise of the three mischief-makers, Popokua makes friends with Odaskwin. She tells him the people need him for his wisdom. Developing a relationship of, in effect, granddaughter and grandfather, they have conversations about life and nature and related subjects. But then she has to leave, though not before she places an argillite necklace of her own making around his neck as a gift. She also promises that she will be back the next day with her best friend, the boy Natanis, and her mother, Pemega. Touched to the quick and alone once more, the old man lies down to sleep – and dies. Thereupon the Little People materialize to carry his body off to the spirit world, their way lit by fireflies. When Popokua shows up the next day, there is no Odaskwin, no cabin, no Little People, nothing. The only thing left is their tittering in the surrounding forest, a sound which, in reality, is the rustling of leaves in the trees. And Popokua plays her magic flute for her friend, the flute which the Memegwesi had given to her friend, Natanis, in the last story.

As with *Natanis*, this is a fairy tale invented by the author based on certain elements of her people's ages-old mythology. The writing and book illustrations are based in an intimate knowledge of the mythology of the Abenaki and echo an oral storytelling tradition. As with all of the Indigenous authors profiled here, the author presents her work, rich in philosophy, imagination, and Indigenous ancestral values of the Indigenous people, in this case, passed on to the next generation through the written word.

L'ours et la femme venus des étoiles

CHRISTINE SIOUI WAWANOLOATH

Abenaki and Wendat from Wendake First Nation,
Odanak First Nation, and Montreal, QC

Published in 2009

The novel's premise is that there once was a time when beings from the sky would come down to Earth to escape danger. Accordingly, it recounts the tale of a little bear named Awassos who falls from the sky to Earth, has various adventures, and meets a human woman who also once fell from the sky. They fall in love, start a family, and found a new race of people.

A mother bear gives birth to a little bear she names Awassos. But then she realizes that a hunter who is in love with the morning star will come after him because the baby bear's fur is made of starlight. She decides, therefore, to send the cub down to Earth for his safety. There, magical creatures made of transparent, undulating light shelter such refugees, and this they do for Awassos. With time, however, Awassos transforms from a sky creature into an Earth creature. This makes it impossible for him to return home. Undaunted, he goes out hunting for a means to find his way home. On this journey, he meets all kinds of creatures, many refugees from the sky like himself. First, he meets a little white spruce tree who once was stardust, fallen from the sky to escape the maw of a celestial eagle. So many other star creatures have followed the little spruce tree's example that together they have formed an entire forest. Awassos next comes upon a rock who is angry because, in falling from the sky as part of a meteor, he has become detached from his family. A spider tells Awassos that the only way to make the rock regain happiness is to roll him back to the place where his family rests. The little bear does so. Then he moves on, gets tired, and lies down to sleep, only to awaken the next morning when some birds, mistaking him for a bush, try to build a nest on him. He learns that he has reached the ocean, a destination he had craved since the start of his journey. And the birds tell him that they have seen a creature like him.

Except that she is female. And human. He asks them to take him to her and they do. They fly while he swims across the ocean to reach the island where this woman lives. Awassos gets cold. The woman, Mkuigo, tells him to sleep in order to keep warm, and so Awassos becomes the first bear to hibernate in winter. Through the course of that season, though, Awassos transforms into a human. He and Mkuigo fall in love, start a family, and found a new race of people to populate the land where they live – until they die of old age. And to this day, there remains an island in the sea not far from the land of the Abenaki (meaning the "people of the dawn") that is shaped like a bear enlaced with a woman.

This is a creation myth that the author herself has created using elements from her people's mythology. As such, it explains the origins of the Abenaki culture. As the creation myths of many Indigenous people, and with them their languages, have disappeared, writers like this one have been obliged to piece things together to try to preserve at least some of the elements of those stories. In doing so, she reconstructs the beauty of her people. So long as these stories and their languages exist – for she uses Abenaki language, if sparingly – the people they speak of will live, she seems to be saying. So long as their "song" remains, they will nullify the colonized status that once was their lot.

EPILOGUE

Besides the 176 works herein cited, another hundred could easily have been added. Included here is a sampling only of what's been published by what I call the first wave of Indigenous Canadian writers. And I say *published* because unpublished work easily adds another hundred to that number; for example, many plays that have been produced but not published (although in the works surveyed here I make two exceptions with the play *Son of Ayash*, by northwestern Ontario's Jim Morris, because of the seminal importance that story has to our people; it is our Gilgamesh, our Odyssey, and *Aitskenanadahate: voyage au pays des morts*, in order to beef up the presence, in this celebration, of Indigenous literature in French). To include all these works, in any case, would have taken me another five years of work, five years I don't have.

Another element that precludes a comprehensive study? The fact that some of the writers whose works are featured are so prolific that to include *all* their works would inflate this volume to double its thickness. And extend its writing, again, to another five years.

As for the inclusion of all those works published up to the year of the publication of *this* book – that is, up to 2017 – that, again, would be impossible for, since that "first wave," there has been an explosion of productivity, of creativity, an explosion that, within the next thirty years, will have tripled the output of Indigenous literature in this country. Suffice it to say that that first wave pried open the floodgates. And there is no stopping the deluge. In fact, if another Indigenous writer as foolish as yours truly ever does a similar "celebration" of that "second wave" come the year 2040, he or she better be ready to work for ten years solid toward its completion; there will be *that* much of it.

This, in any case, is a sampling substantial enough to give readers an idea of what is out there, of what is happening in the field of Indigenous literature in Canada, to give them an idea of the substance and scope of the work that has been written and published by Canada's Indigenous writers in the period herein specified. And it will give them a hint, moreover, of the work these and more Indigenous writers will be producing in the second three decades (from 2010 to 2040) as part of that "second wave." But some four hundred works that exist now when, as little as thirty years ago, there were less than twenty? A remarkable achievement, one has to admit!

Still, let us take a look at the series of questions that were posed in the prologue to this book and see where their answers have gotten us.

What happened here? Well, some four hundred books were written, in French, English, Cree, Innu, and other Indigenous languages by Canada's Aboriginals.

Why that period? This literature was born as a reaction to three seminal events in our recent history: (1) the Canadian government giving us the right to vote in federal elections in 1960, (2) Norval Morrisseau's first exhibition of paintings in 1962, and (3) the White Paper of 1969, the upshot of which was that the special status of Indigenous people in this country was about to be extinguished; we were to be assimilated into the dominant society. In effect, we were about to disappear.

Why that voice, that culture, that literature? Because that voice, that culture, that literature (that is, oral literature) had either been silenced by the dominant society. Or had been ignored, that is, had never been given a chance to express itself.

What previously had quietened that voice? Some five hundred years of victimization by the forces of colonization.

What is it beginning to say, what is its point, its objective? It is saying that we as a people have a literary tradition that is every bit as rich and as powerful as those found in any other country or culture the whole world over. And it bears – no, demands – listening to because it has things of vital importance to say.

Where is it going? Simply put, it is going to save the planet from the Armageddon it is heading straight for.

What has it accomplished? By adding Indigenous subject matter into the curriculum of Canadian educational institutions at all levels, it is keeping Indigenous youth in school. Prior to this, quitting school after grade five and thus falling back on a lifetime of welfare was one of the only alternatives, suicide out of sheer despair the too-frequent final outcome. Since its acknowledgment by schools, this literature has raised the level of literacy and education in Indigenous communities across the country. And in so doing, newly skilled workers such as these graduates are renewing economic development in their communities thus making them healthier, thus making them stronger, thus giving them *and* their residents a viable future.

Has it made a difference in Canadian society, in Canadian thinking, in the life of Canada? If so, what? In what way, what form? We still have a long way to go, it goes without saying, but what this literature has done so far is create more and more functional Indigenous individuals every year, people who have become proud representatives of their country. Today, quite frankly, the "national" – indeed "international" – image of the "drunken Indian" has been, and is being, replaced by images of doctors, dentists, lawyers, entrepreneurs, architects, educators – when I was growing up in northern Manitoba, an Indigenous teacher was unheard of – including many university professors, internationally renowned fashion designers, sports personalities, artists, writers, musicians, actors. Today, we have world-famous stars who get nominated for Academy Awards in Hollywood. Making Indigenous kids very, very proud of who they are. And giving them dreams they *know* can be realized. Without the existence of that literature, this wouldn't have happened.

Beyond that, has it changed the way the world thinks of itself and of its inhabitants, its land, its environment?

If any one element ties all these works together, if any one theme holds the entire body of work together, it is the circle, the circle of the goddess, the circle of matriarchy, the circle of nature, the circle of the Earth.

Because the essence of what happened in 1492 is that the straight line of monotheism punctured the circle of pantheism; the phallus of a one-god system (and a male one, at that) pierced the womb of a system based on nature-as-female. And shattered it. Leaving us Indigenous writers with three important tasks on our hands: either to bend the erection of that phallus into a curve – erections, after all, can last for only so long, and two thousand years might just be enough – *or*, second, to cut it off entirely (which is what happens in my play *Rose*, if read as allegory). Third, our job is to repair that circle, reconnect the gaping holes that were slashed out by what must surely be the most spectacular act of rape in the history of the universe ... before it's too late.

This literature has assisted in the process whereby the world has changed dramatically, in the latter half of the twentieth century in particular, *vis-à-vis* its thinking on gender, just for instance. Because the knowledge that Indigenous languages have no gender has come out of the closet, a reassessment has occurred as to the position of women and transgendered people in the great circle of life, right down to construction of public washrooms for three genders in ever more public venues. And the right of same-sex couples to marry and adopt children. I mean, think of it: why is 95 percent of our prison population heterosexual and male? Because that population comes from totally and utterly dysfunctional, in too many cases horrifying, violence-shattered, heterosexual marriages. There are alternatives, this literature is saying – there exist, for example, more than just two genders in human society.

Questions on climate change – indeed on the preservation of the planet – have been ushered into the circle by Indigenous thinkers when formerly, with European/Christian thinking, the environment was excluded from the straight line of phallic monotheism. Before the emergence of this literature, it had never entered Western minds for even one second that God, at one point in human history, might have been a woman. And might be again. Spirituality, oneness with the Earth-as-garden, even the value of laughter, these too, have been brought back into that circle by this literature. "Taking back our spirits" – all of our spirits, not just Indigenous people's – is what this literature is about. *How, kaachimoostaatinaawow* (I'll tell you a story) ...

Sixty years ago when I was a child in northern Manitoba, that north was heaven. I grew up in a garden of Eden, a garden of the most extraordinary beauty, the most extraordinary joy. If a forest fire happened, one – *one* – would happen perhaps once a decade. If that. And they were minor conflagrations compared to what is happening today. Now, sixty years later, dozens, perhaps even hundreds, of forest fires slash their way across northern Manitoba every summer. It is no longer safe to live up there, not for humans, not for animals. In my day, emergency airlifts were unheard of. Now they are routine – entire communities flown by bush plane to safety in the south. And that's just northern Manitoba. Forest fires clean across the country have already started entering urban centres such as Kelowna, British Columbia; Slave Lake, Alberta; Leaf Rapids, Manitoba; Fort McMurray, Alberta. And it is only a matter of time before they reduce to ashes all of Muskoka,* the Banff National Park, Thunder Bay, North Bay, Ottawa, Toronto, Los Angeles. Northern Manitoba should be declared a national park, a UNESCO World Heritage Site, before it ends up a desert. For if the Amazon jungle is the lung of the southern hemisphere, then the forests of Canada's north are the lung of the northern hemisphere. And our children will need that oxygen to feed *their* lungs. Time is of the essence. Georgian Bay is disappearing, Lake Huron with it – in the sixteen years from 1998 to 2013, that lake alone has gone down about two metres in depth, and it's not stopping. If there is going to be a Muskoka and a Georgian Bay, let alone a planet, left for your children and their children – and their children and children's children – then our thinking has got to change dramatically in the next few decades. Nature must be brought back to life. It must be given its soul back, the one that got taken away from it in that fabled story of eviction from the garden, a story that, by the way, is far from universal. The goddess must be saved before her husband beats her to death, it is as simple as that. And this is what we Indigenous writers, as a collective voice, in one way or other, are saying. To our country. And to the world.

How, keetawm kaachimoostaatinaawow (I'll tell you a story again). *Kayaas, igoospeek kagee-awaaseewiyaan, ootee waathow keeweet'nook Manitoba kaa-ichigaateek aski, keegaach mawch awinuk maana keen'tayschooloo-oo. N'paapaa, n'maamaa, nimoosoom, noogoom, apoochiga nimis igwa nistees mawachi kaak'seewee-ayawichik, mawch keen'tayschooloo-iwuk. Oosaam waathow keeweet'nook eegee-ayaa-ak, kapee maana eegeep'mooteewee-aak, eemaachiyaak, eewanee-eegiyaak, eepagitawaa-ak. Igwa ithigook waathow saawaanook maana eegaa-ayaag'wow igoospeek ischooliwa. Apoochiga kees-pin keen'taytheetaag'wow tantay-schooliwichik, mawch tageegaskeetaawuk. Igwaani, mawch awinuk keeschooloo-oo igoospeek, mawch awinuk keegaskeetow taagathaaseemoot. Nigeegeenee-hithiwaanaan maana poogoo, igaachi nigee-oocheepawnee-imoonaan. Maw maa-a nigeegathaaseemoonaan. Anooch maa-a igwa peetoos. Neet'naan ooskip'maat'suk, neet'naan igwa nigeeschooliwinaan athis p'mithaagaana igwa igootee waathow keeweet'nook eesithaag'wow. Athis waathow keeweet'nook eesithaag'wow igwa oo-oo p'mithaagaana, nigaskeetaanaan igwa neet'naan tantayschooliweeyaak. Igoochi anooch kaageesigaak kaagaskee-taa-ak tagathaasimooyaak taayameechigiyaak meena. Taamasinaa-igiyaak meena. Igoochi meena igwa mawaachi kaatigaskeetaa-ak taweecheewaa-ag'wow n'tooteeminawuk maawachi kwayas tagaskeetaachik tapami-isoochik. Igoochi kaamasinaa-igeeyaak. How, n'gagaatheeseemoon igwa …*

Now sign here with an *X*: _____
Thank you. You've just signed your house away. When can I move in?

You see? It's all in the perspective. It's all in who is writing. About whom. And in what language …

---

* For those not familiar with the province of Ontario, Muskoka is a region that is known for the stunning beauty of its lakes and maple forests. A mere two-hour drive north of Toronto, it has become, over the years, an idyllic summer playground for the well-heeled of Canada's largest city – its hundreds of cottages, many of them palaces, are legendary. Pity that it is about to go up in flames.

ACKNOWLEDGMENTS

The list of people without whose help this book would never have been written is very long. I'm always wary of this exercise – that is, of listing the names – because, no matter what I do, I will always miss someone. But here goes …

Adolphe Bighetty, Delphine Bighetty, Doris Bighetty, Madeline Bighetty, Philip Bighetty, Denise Bolduc, Wayne Booker, Di Brandt, Linda Burridge, Dieter Buse, Judith Buse, Warren Cariou, Rod Clarke, Shirley Clarke, Marilyn Dumont, Renata Eigenbrod, Hilma Fiedler, Peter Globensky, Scott Grills, Louise Bernice Halfe, Daniel Highway, Raymond Highway, Jeanette Highway, Britney Highway, Greg Hill, Chris Hurt, Keith Hyde, Edwin Jebb, Jan Johnson, Stuart Kallio, Pia Kleber, Pat Lacroix, Raymond Lalonde, Richard Lalonde, Ann Lepage, Billy Linklater, Bryan Loucks, Lorraine Mayer, Mary Jane McCallum, Pat McGuire, Sam McKechnie, Brian Merasty, David Merasty, Glen Merasty, Jean-Baptiste Merasty Sr., Louise Merasty, Therese Merasty Sr., Daniel David Moses, Bernice Olson, Noah Para, Ron Phillips, Louisette Pringault, David Ray, Carmen Robertson, Rosa Roig, Armand Garnet Ruffo, Beverly Sabourin, Cecil Sanderson, Agnes St. Pierre, Sara Samuel, Linda Sanderson, Naomi Sarrazin, Mario Scattoloni, Regina Schuller, Gregory Scofield, Danielle Seguin, Kia Skalesky, Brenda Small, Carol Steele, Shirley Stevens, John Stone, Michel Surroca, Michele Surroca, Gabe Vadas and the Norval Morrisseau Estate, Ellen Gould Ventura, and Kevin Williams.

As for institutions, the list includes Algonquin College (Ottawa), Brandon University, Carleton University (Ottawa), Confederation College (Thunder Bay), Lakehead University (Thunder Bay), Mount Royal University (Calgary), National Archives of Canada (Ottawa), Native Earth Performing Arts (Toronto), Ontario Arts Council (Toronto), University College of the North (The Pas, Manitoba), University of Alberta (Edmonton), University of British Columbia (Kelowna campus), University of Calgary, University of Guelph, University of Manitoba (Winnipeg), and University of Ottawa.

In fact, this project started off, away back in the spring of 2007, as a research project at Confederation College, Thunder Bay, in the name of the advancement of Indigenous education and literacy and under the leadership of Brenda Small, Director of Neeganeewin College, and Peter Globensky. And of the two research assistants they hired for it, the author owes a very special thanks to his dear friend and colleague, Ryan Duplassie.

An earlier version of the prologue was published in *Twenty-First Century Perspectives on Indigenous Studies: Native North America in (Trans) Motion*, edited by Birgit Däwes, Karsten Fitz, and Sabine N. Meyer (New York: Routledge, 2015).

And last, of course, come my esteemed editors, Ann-Marie Metten, Jordan Abel, Tilman Lewis, and Chloë Filson, and to the book's designer, Les Smith. *Kwayas mistaa-i kinanaa-skoomiti-naawow, niweechee-waaganuk.*

GLOSSARY

This glossary focuses on key terms related to Indigenous storytelling as well as to political events in the experience of colonization.

Bill C-31. According to the Indian Act, which came into effect in 1876, there are two kinds of Indian: status and non-status. Status Indians are registered members of an Indian band whose members – or rather whose ancestors – signed a treaty with the Crown of England through the Government of Canada. As such, they have a right to live on a reserve and enjoy certain rights and privileges such as free health care, free dental care, free education (including university tuition), and tax exemptions. In fact, strictly speaking, that status Indian *should* live on that reserve. Non-status Indians, on the other hand, are not registered with the federal government or with an Indian band that signed a treaty with the Crown and thus have no right to live on a reserve or enjoy its privileges. According to this Act, a status Indigenous woman lost her status when she married a white man or a non-status Indian. Thus, strictly speaking, she lost her right to live on her home reserve together with the aforementioned rights and privileges. Conversely, when a non-Indigenous woman or a non-status Indigenous woman married a status Indian, she automatically became an Indian in the eyes of the law – *she* had the right to live on that reserve and enjoy certain rights and privileges. Bill C-31 changed all that. Enacted in 1985, it gave the status Indigenous woman the right to keep her status when she married a white man or a non-status Indian. Since 1985, however, an Indian woman has retained her status, as have her children and those children's children – who often are referred to as "Bill C-31 children," named after the new law's designation: Bill C-31.

Helen Betty Osborne. A young Cree woman from the Norway House First Nation in mid-north Manitoba. On the evening of November 17, 1971, when she was seventeen, she was abducted by four non-Indigenous men in the railway town of The Pas, Manitoba, where she attended high school. They then drove her forty kilometres north, dragged her into a forest, and raped her by ramming a screwdriver fifty-six times up her vagina. Then they left her in the snow to bleed to her death. For sixteen years, the case went ignored by the authorities. And when it finally did come up for investigation, only one of the men was indicted. He got one year in prison.

Loup-Garou. The is a figure that exists in the mythology, and therefore the dream world, of many Indigenous peoples, in the west especially. A kind of werewolf – that is, a creature half man and half wolf – his appearance will frequently presage a death. The word has French and, before that, pre-Christian European roots. The word *loup* – pronounced with a silent *p* as in "loo"– is French for "wolf." As for *garou*, it means "man" in an artful melding of ancient English, French, and other northern European languages, thus bringing us to the notion of "wolf/man."

Medicine Wheel. A circle the inside of which is divided into four equal-sized segments each representing: (a) a direction from the physical world and, (b) a slice of human, and humane, spiritual value. In order, these segments go: the east (illumination), the south (humility and trust), the west (honesty), and the north (wisdom). Used for astronomical, ritual, healing, and teaching purposes, these four inner circles, so to speak, are also referred to as "sacred hoops."

Memegwesi. The Little People of Ojibwa mythology are known as *Meme-kwesiwak* in Cree, *Memequasit* in Ojibwa, they are, literally, tiny, little people the size of dwarfs. Or five-year-old children. Central characters in these people's mythologies, in effect they are extensions of the power of the natural world. As such, they appear to traverse, with complete freedom, the border between reality and dream, just as angels do in Christian mythology. The Little People appear to humans when the moment is propitious. They live in trees, rocks, and even ice; the rustle of leaves touched by a breeze, even the cracking and crackling of ice in spring happens when these creatures

From **Oral** to **Written**

giggle. They also exist in most Indigenous North American mythologies that I know of as, in fact, they once did in Celtic (leprechauns), Nordic (trolls), and other pre-Christian European mythologies. The difference between the European and Indigenous North American situations, however, is that the European narrative tradition was effectively reduced to folk tale and thus to irrelevance by the sweeping power of Christian mythology. Meanwhile the Indigenous North American tradition is still very much alive, at least in certain Indigenous communities.

Midewiwin Society. An informal organization made up of men and women who practise medicine. They deal with healing herbs and plants and conduct the sacred ceremonies of the Ojibwa people, the sweat lodge, for instance. Priests of a sort, they connect their communities with the Great Spirit, that is, with god as they understand him or her. In other words, they care for the spiritual health of their communities. The key ingredient, or "seed," in the term "Midewiwin" is "mede" which, in the language of the Anishnabe, is pronounced "meh-deh," somewhere halfway between "midi" and "may day." The word meaning "heart," the term "midewiwin" is therefore sometimes translated into English as "the way of the heart." Still, there are those who would take this notion one step further, thus arriving at the more arcane translation, "the spiritual mystery." The heart and the spirit, after all, have always had an association close enough in the human imagination to make them next to indistinguishable. Does love come from the heart? Or does it come from the spirit? Or does it come from both? The final problem being one that has always confounded all translators – there are words and ideas in all languages that ultimately cannot be translated, at least not in a manner adequate enough to please all people.

Oka Crisis. The Mohawk standoff at Oka, Quebec, against the Canadian army over the building of a golf course on their people's burial grounds. It began in mid-July 1990 and lasted for seventy-eight days, galvanizing Indigenous groups across Canada in support and solidarity.

Residential School. For more than a century, beginning in the 1870s and continuing until the 1980s, Indian residential schools separated more than 150,000 Indigenous children from their families and communities.

Many of the books in this survey reflect on and work to heal the effects of displacement, colonization, and abuse that happened at these schools.

Sixties Scoop. Indigenous children being taken from their families by the federal government and placed in white foster homes to receive "better" raising has come to be known, over the years, as the Sixties Scoop. It is known as such because the majority of adoptions happened in the 1960s, although the government policy continued into the 1980s. According to Origins Canada, a volunteer-run organization serving people across Canada who have been separated from family members by adoption, statistics from Indigenous and Northern Affairs Canada reveal a total of 11,132 status Indian children adopted between the years of 1960 and 1990.

Trickster. The dream world of North American mythology is inhabited by the most fantastic creatures, beings, and events. Foremost among these beings is the Trickster, as pivotal a figure in the Indigenous world as Christ is in the realm of Christian mythology. *Weesageechak* in Cree – though there are different spellings depending on the dialect – *Nanabush* in Ojibway (ditto), *Raven* on the West Coast, *Glooscap* on the East, *Coyote* on the plains, *Iktomi* among the Dakota/Lakota of the north-central United States and the southern edge of the Prairie provinces, this figure goes by many names and many guises. In fact, he can assume any guise she chooses (in the Indigenous languages, there is no gender, hence this flip-flop). Essentially a comic, clownish character who plays tricks on people – just like God, it might be said – he teaches us about the nature and the meaning of existence on the planet, which, first and foremost, is to laugh and laugh like mad. She straddles the consciousness of Man and that of God, the Great Spirit.

His incarnation as Coyote has a visual form, as she does as Raven, as he does as *Iktomi* – a spider – among the Lakota/Dakota. But other than that, he has never been anthropomorphized, just as with the *Weetigo*, just as, for that matter, with the Great Spirit, with God. He has never been invested with the image of a man or a woman in the human imagination, not as has the Christian God who we all tend to think of as a bearded old man with a thunderbolt in hand, for instance, or the Greek trickster-god, Hermes, with his winged sandals or, in that same world,

From **Oral** to **Written**

Pan with his goat's legs and horns. In the pantheistic – as opposed to monotheistic or polytheistic – context dream world that is the collective Indigenous subconscious, the Trickster is simply a bolt of energy, as with electricity, that shoots its way through the universe animating everything and everyone it passes through. So that when the impulse to laugh, and laugh hysterically, hits you in the gut, the bolt of electricity known to us Indigenous people as the Trickster has just zoomed through you. The phenomenon, that is to say, can be proven scientifically. Biologically and quantum-physically.

Still, the most important feature about this remarkable being is the fact that she is insane beyond insane. In fact, the more outrageous the humour or situation he can cause, the happier she is. Meaning to say that if he is the avatar of God's presence here on Earth, then God, in Indigenous mythology, laughs. And laughs like crazy. By comparison, when was the last time you heard the Christian God laugh? Which is where the qualitative – and quantitative – difference between English and Cree, to name but one Indigenous language, originates when it comes to the matter of laughter. In the real world, you notice it the second you enter Indigenous company for, when you do, the laughter quotient triples. And madness is king.

Two-Spirits. People who are both male and female simultaneously. Men who have the souls of women and women who have the souls of men, they had a special place in the matriarchal circle of life. As healers, artists, magicians, visionaries, priests-of-a-sort, they were the people who added the colours of the rainbow to the black-and-white, violence-ridden, and very boring world of heterosexuality. And because the Indigenous languages have no gender – there is no "he" and no "she," just "he/she" (in a sense) – then God not only is female but assumes, on that circle, elements of the masculine as well. Ultimately, the subject needs ten thick books to address in a manner remotely adequate.

Wesakechak. The Cree trickster whose name has many spellings; for example, "Wee-sa-kay-jac" for the Sandy Lake Cree. The Trickster is known by many other names in other cultures; for example, Nanabush in Ojibwa, Glooscap in Mi'kmaq, Raven, Coyote, and so on. The antics of this cosmic clown keep life interesting for his friends those humans.

White Paper of 1969. Officially entitled Statement of the Government of Canada on Indian policy, the 1969 White Paper was a policy paper that proposed ending the special legal relationship between Aboriginal peoples and the Canadian state and dismantling the Indian Act. This White Paper advocated all-out assimilation for Indigenous people and was soundly rejected by Indigenous people across Canada. All this without consulting them.

PUBLICATION HISTORY

Akiwenzie-Damm, Kateri. *My Heart Is a Stray Bullet.* Neyaashiinigmiing, ON: Kegedonce Press, 1993, 2002.

Alexie, Robert Arthur. *Porcupines and China Dolls.* Toronto: Stoddart, 2002. Republished Penticton, BC: Theytus, 2009.

Alfred, Taiaiake. *Peace, Power, Righteousness: An Indigenous Manifesto.* Don Mills, ON: Oxford University Press, 1999.

Anderson, Kim. *A Recognition of Being: Reconstructing Native Womanhood.* Toronto: Second Story, 2000.

Antane Kapesh, An (Anne André). *Je suis une maudite sauvagesse / Eukuan nin matshimanitu Innu-Iskueu.* Montreal: Lémeac, 1976.

———. *Qu'as-tu fait de mon pays?* Ottawa: Éditions impossibles, 1979.

Armstrong, Jeannette. *Slash.* Penticton, BC: Theytus, 1985.

———. *Whispering in Shadows.* Penticton, BC: Theytus, 2000.

Arnott, Joanne. *Wiles of Girlhood.* Vancouver: Press Gang, 1991.

Arthurson, Wayne. *Fall from Grace.* New York: Forge, 2011.

———. *Final Season.* Saskatoon: Thistledown, 2002.

Assiniwi, Bernard. *Le bras coupé.* Montreal: Lémeac, 1976.

———. *Ikwé : la femme algonquienne.* Hull, QC: Vents d'ouest, 1998.

———. *L'Odawa Pontiac : l'amour et la guerre.* Montreal: XYZ, 1994.

———. *La saga des Béothuks.* Paris: Actes Sud and Montreal: Lémeac, 1996.

———. *Windigo et la naissance du monde.* Hull, QC: Éditions vents d'ouest, 1998.

Bacon, Joséphine. *Batons à message / Tshissinuatshitakana.* Montreal: Mémoire d'encrier, 2009. Translated by Phyllis Aronoff as *Message Sticks.* Toronto: TSAR, 2013.

Baker, Marie Annharte (Annharte). *Being on the Moon.* Winlaw, BC: Polestar, 1990.

———. *Exercises in Lip Pointing.* Vancouver: New Star, 2003.

Baskin, Cyndy. *Sage.* Toronto: Sister Vision, 1999.

Blondin, George. *When the World Was New: Stories of the Sahtu Dene.* Yellowknife: Outcrop, 1990.

Bose, Chris. *Stone the Crow.* Neyaashiinigmiing, ON: Kegedonce Press, 2009.

Boudreau, Diane, ed. *Histoire de la littérature Amérindienne au Québec : oralité et écriture.* Montreal: L'hexagone, 1993.

Bussidor, Ila, and Üstün Bilgen-Reinart. *Night Spirits: The Story of the Relocation of the Sayisi Dene.* Winnipeg: University of Manitoba Press, 1997.

Campbell, Maria. *Halfbreed.* Toronto: McClelland and Stewart, 1973.

Cardinal, Harold. *The Unjust Society: The Tragedy of Canada's Indians.* Edmonton: Hurtig, 1969.

Cercle d'écriture de Wendake. *Émergence, débâcle, et mots de givre.* Wendake, QC: Centre culturel Ti-Yarihuten, 2006.

———. *Où vont les vents …* Wendake, QC: Centre culturel Ti-Yarihuten, 2005.

Clements, Marie. *Burning Vision.* Vancouver: Talonbooks, 2003.

———. *Copper Thunderbird.* Vancouver: Talonbooks, 2007.

———. *The Unnatural and Accidental Women.* Vancouver: Talonbooks, 2005.

Clutesi, George. *Stand Tall, My Son.* Illustrated by the author and Mark Tebbutt. Port Alberni, BC: Clutesi Agencies, 1990.

Connolly, Jacinthe. *L'été de Takwakin.* Illustrated by Christine Sioui Wawanoloath. Wendake, QC: Conseil en éducation des Premières Nations, 2002. Also available in English as *Takwakín's Summer Journeys.* Wendake, QC: First Nations Education Council, 2002.

Coocoo, Charles. *Broderies sur mocassins.* Chicoutimi, QC: Éditions JCL, 1988.

Copway, George (Kahgegagahbowh). *The Traditional History and Characteristic Sketches of the Ojibway Nation.* London: C. Gilpin; Edinburgh: A. and C. Black; Dublin: J.B. Gilpin, 1850; Boston: B.B. Mussey, 1851.

Cuthand, Beth. *Voices in the Waterfall.* Vancouver: Lazara Press, 1989. Republished Penticton: Theytus, 1992, 2008.

Dandurand, Joseph A. *Looking into the Eyes of My Forgotten Dreams.* Neyaashiinigmiing, ON: Kegedonce Press, 1998.

———. *Please Do Not Touch the Indians.* Candler, NC: Renegade Planets, 2004.

Deerchild, Rosanna. *This Is a Small Northern Town*. Winnipeg: J. Gordon Shillingford / Muses' Co., 2008.

Dennis, Darrell. *Tales of an Urban Indian*. In *Darrell Dennis: Two Plays*. Toronto: Playwrights Canada Press, 2005.

———. *The Trickster of Third Avenue East*. In *Darrell Dennis: Two Plays*. Toronto: Playwrights Canada Press, 2005.

Désy, Jean, and Rita Mestokosho. *Uashtessiu / Lumière d'automne*. Montreal: Mémoire d'encrier, 2010.

Dickason, Olive Patricia, and Moira Jean Calder. *A Concise History of Canada's First Nations*. Toronto: Oxford University Press, 2006.

Dimaline, Cherie. *Red Rooms*. Penticton, BC: Theytus, 2007, 2011.

Dumont, Marilyn. *A Really Good Brown Girl*. London, ON: Brick Books, 1996, 2015.

———. *That Tongued Belonging*. Neyaashiinigmiing, ON: Kegedonce Press, 2007.

Episkenew, Jo-Ann. *Taking Back Our Spirits: Indigenous Literature, Public Policy, and Healing*. Winnipeg: University of Manitoba Press, 2009.

Favel, Floyd. *Lady of Silences*. In *Staging Coyote's Dream: An Anthology of First Nations Drama in English*, vol. 1. Edited by Ric Knowles and Monique Mojica. Toronto: Playwrights Canada Press, 2003.

Fife, Connie. *Beneath the Naked Sun*. Toronto: Sister Vision, 1992.

Flather, Patti, and Leonard Linklater. *Sixty Below*. In *Staging the North: Twelve Plays*. Edited by Sherrill Grace, Eve D'Aeth, and Lisa Chalykoff. Toronto: Playwrights Canada Press, 1999.

Freeman, Mini Aodla. *Life Among the Qallunaat*. Edmonton: Hurtig, 1978. Republished Winnipeg: University of Manitoba Press, 2015.

French, Alice. *My Name Is Masak*. Winnipeg: Peguis, 1976, 1992.

———. *The Restless Nomad*. Winnipeg: Pemmican, 1992, 1998.

Gatti, Maurizio, ed. *Littérature amérindienne du Québec : écrits de langue français*. Montreal: Éditions Hurtubise, 2004.

Gottfriedson, Garry. *Glass Tepee*. Regina: Thistledown, 2002.

———. *Skin Like Mine*. Vancouver: Ronsdale, 2010.

———. *Whiskey Bullets: Cowboy and Indian Heritage Poems*. Vancouver: Ronsdale, 2006.

Gummerson, Penny. *Wawatay*. Toronto: Playwrights Canada Press, 2005.

Halfe, Louise Bernice. *Bear Bones and Feathers.* Regina: Coteau, 1994.

———. *Blue Marrow.* Toronto: McClelland and Stewart, 1998. Republished Regina: Couteau, 2004, 2005.

———. *The Crooked Good.* Regina: Coteau, 2007.

Joe, Rita. *Lnu and Indians We're Called.* Charlottetown: Ragweed, 1991.

Joe, Rita, with Lynn Henry. *Song of Rita Joe: Autobiography of a Mi'kmaq Poet.* Charlottetown: Ragweed, 1996. Republished Wreck Cove, NS: Breton Books, 2011.

Johnson, E. Pauline. *Flint and Feather: The Complete Poems of E. Pauline Johnson (Tekahionwake).* First published Toronto & London: Musson Book Co., [1912] 1917; republished Toronto: Hodder and Stoughton, 1974.

Johnson, Harold. *Billy Tinker.* Saskatoon: Thistledown, 2001.

———. *Charlie Muskrat.* Saskatoon: Thistledown, 2008.

Johnston, Basil. *Indian School Days.* Toronto: Key Porter, 1988.

———. *Moose Meat and Wild Rice.* Toronto: McClelland and Stewart, 1978, 1987.

———. *Ojibway Heritage.* Toronto: McClelland and Stewart, 1976.

Jones, Peter (Kah-ke-wa-quo-nā-by). *Life and Journals of Kah-ke-wa-quo-nā-by (Rev. Peter Jones), Wesleyan Missionary.* Toronto: Missionary Committee, Canada Conference, 1860.

Josie, Edith. *Here Are the News.* Toronto: Clarke, Irwin, 1966.

Kane, Margo. *Moonlodge.* In *Singular Voices: Plays in Monologue Form.* Edited by Tony Hamill. Toronto: Playwrights Canada Press, 1994.

Kenny, George. *Indians Don't Cry.* Toronto: Chimo, 1977. Republished Toronto: NC Press, 1982. Translated by Patricia M. Ningewance as *Indians Don't Cry / Gaawiin mawisiiwag anishinaabeg.* Edited by Renate Eigenbrod. Winnipeg: University of Manitoba Press, 2014.

King, Thomas. *Green Grass, Running Water.* Toronto: HarperCollins, 1993, 2010.

———. *Medicine River.* Markham, ON: Viking, 1989, 1996, 2005.

———. *One Good Story, That One.* Toronto: HarperCollins, 1993.

———. *A Short History of Indians in Canada.* Toronto: HarperCollins, 2005.

———. *The Truth About Stories.* Toronto: House of Anansi, 2003.

———. *Truth and Bright Water.* Toronto: HarperCollins, 1999.

Kistabish, Richard (Ejinagosi). *Aki / Pour ceux qui aiment la terre.* Val-d'Or, QC: Conseil Algonquin de l'ouest du Quebec, 1986. Published in English as *For the World That Loves the Land.* Val-d'Or, QC: Algonquin Council of Western Quebec, 1988.

Kusugak, Michael. *The Curse of the Shaman: A Marble Island Story.* Illustrated by Vladyana Krykorka. Toronto: HarperTrophyCanada, 2006.

LaRoque (LaRocque), Emma. *Defeathering the Indian.* Agincourt, ON: Book Society of Canada, 1975.

Lawson, Sherry. *Don't Stand Too Close! You Might Get Some on You: More Lessons from My Life.* Orillia, ON: S. Lawson, 2008.

———. *I've Been Shot At, What's Your Excuse? Lessons from My Life.* Longford Mills, ON: S. Lawson, 2007.

Loring, Kevin. *Where the Blood Mixes.* Vancouver: Talonbooks, 2009.

Mahikan, Julian. *Le mutilateur.* Paris: Édilivre, 2008.

Manuel, Vera. *The Strength of Indian Women.* In *Two Plays About Residential School.* Vancouver: Living Traditions Writers Group, 1998. Reprinted Penticton, BC: Living Tradition, 2012.

Maracle, Brian. *Back on the Rez: Finding the Way Home.* Toronto: Viking, 1996.

———. *Crazywater: Native Voices on Addiction and Recovery.* Toronto: Viking, 1993, 1996, 1997.

Maracle, Lee. *Bobbi Lee: Indian Rebel.* Toronto: Women's Press, 1990, 1994.

———. *Daughters Are Forever.* Vancouver: Polestar, 2002.

———. *I Am Woman: A Native Perspective on Sociology and Feminism.* Vancouver: Write-on-Press, 1988. Republished Vancouver: Press Gang, 1996.

———. *Ravensong.* Vancouver: Press Gang, 1993.

———. *Sundogs.* Penticton, BC: Theytus, 1992.

———. *Will's Garden.* Penticton, BC: Theytus, 2002, 2008.

Mayer, Lorraine. *Cries from a Métis Heart.* Winnipeg: Pemmican, 2007, 2015.

McLeod, John. *Diary of a Crazy Boy.* (Toronto) *Theatrum* 19 (June/August 1990): S1–S11.

McLeod, Neal. *Cree Narrative Memory: From Treaties to Contemporary Times.* Saskatoon: Purich, 2007.

———. *Gabriel's Beach.* Regina: Hagios, 2008.

———. *Songs to Kill a Wîhtikow.* Regina: Hagios, 2005.

Mercredi, Duncan. *Wolf and Shadows*. Winnipeg: Pemmican, 1995.

Mercredi, Morningstar. *Morningstar: A Warrior's Spirit*. Regina: Coteau, 2006.

Mestokosho, Mathieu. *Récits de Mathieu Mestokosho, chasseur Innu*. Edited by Serge Bouchard. Montreal: Boréal, 2004, 2017.

Mestokosho, Rita. *Eshi Uapataman Nukum / Comment je perçois la vie, grand-mère*. Goteborg, Sweden: Beijbom, 2010. Translated by Sue Rose as *How I See Life, Grandmother*. Sweden: Beijbom, 2011.

Mojica, Monique. *Princess Pocahontas and the Blue Spots: Two Plays*. Toronto: Women's Press, 1991, 2011.

Morali, Laure, ed. *Aimititau! Parlons-nous!* Montreal: Mémoire d'encrier, 2008.

Morris, Jim. *Son of Ayash*. Unpublished manuscript. First produced at Sioux Lookout, Ontario, February 1982.

Moses, Daniel David. *Almighty Voice and His Wife*. Toronto: Playwrights Canada Press, 2003.

———. *Big Buck City*. Toronto: Exile, 1998.

———. *Coyote City*. Stratford, ON: Williams-Wallace, 1990.

———. *Delicate Bodies*. Vancouver: blewointmentpress, 1980. Republished Madeira Park, BC: Harbour, 1992, 2005.

———. *The White Line*. Saskatoon: Fifth House, 1990.

Mosionier, Beatrice Culleton. *In Search of April Raintree*. Winnipeg: Pemmican, 1983. Republished Winnipeg: Portage and Main, 2008.

Nolan, Yvette. *Annie Mae's Movement*. Toronto: PUC Play Service, 1999. Republished Toronto: Playwrights Canada Press, 2006.

———. *Job's Wife or The Delivery of Grace*. In *Blade, Job's Wife, and Video: Three Plays*. Toronto: Art Biz Communications, 1995. Also in *Staging Coyote's Dream: An Anthology of First Nations Drama in English*, vol. 1. Edited by Ric Knowles and Monique Mojica. Toronto: Playwrights Canada Press, 2003.

Pésémapéo Bordeleau, Virginia. *Ourse bleue*. Lachine, QC: Éditions de la pleine lune, 2007.

Picard-Sioui, Louis-Karl. *Yawendara et la forêt des Têtes-Coupées*. Quebec City: Loup de gouttière, 2005.

Ray, Carl, and James Stevens. *Sacred Legends of the Sandy Lake Cree.* Toronto: McClelland and Stewart, 1971. Republished Ottawa: Penumbra Press, 1995.

Reid, Bill. *Solitary Raven: The Selected Writings of Bill Reid.* Edited by Robert Bringhurst. Vancouver: Douglas and McIntyre, 2000. Revised and expanded as *Solitary Raven: The Essential Writings of Bill Reid.* Vancouver: Douglas and McIntyre, 2009.

Riel, Louis. *The Collected Writings of Louis Riel / Les écrits complets de Louis Riel.* Vol. 4, *Poetry (Poésie).* Edited by Glen Campbell. Collection edited by George F.G. Stanley. Edmonton: University of Alberta Press, 1985.

Robinson, Eden. *Monkey Beach.* Toronto: Knopf Canada, 2000.

———. *Traplines.* Toronto: Knopf Canada, 1996.

Robinson, Harry. *Write It on Your Heart: The Epic World of an Okanagan Storyteller.* Compiled and edited by Wendy Wickwire. Vancouver: Talonbooks / Penticton, BC: Theytus, 1989. Revised Vancouver: Talonbooks, 2004.

Ross, Ian. *fareWel.* Toronto: Scirocco Drama, 1997. Republished Winnipeg: J. Gordon Shillingford, 2002.

Ruffo, Armand Garnet. *At Geronimo's Grave.* Regina: Coteau, 2001.

———. *Grey Owl: The Mystery of Archie Belaney.* Regina: Coteau, 1996.

Scofield, Gregory. *The Gathering: Stones for the Medicine Wheel.* Vancouver: Polestar, 1993.

———. *I Knew Two Métis Women.* Vancouver: Polestar, 1999.

———. *Native Canadiana: Songs from the Urban Rez.* Vancouver: Polestar, 1996.

———. *Sâkihtowin-maskihkiy êkwa pêyak-nikamowin / Love Medicine and One Song.* Vancouver: Polestar, 1997.

———. *Singing Home the Bones.* Vancouver: Raincoast, 2005.

———. *Thunder Through My Veins: Memories of a Métis Childhood.* Toronto: HarperCollins, 1999.

Simon, Lorne. *Stones and Switches.* Penticton, BC: Theytus, 1994.

Sioui, Éléonore. *Andatha.* Val-d'Or, QC: Éditions Hyperborée, 1985.

Sioui, Jean. *L'avenir voit rouge*. Trois Rivières, QC: Écrits des forges, 2008.

———. *Hannenorak*. Illustrated by Manon Sioui. Quebec City: Loup de gouttière, 2004.

———. *Hannenorak et le vent*. Illustrated by Manon Sioui. Quebec City: Cornac, 2008.

———. *Le pas de l'Indien : pensées Wendates*. Illustrated by Lyse Renaud Sioui. Quebec City: Loup de gouttière, 1997, 2005.

———. *Poèmes rouges*. Quebec City: Loup de gouttière, 2004.

Sioui Durand, Yves. *Atiskenandahate / Voyage au pays des morts*. Unpublished manuscript, 1985; performed Montreal, 1988; CBC-TV, 1991; CBC Radio, 1994.

———. *La conquête de Mexico : Adaptation dramatique du Codex de Florence*. Montreal: Trait d'union, 2001.

———. *Le porteur des peines du monde*. Montreal: Lémeac, 1992.

Sioui Wawanoloath, Christine. *Natanis*. Illustrated by the author. Quebec City: Loup de gouttière, 2005.

———. *L'ours et la femme venus des étoiles*. Quebec City: Cornac, 2009.

———. *Popokua*. Quebec City: Cornac, 2008.

Slipperjack, Ruby. *Dog Tracks*. Calgary: Fifth House, 2008.

———. *Honour the Sun*. Winnipeg: Pemmican, 1987.

———. *Silent Words*. Saskatoon: Fifth House, 1992.

———. *Weesquachak*. Penticton, BC: Theytus, 2005. Originally published, 2000, under the title *Weesquachak and the Lost Ones*.

Snow, Chief John. *These Mountains Are Our Sacred Places: The Story of the Stoney People*. Toronto: Samuel Stevens, 1977.

Sterling, Shirley. *My Name Is Seepeetza*. Toronto: Douglas & McIntyre / Groundwood, 1992.

Stonechild, Blair. *The New Buffalo: The Struggle for Aboriginal Post-Secondary Education in Canada*. Winnipeg: University of Manitoba Press, 2006.

Stonechild, Blair, and Bill Waiser. *Loyal Till Death: Indians and the North-West Rebellion*. Markham, ON: Fifth House, 1997, 2010.

Storm, Jennifer. *Deadly Loyalties*. Penticton, BC: Theytus, 2007.

Taylor, Drew Hayden. *400 Kilometres*. Vancouver: Talonbooks, 2005.

———. *The Baby Blues*. Vancouver: Talonbooks, 1999.

———. *The Berlin Blues*. Vancouver: Talonbooks, 2007.

———. *The Bootlegger Blues*. Saskatoon: Fifth House, 1991.

———. *The Boy in the Treehouse*. In *The Boy in the Treehouse / Girl Who Loved Her Horses*. Vancouver: Talonbooks, 2000.

———. *The Buz'Gem Blues*. Vancouver: Talonbooks, 2002.

———. *Girl Who Loved Her Horses*. In *The Boy in the Treehouse / Girl Who Loved Her Horses*. Vancouver: Talonbooks, 2000.

———. *Motorcycles and Sweetgrass*. Toronto: Knopf Canada, 2010.

———. *Only Drunks and Children Tell the Truth*. Vancouver: Talonbooks, 1998.

———. *Someday*. Saskatoon: Fifth House, 1993.

Tyman, James. *Inside Out: An Autobiography by a Native Canadian*. Saskatoon: Fifth House, 1989, 1995.

Van Camp, Richard. *Angel Wing Splash Pattern*. Neyaashiinigmiing, ON: Kegedonce Press, 2002.

———. *The Lesser Blessed*. Vancouver: Douglas and McIntyre, 1996, 2016.

Vanderburgh, R.M. *I Am Nokomis, Too: The Biography of Verna Patronella Johnston*. Don Mills, ON: General, 1977.

Vassiliou, Mélina. *Fou floue fléau : poésie / Nin tshishe ishkuess*. Sept-Îles, QC: Institut culturel éducatif montagnais, 2008.

Wagamese, Richard. *A Quality of Light*. Toronto: Doubleday Canada, 1997.

———. *Dream Wheels*. Toronto: Doubleday Canada, 2006.

———. *For Joshua: An Ojibway Father Teaches His Son*. Toronto: Doubleday Canada, 2002, 2003.

———. *Keeper'n Me*. Toronto: Random House, 1994, 2006.

———. *Ragged Company*. Toronto: Doubleday Canada, 2008.

Weetaltuk, Eddy. *E9-422: Un Inuit, de la toundra a la guerre de Corée*. Edited by Thibault Martin. Translated by Marie-Claude Perreault. Paris: Carnets Nord, 2009. Republished as *From the Tundra to the Trenches*. Winnipeg: University of Manitoba Press, 2017.

Wheeler, Jordan. *Brothers in Arms*. Winnipeg: Pemmican, 1989.

Young, Mary Isabelle. *Pimatisiwin, Walking in a Good Way*. Winnipeg: Pemmican, 2005, 2009.

INDEX BY CULTURAL GROUP

From **Oral** to **Written**

INDEX BY AUTHOR

INDEX BY TITLE

Tomson Highway is a writer from northern Manitoba. His best-known works are the plays *The Rez Sisters, Dry Lips Oughta Move to Kapuskasing, Rose, Ernestine Shuswap Gets Her Trout,* and *The (Post) Mistress,* as well as the bestselling novel *Kiss of the Fur Queen.* He writes in three languages: Cree (his mother tongue), French, and English. As a classically trained pianist (who also writes music), he has studied with some of the finest teachers in Canada, most notably William Aide and Anton Kuerti.